Project and Program Management

Project and Program Management

A Competency-Based Approach,
Second Edition

By Mitchell L. Springer

Purdue University Press, West Lafayette, Indiana

Library of Congress Cataloging-in-Publication Data

Springer, Mitchell L., 1959-
  Project and program management : a competency-based approach / by Mitchell L. Springer. -- Second Edition.
     pages cm
  Includes bibliographical references and index.
  ISBN 978-1-55753-652-5 (hbk. : alk. paper) -- ISBN 978-1-61249-275-9 (ePDF) -- ISBN 978-1-61249-276-6 (ePub)
1. Project management. I. Title.
  HD69.P75S684 2013
  658.4'04--dc23
                              2012051019

About the Author

Dr. Mitchell L. Springer, PMP, SPHR

Dr. Springer currently serves in a dual capacity as the Purdue University College of Technology Executive Director for College of Technology Operations and Strategic Initiatives as well as the Academic Center for Professional Studies in Technology and Applied Research (ProSTAR), located in West Lafayette, Indiana. He possesses over thirty years of theoretical and industry-based practical experience from four disciplines: software engineering, systems engineering, program management, and human resources. Dr. Springer possesses a significant strength in pattern recognition, analyzing and improving organizational systems. He is internationally recognized, has authored numerous books and articles, and has lectured on software development methodologies, management and organizational practices, and program management. Dr. Springer sits on many university and community boards and advisory committees. He received his Bachelor of Science in Computer Science from Purdue University, his MBA and doctorate in Adult and Community Education with a Cognate in Executive Development from Ball State University. Dr. Springer is certified as both a Project Management Professional (PMP) and a Senior Professional in Human Resources (SPHR).

Contents

List of Illustrations

Preface

I was preparing to thank all of those involved in the preparation of this book, when I noticed, without intent, I was writing something I had already written in a similar form in another book. So, with updated thoughts . . .

For over thirty years, I've spent a fair amount of time studying the discipline of gerontology—the study of biological, psychological, and sociological changes as they relate to the aging process. In doing so, I've reawakened to many realities, long since forgotten or simply pushed to the background, some of which I'll share here: (1) Attitude is everything. (2) Put past events behind you—learn from them, but look to the future. (3) Figure out what you're passionate about, because in that passion there exists the opportunity for total personal contribution, which in turn can produce tremendous gratification and contentment. (4) Remember the saying "a bend in the road is not the end of the road, unless you fail to make the turn." This is critically important as we progress through life's ups and downs. (5) Live a little, laugh a lot. (6) When stressed, visualize the worst-case scenario and determine how best to deal with that. Of course the worst case will probably never materialize, but you'll feel more in control and the stress will subside. (7) Live as though there is accountability; you may be a different person. Above all else, (8) recognize our short time on earth is to prepare for the eternity that follows. There'll always be another chapter in the book of eternal life. In being reflective, I've always had a love for life . . . and certainly no more than now.

It would not have been possible to evolve this work without the input of literally hundreds of sources. As much as anyone, I owe the bulk of my thank-you to the multitude of students from whom I have learned so much over the years. Most all have been working professionals, each with their own understanding of theory and practice, representing dozens upon dozens of companies. These many students have provided additional breadth and depth of understanding, as well as massive research and numerous examples of alternative perspectives manifested from the application of assimilated information through projects. To all of these students, I offer my most sincere thank-you.

For my dear, longtime friends at Purdue University Press, none of this would have been possible without your outstanding and unending efforts. Special thanks to Director Charles Watkinson, for his vision and guidance with strategic intent; to Production and Marketing Manager Bryan Shaffer, who has provided invaluable insight; and perhaps most importantly, my very special thank-you to Lead Production Editor Katherine Purple. I have long since come to appreciate how Katherine has more red marks on my manuscripts than I have original black. She has been amazing.

No acknowledgment is complete without thanking those closest to you: my sons, Matthew and Christopher. I am so proud of you both. I am truly blessed.

Introduction

The first edition of this text evolved from nearly 17 years of research, teaching, and writing. It came to be through an iterative process of understanding the research and development phases of the program/project management life cycle of major system product development. The text began with a basic underlying understanding and desire to write about program planning, that being the pre-contract award period of the overarching process for managing programs.

Program Planning was written in 1995. It dealt primarily with the program/project management planning process; again, that being prior to a contract being awarded. It identified a process made up of a series of activities, each with its own attendant products. Back in 1995, the whole discipline of program and project management was just starting to evolve into a recognized and accepted discipline. Now, it can be readily argued that program/project management has been around since the beginning of time, and in fact the most widely recognized credentialing authority, the Project Management Institute, has been around since 1959. The Defense Systems Management College has equally been around since that time. But, program and project management as a recognized and essential discipline didn't really begin to proliferate in literature until around 1995.

Program Planning defined a planning process with multiple time-phased, semi-sequential activities and their attendant products. In retrospect, although somewhat narrow in perspective, the book covered the basics of the quantitative aspects of program/project management. Through teaching program/project management in multiple universities, primarily to working professionals and graduate students, came the realization that a text for planning programs that was entirely quantitatively focused was insufficient. It became clear that the actual practice of program/project management, if taught correctly, needed to include more than the quantitative component; it also needed to include the peripheral disciplines and concepts. This more thorough understanding, evolving from actual teaching experience, led to *Program Management: A Comprehensive Overview of the Discipline*. This book gained recognition internationally and was published in seven countries around the world. Interestingly enough, the title itself brought many questions. How can something be a comprehensive overview? Can't something be less than a comprehensive overview? It was the breadth of the discipline that was gaining the breadth of discussion.

Again, as before, it was the numerous and varied disciplines as represented by the students that led to the natural conclusion that my defense industry background had caused the use of a very defense industry-specific set of terminology and an unnecessarily complex process. The terminology, process, and practice as defined and implemented in the defense industry is the most complex in any industry and certainly doesn't lend itself readily to assimilation from those not in the more acronym-oriented defense industry. What was needed was a much simpler overview and discussion of the process and products themselves. To this end, *A Concise Guide to Program Management* evolved.

The value of *A Concise Guide to Program Management* was that the process and products were discussed in terms of a much simpler industry, one oriented toward something with which a large number of students had at least some familiarity: home building. This book, then, focused on describing program/project management from a commercial perspective, versus the previous attempts at describing the discipline from a defense-oriented perspective.

To summarize, at the time of *A Concise Guide to Program Management*, experience with students had led to an enlarged writing perspective from simply planning programs to describing the comprehensive nature of program/project management to describing program/project management from a commercially oriented perspective. Through additional teaching, it was discovered that students preferred to actually have a little of the defense perspective, with a more detailed discussion involving the commercial perspective. In this sense, both books served to more completely define the program/project management process, such that a more comprehensive understanding could be attained. This was good and would prove to be the winning combination for maximum assimilation and subsequent application.

What is left then to write about on this topic? The answer: another perspective that entails the work previously discussed and now formalizes the knowledge into a structure that allows the exhibition of behaviors believed to be required for success as program managers of the future. In other words, we need a model of competencies premised on behaviors that entail the concepts presented in previous work around planning and other interrelated disciplines: a competency-based approach.

Aren't there already books on competency-based approaches to program/project management? The answer is yes, but they do not include the breadth of discussion required to fully understand the discipline. Other books on competency-based approaches to program/project management simply discuss what the authors feel are required competencies, and not all authors agree.

What differentiated the first edition of this book from other competency-based perspectives, then, was that the book rounded-out the discussion on competencies required for future program/project management success by incorporating the more complex discussion already evolved and expanded on in previous works on planning and the interrelatedness of peripheral disciplines. The first edition of this book used a broader stroke to paint a more complete perspective of not only the process and products identified to be the program/project management process, but equally, placed these elements into a competency-based framework, which could then be tied directly to a competency model and subsequent training.

This second edition of *Project and Program Management: A Competency-Based Approach* really takes the first edition to a new level. To begin with, through years of teaching and writing, there are a number of new chapters, significant expansion of existing ones, and a major shuffling of the order of the material. This revision has expanded and new chapters recognizing the qualitative significance of the discipline—this idea coming directly from the students. Additionally, the many students over the years have helped to evolve a much greater understanding of the competencies required to be a successful program/project manager. This effort is reflected through 315 references to 107 unique companies. Where within those 107 unique companies, there are a total of 54 unique behaviors identified; across those 54 unique behaviors, there are 229 unique skills, where each behavior has two or more skills, and on average around four skills per behavior. This work provides significant insight into the business and industrial perspective of what constitutes a well-rounded program/project manager.

The quantitative chapters, those dealing directly with the program/project management process, activities, and outcomes (products), have been refined to bring together the non-jargon-oriented commercial perspective, then followed by what may be termed a deeper dive. This more detailed perspective provides insight into the complexities of each activity and attendant outputs. The deeper dive is for those who wish a more thorough understanding and the challenges that might arise from a large-scale implementation of the process.

The new qualitative chapters include material dealing with disruptive technologies, leadership and gender, succession planning, change management, and, perhaps most excitedly, providing an insight into what it means to capitalize on the world's collective knowledge. As before, all of these chapters were researched, taught on more than one occasion, and suggested by the many students to be part of this revised edition.

Included in this revised edition is a chapter summarizing the entire program/project management process outputs by identifying in a concise manner the ordered outputs from the many process activities. This chapter, as others, was highly regarded and recommended by the students. It brings together the quantitative discussion from applicable chapters into one brief chapter, with reference to other chapters for further understanding.

Lastly, the material has been significantly restructured and reorganized. To better integrate the qualitative and quantitative material, the students felt the new organization presented in this revised edition supported a greater perceptual flow, which in the end enhanced student understanding and assimilation.

Chapter 1

Program/Project Management Competencies

Every discipline, to be a discipline, must have competencies. Competencies define the behaviors indicative of what is required to be successful in the respective discipline. Competencies, then, allow us to judge ourselves in terms of how much we know about a given competency, which, in turn, allows us to pursue a better understanding of a given competency through training and education. In other words, since competencies are nothing more than manifested behaviors, which we can form through training, competencies are things we can develop in ourselves and others. The question to be asked, however, is what are the agreed-to competencies of a given discipline?

The answer to the question "what are the required program/project management competencies for success in practice?" is not uniformly agreed upon. In fact, looking through the proliferation of literature, it appears there is not a single set of program/project management competencies agreed to by all. What we can do, however, is to pull from the many already defined competencies a set that we can then apply our own experience to create an acceptable set. Certainly, without question, we can define the basic competencies. So, to this end, this book defines the basic competencies and a few others oriented around successful leaders and leadership that is proposed to form a complete set of program/project management competencies.

J. Davidson Frame, in his 1999 book entitled *Building Project Management Competence,* defines eleven competencies program/project managers must possess to ensure at least some facsimile of, or opportunity for, success. These eleven competencies are:

- Be results oriented
- Have a head for details
- Possess a strong commitment to the project
- Be aware of the organization's goals
- Be politically savvy
- Be cost-conscious
- Understand business basics
- Be capable of addressing needs of staff, customers, and management
- Be capable of dealing with ambiguity, setbacks, and disappointments
- Possess good negotiation skills
- Possess the appropriate technical skills to do the job

Frame goes on to separate competencies into three categories: knowledge-based, socially rooted, and business-judgment.

According to Frame, knowledge-based competencies are objective knowledge that individuals are expected to possess in order to carry out their jobs effectively. An Ada programmer should know something about Ada as a programming language; a restaurant owner should know something about running a restaurant; and a builder should know something about building a house.

Socially rooted competencies are more subjective as defined by Frame. He writes, "They focus on abilities such as good judgment and human relations skills. Task leaders who are able to mediate conflicts on their teams possess some measure of socially rooted competence, as do project managers who can motivate borrowed resources to put in needed extra hours of work and technical workers who display sensitivity to their customers need" (p. 6).

The last category of program/project management competencies are business-judgment competencies. These are "tied to the ability of individuals to make decisions to consistently serve the best business interest of the organization. People who are strong in this area are able to assess the risks and rewards associated with decisions they are about to make. They look beyond the immediate impact of their decisions and understand their opportunity costs. Although they recognize the importance of establishing and following good methods and procedures for the effective functioning of the organization, they do not behave like mindless bureaucrats. When they see an opportunity to improve the business performance, they seize it, even when it lies outside the realm of business procedures" (p. 6).

Harold Kerzner, in his 2009, tenth edition book entitled *Project Management: A Systems Approach to Planning, Scheduling and Controlling,* defines ten skills he believes project managers must possess to be effective in their pursuits. These ten skills are:

- Team building
- Leadership
- Conflict resolution
- Technical expertise
- Planning
- Organization
- Entrepreneurship
- Administration
- Management support
- Resource allocation

Kerzner goes on to say that "it is important the personal management style underlying these skills facilitate the integration of multidisciplinary program resources for synergistic operation. The days of the manager who gets by with technical expertise alone or pure administrative skills are gone" (p. 905).

Others, and there are many, have separated a program/project manager's competencies into two categories of leadership and those specific to program/project management, although there seems to be much confusion on a common set of defined competencies. Others have added the following competencies, some derived from the Project Management Institute's (PMI's) definitions:

- Strategic thinking
- Customer focus
- Business alignment
- Domain knowledge
- Decision making
- Ethical behavior
- Self-management
- Global awareness
- Risk and opportunity management
- Program planning and execution

Over the last ten years, professional adult students have been asked to build competency models in much the same manner as is being described here. They were asked to visit online organizations, download their respective competency model for program/project managers, and then compare and contrast their findings. Ultimately, they have been asked to create their own version of a "good" competency model from their research findings and their own personal experiences.

The result of this student research has been 315 references to 107 unique companies. Within those 107 unique companies, there are a total of 54 behaviors identified. Across those 54 behaviors, there are 229 skills, where each behavior has two or more skills, and on average around four skills per behavior. Figure 1.1 depicts the top 20 of 54 identified behaviors of the 107 companies researched.

Behaviors	# of occurrences
Managerial/Leadership	72
Communication	61
Personal Effectiveness / Skills	43
Risk Management	29
Planning & Project Management	28
Impact and Influence	27
Problem Solving	27
Team Development	27
Customer Focus	25
Technological Savvy	24
Shape the Future/Vision	20
Time Management	20
Organization	17
Decision Making	16
Human Resources	15
Achievement and Action	12
Business / Corporate	12
Trust and Respect	11
Cognitive	10
Goal Oriented	9

Figure 1.1. Most Identified Behaviors across Companies

Something most interesting in figure 1.1 is that qualitative behaviors outnumber quantitative behaviors significantly. In fact, depending on how one wishes to argue it, there appears to be 17 qualitative behaviors to just three quantitative ones; in other words, 85 percent of the behaviors of the top researched companies believe qualitative behaviors are at least as important as quantitative, and from the data, more so.

When most of us become program/project managers, we are given key training on the tools and techniques that enable us to monitor our cost, schedule, and technical performance baseline. In other words, we are taught about: (1) scheduling techniques; the differences between Gantt charts and network diagrams, (2) earned value; how to compare a program's actual cost to credit earned for work performed and baseline cost, and perhaps (3) we may be indoctrinated into the organization's departmental budgeting process. Most all of these, as one would notice, are quantitative measures, which while essential, are arguably not the entirety of what is required for successful program/project management.

To provide an example premised on the findings from the above research, I'd like to share a story. Earlier in my career, I was working on a program as the software engineering manager. We were a subcontractor to a larger prime contractor located in the southern United States. At this particular point in our relationship with this prime contractor, the program manager, contracts manager, marketing manager, and I (the software engineering manager) were flying down to see our prime for what is termed fact finding. Fact finding is the process a prime contractor goes through with a subcontractor to determine appropriateness of the subcontractor's cost basis for the subcontractor's bid to do their portion of the job.

After some number of hours and numerous discussions on the many line items that formed the basis of our bid, we stumbled onto a particular document that we felt would take five months of a single person's time to complete. The prime, our customer, felt it should only take two months to complete. After what appeared to be a standstill, their contract manager stood up and said, "We don't think you are negotiating in good faith. We would like you to leave." As my colleagues began to pack, I sat dumbfounded. On seeing this, my contracts manager said, "Let's go. Pack your briefcase. We're leaving." Now the hallway out of this facility was quite long. In fact, it was probably about two city blocks from the building we were in to the exit. The silence was deafening. Nobody spoke a single word. Once outside I asked our contracts manager what we were going to do, as I had never been asked to leave a negotiation session before. He simply replied that we would go back to our hotel and see what developed that evening.

After a nice meal (you always eat well when traveling with marketing people), we went back to the hotel only to receive a phone call from our prime, who asked that we return the next day to continue our discussions.

As requested, the next day we returned. Again we were escorted down the long hallway toward our meeting room. It was amazing how everyone appeared so jolly. People were laughing and joking like nothing had happened. There was great food and drinks for us, and all seemed well. We again began to discuss line items that made up our cost proposal. Again, as in the previous day, we came to that one line item that we disagreed upon.

What happened next is funny now, but back then I was floored. Our contracts manager, not theirs, stood up and said, "We don't think you are negotiating in good faith. We are leaving." I was dumbfounded, a second time! I couldn't believe it. I sat motionless and watched. Again, my contracts manager looked over at me and said, "Let's go. Pack your briefcase."

As we were escorted down the long hallway, my contract manager looked over at me and apparently recognized my puzzlement. He said, "Don't worry, I've been thrown out of better places than this before." My feeling was that I had never been asked to leave a negotiation, and I had never walked out of a negotiation, and above all else, I had never had both of them occur in the same trip!

After returning home, our business area manager was brought up to speed on the turn of events. He made one telephone call to his peer at our prime's organization. I heard them talk. Our manager said, "What do you think, Bob? I heard our boys had some minor difficulty working together. What do you say we split the difference?" The other manager must have said OK, because the next thing I knew our manager was hanging the telephone up and saying, "It's all OK guys, you can get back to work now." I incredulously wondered what had just happened. I thought, "You mean we flew four people to the southern United States, spent time in hotels, ate meals, and then met with up to six of their people for two days, only to have our V.P. spend three minutes on the telephone with their V.P., and all is well?"

As I reflected on this, I wondered, where in my quantitative training did I miss the part about contracts, contract negotiations, politics, and dealing with people? The answer: I didn't! It wasn't covered in my scheduling class, or my cost class, or even my training on reading end of the month budget summaries. It wasn't covered, period.

And this is what this text provides. This text is a look at the breadth of behaviors that make up program/project management as a whole, not simply the quantitative aspects of planning.

So given this, it comes as no surprise that qualitative behaviors and skills are paramount to program/project management success, and are reflected in the data as the top behaviors from the top 20 of 54 companies researched.

So, where are we? We're left with the task of extracting and formulating a set of program/project management behaviors that most generally encapsulate the predominance of those we deem to be applicable to managing successful programs and projects.

Our list then, of program/project management behaviors, will separate the qualitative from the quantitative behaviors, and it looks like the following:

- Qualitative behaviors
  - Understanding the global environment—seeing the bigger picture
  - Understanding leadership
  - Understanding team dynamics and individual personalities—team building and team development
  - Understanding decision making
  - Understanding the business case for diversity and attendant inclusivity
- Quantitative behaviors
  - Domain-specific knowledge—in this context, program/project management

Notice how our list evolves from an outside to inside perspective. By that, we begin by looking to the outer world, by understanding the greater scheme of things. Seeing the bigger picture is imperative in today's world of program/project management. Our program/project managers are being asked to do more today than in previous years. In today's environment, our program/project managers are being asked to function in the capacity of business development professionals. This means our program/project managers must look for new markets or extensions to existing markets for our many products and services that we design, develop, and produce.

As our list of competencies focuses in, we examine the essence of leadership, teams, individuals, decision making, and, ultimately, the very quantitative nature of our discipline, our domain-specific knowledge.

Seldom do we have program/project managers who do not understand the basics of cost, schedule, or technical performance of our programs. In fact, it's quite typical that our program/project managers are more likely to suffer from people-oriented problems than from quantitatively oriented pitfalls. That is not to say our programs don't have enough quantitative or technical problems; in fact, most "Oh, man!" type problems are in fact quantitative/technical in nature. But our inattention to qualitative competencies, coupled with our lack of sufficient training and education of these competencies for our program/project managers, tend to form a very natural environment for failure.

There's a saying that goes something like this: "When you take a good technical person, make her or him a manager, but do not provide that person with the right training or education, then you end up losing on two accounts: you lose a good technical person and you gain a lousy manager." From experience, when good technical people are managing, fall under the stress of the program, and have not been adequately trained as a manager, then those new managers usually resort to what they know best: they begin to micromanage the technical people who work for them. In fact, what's most interesting in this scenario is that the new manager most likely is no longer as good as the technical people who work for him or her, and, to further complicate the scenario, the manager is not doing what we are paying him or her to do, which is manage technical people, not be the best technical person on the team.

Chapter 2

The Importance of Program/Project Management

Program/project management has been around since the beginning of time. The only difference between 300 B.C. and now is that we have crystallized and subsequently formalized our understanding of the many activities one must perform if we wish to bring continuity to our program/project management practices and therefore increase our opportunities for success.

Many times over the years of teaching program/project management, the class participants have discovered that this discipline is not necessarily for rocket scientists alone, although they ideally adhere to the basic principles of it. Instead, the basic activities and products of the program/project management process are followed, or at least thought about, in every single decision made. As we move through the program/project management process, it will become increasingly obvious that we do, in fact, at least think through the various activities of the process, if perhaps for only a few seconds at each point along the way.

Let's take the example of planting a garden. One of the first things we do is to think about how nice a garden might look if planted in that ideal spot in our back or front yards. This concept of "visualizing" is what we might call our "operational perspective." In other words, at this point we are simply collecting our thoughts on why we might want to plant such a garden and how we envision it will look or benefit us in some way.

At some point, once we've decided that a garden would indeed look just fine, especially as the neighbors drove by, we begin to think about what type of plants might look really special and what other supporting plants might bring out the colors we're trying to emphasize. This activity, while still only a daydream, is the beginning of our requirements analysis efforts. That is, we are beginning the process of figuring out exactly what we want to do, what plants would be needed, how many plants might look most acceptable, and the like. We might even consult with an organization that specializes in landscaping. The landscaper, incidentally, is what we would call a specialist organization or function. Function in this sense is an organization with some special knowledge, skills, or abilities and behaves as an expert in the field. In this case, our specialist function is our landscaper.

As we get a little more serious, we begin to make a list of what we might want to purchase, and perhaps we even assign some of the tasks associated with the garden. For example, we might write down that the ground needs to be turned and a mixture of black dirt and fertilizer added and tilled in. We might also think that our brother-in-law, Tom, has a tiller and could help us do that. Further, we might believe our garden should have some type of special stone, and that the stone could be purchased and delivered by the local garden center. The process of defining all of our work and separating it into chunks to be worked by different individuals or organizations is what we would refer to as a "Work Breakdown Structure."

Note that up to this point we may only have been doodling on a piece of scrap paper. We've made no formal notes, written no formal proposals, nor asked for any formal quotes from outside vendors or even our brother-in-law, Tom. We've done nothing more than perhaps eat our lunch and jot down a few thoughts.

Yet even with nothing more than a few loose thoughts and a scribbled up piece of scrap paper, we have proceeded clearly through the beginning phases of the program/project management planning process.

The point is that program/project management is a process with a set of attendant products. Its purpose is to bring consistency, uniformity, and continuity to our program management practices, should we consciously decide to follow them. Even in the case where we do not intentionally follow every activity or generate every formal product, simply being aware of the process helps us to better move in a uniform direction. The value in moving uniformly through the process, whether consciously or unconsciously, is that we minimize the chances for making mistakes and potential rework. For example, had we known that certain plants favor shade over sunlight, we might not have spent the money on them, fearing they would die in the heat of the summer months.

The point of this book, therefore, is to bring a very logical and proven effective process, the program/project management process, into our daily lives so that each of us may benefit from having gained insight into it. In this way, perhaps during our next project, we might stop and think, "I'm beginning to collect requirements, and it might behoove me to think this through a little bit before I begin."

As a program/project manager, seeing the bigger picture is important. We are no longer simply asked to manage our cost, schedule, or technical performance of our programs. We are asked to see permutations of our products or services that can solve our customers' needs. We are, in essence, asked to perform in a marketing or business development role. It has been recognized that our marketing professionals are too limited in number and that our program/project managers acting in a similar marketing capacity can help reach a greater audience because of sheer numbers and the managers' familiarity with the immediate customer. One might ask who better understands the needs of the customer than the program/project manager working side by side with him/her throughout the course of a given job.

Seeing the bigger picture is very similar to the concept of open versus closed systems. In a closed system, the organization or unit only sees within itself, whereas in an open system, the organization takes into consideration the external environment. In the open system, the organization considers the multitude of outside factors that have an influence on the organization, from environmental to competition with other similar organizations within a given industry.

An example to serve this purpose happened many years ago. While working on a real-time embedded software/hardware system, a black box, we were asked by our customer not to bid the technology being proposed. As an organization, we knew what we were proposing was the best technology available and was inherently better than the existing processing box and that of our competitors. The customer, however, recognized the challenges of interfacing our new architecture with existing architecture, and for that reason they picked our competitor's approach. We lost the contract. During our customer debrief, the customer essentially said subtextually that they had not wanted us to bid the box. In this scenario, we didn't see the bigger picture, and perhaps, we lost sight of providing what was needed.

From this perspective, then, it is important we not have a myopic perspective on our efforts. We must see all aspects of our external environment to ensure we are moving with focus and with regard to complicating factors, both internal and external.

How long, then, has program/project management been around? The answer is nearly forever. It simply has existed in an informal and inconsistent manner. The two oldest and most widely recognized organizations are the:

- Project Management Institute (est. 1969), which has over 500,000 worldwide members in 170 countries
- Defense Systems Management College (DSMC, est. 1971), is one of 15 Untied States Department of Defense (DoD) education and training institutions in a consortium known as Defense Acquisition University (DAU)

Is there a demand for program/project management? The short answer is yes.

- More and more companies are asking for it.
- It is gaining international recognition as a growing discipline.
- Major universities are offering courses, certificate programs, and master's degree-level programs.
- There are a growing number of seminars and organizations specializing in it.

From the Project Management Institute Jordan Chapter homepage (2013):

As the number of projects swell, the pool of credentialed talent is not keeping pace. In the Persian Gulf and China Sea regions alone—where entire cities are being built, seemingly overnight—a shortage of 6 million skilled project professionals is expected by 2013. Add to that the fact that, of the 20 million people participating in projects worldwide, just one million have professionally recognized formal training on how to best execute those projects. One thing becomes clear: The demand for skilled project managers is at a critically urgent level.

One of the first advertised requirements from a major company requesting their project managers be certified occurred in 1998 in the Fort Wayne, Indiana, *News Sentinel*, which stated "Project Management Institute certification desired for Project Management positions." In this advertisement, IBM was specifically soliciting the credentialing requirement.

Figure 2.1. IBM 1998 Newspaper Seeking PMI Certification

When we make reference to accredited programs, we are making reference to those colleges and schools accredited through the six regional accrediting commissions of the Association of Colleges and Schools: Middle States, New England, North West, Southern, Western, and North Central.

As we look across these accredited colleges and school, we see there are no bachelor's degrees in program/project management. This is because of the eclectic nature of the program/project management discipline. Program/project management is a discipline, but it is typically not a standalone discipline. Normally, an individual begins in another discipline, such as engineering, finance, or marketing, and then becomes responsible for managing projects within that discipline and across other disciplines. To this end, there are not generally undergraduate bachelor's degrees in program/project management—even though program/project management is, itself, a self-contained discipline.

There are, however, a number of master's level degrees in program/project management. A whole curriculum in program/project management would in some manner include discussion on the following topics:

- Management and Leadership
- Organizational Behavior
- HR, Communications, Ethics
- Accounting, Economics, Finance
- Strategic Management and Marketing
- Risk Management and Tech Performance Measurement
- Management Cost/Schedule Control System
- Scheduling Techniques
- Contracts and Procurement

Notice that each of these topics is itself one or more college-level, semester-length courses. There are related accredited whole degrees, namely:

- Professional Development
- Procurement Management
- Production Management
- Program Planning and Administration
- Organizational Behavior
- Human Resources
- Contract and Acquisition Management

Typical program/project management educational offerings include:

- Accredited/non-accredited master's degree-level programs
- Individual courses
- Certificate programs

Who are the typical students in program/project management classes and courses? Generally:

- Professionals (all occupations)
- Graduate level
- Undergraduate: junior/senior level

Seldom do we see undergraduate, entry-level students. This again is because of the exposure that enhances the learning experience. It is hard to fully appreciate the cross-discipline nature of the program/project management field without having ever experienced it firsthand. After having been involved in training and education for nearly thirty years, it is almost always professionals who populate the classes/courses.

Figure 2.2 depicts an example of what one organization had done to promote the knowledge of program/project management.

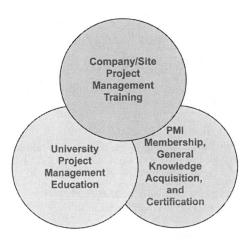

Figure 2.2. PM Education, Training, and Continued Knowledge Acquisition

In figure 2.2, one company supported the acquisition of program/project management knowledge first through formal education. Subsequent to formal general education, the organization trained the participants in the tools and processes of their company. Following successful education and training, the company paid for the students' membership to the Project Management Institute (PMI) and for PMI's Project Management Professional (PMP) certification.

For formal education, the company used a university's certificate in Program Management. A certificate (is):

- Concentrated, specialized study that complements existing knowledge and skills
- Focused on needs to meet job and career requirements and goals
- Highlights emerging areas of technology, tools, and specialization

Benefits to the student of pursuing a certificate include:

- Learning Project Management skills to help be successful in a given occupation
- Preparing the individual for PMP certification
- Networking with project managers from other industries and businesses

Benefits to the company of having their employees pursue a certificate include:

- Consistency and coherency of project management theories and methodologies
- Better trained and more efficient project management workforce
- Project manager training and education programs can be stressed in future proposals
- Improved networking between project managers (internal and external)

Relative to the company's continuing support of project management knowledge:

- Provided to those entering/completing Project Management Certificate Program
- Benefit to project managers:
    - Monthly professional magazine and newsletters
    - Local chapter meets monthly (networking, discipline presentations, and training)
- Benefit to company:
    - Project managers exposed to discipline topics, training, tools, networking, etc.
    - Project management training exposure in proposals

Relative to the company's support for taking the PMP certification exam:

- Sponsorship to take PMI test (for individuals who complete Project Management Certificate Program, or equivalent)
- Passing provides PMI's Project Management Professional (PMP) certification
- Benefit to project managers:
  - Internationally recognized PMI certificate in the Project Management discipline
- Benefit to company:
  - Consistent and coherent theoretical Project Management education
  - Project Management qualification exposure in proposals and to our customers

What, then, is the definition of a program/project? Programs/projects:

- Have a specific product or service (well-defined objective)
- Have a defined start and end date
- Have funding limits
- Consume resources, including dollars, people, and equipment
- Have a customer
- Has a degree of uncertainty

Examples of projects are too numerous to list, but they span every conceivable action requiring some level of organization. Through the many students, variations of projects submitted as part of class assignments include such diverse activities as:

- Hosting a conference or seminar
- Designing a marketing brochure
- Adding a family room
- Holding a high school reunion
- Performing a surgery
- Building a tree house
- Planning a wedding

To this above point, we all manage projects, some with less formality and consistency than others. What is important to recognize, and one of the main thrusts of this book, is that program/project management is a process. As such, it has a series of related activities, where each activity has one or more products.

Chapter 3

Process Management—Evolution and Definition

To better understand the historical significance of process management and to gain an appreciation for process management relative to other general program planning models, this section is organized into two primary categories: a historical orientation and a discussion of general program planning models. Succeeding sections then define process management more explicitly, identify key components of the planning process of this study, and conclude with a discussion of the sources of documentation.

Historical Orientation

To better understand the context in which a process-oriented approach to management exists, it is beneficial to look historically at the relationships between the numerous management philosophies and organizational designs within the U.S. economic, social, and political scenarios. An interesting aspect of organizational design, management theory, and situational contexts is their inherent order and dependency. Generally, U.S. economic, social, and political factors formed the premise for management philosophies. Management philosophies, in turn, formed the underlying premise for organizational design. While this is certainly not an absolute sequential ordering, it would appear that the adage "necessity is the mother of invention" is applicable.

The present historical account examines aspects of management theory, organizational design, and U.S. situational factors from three perspectives:

- The industrialization era. This period is characterized by the scientific management theories, mechanistic models of organizational design, and orientation toward production efficiency and effectiveness.
- The human-relations period. This period moved away from the scientific methods of mass production to consider employee involvement. This period is characterized by process, quantitative, and behavioral approaches to management, an organic organizational design model, with once-small companies evolving into larger companies, and larger companies evolving into conglomerates.
- The international era. This period is decidedly different from all previous ones. It is not marked by continual expansion and prosperity, but rather by increased foreign competition, changes in buyer habits and perspectives, and generally dwindling U.S. manufacturing market shares. Indicative of this period are the contingency and matrix organizational design models, and the systems, contingency, and total quality management (TQM) philosophies.

Over the years, experts have disagreed on exactly how many different approaches to management exist and what each approach entails. Generally speaking, the classical, behavioral, and management science approaches appear in most categorical accounts. Numerous authors, however, categorically discuss the qualitative, contingency, systems, management system, TQM, high involvement, and triangular approaches as well. Within the contingency approaches, an entirely different yet related area of leadership theories exists. While it is not the intent here to compare each of these approaches, our discussion will identify dominant management philosophies and organizational design models indicative of the periods and compare the environments that prompted changes from one management philosophy to the next.

At a macro level, figure 3.1 depicts the overall relationships between the U.S. economic, social, and political environments, management philosophies, and organizational design techniques.

The Industrialization Era

The Industrial Revolution in the United States appears to have been the catalyst for the earliest forms of organizational design and management philosophies. Three advances in technology launched the period: the steam engine (1790–1810), the railroads (1830–50), and the telegraph (1844). These technologies are thought to have been responsible for the proliferation of U.S. entrepreneurship by 1860. Along with these technologies came increasing demand for manufactured goods and industrial markets. During the last half of the nineteenth century, the U.S. economy entered an explosive transition from an agricultural nation to an industrial nation.

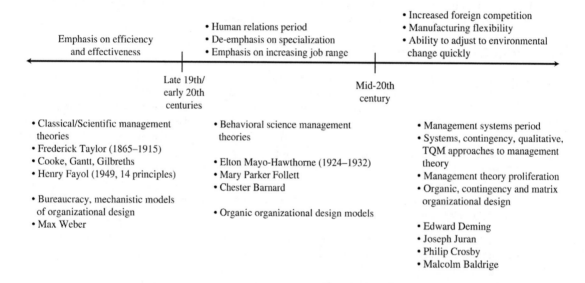

Figure 3.1. Context Diagram

With the transition into an industrial society came demand for more efficient and effective production techniques. The goal of this period was to meet demand. Quality and price frequently gave way to availability. During this time, scientific management unfolded through the efforts of Frederick W. Taylor (1865–1915). Taylor was credited with the scientific management philosophy, which sought to increase productivity and make work easier by scientifically studying work methods and establishing standards. Scientific management, as developed by Taylor, was based upon four main principles (Rue & Byars, 1989):

- The development of a scientific method of designing jobs. This involved gathering, classifying, and tabulating data to arrive at the "one best way" to perform a task or series of tasks.
- The scientific selection and progressive teaching of employees. This was not a generalist perspective, but instead a matching of the job or single task to a single worker. Taylor also

emphasized the need to study worker strengths and weaknesses and to provide training to improve employee performance.

- The bringing together of scientifically selected employees and scientifically developed methods for designing jobs. Taylor believed that new and scientific methods of job design should not merely be put before an employee; they should also be fully explained by management. He believed that employees would show little resistance to changes in methods if they understood the reasons for the change and they saw a chance for greater earnings for themselves.
- A division of work resulting in an interdependence between management and the workers. If they were truly dependent on one another, Taylor felt, then cooperation would naturally follow.

The scientific study of work also emphasized specialization and division of labor. In time, the need for an organizational framework became more and more apparent. The concepts of line and staff were developed. In an effort to motivate workers, most scientific management programs developed wage incentives. Once standards were set, managers began to monitor actual performance and compare it with standards. Thus, the management function of control was launched.

Summarizing scientific management as a managerial philosophy, Taylor saw equal benefits for both management and workers: management could achieve more work in a given amount of time, and workers could produce more and earn more, with little or no additional effort (Rue & Byars, 1989, p. 38). Taylor believed that economic rewards could motivate employees, provided that those rewards were linked to individual performance.

Other scientific management pioneers followed in Taylor's footsteps. Morris Cooke applied scientific management principles to educational and municipal organizations. Henry Gantt created a scheduling technique for production control that utilized a bar chart, coined the "Gantt chart." The Gantt chart is still widely used today. Frank and Lillian Gilbreth combined the study of motion and work methods with psychology. The Gilbreths' work contributed significantly to research in the areas of fatigue, micromotion, and morale.

Yet it was Henri Fayol who first issued a complete statement on a theory of general management. In Fayol's primary work, he introduced 14 principles of management: (1) division of work, (2) formal positional authority, (3) discipline based on obedience and respect, (4) unity of command, (5) unity of direction, (6) subordination of the individual interests to the general interests, (7) dependence of wages on many factors, (8) centralization of authority, (9) scalar chain (line) of authority, (10) an ordered and ensured place for everything, (11) equity, (12) stability of tenured personnel, (13) initiative, and (14) the building of harmony and unity within the organization.

During the early twentieth century—a time of fairly rapid industrialization that encouraged public and private organizations to emphasize production and efficiency as criteria of effectiveness—mechanistic design evolved. Mechanistic design is informed by the hierarchically structured management philosophies of the time. Mechanistic organizational design promotes an effective organizational structure characterized by highly specialized jobs, homogeneous departments, narrow spans of control, and relatively centralized authority. Classical design theory presupposes a single best way to structure an organization to achieve these ends (Gibson, Ivancevich, Donnelly, & Konopaske, 2011).

Max Weber, in describing applications of the mechanistic model, coined the term "bureaucracy." Because authority involves the legitimate right to exact obedience from others, organizational design involves domination. Weber's search for the forms of domination that evolve in society led him to the study of bureaucratic structure (Gibson et al., 2011, p. 497). Gibson says, "According to Weber, the bureaucratic structure is superior to any other form in precision, stability, stringency of its discipline and its reliability. It thus makes possible a high degree of calculability of results for the heads of the organization and for those acting in relation to it. The bureaucracy compares to other forms of organizations as does the machine to other nonmechanical modes of production" (2011, p. 498).

Weber's description of bureaucratic organizational design has the following characteristics: (1) all tasks are divided into highly specialized jobs; (2) each task is performed in accordance with a system of abstract rules to ensure uniformity and coordination of different tasks; (3) each member or office of the organization is responsible for job performance to one, and only one, manager; (4) each employee of the organization relates to other employees and clients in an impersonal, formal manner, maintaining a social distance with subordinates and clients; and (5) employment in the organization is based on technical qualifications and is protected against arbitrary dismissal.

The nature of Weber's characteristics of an organizational bureaucracy is identical to the Fayol's management theory principles. Both describe an organization that functions mechanically to accomplish the organization's goals in a highly efficient manner.

The Human-Relations Era

The Great Depression of 1929 saw unemployment in excess of 25 percent. Afterward, unions sought and gained major advantages for the working class. In this period, known as the golden age of unionism, legislatures and courts actively supported organized labor and the worker. Graff and Krout (1971) described this event:

> The collapse of the stock market was the initial stage of the long and bleak great depression. Unemployment which had been growing since the previous July, continued to increase at an alarming rate following the crash on Wall Street. Spending by consumers, which had been declining since July, continued to slacken. As businessmen stopped building new plants, the number of jobs available decreased. Income was not distributed well enough to keep people employed through an increase in spending by consumers. Farmers found prices lower than ever; millions of working people could neither buy factory goods nor find employment. Middle-class people everywhere could not meet the time payments on their cars, refrigerators or houses. The "prosperity decade" had ended with a sickening thud (p. 631).

During these times of greater employee supply and lesser demand, employers easily solicited efforts from employees. As was the case when quality and price frequently gave way to availability in production decisions during the industrialization period, so too did employers sacrifice the human aspects of the employer-employee relationship during the lean years of the Depression.

Recognizing this problem, emphasis during this time had shifted to attempts at understanding the needs of workers. The human-relations movement arose in the early 1930s, and no activity better exemplifies this philosophy than the famous Hawthorne studies (1924–32) conducted by Harvard University psychologist Elton Mayo. The Hawthorne studies led to an increased interest in the human problems in the workplace and a refocusing on the human factor of production.

Again, as was the case with the efforts of Frederick Taylor, many followed in Mayo's humanistic footsteps to better understand, describe, and document the intangible human relations of the time. One such person was Mary Parker Follett, who from 1920 to 1933 espoused a basic theory that the fundamental challenge for any organization was to build and maintain dynamic, yet harmonious, human relations within the organization. In 1938, Chester Barnard, another follower of Mayo, effectively integrated traditional management and the behavioral sciences. Barnard viewed the organization as a social structure and stressed the psychosocial aspects of organizations.

The International Movement

In this changing context, organizational design and management philosophies are attempting to combat these newly perceived international opportunities or threats. The predominate management philosophies of this period are the systems, contingency, and total quality management (TQM) approaches.

Process management, as a management philosophy, has evolved most notably in this era of internationalization. Process management crosses over both management philosophy and organizational design concepts, as discussed in the next section.

A process is quite simply a series of activities that, when followed, produce a desired result. We have processes for nearly everything we do in life. Even as I wake in the morning, I have a process I follow for showering, shaving, and getting dressed.

Is a process similar to a routine? The answer is yes. A routine is defined by my desk copy of the *American Heritage College Dictionary* as "a prescribed detailed course of action to be followed regularly; a standard procedure . . . a set of customary procedures or activities."

A process is an activity or group of activities that takes an input, adds value to it, and provides an output. The key in having a good process resides in:

- The clearness of the definition of the many activities that make up the process
- The degree of adherence to the process activities
- The adequacy of the process activities to satisfy the desired outcome.

Let's look at an example. Every morning for breakfast I eat cereal and toast. Although it sounds somewhat compulsive, I have worked for years to perfect a process, based on the geographical location of items in my kitchen, that maximizes efficiency. The process I use looks like the following.

- Place bread in the toaster.
- Obtain butter from the refrigerator.
- Obtain cinnamon from the spice cabinet.
- Obtain plate for toast (which is in a different cabinet than the bowl for cereal).
- While toast is browning, obtain bowl for cereal.
- With bowl in hand, obtain spoon from drawer and cereal from cabinet.
- Place cereal in bowl (at this time toast pops up from toaster).
- Place toast (one piece at a time) on toast plate and butter.
- When second piece of toast is buttered, place it upside down on the first piece of toast.
- Holding both pieces of toast, gently tap plate over sink to remove excess toast crumbs from plate.
- On the way to the table, grab milk from refrigerator.
- Place toast on table, pour milk on cereal.
- Replace milk in refrigerator; while milk is softening cereal, remove clean dishes from dishwasher.
- Return to softened cereal and enjoy breakfast.

Now, as compulsive as it sounds, this process is so engrained in my routine that I perform these activities without even thinking about them. My movements around the kitchen are swift and efficient as I proceed from one activity of my breakfast process to the next. The end result is an efficient process, because I have minimized my movements throughout the kitchen, and an effective process, because I have gained the benefit of a nutritional morning breakfast.

By definition, then, the many activities of a process, when executed successfully, produce a consistent end result.

Process management is concerned with making sure the defined process is still efficient and effective, in that it minimizes the activities of the individuals performing the process and that the end result is still what is desired. Process management, then, is simply managing the existing process.

Creating an efficient process involves the elimination of non-value-added activities. In other words, once we identify all of the activities to be performed and the order in which we intend to perform them, we must then look to see if some activities:

- Are redundant and can be deleted
- Are best performed in another sequence
- Can be combined with previous or subsequent activities
- Are potentially missing, which could enhance the efficiency of the entire process

In business and industry, process management, as characterized by R. Choyce (1992) and J. Gioia (1992), provides management with:

- A way of thinking systematically about the behavior of people at work in an organizational setting.
- A vocabulary of terms, concepts, theories, and methodologies that allow work experiences to be clearly analyzed, shared, and discussed.
- Techniques for dealing with many of the problems that commonly occur in the work setting.

Process management is not a new concept. Process management originated as part of the production-oriented statistical quality control movement in the late 1920s and early 1930s. What is relatively new, however, is the transition of process management methods from a manufacturing environment to a total company orientation.

Process management is a continuous effort that recognizes that the work done in an organization is accomplished through a series of processes and charges the organization's managers with ensuring that these processes are clearly defined, healthy, and competitive. It is a comprehensive approach, the goal of which is to increase the effectiveness, efficiency, control, and adaptability of a given organization.

Business process management represents a break from some of the traditional concepts of organizational authority (Stinnett, 1992). It requires a new way of looking at, and thinking about, long-established assumptions concerning hierarchies and organizational structure. For instance, in a conventional organization it would be most unusual for the vice president or director of one group or division to become directly involved in the activities taking place in another group or division. Because process management involves managing processes across divisional and organizational boundaries, as well as within these boundaries, it requires a more flexible management strategy. It also requires close cooperation among managers in diverse functional and operational units to ensure that the process flow is not interrupted by conflicts over lines of authority (King, 1992).

Process management relies on process definition, elimination of non-value-added activities, customer/supplier orientation, and a team approach (Hoban, 1992; Price, 1992). Process management processes utilize continuous process improvement (CPI), which assumes that a measurement baseline has been established. Through CPI, the process is measured forever. CPI accounts for error elimination, innovation, and business changes. All activities of a process are questioned; nothing is sacred.

Process management offers organizations a means of applying to nonproduction functional organizations the same quality improvement and defect reduction techniques used in manufacturing processes. Many engineering, service, and business processes offer an organization the greatest untapped potential for cost savings through quality and productivity improvement (Welsh, 1992). Process management, with its emphasis on business process quality, is the most meaningful way to apply the principle of quality throughout an enterprise (Zells, 1992).

The basic steps in creating an efficient process are:

- Determine what end result is desired.
- Identify the activities currently used to accomplish this process.
- Determine how the current activities are ordered (we call this the interrelatedness of the many activities).
- From the new flow chart created, of activities and their ordering, ask which activities do not seem to add value, could be merged, or seem inappropriately placed in time.

- Create a new flow chart depicting the ideal scenario (don't worry about who currently does which activities or how).
- Identify measurement points in the new process that will allow you to determine how well the new process is working. In my breakfast scenario above, does the toast pop up before I am ready to butter it? If it does, then either the toast will get cold, or I need to modify my process to get me back to the toast in a more timely manner.
- Test the new process. In a business environment, this may mean making people assignments to the activities. It may further mean reassigning individuals or work in a manner not previously assigned.

As stated above, it is only through proper measurement that we can make required changes to an existing process in order to increase either efficiency or effectiveness. Proper measurement requires that we identify sufficient measurement points throughout our process, and, that these measurement points are reflective of how the process is running.

For example, if I were to choose to measure how long it takes to grab the milk from the refrigerator, that would not be as meaningful as determining how long it takes to grab a bowl, spoon, and cereal and to pour the cereal into the bowl, because if the toast pops up before I can get the cereal into the bowl, then perhaps pouring the cereal into the bowl should be done after the toast is buttered.

We can also choose too many measurement points. Too many points can lead to excessive measurement so that all we accomplish is taking measurements.

General Program Planning Models

According to Theodore Kowalski, the program planner can select one of four basic combinations with regard to a program planning format: "(1) a nonintegrated linear model, (2) a nonintegrated nonlinear model, (3) an integrated nonlinear model, and (4) an integrated linear model" (1988, p. 99). Nonintegrated means that attention is being paid solely to the programs being developed without considering the organizational and environmental factors. Integrated models consider criteria from the environment, organization and individual learners. Kowalski refers to integrated models as "systems models" (p. 92). Linear models provide a sequential path that outlines the steps to be completed in performing the program planning. Nonlinear models, however, are not to be construed as being unstructured; they attempt to provide greater flexibility in terms of time and resource allocation.

The important components of successful program planning can be discussed through the systems approach model (SAM), an integrated nonlinear model, articulated by Murk and Wells (1988). SAM consists of five components, which are dynamically interrelated, yet independent. For SAM to be successful, all five components must be used, although not in the traditional linear fashion (p. 45).

SAM's components for program planning are: needs assessment, instructional planning and development, administration and budget development, program implementation, and program evaluation. Edgar J. Boone, R. Dale Safrit, and Jo Jones substantiate these as predominate components in their evaluation of nine of the most prevalent program planning models in adult education (2002, p. 20).

In their discussion of needs assessment as a part of program planning for adult and continuing education programs, Murk and Wells state that "all planners involved should understand the needs, aspirations, and educational and financial limitations of the adult participants," and "as a training coordinator or program planner, you should know the major purposes or rationale behind the development of your program" (1988, p. 46).

Instructional planning and development proceeds from an understanding of what is to be done, that is, the needs have been determined. This phase of program planning is concerned with defining the event or program, identifying meaningful goals, objectives, and outcomes, selecting the appropriate activities, choosing effective instructors, coordinating program logistics, and developing and administering formative evaluation procedures.

Murk and Wells identify administration and budget development as the third component of program planning, which consists of formulating a cost-effective budget, securing a funding source, establishing administrative personnel, developing a competency in marketing techniques, and coordinating the environmental conditions that contribute to a more meaningful learning experience (1988, p. 46).

The implementation phase of program planning attempts to execute the program in accordance with the previously defined plan. During implementation, constant feedback is required, which enables real-time, dynamic program modification. This real-time modification helps the program facilitator to more adequately satisfy the dynamically realized needs of the participants.

The final component to SAM is program evaluation. Program evaluation, as applicable to SAM, is premised on the same principles as those identified in section 2.4.3.2 of this study.

SAM allows components to be executed in the order that makes the most sense. Murk and Wells, in discussing this interrelatedness, identify a situation where the knowledge gained from a previous program is used as the starting point for a similar, more recent version. In this example, the program planner would first look at the program implementation of the already completed program. SAM, as depicted in this example, supports this nonlinear approach to program planning.

Integrated Linear Models versus Integrated Nonlinear Models

There are some nonintuitive theoretical concepts that begin to surface when discussing integrated linear planning models and integrated nonlinear planning models, such as the systems approach model. One must intuitively ask such questions as: How can a program planner perform program development unless it is known what the user wants? And how can one identify a program budget or choose effective instructors unless the program has been conceived or preliminarily developed?

These types of questions lead to the belief that there is an inherent sequentiality to integrated nonlinear models, which perplexes the differentiation between linear and nonlinear models in general. Therefore, this section attempts to resolve that perceived perplexity by offering a different perspective of the relationship between integrated linear planning models and integrated nonlinear planning models.

The remainder of this discussion is based on the premise that integrated nonlinear planning models are really macro-models, and that integrated linear models are really micro-models. They are not separate models; rather, the integrated linear model is a subset of the higher-level, integrated nonlinear model.

This view is justified by the fact that program planning is really composed of numerous subcomponents within the basic framework of the predominantly identified components necessary for successful program planning (see section above for predominant components). It should be intuitive that at a micro level, a needs assessment is required prior to the completion of program development, and that a budget for a program cannot be fully identified until such factors as program length, costs of instructors, and place of instruction are identified. In this sense, there is a sequentiality or linearity to program planning. And from this perspective, a linear model provides a very specific stepwise progression to program planning.

In reality, however, not all activities of program planning progress at the same pace through a linear model. The essence of linearity resides in each subcomponent having a predecessor and successor activity, but at any particular point in time, different subcomponents may be at different stages in the linear model. This important characteristic provides us with the macro view of program planning, and hence, leads us to nonlinear models.

Nonlinear models allow for various activities to be at different stages in the program planning model. Note that this is true even though each activity must, at a micro level, go through a very logical natural progression, as depicted in the linear models. The key to this micro/macro discussion is that final versions of activities (such as budgets and programs) cannot be determined until the required predecessor step is completed. For example, program budgets cannot be fully completed until all costs have been finally identified.

I propose that program planning is a cyclical process, but possesses an inherent sequentiality. The inherent sequentiality is at the micro level and must be adhered to by each of the subactivities, while the cyclical outer process provides us with the macro view we call nonlinear program planning. The outer/macro process provides the framework that allows for the cycling to take place. The final version of end products, however, cannot be generated until the sequential activities have been completed. This does not prevent preliminary or draft versions of end products from being begun or completed; in fact, the macro view encourages the development of intermediate versions of planning products—hence the cyclical nature. Figure 3.2 below depicts this relationship.

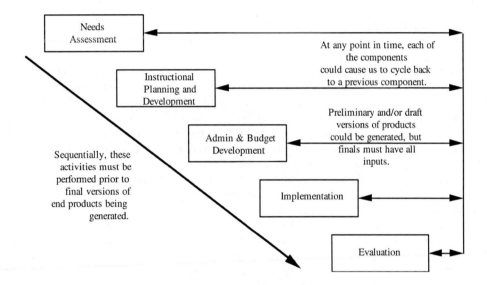

Figure 3.2. Cyclical Nature of a Sequential Process

I have used the components of SAM, as discussed by Murk and Wells, to depict the macro and micro relationships of the planning models. The microview (linear) stipulates that final versions of end products cannot be completed until the planning process has been cycled through at least once. The macroview (nonlinear) allows each component to proceed, recognizing that only preliminary data is available for the generation of component end products.

Evaluation Methodologies and Accountability

Kowalski identifies three types of evaluation methodologies: summative, formative, and ex post facto (1988, p. 151). An adult- or continuing-education program could be evaluated using any of these evaluation methodologies, depending on the purpose(s) of the evaluation.

A summative evaluation is concerned with making judgments. Its intent is to determine, for instance, whether a program is accomplishing its goals. For example, one or more programs may claim to accomplish the same basic goals. In a summative evaluation, the judgment to be made is which program comes closest to accomplishing those goals. The losing program, most likely, would be discontinued.

By contrast, a formative evaluation is not concerned with making culminating judgments, but rather with making improvements to the program under evaluation. This form of evaluation seeks to identify ways in which experience can serve to improve the selected program the next time it is offered (Kowalski, 1988, p. 152).

An ex post facto evaluation is a longitudinal study. Kowalski states, "the purpose is to compare the results of a given workshop with the reported results in another company" (Kowalski, 1988, p. 152). In other words, the company is attempting to achieve the same results already reported by another company. Because the results from the other company have already been reported, the comparison is made after the fact, ex post facto.

In short, "summative evaluation may or may not be comparative. It could be used to select one option from many, or it could be used simply to determine if a program did or did not meet its goals. Formative evaluation seeks to improve a program by identifying the degree to which objectives have been met and by using this information to adjust goals, procedures and the like. It is non-comparative. Ex post facto evaluation is comparative. It compares the results of a given program with the previous results of the same program" (Kowalski, 1988, p. 152).

The accountability so important in program planning "is a relatively new concept to the professional practice of adult education. Accountability refers to the practice of reporting efficiency of planned program operation, primarily to the learners and leaders of the target public, the organization, funding sources, the profession, and, where appropriate, the governance body" (Boone et al., 2002, p. 197). That is, as professionals performing evaluations, we have a responsibility to the stakeholders of the educational program to report accurately and promptly our unbiased findings. Therefore, it is critical that the stakeholders are involved in developing the process and evaluation instruments used in performing the evaluation. Up-front stakeholder buy-in is more likely to generate a receptive audience to evaluation findings.

According to Boone and colleagues, "Three processual tasks related to the accountability dimension of the evaluation and accountability subprocess speak to the adult educator's responsibility to (1) report evaluation results, (2) analyze the organization in terms of evaluation results, and (3) make recommendations, based on evaluation results, to the organization" (2002, p. 198).

The program planning process presented in this book is an integrated linear model developed for a specific industry. The evaluation methodology is non-comparative and summative—that is, the intent is to determine whether the outcomes of the program, as mutually determined by the stakeholders and the evaluator, have been satisfied, and if so, to what degree or level of quality. It is hoped that the evaluation results will be used to improve the planning process; from this perspective, there is an element of formative evaluation.

Composition of a Planning Process

Successful execution of a program is largely based on the development of an accurate and well-documented program baseline, from which cost, schedule, and performance deviations can be readily identified and corrected. Planning is only one of the four phases in an overall management process, which are planning, execution, analysis, and adjustment.

The basic model of the four primary phases of a management process are depicted in figure 3.3.

Simply stated, planning identifies what to do, who is to do it, when it is to be done, and what resources are to be expended. Planning forms the foundation for each of the succeeding phases and is the most important phase of the entire process. Execution is simply the realization of the plan generated in the planning phase. Analysis determines the level of adherence to the plan, and adjustments must be made if there are deviations from the plan. This corrective action is determined by either the program manager or jointly by the program manager and the procuring agency.

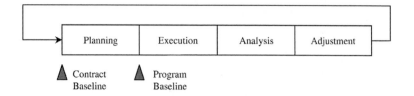

Figure 3.3. Program Management Process Flow

Although it would appear from the process flow that the four program management process phases are sequential, they are not. Planning, of course, must precede execution, analysis, and adjustment. Execution, analysis, and adjustment, however, can—and will—be undertaken simultaneously. A single program may be in each of these phases at the same time, because different activities within the program progress at varying paces.

Program planning is composed of a number of activities associated with defining the program organization: work to be performed; technical, cost, and schedule requirements; and the identification of risks. This study will approach program planning by examining the following activities of the program management planning process: program organization planning, schedule planning, cost planning, and performance planning. Salient features of these activities can be summarized as follows:

- Program organization planning includes the establishment of the planning and program organizations and definition of the work to be performed, known as the work breakdown structure. During the program organization planning phase, the planning work to be accomplished is assigned to the responsible individuals. These assignments are documented in a planning responsibility assignment matrix. Subsequently, when the actual program work has been defined, another program responsibility assignment matrix is created.

- Schedule planning provides the time frame for resource allocation and establishes a baseline for current status and forecasts of completion dates of scheduled work. The scheduling activity consists of a hierarchy of related levels of schedules, with each succeeding, lower level more fully identifying and expanding the tasks necessary to meet the program requirements. The various schedules depict a continuous logical sequence of contract activities and milestones from the master schedule through the intermediate schedule to the detailed schedules.

- Cost planning is primarily concerned with establishing a preliminary budget, with which work progress and actual incurred costs can be compared. Effective cost planning is crucial to the financial survival of the program, organization, and procuring agency. Cost planning entails refining the work breakdown structure and its attendant dictionaries. The dictionaries clearly differentiate the varying work elements defined in the work breakdown structure and describe what the work consists of and what the work might exclude.

- Performance planning is the identification and subsequent documentation of the technical performance requirements. These requirements are stated and/or derived from the contract issued by the procuring agency. Successfully completing the program requires satisfying these requirements. Performance planning also includes the identification of risks. Risk identification includes prioritization according to the probability of occurrence and the extensiveness of the impact on the program. A significant risk is one that has a high probability of occurrence plus a consequential impact.

Chapter 4

Contract Types—
What Type of Contract Should I Enter Into?

There are numerous forms a contract can take on between a buyer and a seller. (A more detailed discussion of contract types can be found in Appendix A.) The three we are going to discuss in this chapter, however, are:

- Fixed price contracts
- Cost reimbursement contracts
- Time and materials contracts

In program management, the program manager will always have certain amounts of risk in the program. How those risks are financially dealt with is determined through the type of contract between the organization and its customer. Early in the bidding phase of the program, the program manager will make many decisions regarding who will assume the cost implications of the potential risks. How risks figure into the equation will be discussed shortly.

In general, contracts are grouped under the heading of two broad categories:

- Fixed price contracts
- Cost reimbursement contracts

When determining which type of contract to select there are many factors involved. Those factors are discussed in the following section. In general, however, and probably more than anything else, the question to ask is, "Can you estimate the amount of effort it takes to complete the tasks?"

If the answer to the above question is "Yes," then a fixed price contract is in order. If the answer to the above question is "No," then a cost reimbursement contract is probably more applicable.

Understanding the amount of effort to perform the task does not mean the work is less defined. It simply means it's more difficult to estimate the level of effort. There is a subtle but significant differentiation in the above statement. Two different contractors may see the same detailed specification but have very different perceptions of what is involved in performing the work to accomplish the tasks. Their differences may be based on experience, understanding of the end-user's operational requirements, or any number of factors.

For example, I was obtaining estimates to have a patio extension placed onto my deck in the backyard. Two contractors were solicited for this estimate. One said he had done many of these type of jobs in the past and figured it would cost X dollars. The other said this really was not something he felt comfortable with estimating, but felt he could do a very good job at it and suggested I pay his labor by the hour for whatever period it took to do the job. The first, therefore, was offering a fixed price to do the job, while the latter was opting for reimbursement of his time (costs).

Factors in Selecting a Contract Type

There may be many factors involved when selecting a type of contract. Some of the more prevalent ones include:

- Price competition
- Type and complexity
- Urgency of the requirement
- Contractor's accounting system

Price Competition

Normally, effective price competition results in realistic pricing. The quantity of competitors has a direct relationship on what type of price an organization can charge. The more competitors there are, the more realistic the price would be expected to be. This is true, unless of course a contractor is attempting to buy into a contract. As an aside, why might an organization "buy" into a contract? There may be many reasons for this, but some of the more prevalent ones include the following.

- Pursuing a new business venture or product line
- Believing there is significant follow-on business
- Protecting an existing business service or product
- Simply having excess cash

The following is a firsthand example of an organization buying into a contract. During the consolidation of the defense industry in the late 1980s and early 1990s, bigger organizations began to bid on government programs that were once bid on and owned entirely by smaller defense contractors. Sometimes, the bigger organizations didn't have the existing product line but firmly believed there was sufficient business opportunity to support the organizations' internal efforts to play catch up. To this end, the larger defense contractors would offer to share the cost of the proposed contract with the government agency. This was a win-win for both the contractor and the government. The government obviously made out, by virtue of having to pay less than would normally otherwise be required, and the contractor made out by obtaining a foothold in a new market niche.

One might ask, why couldn't any of the other smaller contractors have also "bought" into the contract? The answer is that the bigger organizations had deeper pockets. They had considerably greater cash reserves, affording them a greater degree of latitude in their marketing pursuits. To this end, the smaller organizations frequently became subcontractors of the larger prime contractors, who themselves were now answering directly to the government agency.

Type and Complexity

Remember that the more accurate an organization can be on estimating the level of effort of the task, the more the contractor can move toward a fixed price contract versus a cost reimbursable contract. Therefore, as the requirement recurs, or as quantity production begins, the cost risk should shift to the contractor, and a fixed price contract should be considered.

Further discussion is in order here. If you or I were to ask someone to build us a home, they most generally would quote us a fixed price. Say, for example, a two-story, four-bedroom, two-and-a-half-bath home might sell for $150,000. If on the other hand, we ask our friendly builder to build us a nonstandard home, perhaps a log cabin or dome, he or she might not want to quote us a fixed price contract. But if there is a significant demand for log cabins and our builder has now built a number of them, he or she would be more inclined to provide us a fixed price to build that home. The point being, the cost risk associated with performing a task repetitively should be transferred to the contractor, as the contractor now has a firm understanding of what is required to perform the task. A cost reimbursement type of contract, by earlier definition, is used predominantly when the contractor does not have a firm understanding of the level of effort required to perform the task.

A fixed price contract places a risk of cost overrun on the contractor, not the customer. When the builder says your home will cost $150,000, you can generally believe that that is the cost of your home. If there is a cost overrun, that overrun will come from the builder's profits. If, on the other hand, the builder is working under a cost reimbursable type of contract, the risk of cost overruns falls directly on the customer. In this case, if the price of lumber goes up, the customer will be billed the additional costs, not the contractor.

Urgency of the Requirement

If urgency is a primary factor, the customer may choose to assume a greater proportion of the risk or it may offer incentives to ensure timely contract performance.

With urgency may come incomplete specifications or an ambiguous statement of work. A contractor might also expect to see frequent changes, as the requirements of the customer begin to evolve in real time. Under these circumstances, it may be prudent to lock into a cost reimbursement type of contract if you are the contractor.

On the other hand, if you are the customer and you lock into a cost reimbursement type of contract, you should be prepared to incur additional costs as you change the definition of the type of work you wish to have performed.

To demonstrate this concept, let's assume you are having some landscaping done and the contractor agrees with you to be paid for whatever hours it takes to do the job. Now, up front you both agreed to some level of maximum effort required to do the job. But, halfway through the job, you decided to switch tree types, from a one-inch maple to a six-foot blue spruce. As a customer, you should be prepared to not only incur the additional cost of the tree, but the time required to deal with the bigger tree.

Contractor's Accounting System

Cost reimbursement type of contracts require a somewhat elaborate, and—perhaps more important—accurate internal cost collection system. Under a cost reimbursement contract format, the customer is reimbursing the contractor for efforts expended. It is only fair, then, that the contractor be able to produce detailed records, which may only exist because of rigorous procedures. Under the fixed price contract format, the customer does not care what the costs of the contractor may be. The agreement under the fixed price form of contract simply says that any cost overrun will be the responsibility of the contractor.

Many would argue, and justifiably so, that it shouldn't matter which type of contract a contractor has; the accounting system should be equally rigorous. This would seem to be a good argument. But, from the customer's perspective, only a cost reimbursable contract requires the finer attention to detail and subsequent support records. The purpose of having a rigorous system under a fixed price contract scenario is that the contractor can keep more accurate records of expenditures and therefore produce a more accurate bid on future and similar work.

Fixed Price Contracts

A firm fixed price contract provides for a price that is not subject to any adjustment on the basis of the contractor's cost experience in performing the contract. Under this form of contract, a price provided by the contractor to the customer is made up of two components, a cost and a profit. As an aside, price equals cost plus profit. A contractor can reduce the price without suggesting the agreed upon work be modified. However, for a contractor to reduce the cost implies either a modification to the defined work or a further assumption of risks on the part of the contractor. Given this type of contract, if the contractor experiences a cost overrun, then the contractor has to pay for that overrun with profits.

In our house-building example, if the builder determines that he or she has made an error in the required square footage on the ground level, then that cost to extend the ground level should be the responsibility of the contractor, not the future home owner—although the contractor may find another way to make it up later, for example, through customer requested modifications to the original floor plan.

A short story typifies this scenario. When I was building my first home, I received a firm fixed price for the home. In this case the builder did, as just described, underestimate the ground floor square footage requirement as prescribed by the housing addition. He told me that he would simply incur the cost of this error and I was in fact getting a really good deal. Later, as building progressed, I realized I would like to have a ladder installed in my garage for the attic above it. The builder said that would be no problem and the price of this effort, plus material, would be $300. It seemed a little high, but I agreed nonetheless. Another change I wanted to make was to add glass doors to the front of the fireplace. He again agreed to the change and quoted me a price of $300. Again, I agreed and construction continued. I couldn't help but eventually realize that each of the other changes I had requested—patio sliding doors being replaced with French doors, recessed lights versus extended lights, and a windowless full steel garage service door instead of the windowed steel garage service door—had all cost $300 each. I found this either very coincidental or very intentional, perhaps to recover the ground floor estimate made earlier in the construction process. The point being, the builder was bent on recovering the earlier cost overrun. So even though he acted in good faith by eating the original overrun to the ground level, his longer-term intentions were to recover his profits and get financially healthy.

A firm fixed price type of contract provides the maximum incentive for the contractor to control costs and perform effectively.

There are many permutations of this type of contract. The more prevalent ones are identified below and described in subsequent paragraphs.

- Fixed price with economic price adjustment
- Fixed price incentive contracts
- Fixed price level of effort

Fixed Price with Economic Price Adjustment

Fixed price contracts with economic price adjustments, simply stated, provide for the upward and downward revision of the stated contract price based upon the occurrence of previously specified contingencies. Examples of such contingencies include labor and material.

An example of labor contingencies might include pending union negotiations. Under these conditions, it may be known that union talks could produce higher wages, therefore having an impact, either higher or lower, on the overall contract. Given this as a possibility, it would make sense to revisit the contract after such negotiations have been completed.

The case for adjusting the price based on material cost fluctuations is equally applicable. A newly manufactured computer chip will be considerably more expensive on introduction into the market than six months or one year later. Or, in the home-building example, sometimes a builder may say that he knows that the price of lumber is going to rise in price between the time you close on a price and the time the builder purchases your lumber for your home. In this case, the builder may suggest an outside overall price increase and further suggest that your share of that increase may be some amount of dollars.

Under this type of contract, the parties would agree *to* the time and method of calculation in a provision to the contract at the time of agreement. Again, this type of contract may be used when there is serious doubt concerning the market or labor conditions that will exist during an extended period of contract performance.

Fixed Price Incentive Contracts

Fixed price incentive contracts are designed to provide an additional incentive to the contractor for meeting some predefined milestone(s). Milestones may include:

- Cost
- Schedule
- Technical performance

It is important that the performance incentives of this type of contract be balanced such that the contractor does not sacrifice one element in favor of another. For example, if the contractor is incentivized for meeting a schedule requirement, but at the expense of product quality, then the overall objective of a high-quality product within a period of time is of little value. This problem is especially true when additional resources must be spent on meeting the incentivized objective.

Some time ago, Volkswagen had a series of billboards in our town that stated "0 to 60, Yes!" I really got a kick out these billboards. They never said 0 to 60 in five seconds; they simply said, "Sure, we can get there." It may take a while, but it can happen. If Volkswagen was required to perform 0 to 60 miles per hour in five seconds, then probably they could have met this requirement with some supercharged type of engine. But, to accomplish this task, they would have sacrificed cost, most probably schedule, and even some other technical requirements, such as weight or size of the vehicle. For this reason, it is important that incentives be balanced and recognize the potential pitfalls associated with tradeoffs.

Fixed Price Level of Effort

A fixed price level of effort type of contract is designed such that the contractor can provide a specified level of effort in general terms over a specific period of time.

This type of contract is most suitable for investigation or study programs in a specific research and development area. Payment is based on effort expended rather than results achieved. This type of contract is especially good when the contractor, with the customer's help, is trying to define the requirements for a later fixed price type of contract.

For example, perhaps the customer wants to investigate the feasibility of flying people commercially into orbit, circling around the globe, and then returning them safely to earth. And to further the excitement of this, they throw in a free trip to Disney World. If the customer, the organization funding this potential effort, is serious, then they would probably contract with some organization that understands what it takes to fly aircraft outside the Earth's atmosphere. The organization contracted with would probably want to simply do some research to determine the feasibility of such an undertaking. This would make most sense, since running off and building the appropriate type of aircraft would cost billions of dollars, and that's even if they knew what the appropriate type of aircraft was!

In this scenario, the organization doing the investigation might suggest they research the problem for six months with three engineers, a manager, and a secretary. The total full-time commitment would be for five individuals for three months, or fifteen person-months, at a predetermined price. The end result of this effort might simply be a report specifying the feasibility of such an undertaking. Another follow-on study might be performed to determine a ballpark, high-level design and cost. Yet more studies might be performed to determine general population interest or prices people would be willing to pay. It is almost unimaginable how many surveys, investigations, and studies would be performed with this type of undertaking.

Cost Reimbursement Contracts

Unlike fixed price contracts, where the contractor quoted a firm fixed price for the activities of the program or project, cost reimbursement type contracts allow for the contractor to recover actual costs incurred plus some predefined profit. This type of contract is suitable for use when uncertainties involved in the contract performance do not permit costs to be estimated with sufficient accuracy to use any fixed type of fixed price contract.

The conditions of reimbursement are premised on the costs being allowable. In other words, a contractor cannot install in his or her personal home marble flooring and charge the customer, unless of course the customer agrees that putting marble flooring in the contractor's home is part of the overall contracted effort.

Again, as in the case with fixed price contracts, there are many permutations of cost reimbursable contracts. These are identified below and outlined in subsequent paragraphs.

- Cost sharing
- Cost plus incentive fee
- Cost plus award fee
- Cost plus fixed fee
- Cost plus a percentage of cost fee

Cost Sharing

In cost sharing, the contractor simply agrees not to be reimbursed for some portion of the cost incurred. The actual percentage to be shared is determined at contract award and documented in the contract.

The best example of this type of contract was presented earlier. Given the situation where an organization (contractor) might want to enter into a market they had not been in before, cost sharing would be one mechanism for doing this. In this case, the contractor would absorb their share of the costs out of profits from another program or possibly from this program.

Cost Plus Incentive Fee

A cost plus incentive fee contract is a cost reimbursement contract that provides for an initially negotiated fee to be adjusted later by a formula based on the relationship of total allowable costs to total target costs.

The operative terms here are *allowable costs* and *target costs*. On contract award, the contractor has agreed in writing to some target level of expenditure, most generally on a monthly basis, but possibly any interval. Then, at predetermined points in the program, those target costs are compared to actual costs incurred. The relationship of these two costs determines the incentive received by the contractor. When we talk about allowable costs, we are generally grounded in government terminology and definitions.

For example, when working on a government program and having to travel, there are limits to the amount a hotel can cost or you can spend on a meal. These limits seem strange to travelers who do not perform government contracts, but for those of us who have been indoctrinated into this culture, it seems quite normal. One group of people who routinely exceed the government's reimbursable rates is marketing. For this reason, I really enjoy traveling with marketing people. The only times I have ever enjoyed five star restaurants is when I've been with them. Under these reimbursable guidelines, however, the contractor is responsible for costs up and over those identified as reimbursable by the customer.

Cost Plus Award Fee

According to Cibinic (1998):

> The cost plus award fee contract was devised by NASA in the 1960s to introduce incentives for improved performance into major contracts for support services. Since that time it has become one of the major types of contracts used for service contracts including research and development. The cost plus award fee contract provides that the contractor's fee will be determined largely by an award given periodically by a high-ranking official in the procuring agency. While the basic elements to be evaluated in arriving at this award and the evaluation mechanism itself are usually disclosed to the contractor prior to performance, this type of contract is known as a subjective incentive. Since the award official has a significant amount of discretion in establishing the precise amount of award.

This subjectivity has led some contractors to question the use of this type of incentive. But, experiences gathered over the past three decades indicates that cost plus award fee contracts are quite efficient in situations where it is not possible to write a contract specification or work statement that contains a precise description of the work the contractor is expected to perform. (p. 1148)

The major advantage of the cost plus award fee contract is improved communication between parties. In the course of making periodic awards, the customer provides the contractor with a detailed evaluation of the program's cost, schedule, and technical performance, pointing out the program's deficiencies and weaknesses.

The major disadvantage of the cost plus award fee contract is the level of effort it takes to administer the contract reviews, as well as the coordination required to make the awards.

It has become common practice to combine cost plus incentive fee and cost plus award fee contracts. In this scenario, cost plus incentive fee is used to incentivize the contractor for cost control, while the cost plus award fee is used to incentivize the contractor for schedule and technical performance control (Cibinic, 1998, p. 1170).

Cost Plus Fixed Fee

Cost plus fixed fee is a type of contract that provides payment to the contractor of a negotiated fee that is fixed at the inception of the contract. The fixed fee does not vary with actual cost, but may be adjusted as a result of changes to the work to be performed under the contract (Federal Acquisition Regulations System (FAR) 16.306(a)).

Of particular interest here is that the contractor gets zero additional fee for within scope cost growth, plus may earn a bad reputation. If this were not the case, then a contractor would simply have to "grow" the program to earn additional fee (profit).

Cost Plus a Percentage of Cost Fee

Cost plus a percentage of cost fee contracts basically imply that the fee (profit) to be gained by the contractor is tied to the cost incurred by the contractor.

A contractor, then, not only has no incentive to control costs, but in fact could simply increase costs (which are reimbursable under the cost plus contract) and make additional fees in doing so. For this very reason these types of contracts are illegal when dealing with the U.S. government (*Muschany v. United States*, 324 U.S. 49, 1944, 61-62).

Time and Materials Contracts

Time and materials type of contracts are used predominantly when it is not possible at the time of placing the contract to estimate accurately the extent or duration of the work or to anticipate costs with any degree of confidence. This type of contract allows for the acquisition of products or services on the basis of labor hours at predetermined rates and material costs.

Time and material contracts are somewhat limited in their use. They do not provide the customer with any real control over the contractor's work efficiency, nor do they incentivize the contractor to control costs. This does not mean, however, that the contractor has an open pocketbook to expend resources without ramification. An initial "best estimate" or "expected value" is agreed to upfront as part of finalizing the contract.

Labor Hour Contracts

Similar to time and material type of contracts, labor hour contracts are used predominantly when it is not possible at the time of placing the contract to estimate accurately the extent or duration of the work or to anticipate costs with any degree of confidence.

The only real difference between labor hour contracts and time and material type of contracts is that materials are not supplied.

Again, as in the time and material type contract, labor hour contracts are somewhat limited in their use. They do not provide the customer with any real control over the contractor's work efficiency, nor do they incentivize the contractor to control costs.

Letter Contracts

A letter contract is a temporary written preliminary contractual instrument that authorizes the contractor to begin immediately manufacturing products or performing services. It typically has limited dollar value and must be replaced as soon as possible by a definitized contract.

A letter contract basically allows a contractor to begin work now, while the details or bureaucracy can be worked out.

Exercises

Exercise #1

Your customer has asked you to submit a bid to develop a new product. While you have built similar products, you have never built one this complex. The customer has provided a detailed specification and a required finish date. What type of contract will you propose?

Exercise #1 Answer

A firm fixed price contract would be most appropriate in this case. The determining factor is whether you have enough information to accurately estimate what it will take to accomplish the task. With a detailed specification and prior experience you should be able to accurately estimate the cost. Knowing the cost, you can provide a price.

Exercise #2

Assume the scenario of Exercise #1, but in this case the customer does *not* have a detailed specification to provide you. The customer does have, however, a one-page list of desires. What type of contract will you propose?

Exercise #2 Answer

Propose a cost reimbursement type of contract. You no longer have sufficient information to be able to accurately estimate the job. Determining the requirements is essential.

Exercise #3

Your company produces ink pens. In a typical year you manufacture and produce a hundred thousand pens. A new chain of business supply stores has asked you to submit a proposal to have your pens featured in their stores. What type of contract will you propose?

Exercise #3 Answer

Since you can accurately estimate the level of effort to produce this item, a firm fixed price type of contract would be appropriate.

Exercise #4

You have been asked to work as a consultant to a program estimated to last three years. You are currently consulting on several other projects and are concerned as to whether you have sufficient time to devote to this project. If the primary concern to both you and your customer is how many hours you can devote to this project, what type of contract would you propose?

Exercise #4 Answer

At first glance you might think this should be a labor hours or time and material contract, but remember you have concern about your available time. With this concern, a firm fixed price level of effort contract would be most appropriate. The actual level of effort you price becomes the commodity you are selling. Since with this contract the level of effort is agreed to by both parties, there should be no questions regarding the amount of time you are devoting to this project. If time availability is not a problem, simply go with a labor hour or time and materials type of contract.

Chapter 5

The Bidding Process—Obtaining a Price Quote

I was standing in the backyard a while back, looking at the general appearance of the landscaping, and decided I should do some additional landscaping with stone and the like. Recognizing this is not my expertise, it was suggested I get some estimates to perform the work. This process of identifying contractors, asking for something to be done, evaluating the contractor's proposal, and agreeing to have the work done is what we call in this chapter the *bidding process*.

The bidding process begins, therefore, after having identified a need, in this case, the need to have additional landscaping done. Our first step is to define the overall thoughts we have on what we would like to have done; this step is called *requirements identification* and will be discussed in the following section ("Defining the Work to be Performed").

Once we have the general requirements defined, we can call one of the many landscapers in the telephone book and ask for a cost estimate to perform the work. In this step, we are asking for a *request for proposal* (RFP), which is something the customer requests from a potential contractor. The more completely we can describe the work to be done, the more accurate the contractor can be in determining a price for the work. As an aside, note that price is what is presented to the customer, and is made up of the contractor's cost plus profit.

The contractor, with the provided details, will generate a proposal. The proposal may be as simple as a one-page list of materials with number of hours of labor and a total cost, or may be more elaborate, presented in a notebook or folder with company history, major projects or customers, and a discussion of why this contractor is better at performing this type of work than others. In either case, we, the customer, will have something to review and compare to other contractors.

We talk about comparing one contractor's proposal to another contractor's proposal. To do this requires that the proposals be similar. That means the proposals must address the same work to be performed, the same materials (if any were specified by the customer), and the same time period to perform the work. Time period can be especially important, especially in the landscaping scenario. For example, if the landscaper has a slow period during the year, then he or she might be more willing to perform the work for a lesser price than during a more demanding time of the year. It's important, therefore, that both contractors get the same instructions for bidding purposes.

Sometimes, as we talk with a contractor, we learn more about what we really want. In fact, sometimes as we learn more, we may want to go back to the original contractors who already bid the job and ask for an updated bid. Or if we think the contractors might consider doing the job for less if asked, then we might want to give them a call or ask in writing for a best and final offer to do the work. Frequently we ask this question of contractors in the form of "Is that the best price I can get?"

Once the contractors who bid on the job submit their proposals, they go on with other work waiting for our (the customer's) decision. It's not uncommon during this waiting period for the contractor to call us and ask if they can supply any additional information. This is obviously more true in some cases than others. For example, when looking at cars, it is more likely that a car salesperson will call the customer before a landscaper.

It is even possible after we, the customer, have made the decision, are asked by a losing contractor why they were not chosen. It may be as simple as price or even the more delicate issue of personality. This type of conversation is what we call the *post-decision conference*.

Figure 5.1 depicts the above discussion and overall process.

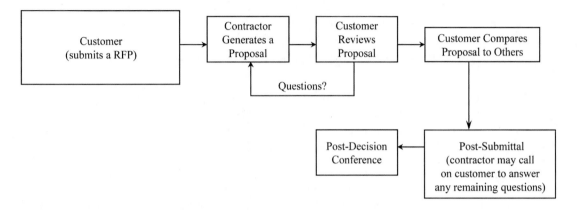

Figure 5.1. Overall Bidding Process

The bidding process is an interesting courtship between the customer and the potential contractors. Figure 5.2 is another depiction of the overall bidding process.

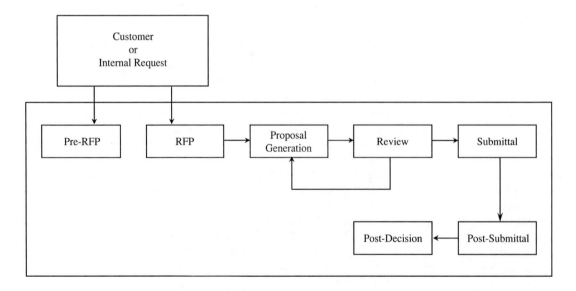

Figure 5.2. Pre-RFP to RFP Interaction

The process begins, sometimes, long before the initial RFP ever gets distributed by the customer. For purposes of this discussion, however, we will begin the process with the customer's receipt of the RFP. The RFP is designed to solicit from a set of potential bidders (contractors) a uniformly created proposal to provide products or services to the customer. The RFP itself is the culmination of an exhaustive—and frequently lengthy—planning, budgeting, and approval process on the part of the customer.

RFPs minimally contain the following information:

- Schedules for product or service deliveries
- Format for providing costs/price
- Technical specifications
- Statement of work (SOW)
- Data deliverables
- Any RFP-referenced documents
- Special instructions
- Award evaluation factors
- Format in which to submit the contractor's proposal

Complex RFPs, those indicative of the U.S. federal, state, or city governments, can contain as many as thirteen major sections, describing all of the above and other more detailed information, such as how to package the contractor's product for delivery to the customer.

Notice that the customer in the above figure can be either an outside customer or an inside customer. If the effort to be performed is an internal research and development program, or something similar, the customer may very well be senior management of the organization. If this is the case, then the contractor is an organization within the same organization.

Once the RFP is received, the proposal generation activity is initiated. During this period, there will likely be one or more peer team reviews of the proposal. On final review, the proposal is ready for submittal to the customer. Once submitted, the effort is not yet over. There is usually an opportunity to fine-tune an initial submittal before a customer decision is made as to which contractor will be awarded the program.

Bid Organization

A proposal is typically made up of three basic volumes—management, technical, and cost—as indicated in figure 5.3.

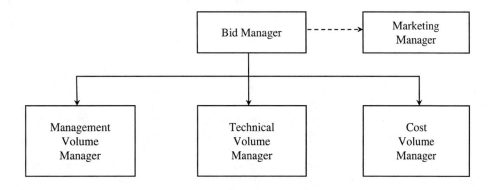

Figure 5.3. Typical Bid Organization

Each volume, depending on the size of the proposal effort, may have its own manager responsible for the generation of that volume. The management volume should, without doubt, describe clearly the following:

- How your organization proposes to obtain and organize its resources to perform on the program
- Who the major players are, with information on their education and experience as it relates to this type of program
- How your program will interface with the customer throughout the life of the program
- How your organization will provide the product and/or service with more efficiency and effectiveness than your competition
- How you can accomplish the program's objectives within cost and schedule constraints
- How you have been involved with other programs of this nature, perhaps in terms of size, complexity, cost, or other pertinent ways

Although the management volume conveys pertinent information about your organization, the technical volume may be most important in terms of your winning or not winning the contract. The technical volume generally is weighted most heavily by your customer. After all, if your product or service is not what the customer wants, then why buy it? The technical volume contains information such as:

- What exactly are you selling to your customer?
- Why is your product or service better than your competition's?
- Specifically, how will your organization build or make this product or service?
- How does your organization intend to satisfy the customer's requirements?

Assuming your organization has sufficiently convinced the customer that it can perform the program as required (management volume) and that it can produce a superior product or service to its competition (technical volume), then the next most critical question is, "What does it cost?"

The cost volume is where the cost and price for the product or service is detailed to the level required by the instruction in the RFP. Typically, the customer will require that all of the bidders prepare their costs in the same format, so that costs for work performed can be compared. The format for the bid is typically outlined as part of a customer-provided work breakdown structure (WBS). The WBS is discussed in subsequent paragraphs. By requiring the contractors to bid their efforts in accordance with a predefined format for predefined work, the customer can then compare apples to apples and oranges to oranges.

This is most obvious by way of an example. If you ask multiple builders to build a four-bedroom home with three baths, on a finished basement, you will most likely get very different prices. This is especially true when moving up and down the quality line of builders. A builder might suggest that it is not fair to compare their price to others' because they use only the finest grade of lumber, or heir studs are only twelve inches apart instead of eighteen. Therefore, when requesting a price from a builder, you typically receive a description of the specifications of the home, detailing each item, its construction features, and its cost. This now allows the home builder to compare, on an equal basis, one builder's price to another's.

The marketing manager is always an integral part of the entire proposal process. It was most probably the marketing manager who identified the opportunity initially. The marketing manager probably knows the customer better than most others and may have some idea of how much the customer is willing to spend for this particular product or service. He or she, therefore, should be an integral part of this proposal team.

Note that in some cases, for example, soliciting a bid to do some landscaping around the house, the three volumes may be simply one sheet of paper. And the marketing manager, volume manager, and bid manager may be the same person.

Responsibility Assignment Matrix

When we talk about a bid and proposal responsibility assignment matrix (RAM), we are generally trying to pictorially depict who has responsibility, and what kind of responsibility, for each activity of the bid process. Figure 5.4 depicts a fictitious bid and proposal RAM.

Notice that for each activity to be performed there is assigned primary, secondary, review, and approval responsibilities. In this example, the bid manager has primary responsibility for those activities involved with generating the proposal, while corporate management and division management have approval responsibility for those items where cost/price is involved. Each of these activities will be reviewed in subsequent paragraphs.

One point of interest is that the functional managers have primary responsibility for conducting preliminary cost reviews. Why would functional organizations have this responsibility and not the bid manager? Functional management is responsible for staffing the programs and bidding the costs for their respective work activities.

Before the Request for Proposal

Figure 5.5 depicts the series of activities that occur before the RFP is received by the contractor.

Notice that there are a series of decisions and activities that take place before the RFP arrives at the potential contractor's facility.

- Is this a business opportunity at this point in time?
- Who is going to be the bid manager?
- What is the anticipated scope of the pending RFP?
- What is the anticipated budget for the RFP effort?
- Who might participate in the proposal effort?

As can be seen from figure 5.5, the marketing manager, business area director, and general manager are the primary players until the bid manager is assigned. Once assigned, the bid manager assumes responsibility for all other activities associated with preparing the initial budgets, determining who will work on the proposal team, and notifying the proposal participants.

When the bid manager and the marketing manager request bid authorization, they are in essence asking permission to spend some number of dollars over a specified period of time to work on the proposal. Notice that the marketing manager, business area director, and general manager are the ones involved in approving such expenditures. Once expenditures are approved, the bid manager prepares and issues a bid request letter that provides authorization for the functional organizations to begin thinking about this program. In other words, the functional organizations know that this proposal effort appears to have management's blessing, at least for some period of time at some predefined expenditure level.

On Receipt of the Request for Proposal

Assuming there was a pre-RFP effort, many decisions including the following would already be established:

- Who the bid (proposal) manager will be
- What the funding limits will be
- What level of effort will be expended
- What the schedule for generating the proposal will be

If there was not a pre-RFP phase, then these activities and decisions will have to take place after the receipt of the RFP. This is most unfortunate if this is the case, because seldom is there sufficient time perform these activities and prepare the proposal, unless of course, the proposal is for a routine product or service that is simpler to bid on.

In fact, in the extreme simpler of cases, as in the case of the individual landscaper, a simple thirty-minute visit to your home may be sufficient. Figure 5.6 depicts the RFP process.

Task	Corporate Management	Division General Manager	Business Area Director	Marketing	Bid Manager	Applicable Functional Organization
Pre-RFP and RFP						
Appoint Bid Manager	R/A	A	P			
Establish Scope/Proposal Plan	R/A	R/A	A	S	P	
Establish Proposal Budget	R/A	R/A	A	A	P	
Make Bid/No Bid Decision		R/A	A	S	P	
Issue Request for Bid Request (BR) Authorization		R/A	A	S	P	
Issue BR Letter				S	P	
Establish Proposal Bid Team			A	S	P	
Develop Proposal Directive			R	S	P	
Prepare for Proposal Kick-off Meeting				S	P	S
Proposal Generation						
Conduct Bid Kick-off Meeting				S	P	
Prepare Draft Proposal			A	A	P	S
Prepare Final Proposal Original Master					P	S
Review and Approval						
Conduct Technical Pink Team Review			R/A	S	P	S
Conduct Technical Red Team Review			R/A	S	P	S
Conduct Preliminary Cost Reviews					R	P
Conduct Business Directorate Review		R	R	R	P	S
Conduct Final Cost Review		R/A	A	A	P	S
Conduct Bid Review	R/A	R/A	A	A	P	S
Submittal						
Publish and Submit Proposal					S	P
Post-Submittal and Post-Decision						
Respond to Questions		R/A	R/A	S	P	S
Submit Response					P	S
Respond to Best and Final Offer (BAFO)	R/A	R/A	A	A	P	S
Prepare Win/Lose Debrief	R	R	R/A	S	P	
Prepare Lessons Learned Report	R	R	R	S	P	S
Close Bid Request Charge Number					P	S

Legend:

P - Primary Responsibility
S - Secondary Responsibility
R - Review Responsibility
A - Approval Responsibility

Figure 5.4. Bid and Proposal Responsibility Assignment Matrix

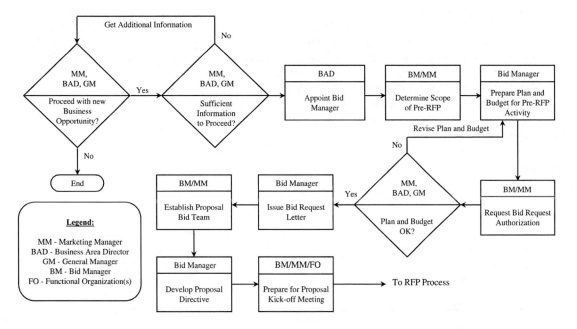

Figure 5.5. Pre-RFP Process Flow

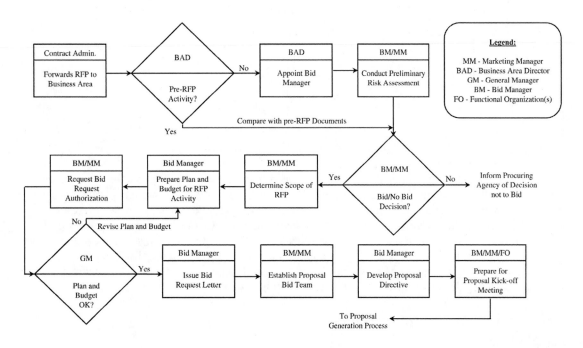

Figure 5.6. RFP Process

Notice that many of the decisions and activities are the same as in the pre-RFP process, if the pre-RFP process was not followed. One new step, after the appointment of the bid manager, is the preliminary risk assessment performed by the bid manager and the marketing manager. Performing a risk assessment on a program is typically the responsibility of the systems engineering functional organization. Any organization, however, can perform a risk assessment. In fact, the program manager will routinely assess the risk/reward aspects of key decisions on the program during program execution.

Also of interest is the RFP came in-house through the contract administrator. The contract administrator is the only individual who should be sending contractual document to, or receiving contractual documents from, the customer.

Proposal Generation Process

The proposal generation process is depicted in figure 5.7.

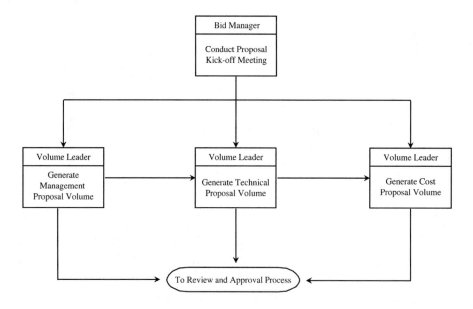

Figure 5.7. Proposal Generation Process

During the proposal generation process, each of the volume leaders is responsible for her or his respective volume of the overall proposal. One mechanism for creating a volume is through a graphics-oriented approach known as storyboarding. Storyboarding is a process where the entirety of what is intended to be said is placed on multiple walls of a proposal room (sometimes referred to as a proposal war room) in the form of an outline. The outline of each volume is made up of major themes and subthemes. The volume leaders then attempt to fill in the story line as it appears in outline form on the walls. The proposal is best depicted pictorially with supporting text. This form of pictorial representation seems to be more appealing than simply reading through page after page of excruciating details.

Review and Approval Process

Figure 5.8 depicts the review and approval process.

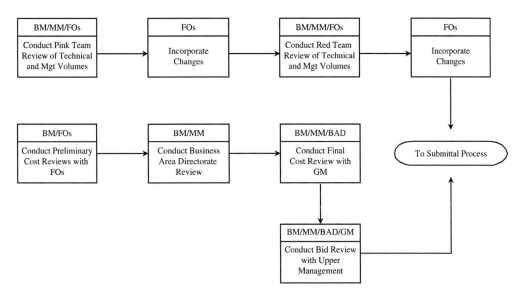

Figure 5.8. Review and Approval Process

Throughout the development of the proposal there will be many reviews of the three basic volumes. The technical and management volumes are reviewed separately from the cost volume.

The number of reviews the technical and management volumes go through is dependent upon the amount of time available before the final submission. In the above process there are two reviews of these volumes. We typically refer to these reviews by names of colors, as in the above where we call them pink and red teams. There have been defined as many four different team reviews:

- Blue/pink team
- Red team
- Gold team
- Black team

The blue/pink team evaluations are early course correction reviews. The fundamental technical architecture and programmatic direction of the company's proposal is evaluated. At this point, format is not the issue as much as identified deficiencies and suggestions for correction. The red team review is intended to critique the proposal for compliance against the RFP instructions and evaluation criteria. The red team looks for consistency and continuity among volumes. The red team is also concerned with presentation themes, graphics utilized, and overall message clarity and crispness. The gold team is typically a final review of the proposal before submission to the customer. The members of the gold team are usually senior managers of the organization. Also, at this point, final aesthetics are assessed. Items such as the table of contents and the like are scanned for correctness. The black team is not a proposal review team, but instead a team designed to "sniff" out information about the organization's key competitors. They perform confidently market analyses and report on the organization's strengths and weaknesses (Frey, 1999, p. 139).

Notice again who the participants are in the pink and red team reviews. The business manager and the marketing manager are leading the strategic direction of the proposal, while the functional managers are concerned with content and adherence to the RFP. The cost volume review process takes a slightly different path, as it moves through the senior management chain. In both cases, the bid manager and the marketing manager are taking the lead. In the final cost review, the business area director and the general manager will be present to offer their input before submission to the customer.

Submittal Process

Once the proposal is written, reviewed, and approved, it is ready to be submitted. Preparation for submittal involves printing and binding the proposal, creating the required transmittal covers, packing the proposal in appropriate shipping containers, and delivering it to the customer. Figure 5.9 depicts the submittal process.

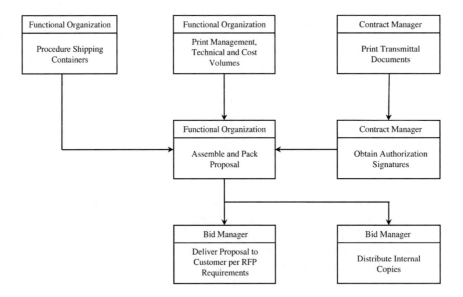

Figure 5.9. Submittal Process

In some instances the deadline is so near that the organization is required to hand-deliver the proposal to the customer. On a major proposal a number of years ago, our proposal was twelve five-inch binders thick. The customer had requested three copies, yielding thirty-six five-inch binders to be delivered. We packaged the binders into relatively small carry-on size boxes and chartered a plane for delivery. I personally loaded the boxes onto the chartered plane, flew to Washington, D.C., our destination, unloaded the boxes into a chartered van, made the delivery, and flew home—all in one long afternoon. Obviously, the projected earnings from this program was rather large, to be able to afford the price associated with this form of delivery.

Notice that a functional organization is responsible for procuring the shipping containers, printing, and packing the proposal. The printing functional organization could very well be the printing department, packing functional organization the packing department, and the functional organization responsible for procuring the shipping containers the shipping department. Functional organizations are those organizations representing major disciplines or functions in the organization. For example, in our home-building example, functional organizations may be plumbers, framers, electricians, or masons.

Post-Submittal Process

Sometimes, after the proposal has been submitted, the customer may request some minor type of change, or the bidding organization may determine that it would have been better to have suggested a different design.

If it is the customer requesting a change, then the customer will most likely ask for a best and final offer (BAFO). The customer may ask any way for a BAFO, even without requesting a change. This provides the contractor one final attempt to massage the bid before a final award decision is made. Figure 5.10 depicts the post-submittal process.

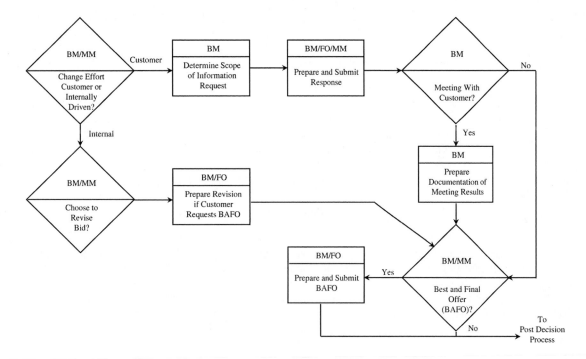

Figure 5.10. Post-Submittal Process

If the customer does not offer the opportunity for a BAFO, then there is a dead period before the customer makes the award decision. If the organization's bid decision was premised on an internal design and/or development effort, which may have part of an internal research and development effort, then the proposal activity may have simply been a small inconvenience to the contractor. In other words, the contractor may see a bigger market for their product or service and may, therefore, continue with their efforts while awaiting an award decision.

Post-Decision Process

Once the contractor's contract administrator receives notice of the customer's award decision, the contractor will either prepare to begin work or request a debrief from the customer as to what the customer may have been looking for. Even if the contractor did win the award, attending a customer debrief is beneficial. Figure 5.11 depicts the post-decision process.

Debriefs by the customer provide valuable information for future proposal efforts with this customer. The debrief frequently will provide information such as:

- How your organization scored in each of its volumes
- Strengths and weaknesses of your proposal
- How to deal, perhaps more effectively, with this customer in the future

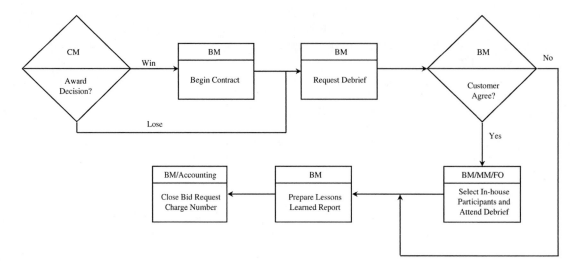

Figure 5.11. Post-Decision Process

At the conclusion of any proposal effort it is always prudent to create a lesson-learned document. This document will help your organization in future proposal efforts by identifying those things that you did right and those things that you would do differently next time.

The last item, if the proposal effort was unsuccessful, is to close the charge number being used by the proposal team members. The charge number was being used for cost collection purposes as long as there was proposal work to be done.

Statement of Work

The statement of work (SOW) is simply a narrative description of the work to be done. It outlines the objectives of the program, a description of the work, a time frame to perform the work, any funding constraints, and details the work in attached technical specifications. The SOW is part of the customer's request for proposal to the potential contractors. A well-written SOW provides enough information so as to avoid any ambiguity during reading (Kerzner 2009, p. 536).

On the surface it may seem rather simple to accurately describe the work to be accomplished in the contract, but on further review it is not always so easy. Examples of ambiguity in wording follows:

> The SOW says to conduct a minimum of 12 tests to satisfy a given requirement. To be safe you bid 18 tests, a 50 percent margin. At the end of the 12 tests the customer says that the results are inconclusive, and asks you to run another 12 tests, at a cost of $500,000 over that bid in your proposal.

This is actually quite real. Having worked as a software engineer and having responsibility for many software-oriented bid efforts, we quickly learned to document in our proposals exactly what we were intending to do. In software engineering, there are three types of software testing that could be performed: black-box, gray-box, and white-box. The difference between black-box and white-box is enormous in terms of costs to the program. Black-box testing simply requires that an output be observed given some predefined form of input. In other words, when I hit a key on my keyboard, the letter typed will show up on my screen. White-box testing, however, requires that each and every path through your software that code could pass must be tested as the keyboard's keystroke flows through the software to ultimately create the letter appearing on the monitor. This form of testing is very intrusive and requires major software test programs and drivers to adequately prove correct. Obviously, black-box testing is considerably less intrusive, simply requiring observation.

Another example follows:

The navy gives you a contract in which the SOW states that the prototype must be tested in water. You drop the prototype into a swimming pool to test it. Unfortunately, the navy's definition of water is the Atlantic Ocean, and it costs you $1.3 million to transport all of your test equipment to the Atlantic Ocean.

Or, how about:

You receive a contract in which the SOW says you must transport goods across the country using "aerated" boxcars. You select boxcars that have open tops so that air can flow in. During the trip, the train goes through an area of torrential rains, and the goods are ruined. The customer wanted boxcars that were aerated from below. Ambiguity over the word aerated is what caused this case to go to court.

It is important, when writing an SOW to stay away from words like *nearly, generally*, or *approximately*. During the heat of my proposal-writing days, I used to like words like *near real-time* and *authentically simulated*. In the world of real-time embedded software and hardware systems, *real-time* is frequently used to describe non-delay type of stimulus-response mechanisms. In other words, it happens not only now, but right now. Not always having explicit direction in the SOW as to what *real-time* meant, in the context of a particular program, I would try to be as accurate as I could by suggesting that in my opinion, the system was performing in *nearly real-time*. Unfortunately, not everybody shared my enthusiasm for the terms. The RFP asked for real-time, not near real-time.

Technical Specification

The technical specification is provided as part of the RFP and provides detailed direction that will allow for proposal costing. It is an exhaustive elaboration of the SOW. Actually, there may be many technical specifications. Kerzner (2009, p. 542) identifies 53 different technical specifications covering nine areas, composed of disciplines such as electrical and civil engineering, and subject areas such as piping and vessels. The reality is that there are literally hundreds of technical specifications used by the U.S. government when it issues an RFP and SOW. Depending on the program type, there are applicable specifications for each discipline involved that are specific to that particular type of product or service being acquired.

A specification provides information having to do with product specifics. For example, the box should weigh eight pounds, be painted green, and be able to relay incoming data to other like boxes in three seconds. If we were looking at building a home, we would have as a part of our specification items such as:

- Solid six-panel poplar doors
- Four-and-one-quarter-inch poplar baseboard
- Hand-stained woodwork with three coats of sealer
- Wood-burning fireplace with thirty-six-inch insert
- Two by four construction—sixteen inches on center
- Roof rafters 2 x 12
- Concrete patio of 12 x 12 feet

Notice the details of our above specification, compared to the more general description of our home. The SOW might simply have said we wanted a four-bedroom, two-and-a-half-bath, two-story home on a slab. One document higher, the RFP might have said we wanted to build a home in the southwest part of town, in a secluded housing addition, and on a cul-de-sac.

Work Breakdown Structure

The work breakdown structure (WBS) is a graphical hierarchical depiction of how the work is organized. It forms the basis for costing, scheduling, and assigning work responsibility.

The WBS must be accompanied by a dictionary for each element of the WBS. The dictionary should stipulate not only what is to be done, but perhaps what will not be done. For example, in an above example I discussed software engineering black-box versus white-box testing. It would be of real value to specify which type of testing was being planned and bid on.

There are many ways to organize the work in a WBS. Below describes some of those ways.

- Functions/Disciplines—with this type of work structure, major functions such as electrical, plumbing, masonry, framing, and the like are identified as key areas where we may wish to collect work together.
- Organizational structure—if the organization is such that different organizations can be uniquely identified and work is separable, then perhaps this type of work breakdown structure might be in order—for example, design engineering and manufacturing.
- Physical location—sometimes an organization may want to organize by site or location—for example, Midwest region, Western region, Southern region.
- Major systems or subsystems is yet another way to organize work. Using this method, an automobile manufacturer might organize work by electrical, braking, transmission, engine, chassis, and the like. The idea is to identify major subsystems of the whole and organize the work along these lines.

An example of a work breakdown structure is depicted in figure 5.12.

In figure 5.12, there are three levels depicted in the WBS. Level #1 is "A—Program." Level #2 is at the horizontal level where "AA," "AB," through "AF" are located. Level #3 has, simply continuing this exercise, three alpha characters as its unique WBS element number ("AAA," "ACA," etc.). There is no requirement to use strictly alpha identifiers. One could use numeric identifiers, or, even a combination of alphanumeric as identifiers. For example: A, A.1, A.1.a.

The customer will generally provide a WBS to the third level and then expect the contractor to extend the customer-provided WBS to a sufficient level to provide adequate execution visibility—usually five levels. Costs, however, are usually reported to the customer at level #3.

From a formality perspective, there are actually three different work breakdown structures when dealing with a formal federal, state, or city municipality. The federal government, for example, might begin with a WBS. From this, a smaller subset of the work might be carved out and identified as a major subsystem to be awarded to a contractor for bidding. This contractor work breakdown structure is referred to as a CWBS. Finally, the contractor is expected to extend the CWBS into what is referred to as an extended contractor work breakdown structure (ECWBS). All of this can be really quite confusing, and not necessary for everyday discussions, so generally, the terms WBS, CWBS, and ECWBS are all referred to as simply the WBS.

Classes of Estimates

An estimate of the cost of the work to be performed may be made based on a number of methodologies, four of which will be discussed here.

- Rough order of magnitude (ROM)
- Top-down

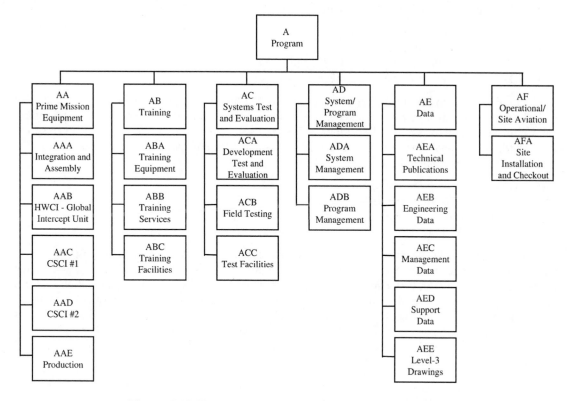

Figure 5.12. Example Work Breakdown Structure (WBS)

- Definitive
- Learning curve

Let's say you are flying home from a meeting with a potential new customer and you are trying to figure out what the proposed work effort for this customer might cost. So, on the back of your drink napkin, you begin to add up numbers for the various parts of the job. When you are done, you have what might be referred to as a rough order of magnitude (ROM).

A ROM is typified as:

- Being made without any engineering detailed data
- Having the potential to have the greatest inaccuracy
- Generally being based on remembering past experiences by the estimator

Using this same scenario, once home, the marketing manager has a discussion with the program manager of a similar effort. After some thought, the program manager of the similar program sits down and creates an estimate of what he or she thinks the cost of the new program might be. This type of estimate is known as a top-down estimate. An example of when this type of estimate might be applicable would be if the new program is, perhaps, 50 percent more difficult than the similar program to which it is being compared.

Characteristics of a top-down approach are:

- An approximate estimate
- Made without engineering data
- More accurate than a rough order of magnitude estimate
- Based on "similar to" previous projects

Continuing our example, if the program manager proceeds to initiate a proposal effort, involving all of the applicable functional organizations and they are involved in generating their respective costs, this effort, then, would be referred to as a definitive estimate. Definitive estimates, then, are bottom-up estimates from the appropriate functional organizations that include man-hours, material, and other resources.

Definitive estimates are indicative of the following.

- Grassroots, bottom-up estimates
- Well-defined engineering data
- Includes plans, specifications, vendor quotes, and the like
- Generally the most accurate

Another form of estimate is the learning curve estimate. Learning curves represent increasingly greater amounts of knowledge over time and are indicative of overall lower costs as we learn how to do something better or more efficiently. If, for example, we manufactured widgets, perhaps millions and millions of them over many years, then one would expect that our first few estimates of what it would cost to manufacture these widgets would be considerably less accurate than our more recent, or last, estimates. This, again, is due to our experience in manufacturing millions of widgets over many years.

Learning curves, therefore, possess the following characteristics.

- Represented graphically as repetitive functions
- Depict reductions in time, resources, and money as a result of continuous learning
- Most generally applied in a manufacturing environment

Chapter 6

Defining the Work to be Performed

A Shortened Perspective

Defining the work means being able to identify and manage what is required to be done. We call this process *requirements management*.

Requirements management involves five steps:

- Identification
- Analysis
- Allocation
- Verification
- Traceability

Requirements identification is the process of collecting stated and derived requirements from both internal and external sources. External documentation that provides a source for program-stated and -derived requirements includes the customer-supplied description of what is needed (recall this was termed a *request for proposal*). Internally, even though the customer never asked for a specific gauge of wiring, the electricians are required by code to install only a certain gauge of wiring. This, therefore, is considered an internal requirement, meaning it came from one of our own people as contractors versus from the customer.

An explicitly stated requirement is one that is stated directly by the customer. For example, "I want a four-bedroom house with two-and-a-half baths." In this case, the two stated requirements are: (1) four bedrooms, and (2) two-and-a-half baths. Now, as a contractor, you know to create four bedrooms requires a whole lot of other activities, namely, many of those depicted in figure 6.1.

These other activities are what we call "derived requirements." They are derived, because the customer did not explicitly ask for them, but they are required to provide the customer what he or she actually did ask for.

Requirements analysis separates similar requirements into groups of higher-level requirements. This activity creates a hierarchical depiction of related requirements. For example, when building a house, major functional organizations might include electrical, plumbing, masonry, framing, and landscaping, as depicted in figure 6.1.

Requirements allocation is the assignment of a given requirement or family of requirements to a functional group of the system for implementation. For example, the requirement to do the wiring of our house would most logically be given to the electricians. The understanding is that the electricians will be responsible for ensuring that this requirement is satisfied. Within the electrical group, the requirement may be further allocated to a specific subset of individuals, such as a younger electrician who might wire only garages. All requirements for each functional organization, therefore, would be associated with that functional organization.

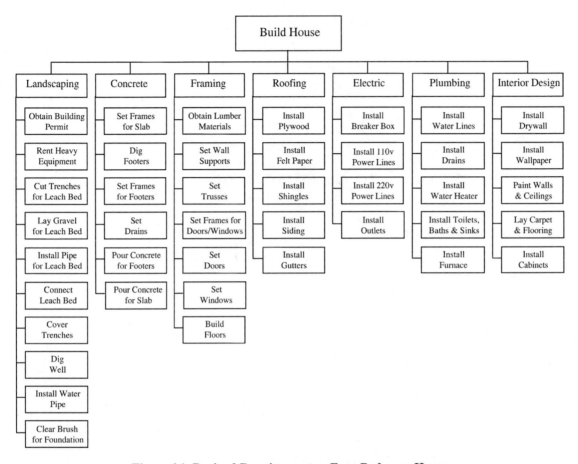

Figure 6.1. Derived Requirements—Four Bedroom House

Further, it's during the proposal preparation phase where the requirements are initially identified, analyzed, and allocated. Once requirements are assigned out, functional organizations would be responsible for the initial proposal costing, all phases of design, and activities associated with satisfying those requirements.

Staying with our current example, the electricians will also identify the type of testing required to demonstrate that the requirement has been satisfied. This verification method may fall into one of four categories: analysis, demonstration, inspection, or test.

Analysis as a verification method can perhaps best be thought of, for example, as performing a desk analysis of a schematic, perhaps a verification of the electrical flow based on schematic drawings.

Demonstration is a form of verification that allows for a physical demonstration of the item to be tested. For example, turning the switch on seems to be a popular test for proper wiring.

Inspection implies a visual inspection of the entity for compliance.

Test implies testing the entity against some predefined standard. In my kitchen, I have nearly the maximum lighting load on a single switch. This makes the switch get hot on occasion, but yet, the switch is manufactured to handle this level of lighting.

The last item dealing with requirements management is requirement traceability. Requirement traceability is the process by which a requirement is traced from its original statement in a contract or request for proposal to the actual piece of the total system that is responsible for implementing a means to satisfy the requirement.

Ready, Fire, Aim

In the expression "ready, aim, fire," the "ready" part is in reference to the upfront planning that takes place, "aim" refers to having common goals, perspectives, and focus, and "fire" refers to the execution of the previously detailed plan.

But have you ever been in a conversation where someone said, "Why did they do it that way? They should have reversed the order. The way they did it was like putting the cart before the horse." All of these expressions and many more are in reference to the sequencing of the activities of the project in question. The culminating tongue-in-cheek phrase for the above is "ready, fire, aim," again meaning, "act before thinking."

Thinking before acting is what this chapter is about. We refer to this step as planning. We plan, so when we begin to implement our plan, our execution of the activities is more defined and, therefore, more efficient. The end result, of course, is a more effective project, one that satisfies what we were trying to accomplish and does so within a planned budget and timeline.

Thinking before acting begins with a basic understanding of the work to be performed. To do this, we begin by listing what we think we have to do (requirements identification). The next thing to do is to create a breakdown of the work, and structure it in such a manner that it can be easily understood, known as the work breakdown structure (WBS). The WBS is a graphical hierarchical depiction of how the work is organized. It forms the basis for costing, scheduling, and assigning work responsibility.

To provide further insight into how work might be organized, figure 6.2 depicts the WBS for hosting a Thanksgiving dinner.

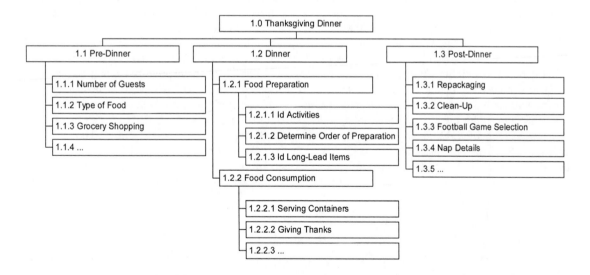

Figure 6.2. Hosting a Thanksgiving Dinner

Notice we defined the work in three basic groupings: pre-dinner, dinner, and post-dinner. This is obviously not the only way to organize the work, but it is acceptable for the manner in which this person thinks and intends to accomplish the work.

Let's look at another example. Suppose you were asked to redesign a process in your company. This type of task is called "business process reengineering" and was very popular in the early 1990s. The WBS for what has to be done might look like figure 6.3.

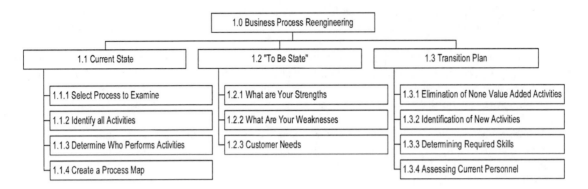

Figure 6.3. Business Process Reengineering

Again, as in the Thanksgiving dinner example, we have chosen to organize our work into three basic buckets: the current state, to be state, and the transition plan for moving between the two. This coincides with the order in which we intend to do work, but is not necessarily the case in all WBS depictions.

Let's discuss another example. Assume you are a builder and have been asked to build a residential home with two floors, four bedrooms, two-and-a-half baths on a basement. You have identified all of the requirements and now wish to depict the work to be performed in WBS format. How might the WBS look? Figure 6.4 depicts one manner in which the work might be graphically depicted.

Notice that the above WBS has been organized by function. In other words, each major function/discipline involved in home building has been identified and work appropriately assigned.

But perhaps our builder thinks differently. Perhaps our builder would have preferred to organize the work by phases in which he or she will perform the work. This is altogether normal, and perhaps most appropriate for this builder. A depiction of the same work organized by planning phase is depicted in figure 6.5.

If we look at the above Thanksgiving example, one of the things we notice is that each box of our WBS has a unique identifier. For example, 1.1 is pre-dinner, 1.2 is dinner, and 1.3 is post-dinner. The idea when creating a WBS is to uniquely identify each box so that we can later reference each box by number as opposed to by name. It doesn't really matter whether our numbering system is entirely numeric, alphabetic, or some combination of the two. For example, the three different approaches would look like the following:

1.0	A	A
1.1	A.A	A.1
1.1.1	A.A.A	A.1.A

It is important that we label our WBS boxes (which we call "elements"), because our next step is to write descriptions for each of our WBS elements. These descriptions are called "dictionaries." Since dictionaries are written for each element of our WBS, the formal and full name of each dictionary is a WBS element dictionary. Therefore, once the work is organized and properly depicted in graphical form, as above, then for each WBS element, for example, "AA," "ACC," or "AF," a written description should be created. In the ideal sense, the dictionary description should include such items as:

- WBS alphanumeric identifier (1.0, 1.1, 1.1.1, etc.)
- Title of the WBS element (e.g., pre-dinner)

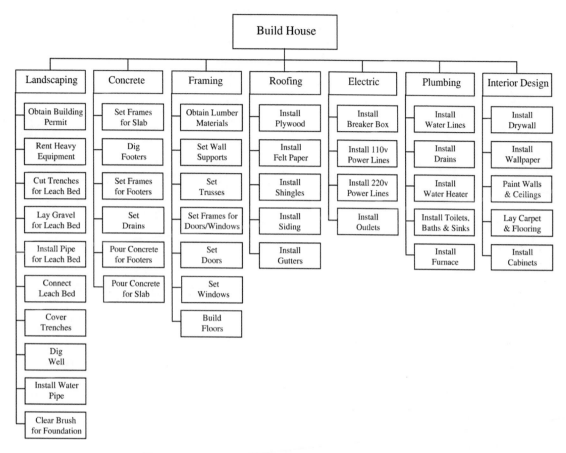

Figure 6.4. WBS for Building a House—by Function

- Revision date representing the most recent date changes were made to this description
- The WBS description (this is the description of the element)
- References back to which customer requirement caused this element to come into existence

Once we have tentatively identified the work to be performed and written dictionary elements for each WBS element, we now must take a stab at identifying who will be tasked to do the work. The result of this activity is called a responsibility assignment matrix (RAM). If there is only one person doing all of the work, such as my landscaper, then the RAM is easy; all work is assigned to that one person. However, if there happen to be multiple individuals or organizations involved in accomplishing the work, then it makes sense at this point to assign out the work to those most capable of performing the activity.

Let's look at another example, which will pull together the whole concept of defining the work (WBS), describing the work (WBS dictionaries), and assigning responsibility for the work (RAM).

Let's assume there is a future bride talking with her future husband. She has provided the following request for proposal (RFP).

She says, "Snookums, I want to get married. I want a church wedding with my family, bridesmaids, rehearsal dinner, reception with music and dancing, and all the trimmings." He replies, "Sweetie, how about we elope?" "Nooo!" she replies. "I want a real wedding. You wouldn't want me to feel

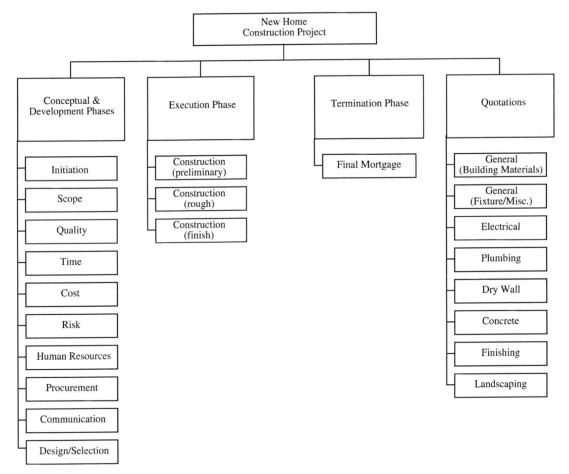

Figure 6.5. WBS for Building a House—by Phase

cheated out of having a pearl and ivory wedding with all the memories, would you?" She adds, "And every time I think of how special our wedding was, I'll have warm and snuggly feelings about you and how caring you are. That's worth something, isn't it?" "Of course it is, Pumpkin," he replies. "I want my little pinky stinker winker bean to be happy. We'll have as big a wedding as you like." "Thank you, my little Pooh Bear! We're going to be happy forever," she concludes.

Our future husband, being fairly astute, decides to enlist the help of an organization known as Heaven on Earth (HOE) Wedding Planners. Following our process as we have defined it so far, HOE begins to identify our future bride's stated requirements. These requirements are typically identified in request for proposals or statement of works as "will" statements. As in, "the contractor will do . . ."

She says, "Snookums, I want to *get married*. I want a *church wedding* with my family, bridesmaids, *rehearsal dinner, reception with music* and dancing, and all the trimmings." He replies, "Sweetie, how about we elope?" "Nooo!" she replies. "I want a real wedding. You wouldn't want me to feel cheated out of having a pearl and ivory wedding with all the memories, would you?" She adds, "And every time I think of how special our wedding was, I'll have warm and snuggly feelings about you and how caring you are. That's worth something, isn't it?" "Of course it is, Pumpkin," he replies. "I want my little pinky stinker winker bean to be happy. We'll have as big a wedding as you like." "Thank you, my little Pooh Bear! We're going to be *happy forever,*" she concludes.

Our italicized portions of the above represent what HOE and our future husband considers to be mandatory, or explicitly stated, requirements. To list them, we would have:

- Traditional church wedding
- Rehearsal dinner
- Reception
- Honeymoon
- Happily ever after

Further examining these stated requirements, HOE and our future husband determined that there were some other, derived, requirements. These are:

- Lots of $$$—money is not necessarily an issue
- Local site—not a thousand miles away
- Christian church of some type—perhaps Lutheran, Catholic, Methodist, etc.
- Photographer (maybe video so she can remember how caring her husband was)
- Nice hotel—for beginning of happy ever after part!

HOE then creates a WBS for the many activities to be performed. It is depicted in figure 6.6.

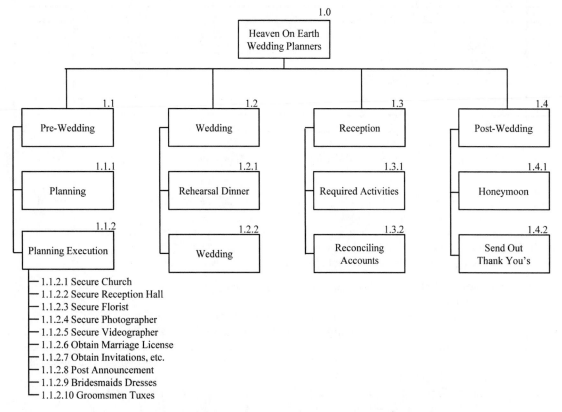

Figure 6.6. WBS—Heaven on Earth Wedding Planners

Approval Signatures (Bride and Groom)	Date		
January Baseline (01 Feb yyyy) Page 1 OF 2　　**Rev A**		Groom	Bride
Total Cost of Wedding	$8,335	6,500.00	1,835.00
1.0 -- Heaven on Earth			
1.1 -- Pre-Wedding	2,300.00		
1.1.1 -- Planning	300.00	300.00	
1.1.2 -- Planning Execution	2,000.00		
1.1.2.1 -- Secure Church	0.00		
1.1.2.2 -- Secure Reception Hall	0.00		
1.1.2.3 -- Secure Florist	500.00		500.00
1.1.2.4 -- Secure Photographer	300.00		300.00
1.1.2.5 -- Secure Videographer	250.00		250.00
1.1.2.6 -- Obtain Marriage License	100.00		100.00
1.1.2.7 -- Obtain Invitations	150.00		150.00
1.1.2.8 -- Post Announcement	100.00		100.00
1.1.2.9 -- Obtain Bridesmaides Dresses	400.00		400.00
1.1.2.10 -- Obtain Groomsmen Tuxes	200.00	200.00	
1.2 -- Wedding	600.00		
1.2.1 -- Rehearsal Dinner	400.00	400.00	
1.2.2 -- Wedding	200.00	200.00	
1.3 -- Reception	2,400.00		
1.3.1 -- Required Activities	0.00		
1.3.2 -- Reconciling Accounts	2,400.00	2,400.00	
1.4 -- Post-Wedding	3,035.00		
1.4.1 -- Honeymoon	3,000.00	3,000.00	
1.4.2 -- Send Out Thank Yous	35.00		35.00

Figure 6.7. Heaven on Earth Wedding Planners Responsibility Assignment Matrix

HOE further continues to define dictionary elements for each element of our WBS. A couple of those dictionary element descriptions are defined below.

Pre-Wedding: This element involves all discussions, activities, and events that lead up to the wedding itself. It does not include the wedding day or any of its activities or events.

1.1.1 Planning: This element includes those items listed below.

- The participation in a Myers Briggs Personality Assessment as administered by a certified professional.
- Meals where last review of personality preferences are examined for compatibility. It is anticipated that there will be a maximum of 10 lunches/dinners of approximately $20 each.
- The purchasing of cases of Coke or Pepsi for late night continuing discussions of mutual goals and aspirations. It is estimated that no more than 20 cases of Coke/Pepsi will be purchased at $4 each (assumes use of coupons).
- Additional discussion topics under this WBS element include, but are not limited to, the when, where, how, and why of the actual event.

- The outcome of this WBS element is a detailed requirements document, which includes both stated and derived requirements, to be reviewed and mutually agreed to by both the bride and groom.

HOE, with the above WBS and attendant dictionaries, creates a preliminary RAM as depicted in figure 6.7.

In this preliminary RAM, HOE has uniquely identified by name who has what activities to perform as well as the initial budget estimate to perform those activities.

From the above, one can see that $8,335 has been allocated to activities of this project. Suppose $10,000 had actually been the target not to exceed. Then $1,665 has been set back in case it is needed. This money set back is called a "reserve," or in the business world a "management reserve."

Management reserve is for in-scope, but yet unanticipated changes to the overall program or project. This money still forms a part of the overall cost of the project and has been set aside. In-scope means that the money will still be used for the wedding versus to buy a new TV. Unanticipated means that costs happened that weren't expected. In summary, then, in-scope unanticipated basically refers to costs that are related to the project but were not seen during the early stages of planning.

With all requirements defined, work organized, costs determined, and tentatively assigned out to be performed, the only thing left of significance is to create a set of schedules. Scheduling is discussed in later sections.

A More Detailed Perspective

Requirements management, as previously stated, involves five steps: identification, analysis, allocation, a means for verification, and traceability. Generating a requirements database necessitates that stated and derived requirements be identified and categorized on being placed into the requirements database and that some basic information be associated with each requirement to enable subsequent traceability to lower-level design activities. One measure of effective program planning and successful execution is the thoroughness of the steps involved in identifying, categorizing, and allocating contractually stated and derived requirements. Figure 6.8 depicts the basic process flow for requirements management.

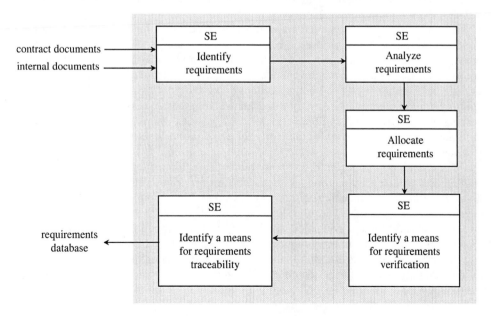

Figure 6.8. Requirements Management Process Flow

Requirements identification is the process of collecting stated and derived requirements from both internal and external sources. External documentation that provides a source for program-stated and program-derived requirements includes the contract statement of work, contract specification, and contract provisions. Internal documentation that provides a source for program-derived requirements includes specific functional organization processes.

An explicitly stated requirement says, for example, that "the programming language used in this program will be the Ada programming language." A derived requirement is one that the contractor has placed upon itself as a result of direction given by the stated requirement. An example of this type of requirement is when the contractor decides to use a Telesoft Ada programming language compiler instead of a VAX Ada programming language compiler. The intention to use the Telesoft Ada programming language compiler is self-imposed, but nevertheless a requirement. The customer only stated that the programming language had to be Ada, not that the Ada programming language compiler had to be Company A's.

Requirements analysis separates similar requirements into groups of higher-level requirements. This activity creates a hierarchical depiction of related requirements. For example, when building a house, major functional organizations might include electrical, plumbing, masonry, framing, landscaping, and the like.

Requirements allocation is the assignment of a given requirement or family of requirements to a functional piece of the system for implementation. For example, the requirement to program the software in the Ada programming language might be given to the software group working on the program. The understanding is that the software group will be responsible for ensuring that this requirement is satisfied. Within the software group, the requirement may be further allocated to a specific subset of individuals, such as the software support group. All requirements for each functional organization, therefore, would be associated with that functional organization. Further, during the proposal preparation phase is when the requirements are initially identified, analyzed, and allocated. On functional organization assignment, functional organizations would be responsible for initial proposal costing, all phases of design (preliminary design, detailed design, integration, and test), and activities associated with satisfying those requirements.

Staying with our current example, the software support group will also identify the type of testing required to demonstrate that the requirement has been satisfied. This verification method may fall into one of four categories: analysis, demonstration, inspection, or test.

Analysis as a verification method can perhaps best be thought of, for example, as performing a desk analysis of an algorithm, perhaps a verification of the algorithms correctness relative to mathematical theorems. Demonstration is a form of verification that allows for a physical demonstration of the item to be tested. For example, a billboard I saw a few months back showed a picture of a Volkswagen automobile and said "0 to 60, Yes!" It didn't say 0 to 60 in five seconds or ten seconds; it simply said, yes, we can get there. This marketing slant carried an interesting testing implication, that is, simply sit in the vehicle and wait until it reaches 60 miles per hour, and the verification by way of demonstration satisfies the requirement. Inspection implies a visual inspection of the entity for compliance. Test implies testing the entity against some predefined standard.

The last item dealing with requirements management is requirement traceability. Requirement traceability is the process by which a requirement is traced from its original statement in a contract or related document to the actual piece of the total system that is responsible for implementing a means to satisfy the requirement.

The requirements database, a collection of all stated and derived requirements, provides the program with a means of tracking all program requirements through each phase of the program's life cycle. A preliminary requirements database is established during the bid and proposal phase.

Once the requirements have been identified, analyzed, and allocated, then it is time to represent the requirements in a WBS.

Work Breakdown Structure

The WBS must be accompanied by a dictionary for each element of the WBS. The dictionary should stipulate not only what is to be done, but perhaps what will not be done. For purposes of completeness an example of a WBS is depicted in figure 6.9.

The program management office has primary responsibility for processing this activity, supplemented by the functional organizations. The process consists of:

- Expanding the contract-provided contractor work breakdown structure (CWBS) to form the extended CWBS. The initial expansion should be to one level below the reporting level. This expansion is generated by incorporating the individual functional organizations' WBS into the program's extended CWBS template. Individual elements of the CWBS do not need to be expanded equally.
- Developing the dictionary, which unambiguously describes the work to be accomplished under each element of the extended CWBS.
- The program manager's review of the extended CWBS and dictionary. If the extended CWBS and dictionary require changes, they are returned to the program management office; otherwise, the program manager signifies approval by signing the extended CWBS and dictionary.

Detailed requirements for generating the extended CWBS and dictionary are as follows:

- For each contract there should be a single CWBS that defines all authorized work.

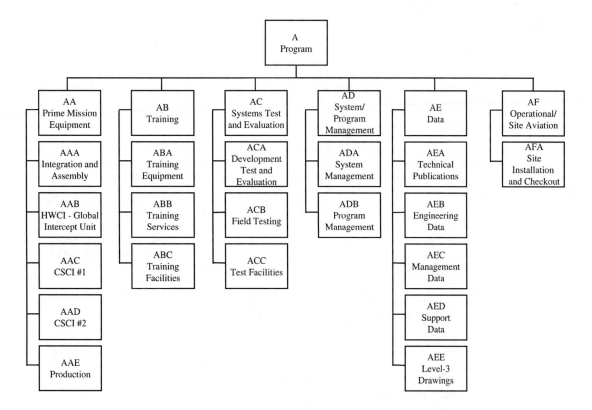

Figure 6.9. Work Breakdown Structure

- Since the CWBS forms part of the contract, it should be defined before the contract is signed. This will generally be accomplished during the proposal and/or negotiation phase of the procurement, since it requires concurrence between the customer and the contractor.
- The program management office representatives on the proposal team are responsible for coordinating the CWBS with the customer. The program management office representatives should make every effort to avoid letting the CWBS divide the work into unnatural or unmanageable packages. Unless otherwise required by the customer, the CWBS should be organized consistently with the product family tree.
- The extended CWBS dictionary correlates with the basis of the work depicted in the intermediate schedules and detailed schedules.
- The program management office, with support from the functional organizations, is responsible for determining the initial top-down costs of the work.
- Each extended CWBS element is categorized under only one higher-level element.
- The degree to which CWBS elements are extended is governed by:
  - contract reporting level
  - the complexity and criticality of elements of work to meet contract requirements
  - the cost of elements of work
  - the visibility needed by management for control of the element of work
- The extended CWBS dictionary identifies quantities of all deliverables, relevant contract line items (CLINs), and data items.
- All work for each subcontractor should be separately identified within the CWBS, using one or more extended CWBS elements according to the nature of the work. Each subcontract should be represented as a cost account. A subcontract should consist of a purchase order that contains a statement of work. A subcontract is required if the supplied item or service is unique, and a purchase order does not sufficiently define requirements.
- The following requirements apply to subcontract cost accounts:
  - The subcontractor's statement of work should include the work described in the extended CWBS dictionary for the subcontract cost account work packages.
  - The subcontractor's cost reporting structure (level) should be the work packages identified within the subcontract cost account.
  - The subcontractor work breakdown structure (SWBS) should be generated for the subcontract cost account and extend to at least the cost account work package level.
  - Monitoring of the subcontract should be in one or more work packages in the subcontract cost account.
  - Cost account managers who use a subcontractor's product in their cost accounts are responsible for monitoring the technical aspects of that product.
  - The subcontract cost account should have a minimum set of items as depicted in figure 6.10.
- Cost account material is any hardware, software, or service that is planned and controlled by an identifying part number, model number, or detailed description. Cost accounts for material should also include:
  - material used for destructive tests or internal setup for pilot runs (overbuy)
  - shrink (anticipated loss, damage, etc., based on historical rates)
  - vendor setup charges
  - vendor burn-in tests
  - minimum buy costs
  - procurement and transportation (material burden)
  - licenses and maintenance fees
  - purchased material inspection, if applicable (based on historical rates)

Item	Derived From	Responsibility
statement of work (SWBS, SDRL, subcontract schedule, etc.)	extended CWBS dictionaries, any cost account planning input documents	cost account manager
specifications	requirements database, any cost account planning input documents	cost account manager/system engineering
subcontract provisions	contract (flowdown), internal requirements	subcontract administration

Figure 6.10. Example Subcontract Cost Account Content

- Cost accounts for material should be a direct charge resource that includes:
  - all assets purchased for a program from sources outside of the company
  - interdivisional purchases
  - internal transfers
- Material planning should:
  - have a cost account that contains BCWS for all material
  - define nonrecurring material—for example, materials used by engineering during product development and built in the engineering lab, including the material for tools and special tests—and classify nonrecurring material as either high-value/critical material or low-value material
  - define low run-rate material as material for systems, modules, tools, and special test equipment that are built in operations, but not in a production environment (flow charts, paced lines, etc.)
- Items in the requirements database at the CWBS level should correspond to the extended CWBS level in accordance with any existing extended CWBS templates of functional organizations. The extended CWBS elements that do not correspond to a requirement should be deleted from the extended CWBS.
- Recurring and nonrecurring efforts should be divided into separate elements. Generally, recurring and nonrecurring efforts should be subsidiary elements under each element to which the distinction applies.
- No work should be associated with summary-level elements.
- If the element identifiers in the extended CWBS are incompatible with the identifiers that the company cost accounting system requires, the extended CWBS should provide a cross-reference between the extended CWBS element identifiers and the company cost accounting system identifiers.
- The extended CWBS should be updated as required. After cost accounts have been fixed, the extended CWBS should be extended to the work package level.
- The dictionary should define the scope of work of each extended CWBS element.
- For each element of the extended CWBS, there should be a description of the technical content, associated risks, and cost category (direct, recurring, nonrecurring, material, etc.) that includes the following information:
  - the program name, extended CWBS identification code, title assigned to the element, job/task number (as applicable), contract line item number, revision date, and revision level

- a definition of the extended CWBS element (associated work and/or product that can be assigned completion dates) and the type of work performed in the extended CWBS element (such as design, development, and manufacturing), as well as its technical content and cost category
- a listing of the specific tasks, or types of tasks, to be included (e.g., component design, tooling, fabrication, structural subassembly)
- a listing of the types of tasks to be excluded (e.g., final assembly)
- name of subcontractor, if applicable
- product completion/acceptance criteria
- a work package description consisting of the following:
  - clear differentiation from all other work packages in the cost account
  - definition of quantifiable tasks in terms of a physical product that can be assigned completion dates
  - specification of the minimum set of documents, resources, or products from other work packages required to start work (start milestone)
  - definition of completion criteria based on accomplishing a specific task
  - identification of the earned value technique selected
  - for the percent complete earned value technique, the formula that provides a ratio of the objective factors to the budget at completion
  - for the apportioned effort earned value technique, definition, and documentation of factors and methods used to apply apportioned effort and identification of the directly related specified work packages are cost accounts by extended CWBS identifier and title

Work Breakdown Structure Dictionary

Once the work is organized and properly depicted in graphical form as above, then for each WBS element, for example, "AA," "ACC," or "AF," a written description should be created. In the ideal sense, the dictionary description should include such items as:

- WBS alphanumeric identifier
- Title of the WBS element
- Revision date representing the most recent date changes were made to this description
- The WBS description
- References back to which stated or derived requirement, identified in the requirements database, caused this element to come into existence

An example of a very complex WBS element dictionary is depicted in figure 6.11.

The process flow for generating the WBS and its attendant dictionary is depicted in figure 6.12.

Recognize, as discussed in the bidding process, that the WBS is really nomenclature for the customer's identification and allocation of the work. The piece of the total system to be allocated to a contractor is typically referred to as the CWBS and the contractor's extension of the CWBS is referred to as the extended CWBS or ECWBS. So, in the above, the more precise nomenclature is to call our WBS an extended CWBS.

Preliminary Responsibility Assignment Matrix

Once the requirements are identified, analyzed, allocated, and organized into a WBS and dictionary element descriptions are written, then we can make an initial stab at depicting costs for each major chunk of work. Chunks of work (or more professionally, collections of related work) are called cost accounts. A cost account, then, is a collection of related work that can be costed, scheduled, performed, and monitored to

Purdue Electronic Systems Company
Extended CWBS Dictionary

Program Name			
Extended CWBS ID	AABB	Title	Preliminary Design
Job/Task Number		CLIN	
Revision Date	27 AUG 20xx	Rev	

Element Description

Develop HWCI architecture. Perform trade studies in accordance with the trade study plan and as required as the process proceeds. Conduct informal walkthroughs to review the proposed concepts and architectures and the supporting analyses. Document the architecture with block diagrams, mechanical sketches, and hardware family trees and place them in the HDF. SOW refer. _____.

Partition the HWCI design. Perform trade studies to evaluate technology and source options for the various design entities. Prepare "long lead" procurement items list for program management. Initiate customer approval of nonstandard parts identified during the development of the design entity requirements. Develop preliminary packaging concept. Perform trade studies to determine packaging concept. Allocate BIT and diagnostics requirements to the design partitions. SOW refer. _____.

Prepare design specifications for all modules and other elements. Maintain and document traceability of all requirements to HWCI B-level or equivalent specification. SOW refer. _____.

Develop a preliminary test plan from the requirements test matrix generated during requirements analysis. SOW refer. _____.

Develop support equipment requirements in conjunction with the logistics and producibility/testability specialty functions. SOW refer. _____.

Update the HDP. SOW refer. _____.

Conduct design walkthroughs. Prepare documentation to support the PDR. SOW refer. _____.

Figure 6.11. WBS Element Dictionary

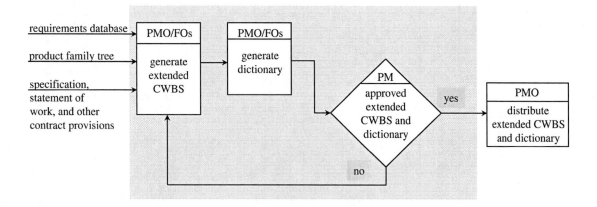

Figure 6.12. WBS and Dictionary Detailed Process Flow

			Amount
Contract Target Cost			91,000,000
Authorized Unpriced Work			0
Contract Budget Base			91,000,000
Management Reserve			9,100,000
Performance Measurement Baseline			81,900,000
Undistributed Budget			193,000
Cost of Money			1,400,000
General & Accounting			13,307,000

Customer CWBS ID	Program Extended CWBS ID/Level 1	2	3	4	5	6	Extended CWBS Title	Allocated Target Budget	Cost Accounts	Charge Number
1	A						program	$67,000 K	67,000,000	
1.1		AA					prime mission equipment	$60,390 K		
1.1.1			AAA				integration & assembly	$2,050 K		
				AAAA			direct/manage integration & assembly	$300 K	$300 K	80100
				AAAB			perform integration & assembly	$1,000 K	$1,000 K	80101
				AAAC			verification	$750 K	$750 K	80102
1.1.2			AAB				global intercept unit	$5,522K		
				AABA			requirements analysis	$585K	$585K	80103
					AABA01		preliminary requirements analysis	$105K		
					AABA02		prepare & execute trade study plan	$140 K		
					AABA03		develop requirements verification plan	$30 K		
					AABA04		update development & interface specification	$60 K		
					AABA05		update hardware development plan	$40 K		
					AABA06		update cost model	$60 K		
					AABA07		requirements analysis verification	$150 K		
						AABA071	walkthroughs	$85 K		
						AABA072	hardware requirements review	$65 K		
				AABB			preliminary design	$445 K	$445 K	80104
					AABB01		develop architecture	$80 K		
					AABB02		derive design entity requirements	$70 K		
					AABB03		develop module/element specifications	$120 K		
					AABB04		develop preliminary test plan	$40 K		
					AABB05		develop preliminary support equip. reqts.	$45 K		
					AABB06		update hardware development plan	$40 K		
					AABB07		preliminary design validation	$60 K		
				AABC			detail design	$1,000 K	$1,000 K	80105
					AABC01		engineering HWCI model build and test	$125 K		

Figure 6.13. Detailed Costed Preliminary Responsibility Assignment Matrix

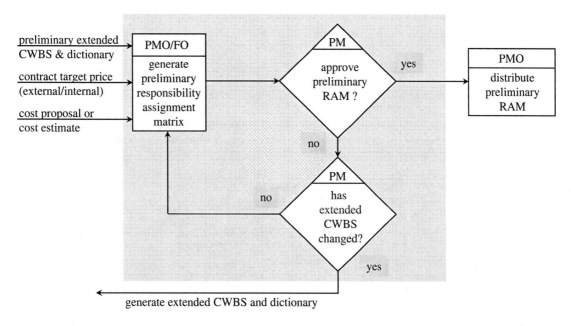

Figure 6.14. Preliminary RAM Detailed Process Flow

completion. To further identify efforts associated with these cost account, an organization might assign a unique charge number for personnel working the cost account to charge their time.

Figure 6.13 depicts a rather elaborate preliminary responsibility assignment matrix.

Note that the allocated target budget is an estimate of what each listed WBS element will cost to design, develop, and deliver. For those items ready to begin work on, charge numbers have been opened and are identified. Notice for each charge number there is a single cost account identified.

The detailed process flow for generating the preliminary RAM is depicted in figure 6.14.

Inputs to this activity are:

- Contract target price (external/internal)
- Cost proposal or cost estimate
- Extended CWBS and dictionary

The external contract target price is generated by a marketing process for the proposal phase, and by the contract manager for an external contract. The internal contract target price is provided by the business area director. The internal contract target price is an internally funded effort by internal research and development, bid and proposal, in direct support of an external contract or other internally funded effort. The cost proposal or cost estimate is generated by accounting to the program management office. The cost estimate is an initial top-down estimate that allocates budget to CWBS elements prior to any bottom-up estimate.

The difference between the preliminary responsibility assignment matrix and the final baseline responsibility assignment matrix are those changes resulting from continuation of the planning process.

This activity is the responsibility of the program management office and functional organization managers, with support of accounting, and consists of several steps.

- The budget is developed (see budget development section below), which consists of:
  - subtracting target profit or fee from contract target price, yielding contract target cost
  - adding the budget of any internally contracted work and authorized unpriced work, yielding the contract budget base (as applicable)
  - subtracting any management reserve from the difference of the contract budget base and the authorized unpriced work, yielding the budget for performance measurement baseline
  - subtracting any undistributed budget
  - subtracting general and administrative (includes general and accounting, internal research and development, bid and proposal, tax, interest, and cost of money) costs, yielding a distributed budget
  - allocating the distributed budget to each extended CWBS element
- Considering the type, magnitude, duration, management visibility/control, and risk of the work and functional organization involved, cost accounts are initially defined to one level below reporting level or the level required to satisfy requirements for a cost account. Costing updates should be reflected in the final baseline responsibility assignment matrix.
- The extended CWBS will be changed if elements are (re)allocated to satisfy requirements for establishing cost accounts.
- The program manager should review the preliminary responsibility assignment matrix. If it requires changes, it needs to be returned to the program management office; otherwise, the program manager signifies approval by signing it.

There are three steps in the generation of the preliminary responsibility assignment matrix.

- Cost accounts are assigned. Initially cost accounts are defined in the extended contract WBS at one level below the reporting level (normally at level number four).
- The distributed target budget is allocated to each cost account to match the work identified in the extended CWBS dictionary, using analysis of historical data.
- A charge number structure based on cost accounts is established. Typically, no charge number should be used for charges on more than one cost account.

Budget Development

Budget development begins with a contract target price provided to the customer. Price is really made up of two elements: contract cost and profit. Once profit is removed, then what remains is the contract's target cost. The contract's target cost then forms the budget base from which all work is performed.

The performance measurement baseline budget is the budget to execute the program, taking into consideration any additions from management reserve (held for in-scope, unanticipated changes). The performance measurement baseline then forms the budget to distribute to the cost account managers once general and administrative costs are removed. The cost and subsequent price had these general and administrative costs added on, and they must be removed before redistributing the budget to the managers responsible for accomplishing the work.

Authorized unpriced work is effort for which definitized contract costs have not been agreed to, but for which written authorization has been received by the contractor.

Undistributed budget is budget applicable to the contract effort that has not yet been identified to the WBS elements at the lowest level being reported to the customer (Fleming, 1992, p. 94).

Figure 6.15 depicts the entire budget development process.

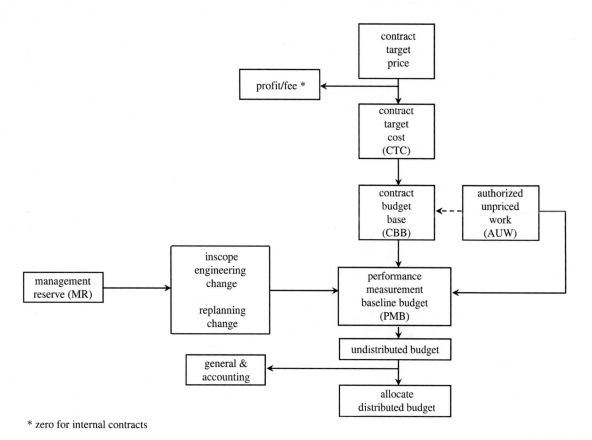

* zero for internal contracts

Figure 6.15. Budget Development Process

Chapter 7

Scheduling and Staffing the Work

Scheduling the many activities that make up your project sounds simple. And, to a large extent, it is. It becomes increasingly more difficult, however, as the number of activities becomes greater. In this chapter we will look at a few "pure" scheduling techniques.

To this point, we have identified stated and derived requirements. From our requirements we created an organization of the work—a work breakdown structure (WBS). Attendant to our WBS we created a dictionary with element descriptions for each work breakdown structure element.

Somewhere in parallel or sequential to the WBS, we must begin to lay out the work identified into a series of increasingly more detailed schedules: master, intermediate, and detailed. Once the work is defined and scheduled, we can create a human resource plan. The human resource plan is a time-phased depiction of resources required to perform the work and accomplish the goals of the program.

Types of Schedules

There are many different types of tools available to help in program/project scheduling. These tools range in price from very inexpensive to very expensive. Prices can be as low as $10 to as much as $50,000 or more. The price varies, typically, in accordance with the level of functionality of the tool. Simpler tools may only do simple bar charts, while the more complex tools will:

- Depict schedules in network diagrams using multiple formats (discussed later in this chapter).
- Allow for resources to be identified against schedule activities.
- Create human resource plans automatically from the data.
- Allow for costs to be associated with the scheduled activities.
- Support the creation of a cost and schedule baseline.
- Allow the cost and schedule baseline to be statused.
- Generate reports identifying cost and schedule deviations from the plan.

To say the least, there are literally hundreds of tools with incalculable permutations of the above capabilities. One tool, which I use in my program management classes, is Microsoft Project—the most recent version. It supports all of the above mentioned capabilities to some degree or another.

When discussing scheduling techniques we usually refer to the pure techniques:

- Program Evaluation and Review Technique (PERT)
- Critical Path Method (CPM)
- Gantt Charts
- Milestone Charts

Generally, however, no tool uses a pure technique. Instead, most tools use some permutation of one of the pure techniques. Fundamentally, when we discuss schedules, there are really only two primary schools of thought:

- Scheduling techniques that depict the interrelatedness of scheduled activities
- Scheduling techniques that do *not* show the interrelatedness of scheduled activities

Over the succeeding paragraphs, we are going to examine the pure techniques in more detail, looking at the advantages and disadvantages of each.

Gantt Charts

Gantt charts were developed by Henry Laurence Gantt (1861–1919) during the World War I era. Fundamentally, they depict scheduled tasks with hollow bars over a horizontal time scale. The many activities are on the vertical axis and their corresponding hollow bars are filled in to reflect progress of the activity.

Figure 7.1 depicts the typical Gantt chart.

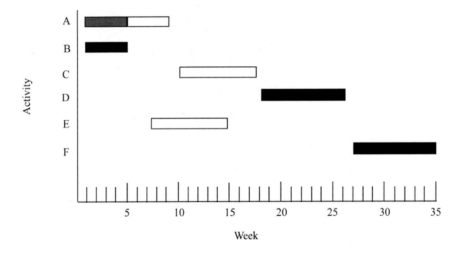

Figure 7.1. Gantt Chart

Gantt charts exhibit many advantages and disadvantages, as identified below.
Advantages

- Easy to understand
- Inexpensive to prepare
- Ideal for repetitive work that can be measured quantitatively

Disadvantages

- Potentially subjective
- Interrelationships among the schedule activities are not depicted
- No follow-on implications from schedule movements.

Gantt charts, as indicated above, are very inexpensive to prepare and easy to read. In fact, a good spreadsheet tool typically allows for some form of drawing that enables one to create Gantt charts on spreadsheets. In this scenario, an individual wouldn't even have to buy a scheduling tool if Gantt charts were the only form of scheduling required. Doing repetitive work that can be counted accurately with some form of quantitative measure is a good use of Gantt charts. Every day, week, or month all that needs to be done to status an activity is to count the items produced, delivered, or completed, whichever measure is appropriate. Once counted, the scheduler simply needs to take appropriate credit by filling in the hollow bar.

As can be seen from the above example, however, if the activities being statused were not quantitative in nature, then the measure becomes quite subjective. For example, as a young software engineer in a discipline that was just beginning to come into existence, I would routinely provide my status in non-quantitative measures. When asked how we were doing in meeting our schedule dates for software being designed and developed, we would simply say, "Everything seems to be pretty much on schedule." What did this mean? In reality, it might mean, and frequently did, that even though only 20 percent of the work remained, it most probably represented 80 percent of the total effort. In our earlier years, we didn't realize this of course, but as time went on, it quickly became a fact based on historical data.

The biggest disadvantage of Gantt charts is that the activities are *not* depicted in such a manner as to represent their interrelatedness. In other words, how the activities are tied together is not represented in the Gantt chart. This being the case, if one activity were to slip into the schedule, we would not know what impact that might have on the other activities. If the program was small enough, and the activities were relatively few, then we intuitively may know the answer to this.

Milestone Charts

While Gantt charts are activity-oriented, milestone charts are event-oriented. Key program/project milestones are identified and placed on a schedule at the time at which they are due to occur. Then, at a predefined time—daily, weekly, or monthly—the milestones are statused as either being completed or not.

Milestone charts have their own set of symbols that describes the status of the many milestones. Figures 7.2 and 7.3 depict symbols used in milestone charts and an example with the use of those symbols.

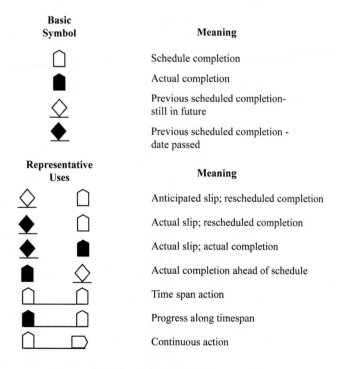

Figure 7.2. Symbology of Milestone Charts

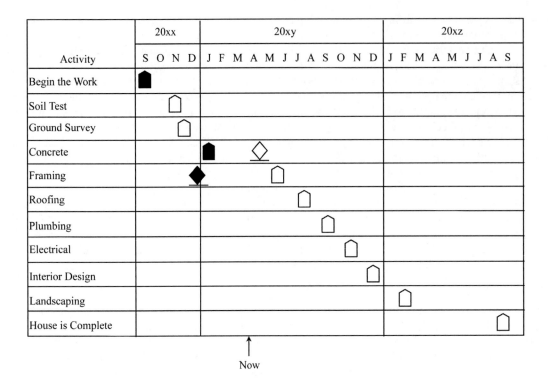

Activity	20xx				20xy													20xz							
	S	O	N	D	J	F	M	A	M	J	J	A	S	O	N	D	J	F	M	A	M	J	J	A	S
Begin the Work	■																								
Soil Test			⌂																						
Ground Survey			⌂																						
Concrete					■				◇																
Framing					◆						⌂														
Roofing														⌂											
Plumbing																⌂									
Electrical																	⌂								
Interior Design																		⌂							
Landscaping																				⌂					
House is Complete																									⌂

Now

Figure 7.3. Example Milestone Chart

From figure 7.3, notice that framing has experienced an actual schedule slip with a rescheduled completion date. Notice as well that the concrete effort has actually been completed ahead of schedule.

Again, "pure" milestone charts may appear somewhat confusing to read, but once a scheduler gets used to the symbols, milestone charts become quite easy to use.

The many advantages and disadvantages are discussed below.

Advantages

- Effective method of communication
- Symbols are standard and simple to use
- Presents actual progress against a baseline plan

Disadvantages

- There may be surprises when there are too few milestones
- Doesn't show schedule activity interdependencies
- No follow-on implications from schedule activity movements

Looking at the symbols used in creating milestone charts, it appears that there are only a handful of commonly used ones. For individuals using this type of scheduling technique, it really does not take long for them to get used to this basic set of symbols. From the outside looking in, however, the symbols seem somewhat confusing and awkward to grasp. As well, milestone charts suffer from the same problem as did the Gantt charts. That is, neither of them reflects the interrelatedness of the many schedule activities. Therefore, just as in the case with the use of Gantt charts, if one schedule activity slides out in time, the parties involved would have no idea of what the impact to the remaining schedule activities would be.

It is perfectly natural to combine the Gantt chart with the milestone chart. Figure 7.4 depicts this permutation of the pure forms of each.

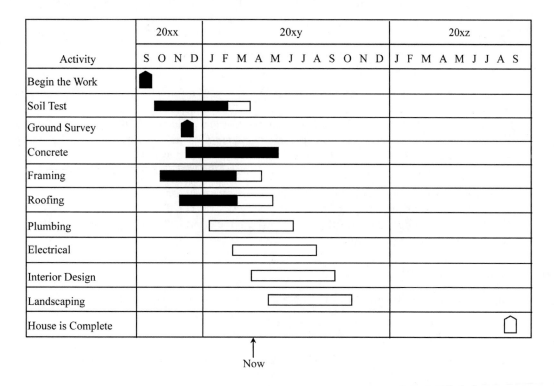

Figure 7.4. Permutation of Gantt and Milestone Chart

Network Schedules

Network scheduling involves identifying the schedule activities in such a way that the activities are tied to each other. In this manner, if one activity is moved, in one direction or the other, then all related/dependent activities are also moved accordingly.

When talking about network schedules, two dominant techniques are discussed:

- Program Evaluation and Review Technique (PERT)
- Critical Path Method (CPM)

PERT was developed in 1958 under sponsorship of the U.S. Navy Special Projects Office. It was developed as a special management tool for scheduling and controlling the Polaris missile program. The Polaris missile program involved 250 prime contractors and more than 9,000 subcontractors. PERT is credited with saving the program over two years in schedule and bringing the Polaris missile submarine to combat readiness.

PERT basically works by computing the mode of the beta distribution using three estimates:

- Most optimistic time
- Most likely time
- Most pessimistic time

PERT was intended to increase control in situations where time estimates were difficult to make with confidence.

PERT experienced a rapid rise, then an abrupt decline in usage around the 1970s. Two reasons were often cited for this:

- PERT was over-applied.
- PERT was combined with cost data or other non-scheduling aspects of program management, and it became cumbersome to manipulate.

PERT has experienced a resurgence in use, primarily due in part to software running PERT on personal computers.

CPM was developed in 1957 by J. E. Kelly of Remington-Rand and M. R. Walker of DuPont to aid in scheduling maintenance shutdowns in chemical processing plants. CPM is superior to PERT when time can be estimated closely and labor and material costs can be calculated quite accurately early in the program.

In CPM, two time and cost estimates are given for each activity in the network. These estimates are:

- Normal estimate—the cost of finishing the program in normal time.
- Crash estimate—the time required to finish an activity if special effort is made to reduce program time to a minimum. It's the cost to perform the effort on a crash basis in an attempt to minimize time to completion.

Network Approaches

Network approaches to scheduling generally fall into two basic categories:

- Activity-on-Arrow (AOA)
- Activity-on-Node (AON)

AOA is most closely associated with PERT, but can be applied to CPM as well. This method is sometimes called activity-on-arc or arrow diagramming method.

AON is most closely associated with CPM and is the basis for most computer scheduling applications. This method is sometimes called precedence diagramming method.

AOA is based on three rules.

- Each activity is represented by one and only one arrow in the network.
- No two activities can be represented by the same head and tail events.
- To ensure correct representation, the following questions must be answered as each activity is added to the network:
  - Which activities must be completed immediately before this activity can start?
  - Which activities must immediately follow this activity?
  - Which activities must occur concurrently with this activity?

Figures 7.5 and 7.6 depict the first and second rules: each activity is represented by one and only one arrow in the network, and no two activities can be identified by the same head and tail event.

Dummy activities are a way to show parallel activities without violating the second rule. In figure 7.7, suppose tasks "A" and "B" must precede "C," while "E" is preceded only by "B." Note the wrong way to depict this scheduling requirement on the left, while the right accurately depicts the requirements with the addition of the dummy activity "D1."

Let's try an example. In Exercise #1, suppose we had the following requirements: draw the AOA diagram so that the following precedence relationships are satisfied:

- "E" is preceded by "B" and "C"
- "F" is preceded by "A" and "B"

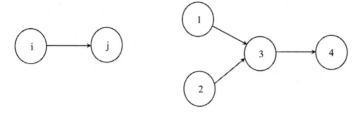

Figure 7.5. AOA Rule #1—One and Only One Arrow in the Network

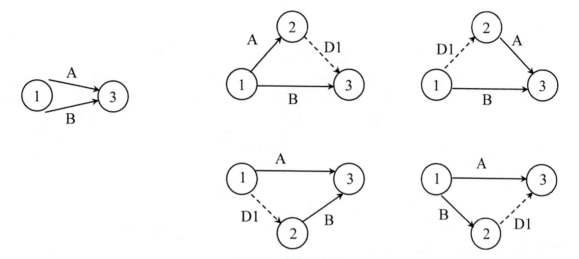

Figure 7.6. AOA Rule #2—No Two Head and Tail Events

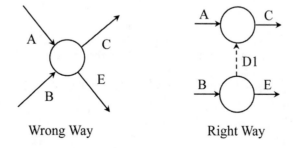

Wrong Way   Right Way

Figure 7.7. Dummy Activities are Like One Way Water Pipes Full of Data

On the surface, figure 7.8 would seem to satisfy these two requirements.

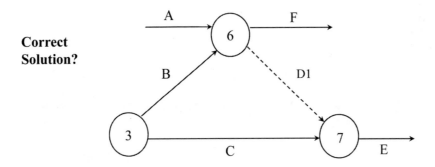

Figure 7.8. Is "E" Preceded by "B" and "C" Alone?

What we discover in figure 7.8 is that "D1" was inserted to allow "B" to precede "E"; in doing so, however, "A" now also precedes "E." Figure 7.9 is the correct solution.

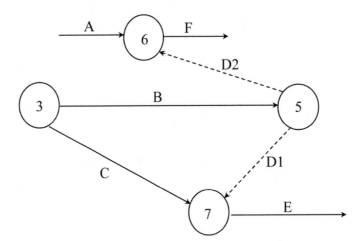

Figure 7.9. Exercise #1—Correct Solution

Let's try another. In Exercise #2, suppose we were asked to draw the precedence diagram for the following conditions:

- "G" is preceded by "A"
- "E" is preceded by "A" and "B"
- "F" is preceded by "B" and "C"

The question becomes, is figure 7.10 correct?

Figure 7.10 is not correct. It implies "A" also precedes "F." That is, the pipeline "D1" also allows "A" to flow through "D2" on its way to "F." The correct solution is depicted in figure 7.11.

The AON scheduling method is characterized by the following.

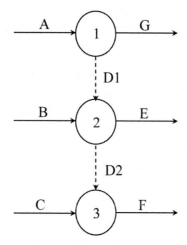

Figure 7.10. Exercise #2—Correct Solution?

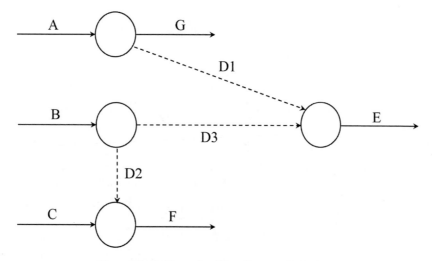

Figure 7.11. Exercise #2—Correct Solution

- AON is the basis for most computer scheduling applications.
- Arrows are used to denote precedence relationships among activities.
- There is no need for dummy activities.
- All nodes, with the exception of the terminal node, must have at least one successor.
- All nodes, except the first, must have at least one predecessor.
- There should be only one initial and one terminal node.
- No arrows should be left dangling. Notwithstanding rules #4 and #5 above, every arrow must have a head and a tail.

- An arrow specifies only precedence relations; its length has no time duration significance relative to either of the activities it connects.
- Cycles or closed loop paths through the network are not permitted. They imply that an activity is a successor of another activity that depends on it.

AON and AOA share the same formula for calculating early start and early finish times. Early start is the earliest the activity can start given the latest finish time of the activity's predecessor. Early finish is the earliest the activity can finish and is based on when it can start and how long the activity is. Early start and early finish times are planned by calculating forward through the schedule's activities.

Forward pass

- $ES(J) = max[EF(I)$, where I is an immediate predecessor of J]
- $EF(J) = ES(J) + L(J)$

The schedule activity's latest finish and latest start times are based on the successor's latest start time. Formulas for calculating latest finish and latest start times are:

- $LF(J) = min[LS(I)$, where I is the successor of J]
- $LS(J) = LF(J) - L(J)$

Figure 7.12 depicts an example of early start, early finish, latest finish, and latest start times.

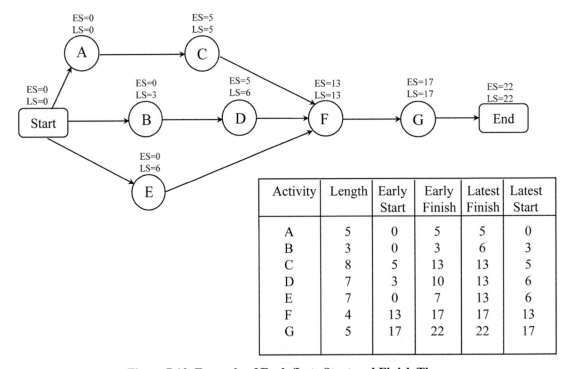

Activity	Length	Early Start	Early Finish	Latest Finish	Latest Start
A	5	0	5	5	0
B	3	0	3	6	3
C	8	5	13	13	5
D	7	3	10	13	6
E	7	0	7	13	6
F	4	13	17	17	13
G	5	17	22	22	17

Figure 7.12. Example of Early/Late Start and Finish Times

Total slack of an activity is calculated as the difference between its late start (or finish) and its early start (or finish). The free slack is the difference between the earliest among the early start times of its successors and its early finish time. That is, for each activity J:

- $TS(J) = LS(J) - ES(J)$
- $FS(J) = min[ES(I)$, where I is the successor of J] $- EF(J)$

Activities with zero total slack fall on the critical path. Figure 7.13 provides an example with slack time calculated. Notice the critical path runs through nodes "A," "C," "F," and "G."

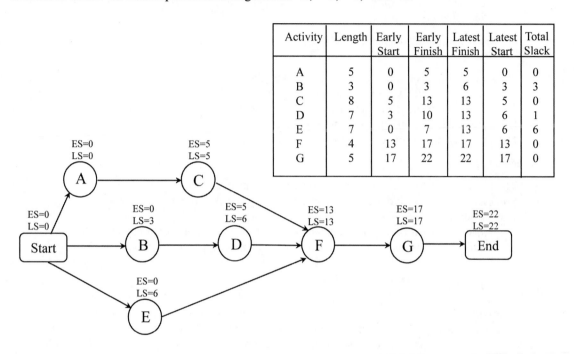

Activity	Length	Early Start	Early Finish	Latest Finish	Latest Start	Total Slack
A	5	0	5	5	0	0
B	3	0	3	6	3	3
C	8	5	13	13	5	0
D	7	3	10	13	6	1
E	7	0	7	13	6	6
F	4	13	17	17	13	0
G	5	17	22	22	17	0

Figure 7.13. Example with Total Slack Calculated

Closing Thoughts on Developing a Network Diagram

Although CPM and PERT are conceptually similar, symbols and charting techniques vary. PERT historically has utilized probability techniques, while, in general, CPM has not. The following procedures apply to both CPM and PERT.

- Identify all individual tasks comprising the program.
- Determine the expected time to complete each activity.
- Determine precedence and interrelationships among activities.
- Develop a network diagram presenting these activities in proper sequence reflecting any dependency relationships.
  - Activities indicated by lines
  - Events or milestones by circles
  - Dependencies or sequencing on separate paths by dotted lines
- Complete and annotate the cumulative time required to reach each milestone along the paths. This will indicate the earliest time work can start on the next activity. The final time will indicate the total time required to complete a particular path.
- Identify the critical path. This is the sequence of events taking the longest time to complete.

- Starting at the program completion milestone on the farthest right, begin working backward and compute latest time an activity can start without delaying the overall program. For example, if the total program takes forty weeks and the last activity takes five weeks, then the final activity cannot begin later than thirty-five weeks. The difference between the earliest start time and the latest time for each activity is the slack time or float. The critical path contains no slack time, that is, free time.

The advantages and disadvantages of network diagrams are listed below.
Advantages

- Network diagrams organize what otherwise would be confusing.
- They are essential for complex systems, ship construction, missiles, and the like.
- They allow managers to predict shortages and act on them early in the program.
- Once prepared, network diagrams are easy to update and rework.
- Network diagrams provide more control over activities and events.

Disadvantages

- The activity times are only as good as the estimates provided.
- Sometimes the network diagrams are hard to follow; they possess too many lines and intersections.
- Sometimes the network diagrams become the focus of too much attention, while other issues may be the root cause of the problems, for example, management/labor relations.

Master Schedule

Schedules provide the time frame for resource allocation and establish a baseline for current status and forecasts of completion dates. A program contains a hierarchy of related levels of schedules, beginning with the master program schedule, with each succeeding lower level more fully identifying and expanding the activities necessary to meet the program requirements.

Management of these activities begins with the master program schedule, incorporates the intermediate schedule, and culminates in the detailed schedules. As a management tool, the intermediate schedule and detailed schedules are typically depicted as an interdependency network, a network diagram that depicts the interrelationships among the numerous program activities.

A program's master schedule is incrementally created, beginning with the identified activities and milestones specified in the contract.

Figure 7.14 depicts a typical master program schedule.

Remember, to generate the master program schedule means that we already know what works has to be done. This implies that we already know what our stated and derived requirements are. Again, stated requirements are those things explicitly asked for, while derived requirements are those things we must do to satisfy the stated requirements. Derived requirements are those requirements we place on ourselves to do the work we believe is being asked of us.

Intermediate Schedule

Intermediate schedules are a hierarchically lower resolution of the work to be performed than initially depicted in the master program schedule. The intermediate schedules simply continue to separate the activities depicted in the master program schedule into lower-level subactivities. This further evolution of identified work culminates in the lowest level of schedules produced, detailed schedules.

Figure 7.15 depicts a typical intermediate schedule.

Activity/Event	20xx												20xy		
	J	F	M	A	M	J	J	A	S	O	N	D	J	F	M
Begin Building House	^														
Concrete Inspection					^										
Framing Inspection							^								
Wiring Inspection								^							
Final Walkthrough Inspection														^	
Perform all Masonry Activities	█	█	█	█											
Frame the House					█	█									
Install all Wiring							█	█							
Install all Plumbing	█	█	█	█	█	█	█	█	█						
Install all Drywall									█	█	█				
Perform Finishing												█	█	█	

Figure 7.14. Example Master Program Schedule

Activity/Event	20xx											
	J	F	M	A	M	J	J	A	S	O	N	D
Begin Building House	^											
Concrete Inspection				^								
Framing Inspection							^					
Wiring Inspection									^			
Install Plumbing in Slab	█	█	█	█								
Install Plumbing in Garage								█				
Install Plumbing in Kitchen								█				
Install Plumbing in Baths								█				
Install Plumbing in Utility Room								█				
Finish Plumbing Activities								█				

Figure 7.15. Example Intermediate Schedule

Notice in the intermediate schedule that the plumbing activity, which was a single line item in the master schedule, has now been expanded. This is the intent of the intermediate schedule—to expand on the higher-level master schedule activities.

Notice also that the above intermediate schedule is easy to read, but it does not provide sufficient detail to show what happens when one of the activities slips out in time. In other words, what is the overall impact to the whole schedule if, for example, installing plumbing in the kitchen happens to slip?

The above, then, is a good depiction of a combination Gantt and Milestone chart, and is easy to read, but does not show the interrelatedness of the many activities.

Detailed Schedules

Detailed schedules are the bottommost schedules in the schedule hierarchy. The purpose of developing lower-level schedules is to identify small, manageable elements of work.

The detailed schedules expand each intermediate schedule summary/subproject into multiple activities, to the extent necessary or desired, and add schedule events that satisfy the requirements of the intermediate schedule. The detailed schedules are working schedules that depict horizontal dependencies and therefore are used on a daily basis by the managers to manage their work. Figure 7.16 depicts a typical detailed schedule.

Activity/Event	20xx											
	J	F	M	A	M	J	J	A	S	O	N	D
Begin Building House	^											
Concrete Inspection					^							
Framing Inspection								^				
Wiring Inspection									^			
Install Plumbing in Slab	▓▓▓▓▓▓▓▓▓▓											
Detail Plan for Plumbing	▓▓▓											
Trench Stone		▓▓										
Lay Required Pipe			▓▓									
Connect Pipe			▓▓▓									
Level Stone			▓▓▓▓									

Figure 7.16. Example Detailed Schedule

Notice that just as was the case in transitioning from master to intermediate schedules, again we have dug one level of detail to the next in transitioning from the intermediate to detailed schedules.

Notice as well the overlapping of activities in the above detailed schedule. Notice how trenching, laying pipe, connecting pipe, and leveling stone seem to have some degree of overlap. One can only guess that this is acceptable, but again we have to wonder what would happen if one of these slipped out in time.

When defining how the activities of a schedule are related, we typically refer to one of three basic relationships (figure 7.17): (1) start-to-start, (2) finish-to-start, and (3) finish-to-finish.

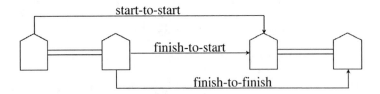

Figure 7.17. Lead and Lag Relationships

Start-to-start means that the second activity cannot start until the first activity starts. Finish-to-start means the second activity cannot start until the first activity finishes. And finish-to-finish means the second activity cannot finish until the first activity finishes. The most popular relationship, and the one most scheduling tools assume you want and therefore applies, is the start-to-start relationship.

Human Resource Plan

As discussed in the above detailed schedule, there are numerous overlapping activities. What we want to know is whether this is one person working a lot of hours, or many people each doing their specific part of the whole job.

The objective of generating a human resource plan is to formulate a concise, meaningful, and practical program-level strategy for managing human resources in the manner most suitable to fulfill the program goals.

Resource planning as a philosophy requires that resources be identified for each detailed schedule activity and assigned in the program's scheduling tool. The human resource plan, then, is a time-phased report, by activity, WBS element, or program.

Figure 7.18 depicts an example of a human resource plan.

Project Name: Build a House													Status Date: December 18, 20xx Run Date: January 23, 20xy		
Person or Group Name	Function/Discipline	Jan	Feb	Mar	Apr	May	Jun	Jul	Aug	Sep	Oct	Nov	Dec	Total
Mike Gradle	Plumbing	1	1	1	1									4
Sally Smith	Plumbing	0.25	0.25	0.25	0.25									1
George Angus	Plumbing Designer	0.5	0.5											1
Sara Likert	Plumbing Stone Trencher		0.25	0.25										0.5
Miguel Alvarez	Plumbing Pipe Layer		0.25	0.25										0.5
Mike Gradle	Plumbing			0.25	0.25									0.5
Sara Likert	Plumbing Stone Leveler			0.25	0.25									0.5
														0
		1.75	2.25	2.25	1.75	0	0	0	0	0	0	0	0	8

Figure 7.18. Example Human Resource Plan

Figure 7.18 is for the plumbers only. Notice that the individuals in the human resource plan are tied to the detailed schedule in the above section. Now, in answer to our opening question, "Is this is one person working a lot of hours, or many people each doing their specific part of the whole job?" we can readily see that there are numerous people doing different tasks. We can also see when these individuals are expected to perform their efforts and what percent of their time will be dedicated to this activity.

A More Detailed Perspective

Master Schedule

Schedules provide the time frame for resource allocation and establish a baseline for current status and forecasts of completion dates. A program contains a hierarchy of related levels of schedules, beginning with the master program schedule, and with each succeeding, lower level more fully identifying and expanding the activities necessary to meet the program requirements. Management of these activities begins with the master program schedule, incorporates the intermediate schedule, and culminates in the detailed schedules. As a management tool, the intermediate schedule and detailed schedules are typically depicted as an interdependency network, a network diagram that depicts the interrelationships among the numerous program activities.

A program's master schedule is incrementally created, beginning with the identified activities and milestones specified in the contract.

Figure 7.19 depicts a typical master program schedule.

Figure 7.20 depicts the detailed process flow for generating the master program schedule and should be referred to when reading the following paragraphs.

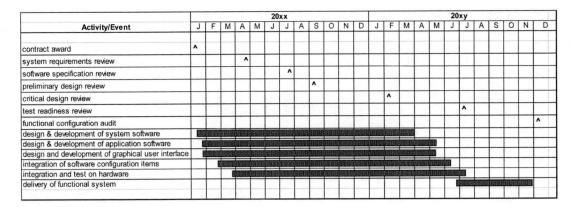

Figure 7.19. Example Master Program Schedule

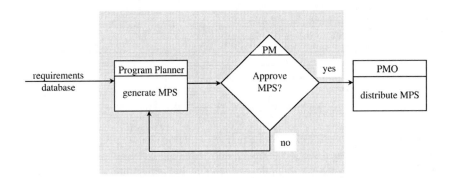

Figure 7.20. Master Program Schedule Process Flow

Input to this activity is the requirements database, which contains stated and derived schedule requirements. Stated requirements are derived from the contract or request for proposal. Internally derived requirements are defined from within the processes of the functional organizations within the program. For example, the design engineering organization process specifies that a review is required (such as a preliminary design review). Even if there is no stated external requirement for such a review, the preliminary design review should be included on the appropriate schedules as an event, and it should occur unless the program manager and the functional manager agree to delete the requirement.

Processing for this activity is the responsibility of the program planner, who utilizes the requirements database.

The schedule includes:

- contract deliveries
- major customer review/decision points and major contractual schedule events
- buyer furnished equipment/material and delivery dates
- buyer review/approval dates
- summaries of all program activities and key schedule events
- schedule reserve

The program manager reviews the master program schedule. If the master program schedule requires changes, it will be returned to the program planner; otherwise, the program manager will demonstrate approval by signing the master program schedule.

The master program schedule should be generated in accordance with the following considerations:

- The master program schedule should be depicted as an interdependency network, or Gantt chart.
- Early, late, and baseline dates for each summary and event should be identified.
- The scheduling process should be performed with approved tools. Approved tools will ensure the use of a consistent format throughout the company.
- The schedules should be generated utilizing top-down development. The master program schedule should be generated and approved before generating the intermediate schedules. The intermediate schedules should be generated and approved before generating detailed schedules.
- Traceability exists from each lower-level schedule element to a uniquely identifiable upper-level schedule element; that is, a lower-level schedule element completely supports the next-higher schedule element.
- Since the master program schedule functions as a reporting tool to company management and to the customer, it should occupy only one page. When adequate space for contract data requirements lists and contract line item numbers is precluded by the one-page format, then the master program schedule may be augmented by supplemental schedules.
- The master program schedule should be released with schedule reserve indicated (if applicable). Schedule reserve consists of time retained for later use, when unplanned activity occurs. Unplanned activities would negatively affect the schedule of in-scope work if the schedule reserve has not been planned at the start of the program. The inclusion of a schedule reserve is at the discretion of the program manager and can eliminate the later need to submit a change request to the external customer or business area director. Lower-level schedules should be generated to show completion of the activities no later than the dates of the accelerated schedule activities created when the schedule reserve was taken.

As discussed earlier, while the master program schedule is being generated, the WBS provided by the customer may be extended to reflect the current understanding of the work and its organization. Accompanying the WBS are dictionaries that describe the work to be performed, as depicted in the currently extended work breakdown structure.

Extending the WBS and creating dictionaries is the first step in planning the costs of the program. Cost planning is concerned with defining the relationship between the elements of work to be performed under the contract, allocating budget to the elements of work, defining who is responsible for performing the work, and selecting preliminary cost accounts.

The cost account is the management control point at which actual costs can be accumulated and compared to budgeted costs for work performed. It is also a control point for cost, schedule, and technical performance planning, work execution, and performance measurement. Cost account responsibility is assigned to a cost account manager.

Intermediate Schedule

The intermediate schedules are a hierarchically lower resolution of the work to be performed than initially depicted in the master program schedule. The intermediate schedules simply continue to separate the activities depicted in the master program schedule into lower-level subactivities. This further evolution of identified work culminates in the lowest level of schedules produced—detailed schedules.

Figure 7.21 depicts a typical intermediate schedule.

Activity/Event	20xx												20xy		
	J	F	M	A	M	J	J	A	S	O	N	D	J	F	M
contract award	^														
system requirements review					^										
software specification review							^								
preliminary design review									^						
critical design review														^	
design & development of operating system			█	█	█	█	█	█	█	█	█				
design & development of database management system			█	█	█	█	█	█	█						
design & development of query language			█	█	█	█	█	█	█	█					
design & development of description lanaguage			█	█	█	█	█								
database management system integration							█	█	█	█	█	█			
system software integration						█	█	█	█	█	█	█	█	█	█

Figure 7.21. Example Intermediate Schedule

Figure 7.22 depicts the detailed process flow for generating the intermediate schedule and should be referred to when reading the following paragraphs.

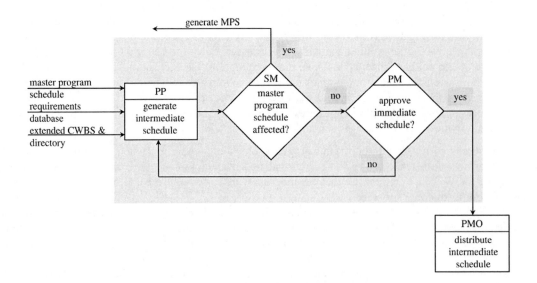

Figure 7.22. Intermediate Schedule Detailed Process Flow

Processing for this activity is the responsibility of the program planner and consists of the following.

- Developing the summary-level activities on the master program schedule in greater detail.
- Identifying the following features associated with these further developed summaries/ subprojects:
  - key events
  - duration of summaries/subprojects
  - fixed start/completion dates

- Changing the master program schedule when any date is changed as a result of intermediate schedule development.
- The program manager's review of the intermediate schedule; if the intermediate schedule requires changes, it is returned to the program planner. Otherwise, the program manager signifies approval by signing the intermediate schedule.

The intermediate schedule should:

- Depict the intermediate schedule as an interdependency network
- Identify early, late, and baseline dates for each summary, subproject, and event
- Identify relationships (dependencies, successor/predecessor) among key events
- Identify the float (slack time) of each summary and event
- Identify the critical path(s)

Detailed Schedules

Detailed schedules are the bottommost schedules in the schedule hierarchy. The purpose of developing lower-level schedules is to identify discrete, manageable elements of work.

The detailed schedules expand each intermediate schedule summary/subproject into multiple activities, to the extent necessary, or desired, and adds schedule events that satisfy the requirements of the intermediate schedule. The detailed schedules are working schedules that depict horizontal dependencies and therefore are used on a daily basis by the cost account managers to manage their work.

Figure 7.23 depicts a typical detailed schedule.

Activity/Event	20xx											
	J	F	M	A	M	J	J	A	S	O	N	D
contract award	^											
system requirements review					^							
software specification review							^					
preliminary design review								^				
design and development of operating system												
design and development of context scheduler												
design and development of time management function												
design and development of file manager												
design and development of input/output function												
operating system integration												

Figure 7.23. Example Detailed Schedule

Figure 7.24 depicts the detailed process flow for creating preliminary detailed schedules and should be referenced when reading the following paragraphs.

Two things could happen as a result of creating the detailed schedules: the end dates in the interdependency network may no longer be acceptable, and the intermediate schedule may have been affected. All processing activities below are associated with these two potential problems.

Processing for this activity is the responsibility of the cost account managers.

- The cost account managers develop the summaries/subprojects identified on the intermediate schedule in greater detail (activities), in accordance with the following requirements:

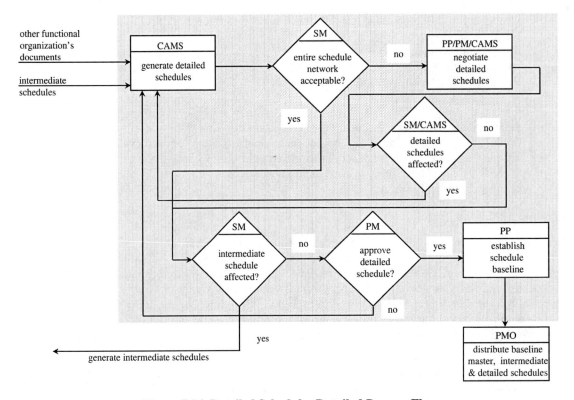

Figure 7.24. Detailed Schedules Detailed Process Flow

- distinguishing each activity from all other activities in the cost account
- defining quantifiable activities in terms of a physical product that can be assigned a completion date
- making each activity the responsibility of a single functional organizational element
- specifying the minimum set of documents, resources, or products from other activities required to start work (start event)
- clearly defining completion criteria based on accomplishing a specific task (completion event)
- identifying activity duration
- identifying fixed start and/or completion dates
- defining predecessor (products required to start the activity) and successor (products produced by the activity) relationships with associated lead/lag times

It is imperative that contractual requirements not be modified during this process.

- The cost account managers answer the following when generating activities:
    - Is work missing or not required?
    - Does the work definition need modification to satisfy the requirements of the cost account?
    - Should the work be broken down further?
    - Should the requirements be broken down further?

- The cost account managers include material-support activities (events) on the detailed schedules as appropriate. Such activities include:
  - generating engineering bills of material
  - generating manufacturing bills of material
  - material procurement planning
  - generating requisitions
  - generating a stocking plan
  - scheduling
  - expediting support groups
  - expediting receiving's distribution of material
  - inspecting/accepting material
  - rejecting/returning material
  - committing material
  - inspecting material
  - releasing material
- The cost account managers determine whether the interdependency network is acceptable, based on the following criteria:
  - all detailed schedule dates support all intermediate schedule dates
  - all activities have at least one predecessor and successor
  - all activities are mapped to the extended contract WBS
  - all events are connected to activities
- The cost account managers determine whether the intermediate schedule is affected (i.e., whether any intermediate schedule date is changed as a result of detailed schedule development).
- The cost account managers submit the detailed schedules to the program manager. If the detailed schedules require changes, they are returned to the program planner. Otherwise, the program manager signifies approval by signing the detailed schedules. If dates on the detailed schedules do not correspond to the dates established by the intermediate schedules, then the following options are available for reconciling differences:
  - identifying alternate plans for accomplishing the work
  - reevaluating interpretations of the requirements to ensure the requirements are satisfied but not exceeded
  - considering additional or more highly skilled resources to accomplish the work
  - reevaluating schedule/risk tradeoffs

The detailed schedules should:

- Be depicted as interdependency networks or Gantt charts
- Identify early, late, and baseline dates for each activity and event
- Identify relationships (dependencies, successor/predecessor) among activities and events (start-to-start, finish-to-start, and finish-to-finish), as illustrated in figure 7.17
- Identify the float (slack time) of each activity and event
- Identify the critical activities and events
- Identify lead and lag times between activities and events

Generating the preliminary detailed schedules may involve negotiation when the interdependency network is unacceptable and the cost account managers have attempted to reconcile the differences. This activity is the responsibility of the program planner and cost account managers and consists of:

- Negotiating the adjustment of intermediate schedule date(s)
- Negotiating the adjustment of detailed schedule date(s)
- Determining whether the detailed schedules are affected (i.e., whether any detailed schedule date is changed as a result of negotiating detailed schedules)
- Determining whether requirements have been changed as a result of this activity, which happens when they have been reallocated or reinterpreted (if requirements change, the requirements database should be modified)

Once the detailed schedules have been deemed acceptable and no effect on either the intermediate or master schedules is perceived, work packages and planning packages should be identified from the detailed schedules. Processing for this activity is the responsibility of the cost account managers and consists of seven steps:

- The cost account managers examine the cost account's requirements and define the work packages/planning packages by determining whether:
  - work is missing or not required
  - the work belongs in this cost account
  - the work belongs in the work package/planning package
  - the work definition needs modification to satisfy the requirements of the extended CWBS
  - the work should be broken down further
  - the requirements should be broken down further
- The cost account managers assign to each activity a unique identifier for each element in the extended CWBS.
- The cost account managers assign each work package/planning package a unique extended CWBS element title.
- The cost account managers convert planning packages to work packages within the approved cost account budget at completion, cost account supplemental schedule events, and cost account requirements identified in the requirements database. This conversion must be accomplished prior to starting the effort identified in the planning package.
- The cost account managers determine whether the extended CWBS dictionary is affected (i.e., whether a work package/planning package description has been generated or modified or whether extended CWBS elements have been added or deleted).
- The cost account managers ascertain that each planning package/work package consists of:
  - a description (located in the applicable extended CWBS dictionary)
  - requirements (located in the requirements database)
  - a schedule
- The cost account managers assign each work package/planning package identified to one and only one functional organization.

Once the detailed schedules have been approved and it has been verified that the intermediate and master schedules are consistent, then the schedule baseline is established and is ready for the program manager's approval. The program planner is responsible for establishing the schedule baseline by recording all early dates as baseline dates.

Keep in mind that having a program planner assumes the program is of sufficient size to be afforded this luxury. In the prior examples of simply obtaining a landscape estimate, the estimator was the program manager as well as the scheduler. In this scenario, the program manager was also the proposal manager, cost manager, cost account manager, and all others not otherwise assigned a responsibility.

Human Resource Plan

The objective of this activity is to formulate a concise, meaningful, and practical program-level strategy for managing human resources in the manner most suitable to fulfill the program goals.

Resource planning as a philosophy requires that resources be identified for each detailed schedule activity and assigned in the program's scheduling tool. The human resource plan, then, is an automated, time-phased report, by activity, CWBS element, or program, generated by the program planner utilizing the program's scheduling tool.

Development of the human resource plan is an iterative process. A first-look, high-level, initial plan is done early in the program planning stage. After cost account plans have been generated, an updated plan is developed using the cost accounts as a basis.

Figure 7.25 depicts an example of a human resource plan.

Figure 7.26 depicts the process flow for generating the human resource plan and should be referenced when reading the following paragraphs.

Processing for this activity consists of six steps:

- The functional organization planning resources, together with the program management office, identify human resources, utilizing the extended CWBS and dictionary and the preliminary responsibility assignment matrix. Processing consists of determining functional organization personnel requirements and preparing an individual functional organization input, in accordance with the resource-loading procedures for the program's scheduling tool.
- The program planner, utilizing the individual functional organization inputs and the intermediate schedule, integrates the functional organization inputs into the resource plan.
- The functional managers/business area directors, cost account managers, and program planner assign resources by name, utilizing the individual functional organization inputs. This activity consists of two steps.
  - The functional manager/business area director assigns resources by name, usually three months prior to the scheduled start date of a work package. This activity is processed outside the program management planning process and, therefore, is done in accordance with the given functional manager's or business area's process.
  - The cost account manager/program manager reviews assignments. If changes are required, then the cost account manager/program manager negotiates with the functional managers/business area director. Otherwise, the program manager approves the assignment of resources.
- The program manager determines whether the human resource plan meets program requirements by considering the following:
  - budget
  - schedule
  - performance
  - identification and reduction of resource loading peaks and valleys
  - method of resource acquisition (human resources organization approval as applicable)
  - duplication/discontinuation of resources
- Two additional details for consideration after resources have been loaded are whether the intermediate schedule has been affected and whether the preliminary responsibility assignment matrix has been affected. If either the intermediate schedule or preliminary responsibility assignment matrix has been affected, then modifications are required.
- The program manager reviews the human resource plan. If it requires changes, it is updated. Otherwise, the program manager signifies approval by signing it.

Project Name:
Status Date: December 28, 20xx
Run Date: December 31, 20xx

Budget	Code/Description	Resource	Code/Description	Year	May	Jun	Jul	Aug	Sep	Oct	Nov	Dec	Total
063GBN	Grace Numbrick	U7	TRAVEL	20xx Hrs	0	0	4	12	81	0	0	0	97
		XD	ENG/ASSOC ENG	20xx Hrs	76	102	166	144	179	137	129	142	1075
373-PB	Production Engineer	PB	PE STAFF/PRINCPL	20xx Hrs	0	0	80	0	160	0	0	0	240
530-XC	Dept 530, XC	XC	SR ENG/SR ASSOC	20xx Hrs	0	0	0	37	48	59	72	88	303
533-W1	Repro Material Dollars	W1	ENG MATERIAL	20xx Hrs	0	0	0	0	0	0	0	0	0
536PLD	Peter Deroach	XN	DATA SPECIALIST	20xx Hrs	176	168	212	176	152	120	103	119	1226
539KH	Karma Hedstone	XW	STAFF SFTW ENG	20xx Hrs	80	88	0	0	0	0	0	0	168
551-XB	XB-551, Config Mgt	XB	STAF/PRINC/STF A	20xx Hrs	6	59	13	59	6	0	0	6	150
613-XK	Dept 613, XK	XK	DESIGNERS	20xx Hrs	0	0	790	707	915	776	735	940	4863
615MLM	Matt McMormick	XE	PROGRAM DIRECTOR	20xx Hrs	144	136	173	151	180	137	130	144	1194
615NWG	Nancy Gladstone	XE	PROGRAM DIRECTOR	20xx Hrs	144	136	173	151	180	137	130	144	1194
615SMR	Steven Roberts	XE	PROGRAM DIRECTOR	20xx Hrs	144	136	173	151	173	137	129	144	1187
615TEW	Tom West	XA	SR STAFF/SR PRN	20xx Hrs	38	35	47	0	0	20	0	0	140
615-XD	Dept 615, XD	XD	DATA ENT/WRD PRC	20xx Hrs	144	136	173	151	173	137	129	144	1187
637-XA	Dept 637, XA	XA	SR STAFF/SR PRN	20xx Hrs	0	0	0	0	2	0	0	0	2
637-XC	Dept 637, XC	XC	SR ENG/SR ASSOC	20xx Hrs	0	0	41	114	22	0	0	0	177
643-PM	PF-643, Assem Shop	PF	PE PRD PLN/SRTLD	20xx Hrs	0	0	0	0	0	0	16	8	24
647-XB	Dept 647, XB	XB	STAF/PRINC/STF A	20xx Hrs	0	0	0	0	1	15	10	22	48
649AMT	Antonio Tomaro	GA	SR Q A ENG	20xx Hrs	71	67	114	62	65	49	48	65	540
650-XB	Dept 650, XB	XB	STAF/PRINC/STF A	20xx Hrs	48	43	75	136	311	227	162	269	1272
650-XF	Dept 650, XF	XF	SR TECH/FOREMAN	20xx Hrs	0	0	0	0	0	0	63	102	165
658-XA	Dept 658, XA	XA	SR STAFF/SR PRN	20xx Hrs	0	11	16	13	5	0	1	1	47

Figure 7.25. Example Human Resource Plan

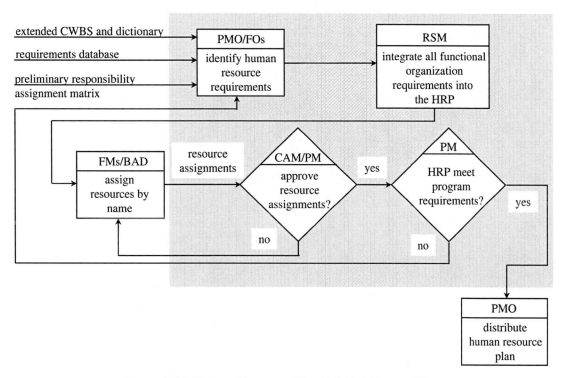

Figure 7.26. Human Resource Plan Detailed Process Flow

Chapter 8

Risk Management—Mitigating the Impact

Risk management is really a permutation of the words *risk* and *management.* That is, risk management is really a formal process for managing program risks.

Risk can be defined as the probability of an undesirable event or situation occurring and the significance of the consequence of the occurrence.

For example:

- A stock price drop causes a paper loss.
- An interest rate increase causes higher home payments.
- A plane crash causes multiple casualties.

When discussing risk we must also address rewards. There must always be some potential gain from successfully executing an activity with risk. As the potential gain increases, so does the acceptability of higher levels of risks. If the consequence of the risk occurrence decreases, the acceptability of assuming the risk increases.

Figure 8.1 reflects this relationship.

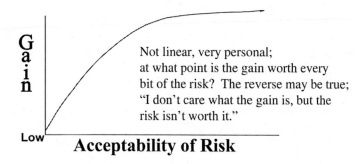

Figure 8.1. Gain versus Acceptability of Risk

Additionally, there is the consequence versus acceptability of the risk. In this trade-off, the higher the consequence of the risk, the lower the acceptability of the risk, and vice versa. Figure 8.2 reflects this relationship.

Risk management is a process composed of four distinct, yet dependent, activities:

- Risk planning
- Risk assessment
- Risk analysis
- Risk handling

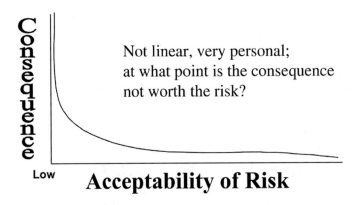

Figure 8.2. Consequence versus Acceptability of Risk

Risk Planning

The intent of risk management planning is to force organized intelligent thought on the tasks of identifying risks, and subsequently, on eliminating, minimizing, or controlling the expected consequences of risk occurrences.

The planning aspect of risk management requires some basic support from other individuals/functional organizations as well as a focused effort.

- Management buy-in: management must provide the necessary resources to perform the required program risk planning. In other words, managing risk is not free. There is effort involved in identifying, quantifying, prioritizing, and monitoring potential risks. Even if you are a one-person show, running your own program and performing all of the activities, there is still some level of risk in what you do. For example, if I'm my own landscaper, I might decide to buy gloves to minimize the risk of getting blisters from shoveling. The act of buying gloves was a risk mitigation activity. The fact that I recognized the risk of blisters was a conscious decision on my part to think through the blister risk.
- Functional management buy-in: functional management are the most knowledgeable individuals on discipline-specific risks. Staying with our landscaping example, suppose I wanted to know what the risk was of planting a certain type of tree in the fall. I would most likely ask an expert at a nursery or at a local university.
- Key areas should be targeted for the risk management process. In our landscaping example, key areas might be risks associated with trenching or risks associated with bedding or brick-laying. A key area is a set of activities, which in and of themselves form a major initiative.

Risk, again, is defined as the probability of an undesirable event occurring and the significance of the consequence of the occurrence. Figure 8.3 depicts this relationship.

Notice from figure 8.3, if the probability of the risk is low and the seriousness is equally low, then the risk is basically negligible. In other words, if it occurs, we will handle it through normal decision making. As the probability of occurrence goes up and the seriousness of the occurrence goes up, risks move from moderate to significant.

Formal risk mitigation is the process of determining what preventive actions should occur to reduce the probability of the risk occurring, what type of risk monitoring systems exist to detect when the risk occurs, and what contingent actions can be applied to reduce the seriousness should the risk materialize.

		SERIOUSNESS		
		HIGH	**MEDIUM**	**LOW**
PROBABILITY	**HIGH**	**SIGNIFICANT RISK** Formal Risk Mitigation required	**SIGNIFICANT RISK** Formal Risk Mitigation required	**MODERATE RISK** Formal Risk Mitigation should be considered
	MEDIUM	**SIGNIFICANT RISK** Formal Risk Mitigation required	**MODERATE RISK** Formal Risk Mitigation should be considered	**NEGLIGIBLE RISK** Manage Risk through routine processes
	LOW	**MODERATE RISK** Formal Risk Mitigation should be considered	**MODERATE RISK** Formal Risk Mitigation should be considered	**NEGLIGIBLE RISK** Manage Risk through routine processes

Figure 8.3. Probability versus Seriousness of the Risk

Risk Assessment

Risk assessment is concerned with identifying the risks and then quantifying them, so as to be able to address only those that pose the greatest probability of occurrence and the greatest seriousness should they occur.

Risks can be identified through any number of sources:

- Expert opinion
- Analogy comparisons
- Evaluation of program plans

Quantification is characterized as:

- Creating a rating system for identified risks
- Getting all parties to agree on the rating system
- Keeping the rating system relatively simple (high, medium, low)

In general, at the highest level, we are attempting to move risks through various known states as follows:

- Knowns—events or situations containing no uncertainty.
- Known unknowns—we know they exist, but don't know much about them. For example, I know that the scientific discipline of bioengineering exists, but I don't know much about it.
- Unknown unknowns—typified as events or situations that could not have even been imagined, such as diseases.

Further, risks exist in every discipline or function (e.g., plumbing, electrical, framing, etc.). Below identifies typical program-related risks.

Corporate business risks:

- Business risk—includes the chances of both profit and loss.
- Pure or insurable risk—includes only the chance for loss, not profit.
    - direct property (fire, storm, flood)
    - indirect property (renting alternative equipment)
    - liability (bodily injury, personal injury, property damage, lawsuits)
    - personnel (loss of key individuals)

Program/project risks:

- Technical risks (performance-related)
    - material properties (metal, plastic, fiberglass)
    - physical size of the entity (6 pounds, breadbox size)
    - speed of the entity (0 to 60? Yes!)
    - operating environment (nuclear threat, salt, sand, sun, moisture, etc.)
    - system complexity (design/integration issues)
- Program risks (resource-oriented)
    - material availability
    - personnel availability
    - communication problems
    - labor conflicts (strikes, walkouts, slowdowns)
    - personnel skill mix
        - what's required
        - what do we possess
        - what do we need
- Supportability risks (associated with fielding or maintaining the system)
    - reliability and maintainability
    - field training
    - interoperability with other systems
    - transportability
    - system safety
- Cost risks (concerned with program cost growth)
    - overhead rates
    - estimating errors
    - sensitivity to other risks
        - technical
        - programmatic
        - supportability
        - schedule
- Schedule risks (concerned with program schedule issues)
    - activity parallelism
    - quantity of elements on the critical path
    - estimating error
    - interdependencies of complex activities
    - dependencies on complex activities
    - sensitivity to other types of risks

Risk Analysis

Risk management analysis is concerned with further definition and description of the identified risks. During this phase of the risk management process we determine:

- The likely causes of the risks
- Variation of the risks
- Magnitude of the risks
- Consequences of the risks
- Possible ways of dealing with the risks

There are many ways to analyze the risk. Techniques for dealing with the risks include:

- Decision analysis
- Estimating relationships
- Network analysis
- Life cycle cost analysis
- Risk factors
- Performance tracking
- Cost performance report analysis
- Independent technical assessment
- Independent cost estimates

As previously stated, there are many ways to analyze risk, ranging from making a quick assessment based on past experience to more scientific techniques. One technique is called decision analysis.

Decision analysis is also known as expected monetary value technique. It computes the expected value for each alternative and uses decision trees to depict the relationships.

For example, as an organization, should we conduct 100 percent of the tests of our 500 widgets we have to produce?

Givens:

- Field failure rate is 4 percent
- $10,000 per widget for testing (500 widgets x $10,000 = $5 million)
- If tested, there are reassembly costs of $2,000 for each passed widget
- If tested, the cost to repair a failed widget is $23,000
- A fielded failed widget costs $350,000 to repair

Figure 8.4 depicts a decision tree for this problem.

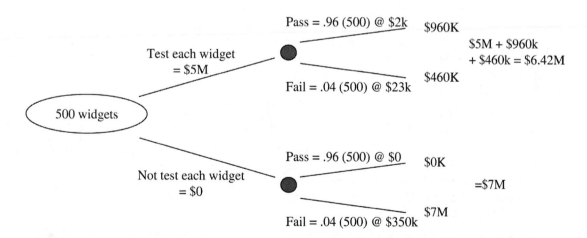

Figure 8.4. Decision Analysis Decision Tree

If our objective is to minimize cost, then we would select the alternative with the lowest expected monetary value, which, in this case, would be to test each widget.

Estimating relationships is an analysis method characterized by the following:

- Review characteristics from previous programs that exhibited cost problems
- Create a model relating characteristics and cost implications (problem = % cost overrun)
- Compare current program characteristics to those in the model
- Reserve sufficient funds for this program

Network analysis, as a risk management analysis technique, is based on network diagramming, and it utilizes the following activities:

- Identify tasks based on the work breakdown structure
- Depict interrelatedness of activities
- Assign resources
- Review durations and critical path
- Examine dependencies
- Assure work is accounted for
- Examine resource loading

Life cycle cost, as a risk management analysis technique, is based on the life cycle cost of a similar project. There are two basic steps in this technique.

- Perform single variable sensitivity analysis, varying:
    - production rates and quantities
    - design trade-offs
    - resource projections
    - repair and warranty variables
    - reliability growth
- Examine the whole project from cradle to grave

Risk factors, as a risk management analysis technique, are intended to estimate the added costs due to identified risks. It is characterized as follows:

- Determine program costs as broken out by work breakdown structure element
- Determine the % additional cost per element due to risk
    - each element may have a different weighted factor
    - weighted factors are multiplied by risk costs
- Recalculate new program costs with the increase due to risk estimates

Performance tracking, as a risk management analysis technique, is really what we refer to as technical performance measurement, and is discussed later in this chapter. In a nutshell, the basic activities are:

- Identify and baseline technical performance parameters (a list of some typical performance parameters are identified below)
- Make monthly assessments of progress toward achieving those parameters
- Note variations from the baseline parameters
- Determine corrective actions

Typical technical performance parameters for performance, reliability, producability, maintainability, quality assurance, and supportability are detailed below.

- Typical technical parameters (performance) are:
    - Speed (miles per hour)
    - Weight (pounds)
    - Range (miles)
    - Power (kilowatts)

- Climb rate (feet/second)
- Takeoff distance (feet)
- Turn rate (degrees/second)

Typical technical parameters (reliability) are:

- Meantime between failures (hrs/days)
- Meantime to repair (hrs/days)
- Probability of component/assembly failure (0 - 1.0)
- Life cycle cost analysis ($)
- Design to cost ($)

Typical technical parameters (producability) are:

- Capital ($)
- Manpower (people count)
- Facilities (square feet)
- Material ($)
- Equipment (machinery required)
- Schedule (time)
- Risk (0 - 1.0)

Typical technical parameters (maintainability) are:

- Standardization (%)
- Modularity (%)
- Update ability (0 - 1.0)
- Special equipment ($)
- Frequency (schedule, time)
- Costs ($)

Typical technical parameters (quality assurance) are:

- Scrap, rework, and repair (% of labor)
- Yield (% of first-time inspection successes)
- Supplier rating (%)
- Customer satisfaction (0 - 1.0)
- Software (lines of code in violation per 1,000 lines of code)

Typical technical parameters (supportability) are:

- Parts inventory ($)
- Costs ($)
- Resources (manpower, equipment, facilities)
- Modularity (%)
- Operational availability (%)

Cost report performance, as a risk management analysis technique, is a review of the cost and schedule variances from the baseline plan. Its basic activities are highlighted below, and it is discussed in considerably more detail in the chapter on management cost/schedule control systems.

- Determine baseline for cost and schedule
- Review monthly and cumulative variances
- Review performance trends (past, present, and future)
- Review written explanation of variances

Independent technical assessment, as a risk management analysis technique, is the same as the cost report performance technique, except with an outside, or independent, party. The basic activities are the same as with the cost report performance technique identified above.

Independent cost estimates, as a risk management analysis technique, look at the cost and schedule estimates by an independent source. Basic activities and features of this technique include the following:

- Cost and schedule estimates are developed by an organization outside of the program office
- Independent organization cross-checks program office estimates
- Helps to prevent overlooked costs or optimistic estimates

In transitioning from risk management analysis to risk management handling, we must remember there are three basic things we need to focus on:

- Preventive actions—those things we can do to reduce the likelihood of the problem occurring
- Risk monitoring systems—those systems put in place to raise a red flag should the problem begin to occur
- Contingent actions—those actions we need to take should the risk actually occur

A model depicting the interrelatedness of these items is depicted in figure 8.5.

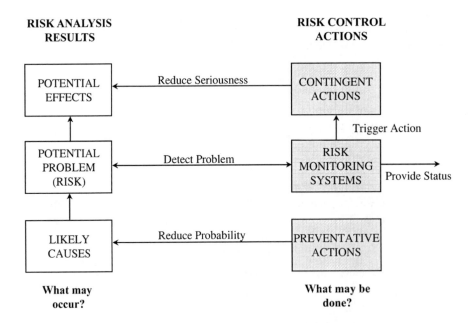

Figure 8.5. Risk Management Analysis to Handling

As depicted in Figure 8.5, preventive actions help us to reduce the probability of the risk occurring. Risk-monitoring systems help to detect the risk should it materialize. Contingent actions help to reduce the seriousness of the occurred risk.

Risk Handling

Once risks have been identified and quantified, there are four ways to handle the risks.

- Avoidance—accept a lower-risk choice. Avoid the higher-risk choice.
- Control—best stated as, "I am aware of the risk, and I will do my best to mitigate the occurrence and effect."
- Assumption—accept the consequences should the risk occur. One mechanism to minimize the impact of assuming the risk is to share the risk with the customer. In the home-building example, the builder might suggest that should the price of lumber go up, the customer would kick-in half of the total cost impact.
- Knowledge and research—this is a continuing process to understand the risks and their impacts, as well as how to curb the events that might trigger the risk's occurrence

Let's look at an example of how all of this fits together. The Software Engineering Institute has a capability maturity model (CMM) for software, which helps an organization to determine the maturity level of their software processes. One key area of the CMM is called "software project tracking and oversight."

The purpose of software project tracking and oversight is to provide adequate visibility into actual progress so that management can take effective actions when the software project's performance deviates significantly from the software plans.

Software project tracking and oversight involves tracking and reviewing the software accomplishments and results against documented estimates, commitments, and plans, and adjusting these plans based on the actual accomplishments and results.

To satisfy these requirements we proposed an integrated dual approach composed of the following.

- Track high-risk events that could cause cost, schedule, and technical performance problems. These are risks with a:
  - high probability of occurrence
  - high seriousness should they occur
- Track standard performance metrics as part of each phase of the software development life cycle.

The key, therefore, to software project tracking and oversight, is the identification, quantification, baselining, and statusing of high-risk events. From previous discussions, these objectives are accomplished through the following:

- Risk management
  - risk planning
  - risk assessment
  - risk analysis
  - risk handling
- Technical performance measurement
  - identification of key performance parameters
  - definition of a technical performance measurement baseline
- Earned value management (discussed in the next chapter)
  - monitoring of technical performance
  - signaling when performance deviates from the plan
  - identification of the need for corrective action

Summarizing risk management, then:

- Risk planning—sets out the requirements for performing risk management
- Risk assessment—is the process of identifying and quantifying program risks
- Risk analysis—is the process of evaluating program impacts as a result of risk assessment
- Risk handling—is the process of executing management actions to mitigate or eliminate the unwanted results of risks
- Risk management—is a continual process through all program phases and the umbrella function of the above five steps

Figure 8.6 depicts the basic risk management phases.

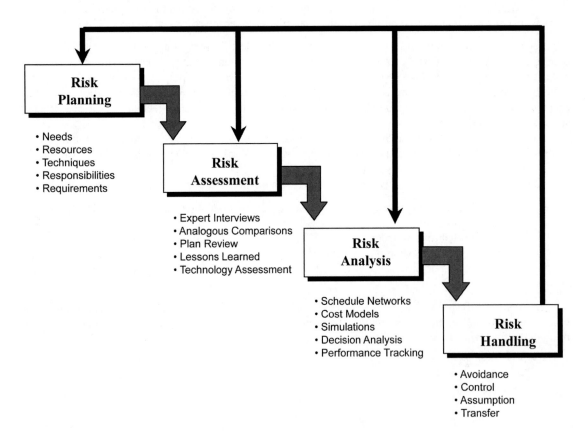

Figure 8.6. Risk Management Phases

Chapter 9

Disruptive Technologies—Thinking Outside of the Box

To a large extent, innovation and the manifestation of the innovation process is intrinsically interconnected to the role of the systems integrator. Systems integration is the higher level of cognitive understanding of the many separate yet highly related disciplines/functions of a product or service. The basic element of successful systems integration is the vision of interrelatedness of these many attendant knowledge domains—vision, which acts as the common thread through the innovation process. The evolution of this concept resides between the philosophical underpinnings of leadership and innovation, and the tactical realities of curriculum design, development, and implementation.

In thinking about innovation, there are numerous separate yet highly integrated concepts that form the underlying premise most often referred to as disruptive technologies—the end result of an innovation process spanning multiple "pure" disciplines/functions.

Disruptive technologies are those things we simply never saw coming. They were not, as the saying goes, on our radar screen. Generally, the literature is replete with oratory, and examples abound, that pure disciplines will no longer singularly yield disruptive technologies. Disruptive technologies have and will continue to evolve from the integration of multiple pure disciplines (i.e., in the gaps). Most new products, such as the iPad, are examples of this concept in that software engineering, hardware engineering, mechanical engineering, chemical engineering, and material scientists all come together to evolve a technology that no single discipline could have possibly evolved. Most new and disruptive technologies have now come into existence because of the combinatorial strength of multiple pure disciplines. As systems grow in complexity, they require a greater understanding of the connectivity of the many required interfacing disciplines. We evolve through a collaborative and ever more connected understanding of others—disciplines, people, cultures, economies, and like, similar once stand-alone thoughts.

What type of ideas exists? Ideas can be categorized into two broad categories: directional and intersectional (Johansson, 2004, p. 17). Directional ideas are those ideas that evolve through the recognized and accepted "normal" process of advancing the basic body of a given discipline's knowledge. Directional ideas are most identified as improvements of a given product or service in a fairly predictable way along defined measures and dimensions.

Intersectional ideas evolve through the combining of knowledge between and across multiple "pure" fields of study or disciplines. Intersectional ideas are those ideas that change the way we perceive the world. They evoke the "wow, I didn't see that coming," or, "that is really cool" type of response.

An excellent example of intersectional ideas capitalizing on the strength of combining multiple pure disciplines is provided in a project involving Rhesus monkeys (Serruya, Hatsopoulos, Paninski, Fellows, & Donoghue, 2002). A few years back, a Rhesus monkey was trained to move a mouse and attendant yellow cursor around a computer screen to catch a red dot, as the red dot moved around the computer screen. As the story goes, the monkey was rewarded for how often he could catch or closely follow the moving red dot. The scientist then, sometime later, subsequently demonstrated a modified version of this experiment. The monkey still chased the red dot around a computer screen, however this time, the monkey never moved a muscle, never moved a hand or raised an arm. The monkey moved the yellow cursor around the computer screen chasing the red dot by simply thinking about the act of doing so. A combination of neuroscientists, medical professionals, mathematicians, and computer scientists had worked to identify which neurons were active with electrical current during the whole process of raising the arm, moving the hand and fingers, and subsequently chasing the red dot. Then they surgically created the capability to follow the thoughts of the subject into actions on the computer screen, without the monkey having to do anything other than think about the activity of chasing the red dot. This, from any perspective, is an amazing feat and is truly indicative of what we would refer to as a disruptive technology and one that encompasses the collective intelligence of multiple pure disciplines.

If we think for a moment about the implications of such a feat, it has tremendous subsequent "directional ideas" or applications as it relates to those with limited mobility. This original concept effort has led to a recent reported study where a man and woman have both been able to control the robotic movement of an arm through nothing more than their thoughts (Vergano, 2012). The article reported, "A fully paralyzed man and woman have demonstrated the ability to hold a ball or grab a cup of coffee using their brain signals to control a robotic arm," In this study, headed by a neuroscientist, the patients were able to use brain implants to control computer controls. Both patients were stroke victims, unable to speak. Both were able to control a right-handed robotic arm by signals sent from brain implants. The brain implants as reported "are about the size of a baby aspirin, have 100 thin wires that slightly protrude into the covering of the patients' brains, centered over the regions connected to arm movements." The implants picked up signals from brain cells.

Continuing along these lines, intersectional ideas and technologies would appear to feed a plethora of directional ideas and subsequent applications. And it would seem appropriate to further assume that in time, directional ideas themselves, based on previous intersectional ideas, would begin to feed circularly into additional intersectional ideas, therefore blurring the line of distinction between intersectional and directional ideas.

Figure 9.1 comically reminds us of the power of intersectional ideas when addressing the once disruptive technology of the iPhone.

Disruptive technologies have existed for some time. Below identifies just a few of those historical and current products and services.

- Light bulb, 1881
- Henry Ford's assembly line
- Apple Macintosh
- Commercial electricity
- Nanotechnology—nanometer (1 billionth of a meter) technology; biobots (Trojan horse)
- Photovoltaics—capable of producing energy when subjected to light (solar power); solar cells embedded in thin sheets of plastic versus silicon-based
- Hard drive technology—extremely competitive commodity market; old electrical mechanical (+65 percent to $30B) to digital solid state chip flash drives (+600x to $11.4B to 80GB by 2008)
- Microfluidics—science of moving liquids through tiny channels the thickness of a human hair

The original Apple Macintosh came about around 1984 (figure 9.2). It basically was a black and white nine-inch screen the size of a smaller current-day printer box. The entire operating system fit onto a 128k floppy drive, which wasn't really floppy at all (it was a hard-cased 3.5-inch disk). The floppy, at 128k, held the operating system and application software required to create presentations, write reports, and do Excel-equivalent operations. All personal data files were also stored on this one 128k floppy disk. This original machine was the first recognizable laptop. You would place your Macintosh into a thick computer bag and lift it over your shoulder to carry it home. At roughly 30 pounds or so, it allowed employees to take their

The iPhone is more than just a gadget. It's a genuine handheld computer, the first device that really deserves the name.

Time, November 12, 2007

Figure 9.1. iPhone as a Disruptive Technology

work home. This very primitive device sold for roughly $3,500. It was indeed a beautiful and powerful piece of computing equipment. Today, one can buy a machine with 8GB of RAM and 1TB of hard drive space for $699.

Apple Macintosh Computer
Introduced on January 24, 1984

Figure 9.2. Apple Macintosh

Other disruptive technologies from the above include biobots. Biobots are cells that essentially carry drugs (think Trojan horse) designed to attach to "bad" cells and subsequently inject the poison to kill the bad cells, or alternatively, contain medicine to help heal damaged cells. Photovoltaics are the panels used on the tops of homes to collect sun rays and reduce heating costs. Currently, these once mammoth panels are being literally printed off printers on sheets of "paper" the thickness of thin sheets of plastic. Hard drives are another advancing technology. In 2007, William Watkins, then CEO of Seagate Technology, was doing what most company CEOs do when in a growth mode: looking for acquisitions or other places to invest in technology-oriented initiatives. Eventually they acquired Maxtor, a competitor, but during the process one of Seagate's confidants suggested they look at thumb drive technology—that being digital solid state chip versus the older electro-mechanical devices. As the story goes, Watkins discarded the thought of solid state as never being a feasible competitor to the electro-mechanical alternatives of Seagate and Maxtor. At to-day's writing, however, solid state has made significant inroads into the consumer market and as third party providers of devices for everything from cameras to phones and home products. The solid state market has grown 600 times to a 2007 market value of roughly $11 billion. What started out as thumb drives with a capacity of 128k are now 80GB and growing for a low sale price roughly $40. In thinking about the growth of solid state drive technology, Watkins (Brown, 2007) provided an "ah ha" moment, saying, "It finally dawned on me that moving digital content would be the most important thing in our lives, and if that were true, it didn't matter if it were a hard drive or flash" (p. 94).

If I wanted to provide yet one more example of disruptive technology, I might open the discussion to cloning. As many of us know, we have crossed a jellyfish with a rabbit, and now we have a rabbit that glows in the dark. In addition, we have cloned everything from sheep to mice, goats, pigs, bulls, gaurs, cats, mules, rats, wildcats, dogs, buffalos, horses, ferrets, and wolves. We have cloned more animals than most of us realize. There are companies that you can hire to clone your dead dog or cat, providing you with identical comfort, therefore minimizing your sense of loss. Cloning, as one would guess, is clearly a disruptive technology.

Chapter 10

Cost, Schedule, and Performance Management—A Quantitative Premise

This is an interesting chapter, in that here we are most concerned with managing the program's overall cost. (A more detailed discussion of program/project cost control and management is found later in this chapter.) To manage the program's cost means we have to:

- Define an initial budget, which entails identifying the cost for each of the activities that are to be performed, including labor and material.
- Determine how we are performing against the original work on our program's activities.
- Keep track of actual costs and be able to compare them against the original budgeted costs.
- Determine if we are on schedule and within cost, and, if not, why not and how we get back on schedule and within our original cost.

Defining the Initial Budget

Let's begin by assigning a cost to each activity we are going to perform. For example, let's assume we are building a house. Further, building the house will be accomplished in three phases. At the end of each phase, the bank will pay the builder some fixed, previously agreed to amount of money. At the end of the third phase, the bank will have paid the builder the total amount agreed to between the buyer and the home builder. Figure 10.1 reflects this scenario.

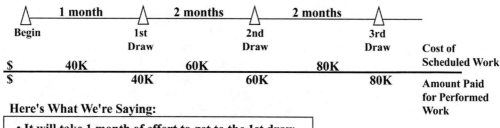

Here's What We're Saying:

- **It will take 1 month of effort to get to the 1st draw**
  - **1st draw milestone is valued at $40K.**
- **It will take 2 months of effort to get to the 2nd draw**
  - **2nd draw milestone is valued at $60K.**
- **It will take 2 months of effort to get to the 3rd draw**
  - **3rd draw milestone is valued at $80K.**

Figure 10.1. Setting the Cost Baseline; Identifying the Value of Each Activity

In Figure 10.1, the builder has established that the first draw is worth $40,000. This number came from looking at labor and material cost for that work required to get to the first draw. The second draw is valued at $60,000, and the third draw is valued at $80,000.

When the builder successfully accomplishes the work for the first draw, the bank sends out an inspector to verify the work was successfully completed. If the work meets building code, then the bank will pay the builder the agreed to amount.

Let's assume at the third draw that the inspector comes out to the house at the five-month date, and the work is not complete. Will the builder receive the $80,000? The answer is no. The builder will only receive the $80,000 when the work is accomplished successfully and inspected.

So if we were to take this concept to the next logical step, at each build date (milestone) we should be able to determine if the builder is on schedule or not, by knowing whether the bank paid the builder for the successful completion of the work identified for that milestone or not.

Determining How We Are Performing against the Initial Budget

Figure 10.2 reflects how the builder will actually be paid as work is completed.

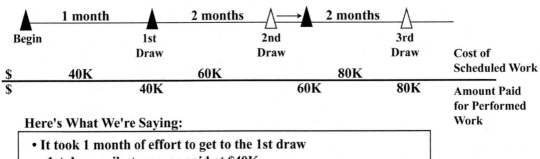

Figure 10.2. Amount Paid for the Work Performed

As reflected in Figure 10.2, the builder will be paid the second draw when the work is successfully accomplished. In this case, the builder will be paid the second draw one month later than expected.

Again, we can determine if the builder is on schedule or not simply by looking at how much the builder has been paid at the time when each bank draw is supposed to be made. In this case, at the third month, the builder should have been paid $100,000 in total, but actually was paid only $40,000. This tells us directly that the builder is behind schedule.

In fact, if we look at each time the builder is to be paid a draw from the bank, and subtract what the builder should have been paid from what the builder actually was paid, we can determine if there is a schedule variance from the original plan. The formula would look something like:

Amount paid for work performed—Cost of scheduled work = X, where, if X is negative, then the builder is behind schedule. But if X is positive, then the builder is ahead of schedule. And if X is zero, then the builder is on schedule.

Keeping Track of Actual Costs

Up to this point we have focused on what the original was to perform the work and when the builder would be paid for performing the work. Notice that what the builder received for performing the work was the actual original estimate to perform the work. In other words, the builder received a fixed amount to perform the work, which was the originally agreed to amount, not necessarily the amount it actually cost to do the work.

This concept of being paid a fixed amount to do a job versus what it actually cost to do a job was discussed earlier in the section "What Type of Contract Should I Enter Into?"

Figure 10.3 depicts a continuation of our example, only this time we add the final concept of actual costs.

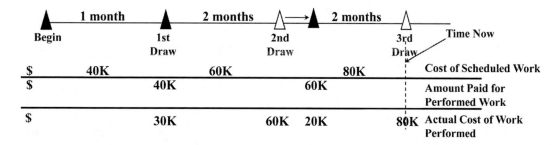

Here's What We're Saying:

- The builder received $40K for accomplishing the 1st draw on schedule –
  - The builder only spent $30K. Therefore, pocketing $10K
- The builder received an additional $60K for accomplishing the 2nd draw late –
  - but the builder spent an additional $80K ($20K more than planned). The builder is now $10K overspent
- The builder is performing to accomplish the 3rd draft and is behind schedule –
  - but the builder spent an additional $80K (out of the planned $80K).
- Schedule is behind, and the builder is overspent.

Figure 10.3. Actual Cost to Do the Work

Notice that builder only actually spent $30,000 to reach the first milestone, the first draw. That means the builder had actually gained an additional $10,000 over original projections to perform this quantity of work.

By the second draft, however, the builder had actually spent $80,000 more dollars, but had only received $60,000 more dollars for performing the work as originally defined and agreed to. This means the builder at this point had received a total of $100,000 as agreed to, but had actually incurred costs of $110,000—that's a $10,000 overrun in costs.

Now look at "Time Now." According to the original schedule, the builder should have been done with all the work at this point and should have received the final bank draw of $80,000. The builder did spend the planned $80,000 to get to "Time Now," but unfortunately, he or she has not finished all of the work agreed to. Without doubt, then, the builder has a serious cost issue, in that the builder has incurred actual expenses of $190,000 to date and is not yet done. And, further, the builder has only received $100,000 in bank draws. Obviously, the builder has a problem, which if the builder doesn't have deep pockets such that the builder can absorb the overrun, might become the buyer's problem. This is what court cases are made of.

A new formula to look at, then, is the difference between "Amount Paid for Work Performed" minus "Actual Cost of Work Performed." If this difference is negative, then the builder (program/project manager) has a cost overrun. If this difference is positive, then the builder is making money. And if this difference is zero, then the builder is on budget.

Getting Back on Schedule and Within Cost

Summarizing our two formulas, we have:

- Schedule variance = "Cost of Scheduled Work" - "Amount Paid for Work Performed"
- Cost variance = "Amount Paid for Work Performed" - "Actual Cost of Work Performed"

The question then becomes "If we have a cost or schedule problem, how do we get back on track?" The answer may be:

- We can assign more people to work the job, which of course would have cost consequences.
- We can simply work faster.
- We can become more efficient.
- We can get lucky and have no more problems.
- We don't—which simply means we have to deal with the realities of having a cost or schedule overrun.

Let's look at the bigger picture. Figure 10.4 reflects the whole story so far.

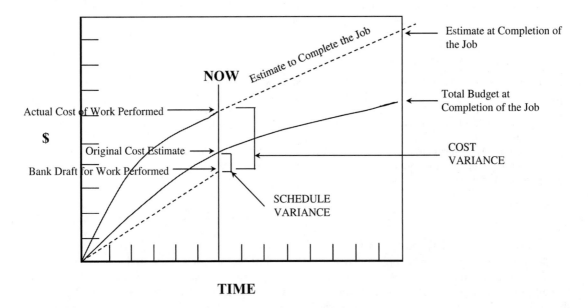

TIME

Figure 10.4. Estimate at Complete

In figure 10.4, we can see our previously defined schedule variance and cost variance. What's been added is an estimate to finish the job. This is what we refer to as an estimate to complete. When we add our actual costs to date and our new estimate to complete the job, the end result is an estimate at complete for all work performed.

Therefore, on a periodic basis, we may be asked as program/project managers to supply an estimate to finish the job. Depending on the type of contract we have, that estimate to finish the job plus the actual costs already incurred may come as a surprise to the buyer of the home.

A More Detailed Perspective

A management cost/schedule control system and the government's terminology of earned value management are synonymous concepts. Both are defined as a disciplined framework in which complete program planning takes place, work is authorized and scheduled consistent with the contract, performance is measured against a predetermined plan, and significant variances to either budget or schedule highlighted for corrective action.

Concept Examples

First, a few examples to help lay the foundation for concept development.

Your child has come home from college after two semesters. You are delighted to hear that she or he has only spent $7,000 of the $10,000 you had budgeted. The question here is, "Are you happy?"

You had agreed to a negotiated price of $100,000 for a new home that was to have been built in five months. After *four* months your builder says he spent $95,000. Are you happy?

In both of the above scenarios, we ask the question, "Are you happy?" In both cases you have cost ($7,000 out of $10,000 and $95,000 from a budgeted $80,000) and schedule (two semesters and four months) information. But what's missing?

What's missing is an element of performance. In the first scenario, what your child didn't say was that she or he flunked all of her or his courses and it will take five years to graduate. In the second scenario, what the builder didn't say was that your new home is complete and you will not have to spend another dime. Now how do we feel?

Features and Benefits

A management cost/schedule control system, or earned value management, has a number of features and benefits.

- Adds more discipline to the planning process
- Places predetermined value on measured performance
- Compares work scheduled to work performed
- Compares work performed to money spent

Additionally,

- Detailed planning forces need dates from other managers and interfaces
- Detailed planning finds things "not thought out" in the proposal phase
- Monthly performance data identifies early and quantifies problems, which helps make improved decisions
- Monthly performance data analysis reinforces functional management commitment and monitoring
- Improves communications internally and with the customer
- Project is much better controlled

Historically, earned value management originated with the government's Department of Defense in 1967. It began as the cost/schedule control systems criteria, and it has since been referenced under numerous names (C/SCSC, Cspec, EV, CS Squared, performance measurement, The Criteria). In any case, earned value management is really not a system by definition, but instead a set of 35 management system requirements. These 35 requirements are broken into five logical groupings:

- Organization—to define the contractual effort with use of the work breakdown structure (WBS), assign responsibilities for the performance of the work, and accomplish within an integrated management cost control system.

- Planning and budgeting—to establish and maintain a performance measurement baseline for control of the work.
- Accounting—to accumulate cost of work and materials, such that comparisons can be made to the baseline.
- Analysis—to measure earned value, to analyze variances and develop cost at completion.
- Revisions and access to data—to incorporate changes and to allow access by the customer to the data.

For discussion purposes, we are simply trying to bring consistency and formality to a process in which products may not necessarily be produced in a consistent or formal manner.

Definitions

Before continuing, a few definitions are in order.

The program manager's role and responsibilities include:

- Responsibility for program profit or loss
- Single management focal point for the program
- Coordinates the program's resources for allocation
- Approves program budget
- Authorizes the accomplishment of work
- Selects and manages cost account managers
- Ensures proper earned value management discipline is followed
- Uses earned value management to isolate problems and stimulate timely corrective action

The cost account manager's role and responsibilities include:

- Plans the work for the discipline for which he or she is responsible
- Manages the work to the plan
- Monitors cost and schedule to the plan
- Uses earned value management to report performance
- Responsible for developing corrective action plans

The program planner and cost administrator may be the same person or two people, depending on the size of the program. They have the following roles and responsibilities:

- Responsible for maintaining the program's cost, schedule, and performance baseline
- Responsible for generating monthly schedule and cost performance reports
- Ensures a controlled baseline change process
- Assists program manager (PM) and cost account manager (CAM) in analyzing program variances and ensures corrective action entries are in accordance with control process

WBS, Dictionary, and Schedules

Remember, at this point we have created a WBS with attendant dictionaries and developed master, intermediate, and detailed schedules. The schedule development is from the top down, but the statusing of the schedules is from the bottom up. Figure 10.5 depicts this relationship.

It's now time to focus on the simplicity of the earned value management concept. In theory it really is not very difficult to comprehend; in practice, however, implementing a system that satisfies the 35 management system requirements discussed earlier can be quite complicated and require great discipline.

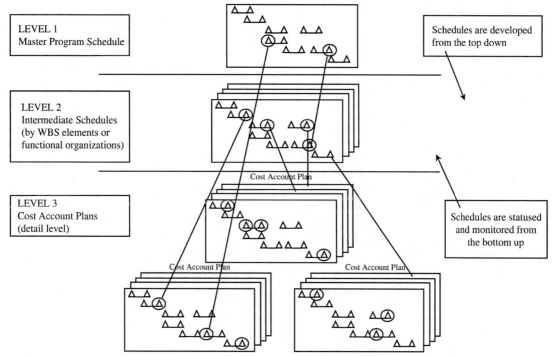

All lower-level schedules are derived from and are consistent with higher-level schedules.

Figure 10.5. Schedule Hierarchy Development and Statusing

"ABC"s of EVM Are "S," "P," and "A"

Truly, the "ABC"s of EVM are "S," "P," and "A." To expand, earned value management and all of its calculations are centered around what is commonly referred to as the budgeted cost of work scheduled (S), the budgeted cost of work performed (P), and the actual cost of work performed (A). These and other concepts are discussed in the following pages.

Let's begin by looking at Figure 10.6.

In Figure 10.6, looking only at the budgeted cost of work performed (BCWS) line, as a cost account manager, I was asked to provide how much effort (person-months) it would take to go from contract award to the preliminary design review (PDR). In this example, I would have said four man-months (MM). The cost manager, knowing that each man-month was worth $10,000, assigned $40,000 to the accomplishment of this work at PDR. Therefore, on the budgeted cost of work scheduled line you see the $40,000. Again, I may have provided six MM to get to the critical design review (CDR) and eight MM to get to the test readiness review (TRR). Again, on the BCWS line you will see that $60,000 and $80,000 have been identified as the worth of those respective efforts.

Now looking at the budgeted cost of work performed line (BCWP), we see that once we get to PDR, CDR, and TRR, and the work is truly completed, as a cost account manager I get credit to the amount that I said it would take to accomplish those milestones.

So as one might expect, if we were to look at the mapping of BCWS to BCWP, it would look somewhat like Figure 10.7.

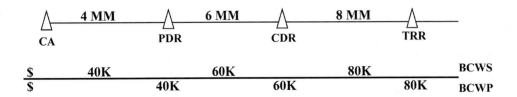

Saying:

Saying:

> • It will take 4.0 person-months of effort to get to PDR
>   - PDR milestone is valued at $40K.
> • It will take 6.0 more person-months of effort to get to CDR
>   - CDR milestone is valued at $60K.
> • It will take 8.0 more person-months of effort to get to TRR
>   - TRR milestone is valued at $80K.

Figure 10.6. Planned Schedule Timeline

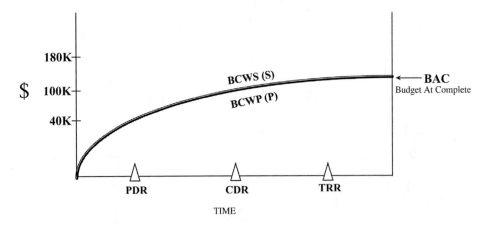

Figure 10.7. Worked Scheduled and Performance Credit

In figure 10.7, we see credit earned for work performed tracks to the value of the work that I, as a cost account manager (CAM), said it would take to do the work. Notice that the total of the BCWS dollar amounts ($40,000, $60,000, $80,000) equals the budget at completion of the program for this cost account.

Figure 10.8 depicts how work is actually accomplished and the introduction of actual costs.

Notice in figure 10.8 that PDR has been blackened in. This means we accomplished PDR at the scheduled time. At the time we accomplished PDR, we received the $40,000 credit we had planned to receive. This is depicted on the BCWP line. If we look just below the BCWP line, we see that the actual cost to perform that work was only $30,000. Therefore, at that time, we were actually ahead by $10,000.

Notice that CDR slipped a little in time. On completion of CDR, however, we received the $60,000 worth of performance credit we said it would take to get there. Notice we do not get the $60,000 until we accomplish the CDR, even if the CDR slips in time. Looking down at the ACWP line at actual costs, we

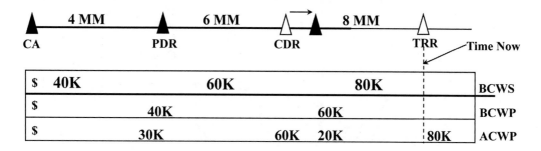

Saying:

- **We received $40K in BCWP for accomplishing PDR on schedule**
  - and we only spent $30K.
- **We received an additional $60K in BCWP for accomplishing CDR late**
  - but we spent an additional $80K ($20K more than planned).
- **We are performing to accomplish TRR and are behind schedule**
  - but we spent an additional $80K (out of our planned $80K).
- **Schedule is behind, and we are overspent.**

Figure 10.8. Work Performed and Actual Costs

see that we really did spend $60,000 to get to the original completion date, and in fact spent an additional $20,000 to get to the completed CDR, for a total of $80,000. Therefore, at CDR, we actually spent $110,000 and have only received credit for our scheduled $100,000 worth of work.

Now looking at TRR, we see that TRR is not filled in, which means it has not yet been completed at time now, and therefore, we do not get our remaining $80,000 worth of performance credit. Why? We did not get it, because we did not complete our performance of TRR yet. Once TRR is completed, we will get our $80,000 worth of performance credit. So looking only at budget cost for work scheduled and budgeted cost for work performed, we see that at this point in time, we should have credit for $180,000, but only have credit for $100,000. This says that we are behind schedule. If we were not behind schedule, then BCWP (work we performed) would be exactly like BCWS (work we had scheduled to have complete at this time). So comparing BCWS to BCWP at any one point in time will tell us if we have a schedule problem.

Now look at the actual costs incurred at time now. We see that we actually spent $190,000 to get to TRR, and we are not finished yet. Comparing, then, the credit we received for work performed (BCWP) to the actual cost of performing the work (ACWP), we see that we have over spent our budget, or in other words, we have a cost overrun.

So in figure 10.8, we see that we are behind schedule and over budget.

Looking at this scenario in another depiction, we see figure 10.9.

What figure 10.9 depicts is a number of things:

- BCWP is really not a direct one-for-one mapping to BCWS. In fact, BCWP is a stair-step function that gets incremented as credit is actually earned.
- The actual cost dollar amount at time now is $190,000.
- Once TRR is accomplished, then BCWP will be equal to BCWS, which is how we know when all of the work has been completed.

Cleaning up figure 10.9 more, we see figure 10.10.

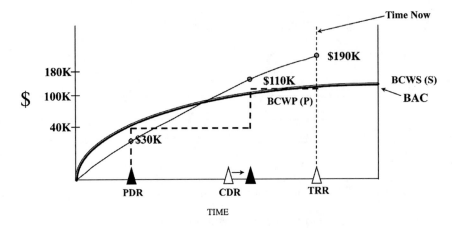

Figure 10.9. Actual Costs—Cumulative Representation

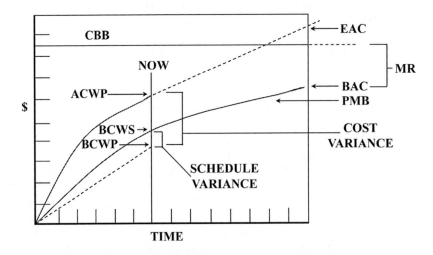

Figure 10.10. Earned Value Management Concepts Chart

In figure 10.10, we see:

- The difference between BCWS and BCWP is schedule variance.
- The difference between BCWP and ACWP is cost variance.
- The ACWP plus the estimate to complete the remainder of the work is equal to the estimate at completion (EAC).
- The contract budget base (CBB) minus management reserve (MR) is the performance measurement baseline (PMB), or what we refer to as the budget at complete (BAC).

Types of Variances

There are three basic variances:

- Schedule variance (current and cumulative)
  - Schedule Variance (SV) = BCWP - BCWS
  - (a negative answer is unfavorable)
- Cost variance (current and cumulative)
  - Cost Variance (CV) = BCWP - ACWP
  - (a negative answer is unfavorable)
- Completion variance
  - Variance at Completion (VAC) = BAC - EAC
  - (shows estimated overrun or underrun)

The estimate at Complete (EAC) is the actual cost of work to date plus the cost of remaining work. EAC = ACWP + ETC (estimate to complete).

This is also referred to as the Latest Revised Estimate (LRE).

EAC is a very subjective estimate and must be generated in a rational, consistent manner. When estimating an EAC, consider:

- Performance to date (current and cumulative variances and efficiencies)
- Impact of approved corrective action plans
- Known/anticipated downstream problems
- Best estimate of the cost to complete remaining work on this cost account

A summary, then, of the earned value language we have used so far is depicted in figure 10.11.

Element	Term	Acronym
Work Planned	Budgeted Cost for Work Scheduled	BCWS
Work Accomplished/ Earned Value	Budgeted Cost for Work Performed	BCWP
Cost of Work Accomplished	Actual Cost of Work Performed	ACWP
Work Authorized	Budgeted Cost at Completion	BAC
Estimate of Final Cost	Estimated Cost At Completion Latest Revised Estimate	EAC LRE
Cost Variance	BCWP minus ACWP	CV
Schedule Variance	BCWP minus BCWS	SV
Completion Variance	Variance at Completion (BAC minus EAC)	VAC
Contract Value less Fee	Contract Budget Base	CBB
Baseline	Performance Measurement Baseline	PMB
Reserve Funds	Management Reserve	MR

Figure 10.11. The Language of Earned Value Management

Past Performance Variances

Past performance variances are considered to be the following:

- Cost Variance (CV = BCWP - ACWP)
- Schedule Variance (SV = BCWP - BCWS)
- Variance at Completion (VAC = BAC - EAC)

The program's percent complete can be calculated by dividing the cumulative credit earned (BCWP) by the total budget at complete (BAC).

Percent Complete = (cumulative BCWP) / BAC

What this says is that the program is X percent complete based on cumulative performance to date and the budget at complete.

Past Trends

It's good to know if we have a cost or schedule variance, and what the new estimate is to complete the entire effort. It is also good to know what percent of the overall program is complete according to the original budget to complete the program. Additionally, however, we really would benefit from knowing what efficiencies we have been performing at. In other words, have we been performing at 100 percent efficiency, or have we been performing at a mere 50 percent? The past efficiencies will give us some insight into what efficiencies we can expect to perform at in the future, given everything remains relatively stable.

There are two past efficiency indexes:

- Cost Performance Index (CPI) = (cumulative BCWP) / (cumulative ACWP)
  This index says for each dollar spent, X amount of performance was earned.
- Schedule Performance Index (SPI) = (cumulative BCWP) / (cumulative BCWS)
  This index says for each dollar spent, X amount of schedule was achieved.

Future Trends

There are also two future trends that predict the efficiency we would have to perform at for the remainder of the program in order to meet our newly revised estimate to complete the program.

The first future trend is the to complete performance index (TCPI).

- TCPI = (BAC - (cumulative BCWP)) / (LRE - (cumulative ACWP))

This says the remaining baseline budget divided by the remaining estimated funds determines the efficiency factor necessary to complete within the LRE.

There are other variations on this future prediction. One in particular places greater weight on the cost performance index than the schedule performance index. This is called an independent estimate at complete (IEAC) and reads as follows:

- IEAC = Actuals + ((BAC - (cumulative BCWP)) / (.8CPI + .2SPI))

Based upon past cost and schedule efficiencies, this formula predicts the program's cost at completion.

Exercise

For each BCWS/BCWP/ACWP row in figure 10.12, place an "X" in appropriate schedule and cost columns.

Figure 10.13 depicts the correct answers.

Selection of Earned Value Techniques

In earned value management the time-phased distributed budget is made up of the sum of the cost accounts, and cost accounts come in two distinct flavors: discrete and level of effort.

BCWS	BCWP	ACWP	On Schedule	Ahead Of Schedule	Behind Schedule	On Cost	Underrun	Overrun
$100	$100	$100						
$100	$200	$100						
$300	$200	$100						
$100	$200	$200						
$100	$100	$200						
$100	$200	$300						
$200	$100	$100						
$200	$200	$100						
$200	$100	$300						

Figure 10.12. BCWS/BCWP/ACWP Exercise

BCWS	BCWP	ACWP	On Schedule	Ahead Of Schedule	Behind Schedule	On Cost	Underrun	Overrun
$100	$100	$100	X			X		
$100	$200	$100		X			X	
$300	$200	$100			X		X	
$100	$200	$200		X		X		
$100	$100	$200	X					X
$100	$200	$300		X				X
$200	$100	$100			X	X		
$200	$200	$100	X				X	
$200	$100	$300			X			X

Figure 10.13. BCWS/BCWP/ACWP Exercise Solutions

The earned value technique and milestone definition are part of the performance measurement baseline. There are four rules that apply to the calculation of earned value:

- Performance measurement must take place at the lowest possible level, work packages, and must be objective.
- The calculation of earned value (BCWP) must be done using methods consistent with the way the plan (BCWS) was established.
- Once the BCWP is reported to the customer and to management, no retroactive changes may take place, except for the adjustment of legitimate accounting errors.
- Each work package has a single earned value technique.

To this point, then, we have already completed the following:

- Master program schedule, intermediate schedule, and detailed schedules
- Work breakdown structure and attendant dictionaries
- Responsibility assignment matrix
- Cost accounts and work packages
- Resources identified and assigned to activities
- Each work package has been assigned one earned value technique

During this phase, the following efforts must be completed:

- Identify earned value technique for each work package
- Identify earned value milestones for each work package
- Review assigned techniques for adequacy
- Review and approval of baseline data

There are basically six major types of earned value techniques.

- X/Y technique
  - 0/100 (usually one month or less)
  - 25/75 (two months or more)
  - 50/50 (two months or more)
  - 40/60 (two months or more)
- Milestone weights
- Milestone weights with percent complete
- Percent complete
- Apportioned effort
- Level of effort

Of the above six types of earned value techniques, all are discrete with the exception of the last, level of effort. A discrete milestone is a milestone that has a definite, scheduled occurrence in time.

Discrete work packages can be thought of as being in three distinct categories:

- If the work package is in the future, and has not yet started, then BCWP = 0 percent of the BAC. This implies no credit has been awarded for work performed.
- If the work package is in progress, then BCWP will be greater than 0 percent but less than 100 percent of the BAC. Remember, 100 percent means all work is complete.
- If the work package is complete, that is, no work remains to be completed, then BCWP will be 100 percent of BAC.

X/Y Technique

In the X/Y technique, some percentage of full credit will be earned on initiation of the activity and the remainder of the performance credit will be earned on completion of the activity. The milestone signifies the initiation and completion of the activity.

If the activity is one month in duration, then a 0/100 technique is most appropriate. If the activity is planned to occur in two subsequent periods, then the X/Y method that most closely resembles the planned level of effort (BCWS) should be used.

Figure 10.14 depicts an example of this type of technique. It is an example of a 25/75 application.

The point illustrated by figure 10.14 is that 25 percent of the total performance credit is earned when the activity begins, and 75 percent performance credit is earned when the activity is completed. Note that performance credit, when discussing X/Y methods, is always associated with start or completion milestones.

EXAMPLE #1: START AND COMPLETE ON TIME

S			250	750	
P			250	750	

EXAMPLE #2: START ON TIME AND COMPLETE ONE MONTH LATE

S			250	750	
P			250		750

Figure 10.14. 25/75 Earned Value Management Technique

Again, in the second example of figure 10.14, the completion did not occur on the scheduled completion date, even though BCWS (S) indicated it should have. The performance credit, therefore, was not awarded until one period later, when the work was complete. As before, since the amount of performance credit that should have been earned at the original completion date was not the same as the amount of credit actually earned (P), we can immediately tell that we have a schedule variance from plan.

Milestone Weights

Milestone weights simply means that some predefined weight has been assigned to each milestone in the activity. The amount of performance credit earned, therefore, is the weight of the milestone times the total amount of performance that could be earned for the entire activity.

Milestone weights are used if the activity is greater than two months. In this scenario, monthly milestones are recommended. Figure 10.15 depicts an example of the milestone weights technique.

Notice that "S," the planned effort, represents the dollars required to accomplish the respective milestone. "P," the planned performance credit, is earned when the milestone is completed. In the event a milestone slips out in time, "P" will be earned when the milestone is completed.

What is a sufficient milestone? A milestone should be:

- Objective—milestones should be explicitly defined based upon a predetermined criterion or a tangible product.
- Auditable—the value of work associated with a milestone should be determined by quantitative analysis producing a result that is repeatable.

Milestone Weights with Percent Complete

Basic practices of this technique are:

- Used if an activity is greater than two months
- Used if each milestone represents the completion of products with essentially equal value
- Milestones are monthly (recommended)

MONTH ONE (JUNE): BEGIN WORK

	1	2	3	4	5	6
S	75	160	40	240	85	175
P	75					

MONTH TWO (JULY): COMPLETE MILESTONE #2

	1	2	3	4	5	6
S	75	160	40	240	85	175
P	75	160				

Figure 10.15. Example of Milestone Weights

- Work performance is based on an objective measurement of how much work toward the milestone has been accomplished
- Requires objective measurable milestones

The utilization of this technique requires an objective measurement criterion. For example, let's say we are building 100 widgets in the factory. The plan is 20 per month. Each milestone would have a value of 20 widgets. If we only build 18 the first month, 90 percent of the milestone value would be reported as earned value (BCWP).

Figure 10.16 provides an example of this technique.

Month 1 Status

	1	2	3	4	
S	100	100	175	125	
P	85				

Month 2 Status

	1	2	3	4	
S	100	100	175	125	
P	85	90			

Figure 10.16. Milestone Weights with Percent Complete

Referencing figure 10.16, for simplicity of discussion, let's assume for milestone #1, 100 units each valued at $1, are to be completed. By milestone #1, only 85 units are complete; therefore, $85 of performance credit is awarded. By milestone #2, 90 units more have been completed. Note that of the 90 units completed, 15 went toward the first 100 in milestone #1, and 75 went toward the 100 units of milestone #2.

Percent Complete

Basic rules for the percent complete earned value technique are:

- Used if activity is greater than two months.
- Work can be divided into objective factors, for example, the number of drawings completed divided by the total number of drawings planned.
- A formula is required that computes performance as a percentage of total BAC. The formula is established at the time the technique is selected and must be recorded in the work package dictionary. The formula must be applied consistently over the life of the work package.

This approach allows for a monthly estimate of the percentage of work completed always on a cumulative basis. This technique, while initially appearing to allow for varying degrees of latitude in subjectivity, is actually utilized only with an attendant, objective, quantifiable formula for determining the progress of the effort. Examples of situations in which this technique is applicable include lines released and drawings issued.

Apportioned Effort

Apportioned effort should be used when the activity is greater than two months. It should also only be used when a task has a direct relationship to another task.

Apportioned efforts are those efforts that have a direct performance relationship to some other discrete activities called their reference base. When determining either the monthly or cumulative earned performance credit (BCWP) for the apportioned effort, the value will always reflect the same percentage as its referenced base.

With respect to schedule variances, apportioned effort always reflects the position of the related base work package. With respect to cost variances, however, they reflect their own cost performance, as related to the BCWP of their respective bases. Figure 10.17 depicts the utilization of this technique.

What is apportioned is the performance credit (P) of the apportioned work package to that of the reference-based work package, that is, if the reference-based work package receives 10 percent performance credit, then the apportioned work package will receive 10 percent performance credit.

Cost Account Plans

The last activity in the program management planning process is the generation of cost account plans. This activity is represented here as a post-contract award activity, because final contract information related to requirements, schedules, and costs is not known until after the contract has been awarded/definitized. Although it is possible to create cost accounts prior to contract award, these cost accounts would simply have to be revisited after contract award, so creating cost accounts prior to contract award provides little benefit.

The cost, schedule, and technical performance measurement baseline is not complete until the cost accounts have been generated.

Generating cost account plans involves the detailed planning of the contract statement of work, budget, and schedule, via work packages and planning packages. A cost account is a control point for cost, schedule, and performance planning, work execution, and performance measurement. Cost account responsibility is assigned to a cost account manager. Cost accounts simply contain information about the work to be accomplished, milestones, milestone techniques, predicted start dates, and possibly any resources associated with the work.

| Work Package Number | ORIGINAL PLANNING: NO BCWP CREDIT 20xx | | | | | | | | Work Package and Milestone Description |
	MO	JUN	JUL	AUG	SEP	OCT	NOV	DEC	
02683		¹△	²△	³△	⁴△	⁵△			Power Supply Material
	S	50	100	150	100	50			
	P								
10765		△————————————————————△							Apportioned Effort Based on 10% of BCWS & BCWP Input for Work Package No. 02683
	S	5	10	15	10	5			
	P								

Figure 10.17. Apportioned Effort Example

Successful completion of this process concludes the planning phase of the program management planning process and therefore establishes the program's performance measurement baseline.

Figures 10.18 and figure 10.19 depict an example cost account plan and the process for generating the cost account plans. Note that the cost account plan example in the below figure is specific to a given tool and company. It is provided here for example purposes only. As other systems are used and other tools, the format will be different.

Cost account plan detailed processing, as depicted in figure 10.19, consists of the following subprocesses.

- The cost account manager schedules and costs all resources, utilizing the work package descriptions from the extended CWBS dictionary and human resource plan. There are eight steps in this subprocess:
  - scheduling resources by month in accordance with the planning package/work package level
  - specifying each human resource item by resource code
  - identifying, in the performing department field, the specific human resources required to execute a planning package/work package (this identification should be used consistently wherever this resource appears)
  - leveling the resource loading for the cost account by adjusting planning package/work package schedules where schedule float exists (peaks or valleys in the resource loading should be resolved by changing planning package/work package dependencies and durations when possible)
  - providing the list of scheduled resources to the project accountant, who generates the resource costs for the cost account; these costs make up the package's budgeted cost for work scheduled
  - determining whether the target cost is exceeded, that is, whether the planned cost account budget at completion exceeds the target cost

WBS ID: ANAA01	Earned Value Method Milestone		Year	20xx		20xy						
Desc: RCVR MODULES 64397	Perf. Org.: 328 Ground Support		Month	N	D	J	F	M	A	M	J	BAC/LRE
Milestone Desc.	Scheduled	Forecast	Weight									
STRT PROT DVT	27-NOV-	27-NOV-	10									
LAYOUT IF CCA	31-DEC-	15-JAN-	10									
LAYOUT RF CCA	27-JAN-	15-FEB-	10									
FAB/TEST IF CCA	24-FEB-	24-FEB-	20									
FAB/TEST RF CCA	31-MAR-	31-MAR-	10									
INTEGRATE LRU	28-APR-	28-APR-	10									
HALT/EMI DVT	26-MAY-	26-MAY-	10									
COMPL DVT	30-JUN-	30-JUN-	20									
EOC		RESOURCE										
LABOR	Hrs	XC, SR ENG/SR A	BCWS	68.0	152.0	152.0	160.0	160.0	121.6	128.0	96.0	1,037.6
			LRE	27.0	208.0	152.0	160.0	160.0	121.6	128.0	96.0	1,052.6
		XF, SR. TECH/FO	BCWS	68.0	152.0	152.0	160.0	160.0	121.6	128.0	76.8	1,018.4
			LRE	72.0	146.0	152.0	160.0	160.0	121.6	128.0	76.8	1,016.4
OTHER DIRECT COSTS		U5, CADAM	LRE		0.2							0.2
BCWS				6.3	14.0	15.1	15.9	15.9	12.1	12.7	8.7	100.7
BCWP				10.1								
LRE				4.3	17.2	15.2	16.0	16.0	12.2	12.8	8.8	102.5

Figure 10.18. Example Cost Account Plan

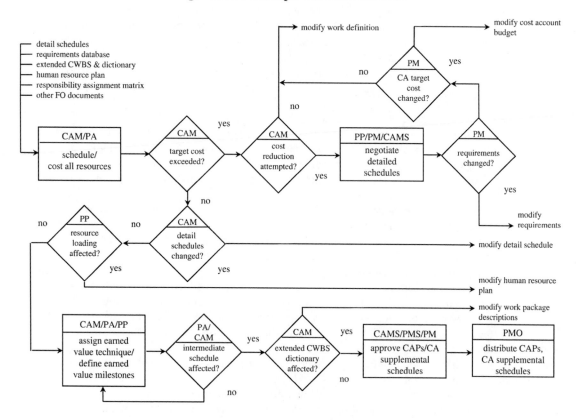

Figure 10.19. Cost Account Plan Detailed Process Flow

- determining whether cost reduction has been attempted by:
  - substituting lower-cost resources
  - using alternate plans, including rescheduling
  - minimizing the work to meet the requirements
  - reevaluating the interpretations of the requirements to ensure the requirements are satisfied but not exceeded
  - reevaluating the cost/risk tradeoffs
    - determining whether detailed schedules need to be changed, that is, whether resource leveling violates the detailed schedules
- The cost account manager(s), program manager, and functional organizations resolve the cost account scope if the cost account target cost is exceeded and cost reduction has been attempted by the cost account manager. This activity consists of three steps:
  - waiting until all cost account managers have completed the scheduling and costing of all resources
  - exploring the potential for an increased cost account target cost
  - exploring the potential for a reduction in cost account scope
    - If requirements have changed, then the requirements database needs to be changed. If cost account target costs have changed, then cost account target cost in the responsibility assignment matrix may need to be reallocated; otherwise, work definition changes.
- The cost account manager and the project accountant assign an earned value technique and define the earned value milestones. This activity follows the program manager's approval of the human resource plan for the cost account, the intermediate schedule, and the cost account budget and consists of seven steps:
  - evaluating planning packages (earned value techniques/milestones are only required for work packages, not planning packages, because performance is not measured against planning packages)
  - specifying a single earned value technique for each work package
  - providing a description for each earned value milestone that is documented as part of the cost account plan; is explicit and based upon predetermined criteria or a tangible product; and is quantified such that the result is repeatable
  - selecting the percent complete earned value technique for material cost accounts/work packages
  - scheduling earned value milestones associated with travel in relation to the technical work that they are supporting
  - evaluating the earned value techniques, earned value milestones, and the cost account plan (earned value techniques are correct when they meet the requirements stated in company guidelines; earned value milestones and attendant descriptions are correct when they are defined in accordance with the requirements stated in this activity; the cost account plan is correct when the cost account manager has confirmed its completeness and accuracy in accordance with the organization's program management process)
  - updating the extended CWBS dictionary whenever a work package description is modified
- The program manager and the project accountant establish cost and schedule variance thresholds. Cost and schedule variance thresholds should:
  - be imposed by contract and/or self-imposed by the program manager
  - be established within one of several time frames: cumulative to date, reflecting performance on a cumulative or total basis through the current reporting period; the current

month, focusing only on the last accounting month of performance; or the variance at completion, which incorporates all actuals to date and makes a projection to the end
- be determined by establishing plus and minus percentage and dollar amounts with respect to functional organization, element of cost, level of extended CWBS, and stage of the program
- be communicated via a program directive
  - The establishment of higher thresholds for under-run or ahead-of-schedule conditions should be considered to minimize the generation of analyses and explanations of variances that do not have potential for adverse impact.
- The cost account managers, functional organization(s), and the program manager approve the cost account plans by signing them. This becomes a contract between the cost account manager and program manager and authorizes the work.

Chapter 11

Multiple Generations in the Workplace— It's How We Grew Up

I've been teaching, facilitating discussion, and presenting on the topic of cohort groups in the workforce and their attendant gerontological life phase since 1990. Of all topics to discuss, I find this topic the most fascinating and enjoyable. In fact, the material and discussion is so intriguing to the participants that it really is quite hard to mess up the presentation. This is a really cool topic! As an aside, you may think I've already dated myself by using the word *cool*, but as we'll discuss later, *cool* has been around since 1948 and is the only slang term to withstand the test of time.

When we talk about gerontological phases of human life, we are actually talking about changes to our biosocial, cognitive, and psychosocial development as we chronologically mature over time. These three perspectives can be thought of as domains of human development.

Biosocial changes are those changes having to do with physical growth and development, as well as the family, community, and cultural factors that affect that growth and development. Cognitive changes address the mental processes through which the individual thinks, learns, and communicates. Psychosocial changes include emotions, personality characteristics, and relationships with other people.

Our discussion of like groups within the workforce centers on groups having similar ages, therefore sharing similar experiences and defining moments (Levinson, 1978, p. 56). Defining moments are those instances where something catches the attention and hearts of hundreds, if not thousands, of individuals at the same basic time in their formative lives.

The list below combines life phases (gerontology) with similar age-related cohort groups in the workforce.

- Late adulthood (60+ years old); Veterans
- Middle adulthood (40–60 years old); Baby Boomers
- Early adulthood (20–40 years old); Generation Xers
- Adolescence (10–20 years old); Nexters
- The school years (7–11 years old)
- Early childhood or preschool (2–6 years old)
- Infants or toddlers (0–2 years old)

Note that our discussion will focus on adolescence (Nexters) through late adulthood (Veterans).

Gerontological Phases (Late Adulthood)

For purposes of this book, when we refer to gerontological phases we are referring to the scientific study of human development. The scientific study of human development is the science that seeks to understand how and why people change, and how and why they remain the same, as they grow older (Berger & Thompson, 1998, p. 4).

To help individuals to better understand the developmental changes we experience as we grow older, there have been established three domains of human development: biosocial, cognitive, and psychosocial.

Biosocial development includes all of the growth and changes that occur in a person's body, and the genetic, nutritional, and health factors that affect those developments, as well as motor skills, everything from grasping a rattle to driving a car. Social and cultural factors that affect these areas, such as duration of breastfeeding, education of children with special needs, attitudes about ideal body shape, and health habits that extend or shorten human life, are also part of biosocial development.

Cognitive development includes all the mental processes that are used to obtain knowledge or to become aware of the environment. It can include perception, imagination, judgment, memory, and language, the processes people use to think, decide, and learn. Education—including the formal curriculum within schools, informal tutoring by family and friends, and the results of individual curiosity and creativity—is also part of this domain.

Psychosocial development includes development of emotions, temperament, and social skills. The influences of family, friends, community, culture, and the larger society are particularly central to the psychosocial domain. Thus, cultural differences in the value afforded children, or in ideas about "appropriate" sex roles or what is regarded as the ideal family structure, are primarily explored in this domain (Berger & Thompson, 1998, p. 5).

This group of individuals goes by many names: senior citizens, sunset group, the Veterans, and the like. All of these names refer to this set of individuals born basically between 1920 and 1945, which at this writing would be between 68 and 93 years of age.

A number of terms are relevant to this age cohort.

- *Ageism* is a term that refers to prejudice against aged individuals. Its effects are similar to racism and sexism, in that ageism reduces opportunities for elder individuals, which might not normally be withheld had they not been classified as such.
- *Gerontology* is the study of the aging process. It is one of the fastest-growing fields of study, especially in light of the large number of Baby Boomers quickly moving toward their sunset years. Some gerontologists attempt to draw a distinction between the young-old and the old-old. The young-old are those seniors who make up the large majority of the old. They are generally financially fit, basically healthy, and well integrated into their families and the communities in which they live. The old-old are those who suffer major physical, mental, or social losses and are the most likely to require support in one form or another as they continue to age.
- *Primary aging* involves irreversible changes to living organisms as they grow old. *Secondary aging*, on the other hand, involves physical illnesses or conditions that are more common in aging but are caused by health habits, genes, and other influences that vary from person to person. Recently, however, there has been significant research that indicates that perhaps primary aging can be slowed or, even more interestingly, reversed. This topic is discussed in more detail in later sections.

There are certain biosocial changes associated with this age group: their hearts begin to beat more slowly, their arteries begin to harden, their digestive organs become less efficient, their lungs lose capacity, sexual responses become slower, sensory organs begin to slow, and the like. These changes and more take place over many decades of this age group. It's not uncommon, for example, for seniors in this age category to have vision problems. Vision diseases in the elderly account for over half the cases of legal blindness in the United States (Berger & Thompson, 1998, p. 611). As this group ages, the pace of these declines increases.

In fact, the death rate for this age group, of the eight leading causes of death, is significantly higher than that for their younger counterparts. In comparison to younger adults, those age 65 are:

- nine times more likely to die from heart disease
- five times more likely to die from cancer
- eight times more likely to die from stroke
- nine times more likely to die from pneumonia/flu
- seven times more likely to die from diabetes
- ten times more likely to die from arteriosclerosis

Worth noting, however, is that this age group is only two times more likely to die from accidents and only two times more likely to die from suicide.

Cognitive discussion begins with an understanding of our sensory system. The sensory register is a part of our memory system that functions for only a fraction of a second during our sensory processing. It retains a fleeting impression of a stimulus that has just been introduced into one of our sense organs. For example, if a person looks at something for a moment and then closes his or her eyes, the image remains briefly for later processing. A significant portion of what gets temporarily stored in the sensory register is transferred to our working memory.

As we age, our sensory registers take longer to store sensed stimulus, and once stored, it fades more quickly. This, coupled with a general overall decline in our sensory systems (eyes, hearing, touch, etc.), leaves some information not only undetected, but that which is may not get registered. Another effect of aging is that we tend to lose our working memory (it's like the RAM in our computers at home). As well, our short-term and long-term memory begin to diminish with age. As we pass through the decades that compose this period of life, we also experience difficulty in processing multiple simultaneous inputs, that is, our ability to parallel-process is slowed.

At this time in our lives, our decision making begins to slow as we take longer to interpret the data we have in memory. This is caused by the gradual dying off of our brain neurons. Brain neurons do not reproduce; they die throughout our lives. They die at an increasing rate after the age of 60. During this time, the brain's communication processing slows noticeably, especially after the age of 55. This causes a general slowing of thought reaction time. As individuals, we can slow the deterioration of the brain by increasing the blood flow to the brain. This can be done by eating the right foods and exercising.

Some studies have shown that antioxidants such as vitamins C and E and replacement of estrogen in women help maintain brain functioning. In addition, studies of certain individuals who have taken anti-inflammatory steroids, such as aspirin and ibuprofen, for extended periods show that these medications may have an unexpected side effect: better and longer-sustained cognitive function in old age (Berger & Thompson, 1998, 641).

From a psychosocial perspective, those in late adulthood who are still working, or even retired, usually remain active. Their activities may include volunteering, pursuing additional education, or being politically involved.

On the whole, married elders tend to live longer and experience happier and healthier lives than unmarried elders. The single greatest stress for elders is the loss of a spouse. The remaining elder, after the loss, is more likely than not to experience some form of health problems.

One of the biggest problems facing elders, which also has a large potential impact on the families of elders, is their frailty, that is, elders' inability to care for their own daily needs.

Cohort Group (Veterans)

It is argued that one of the greatest challenges in our workforce is reconciling the varying values, ambitions, views, and mind-sets. From casual observation in this chapter and others to follow, however, one might argue that there has always been multiple generations at work at the same time in our workforce. The difference between past and present conditions lies in the type of work that was performed.

In past times, we were an industrialized nation. This directly implies the use of a mechanistic management philosophy coupled with a very structured organizational design. Our styles of management were very much command and control, with significant formality. Most senior employees worked in the front offices, whereas middle-aged employees worked in the higher-skilled jobs, and the youngest and most physically fit were relegated to the factory floor. This is not the case today, in our postindustrial, information-oriented, high-tech, and skill-based society.

Seniors today are living and working longer. According to the U.S. Census 2001 survey, men are living to an average age of 74, while women are living to an average age of 80. That's compared to 66 and 72 in 1950. As a direct result of this longer life span, a number of seniors are staying in the workforce longer. Factors contributing to their retiring later include the following:

- Changes in life expectancy (74 and 80)
- Healthier lifestyles
- Work is knowledge-based, versus previous more physically oriented work
- Technology can be learned by old and young alike

Because of the period in which they matured, Veterans have been subjected to significant struggle and strife. This age group was most likely impacted in some way by World War I and II. The core values of this age group, therefore, might best be summarized as follows.

- Dedication and sacrifice
- Hard work
- Conformity
- A belief in law and order
- Respect for authority
- Exercising patience
- Delaying rewards
- Believing in duty before pleasure
- Adherence to rules
- Above all, honor

Events that shaped this age group include:

- 1927—Charles Lindbergh completed first transatlantic flight
- 1929—Stock market crashed
- 1930—U.S. Depression deepened
- 1931— "Star Spangled Banner" became the National Anthem
- 1932— President Franklin D. Roosevelt elected
- 1933—The Dust Bowl
- 1933—The New Deal
- 1934—Social Security system established
- 1937—*Hindenburg* tragedy
- 1937—Adolf Hitler invaded Austria
- 1940—U.S. prepared for war
- 1941—Pearl Harbor

A brief sidebar on Social Security provides for interesting discussion. Because of the stock market crash of 1929 and the Great Depression of 1930, around 1934, President Franklin D. Roosevelt knew he had to do something to provide some form of safety net for elderly individuals stricken by a sickening economy. Roosevelt looked at the model of Social Security enacted in Germany in the late nineteenth century (1883) by Chancellor Otto von Bismarck. Bismarck believed that if people lived to the age of 65, then they should be provided some form of safety net to keep them from living in poverty for their remaining years of life. So in 1935, Roosevelt enacted what today is known as the Social Security Administration. The idea behind it was to provide, just like the German model, some form of safety net to those who reached the retirement age of 65. Now, interestingly enough, the life expectancy for males and females in 1935 was 59.3 for males and 63.3 for females. In other words, we were not expected to live to be 65. Now, recall from previous discussion that the life expectancy today for males and females is roughly 78 and 82, but, for the most part, we can still claim full benefits at 65 and reduced benefits at 62. This isn't the original intent of the 1934 enacted law for Social Security. In fact, if we used the model as it was intended to be used in 1935, we wouldn't be eligible for full Social Security until roughly 80 years of age, which one could easily argue is why we have problems today.

To continue this sidebar, in 1940, the first monthly Social Security check was issued (Social Security Administration, 2005, p. 6). It was issued to Ida May Fuller, a retired paralegal. In 1940, there was no early Social Security benefit, so you had to be 65 years of age to begin drawing from it. Fuller lived to the ripe old age of 100 and ended up collecting Social Security for some 35 years before dying in 1975.

Cultural memorabilia for this age group includes:

- Kewpie dolls
- Mickey Mouse
- Flash Gordon
- The golden era of radio
- Wheaties
- Charlie McCarthy
- Tarzan
- Jukeboxes
- Blondie
- The Lone Ranger

I remember my mom talking about how she and her sisters would huddle on the living room floor to listen to the radio on a Saturday night. They would listen to a show called *The Shadow*. According to Wikipedia, *The Shadow* radio program, intoned by actor Frank Readick, Jr., has earned a place in the American idiom: "Who knows what evil lurks in the hearts of men? The Shadow knows!" These words were accompanied by a haunting theme song. My mom said they would all shiver at the sound and gasp with anticipation.

Heroes of this period include:

- Superman
- Franklin Delano Roosevelt
- Douglas MacArthur, George S. Patton, Bernard Montgomery, William Halsey, and Dwight D. Eisenhower
- Winston Churchill
- Audie Murphy
- Joe Foss
- Babe Ruth
- Joe DiMaggio

What do MacArthur, Patton, Montgomery, Halsey, and Eisenhower all have in common? They were all significant military leaders. Again, this is indicative of this generation's mind-set.

The personality of those individuals in this age group is reflective of the events of this period, namely, World War I, World War II, the industrial economy in general, and the type of command and control management style prevalent of the time. Their personalities can be summarized in the following:

- They prefer consistency and uniformity.
- They like things on a grand scale—trains, larger automobiles.
- They are conformers. They learned this from their Boy Scout leaders, drill sergeants, and President Roosevelt.
- They believe in logic, not magic. They tend to avoid "personal" conversations. They would rather watch violence on TV than love scenes or those with sexually explicit content. Some of this, coincidentally, may not necessarily be simply because of the violence exposed to from the war, but also because our attention to sexually oriented medium in general tends to wan as we chronologically mature.
- This group is very disciplined. They created the term *snafu*, which stands for "situation normal, all fouled up." They are also more willing to put up with frustrations than their younger cohorts. They tend to suffer silently, which is why this age group has occasionally been referred to as the "Silents."
- This group tends to be past-oriented and history-absorbed. They tend to look to the past to find successful precedents, that is, what worked and what didn't.
- They believe in law and order; the chaos of war and thuggery of the Great Depression taught them the value of law and obedience. They also generally favor stricter laws and longer jail sentences as deterrents to crime.
- This group's spending style is generally very conservative. They would rather save and pay cash than use credit. They tend to have strong brand loyalty, in other words, they will generally stay in a product line: Chevy to Cadillac, Ford to Lincoln.
- Their preferred reading is *Reader's Digest, USA Today, Time,* and the *Wall Street Journal.*

The most enduring workplace legacy of this particular group is likely to be their older command and control style of management. This is something most familiar to them, and it is what they learned from their war year experiences.

On the job, this age group is tremendously strong. As assets, they:

- Are stable with a stick-to-it mentality
- Are detail-oriented and generally not afraid to "dig" into it
- Are very thorough
- Are loyal
- Are hardworking—they tend to value obedience over individualism
- Gain satisfaction through the work itself, as opposed to any other form of office politicking

Their liabilities stem directly from their experiences and their desire to be obedient and conforming. They are:

- Awkward with ambiguity and change
- Reluctant to buck the system
- Uncomfortable with conflict

Messages that motivate this particular group include such phrases as "your experience is respected here," "it's valuable to the rest of us to hear what has and hasn't worked in the past," and "your perseverance is valued and will be rewarded."

About this generation, the Baby Boomers would say, "they're dictatorial," they're rigid and need to learn flexibility and adapt better to change," "they're inhibited," "they're technological dinosaurs," and "they're narrowly focused." The Generation Xers would say, "they're too set in their ways," "they don't even know how to use e-mail," "they too will pass," and "they've got all the money." Finally, the Nexters would say, "they are trustworthy," "they are good leaders," and "they are brave."

Note that the Nexters, who are the children of the Baby Boomers, favor their grandparents more than their parents favor their own parents. Some of the reasons for this might be that the Nexters have really had to grow up with both parents working, more so than any other generation. To this end, the grandparents may have played a more active role raising or babysitting these young individuals.

Key things to think about when recruiting, orienting, providing opportunities for, developing, and motivating include the following:

Recruiting:

- Use older employees as part-time employees.
- Speak to family, home, patriotism, and traditional values.
- Let them know their age and experience are assets.
- Use good grammar. Say "please" and "thank-you" and avoid profanity. Worth noting is that younger employees seem to be moving in this direction.

Orienting:

- Allow lots of time to orient. This group prefers to know what is expected, what the policies are, and who is who.
- Convey the company history. This shows the bigger picture.
- Emphasize long-term departmental and organizational goals. Show them how they will contribute to the long-term strategies of the organization.

Opportunities:

- Stress the long haul—months and years, not weeks.
- If your customers are seniors, then your workforce should be too.
- Keep gender roles in mind. Lifestyles of men and women in their 60s, 70s, and 80s differ more than any other group. Veteran men die younger, the women often remarry, and men are most likely to be married.

Developing this age group:

- You're likely to need to train this group in the use of current technology.
- This group appreciates logic, but the logic of technology isn't always obvious, as they did not grow up with it.
  - 1 in 10 has a PC at home (Generation Xers—3 in 10 has one at home)
  - less than 1 in 10 watch videos regularly (Generation Xers—5 in 10)
  - 2 of 10 have ATM cards (Generation Xers—6 in 10)
- Use older trainers; they share a common language, move, talk, and think at a common pace.
- Use large print in text materials.
- Once trained, Veterans like to continue their learning. They are very patient and persistent.

Motivating:

- Use a personal touch. They prefer humans to e-mail or voicemail.
- Provide traditional perks—visual symbols of status such as plaques or a photo with the CEO work best.

To reiterate, average life expectancy is quickly approaching 80+ years of age (Boyd & Bee, 2011, p. 394; Sheehy, 1998, p. 9). This group can expect to live 20 to 25 years beyond what is traditionally called "retirement," and half of all retirees would prefer to continue to work. Figure 11.1 presents a final thought on the fact and fiction of this age group.

Myths:	Facts:
• They have more accidents and they get sick more often	• Older persons have fewer on-the-job accidents, and insurance claims by older workers are not different than for all employees.
• They can't learn technology.	• Seniors are willing students when the training is done right (respectfully, with low stress).
• They don't want to work.	• Many retirees say they'd prefer to be working, at least part time.
• They're not as productive as younger employees.	• The U.S. Department of Health and Human Services reports that older workers are every bit as productive as younger ones.
• They're not as bright as their younger counterparts.	• The American Management Association reports that psychologists find that intelligence remains constant until at lease age 70.

Figure 11.1. Myths and Facts About Aging—Veterans

Gerontological Phases (Middle Adulthood)

This group of individuals represent a cohort group called the Baby Boomers. They are far and away the single largest group of people in our workforce today. According to the government's 2001 U.S. Census data, 27.6 percent of our population fall into this age group, compared to 19.6 percent age 60 and over, 26.5 percent from 20 to 40 years of age, and 26.3 percent from 0 to 19 years of age. Collectively, the 35–60 age group may account for as much as 34–35 percent of our total population.

This can be a trying age group. It's generally around the age of 40 that most people begin to notice that they aren't as young as they once were. Nobody can attest to that more than I. At forty, I required bifocals for the first time. And after showing my son how to high jump for middle school track, he reminded me, while I was still gloating about my best height, that my best height was not even the starting height for middle school girls. I might add that I was sore for days afterward. Perhaps others have also noticed how Baby Boomers seem to forget things before that they would not have—for example, "What was his name?"

This phase of life generally begins to experience the decline of the sensory systems (Berk, 2009, p. 489). Hearing and vision seem to be the first to weaken. Hearing in women begins to show a decline by age 50, while in men it begins much earlier at age 30. Relative to vision, eyes lose elasticity, therefore impacting depth perception and the ability to adapt to darkness. Both of these are noticeable by the age of 50 (Berk, 2009, p. 490).

Vital body systems show noticeable declines in efficiency. Heart, lungs, digestive systems, and immune systems begin to show deterioration. Perhaps most noticeable to women and men alike are changes to the sexual reproduction system. Between the ages of 42 and 58, most women will reach menopause—their menstrual cycle stops, ovulation ceases, and levels of estrogen are reduced. In men, sexual responses continue to slow, sometimes taking longer to respond to a given sexual stimulus (Boyd & Bee, 2011, p. 397).

Cognitively, overall intelligence improves through early middle adulthood, and intelligence remains stable through middle adulthood. Fluid intelligence, the speed of thinking, experiences small decrements that continue through the early 40s. The speed of decrements increases in speed in later middle adulthood. Crystallized intelligence, which is the practical intelligence, continues to improve with experience, education, and social interaction through the age of 60.

Relative to psychosocial development:

- Baby Boomers recognize midlife, which is as many years remaining as have already passed.
- If they haven't already, Baby Boomers tend to reexamine their goals, accomplishments, and commitments. This sometimes leads to the infamous midlife crisis. At one point, a women pointed out to me how many red sport cars were lined up in our middle/senior management parking spaces (translated, 40- to 60-year-olds).
- Family dynamics are frequently unique, in that Baby Boomers have growing children and aging adult parents. This has caused this generation to be coined the "sandwich generation."
- There tends to be a general shift toward self-improvement. Boomers may enroll in classes at the local universities to take piano lessons or cooking and the like.
- There tends to be a gender crossover within this age group. Women become more assertive, while men are able to express tenderness or sadness more openly.
- Generally, middle adulthood women are less likely to find another spouse than earlier in life as there are fewer available men.

Cohort Group (Boomers)

This Baby Boomer group was actually named because they represent the largest population of individuals in the current workforce. Their birth years actually span from 1946 to 1964, but in terms of similar experiences and defining moments, the period of 1943 to 1960 is used (Smith & Clurman, 1997, p. 42).

This particular group of individuals grew up in much different circumstances than did their parents. (Veterans). The first documented war for this group was the Korean War, when the oldest among them was 10 years old. The country had just gone through some of its most difficult times; with World War I, World War II, and Korea behind them, there was a pent up-demand for products and services that had never before been seen. During this, the nation experienced its greatest economic expansion ever experienced before or after this time to date. Therefore, the environment this particular group was raised in was one of extreme optimism and positive sentiment. Some of the major events shaping this group include the following:

- 1954—Joe McCarthy House Committee on Un-American Activities hearings began
- 1955—Salk vaccine was tested on the public
- 1955—Rosa Parks refused to move to the back of the bus in Montgomery, Alabama
- 1957—First nuclear power plant was built
- 1957—Congress passed the Civil Rights Act
- 1960—Birth control pills were introduced.
- 1960—John F. Kennedy was elected president of the United States
- 1961—Kennedy established the Peace Corps
- 1962—Cuban Missile Crisis
- 1962—John Glenn circled the earth
- 1963—Martin Luther King, Jr., led a march on Washington, D.C.
- 1963—Kennedy was assassinated
- 1965—Combat troops were sent to Vietnam
- 1966—National Organization of Women was founded
- 1967—American Indian movement was founded
- 1968—Martin Luther King, Jr., and Robert Kennedy were assassinated
- 1969—First lunar landing
- 1969—Woodstock
- 1970—Kent State University shootings

Who could forget Woodstock of 1969? This was the real Woodstock, not that wannabe Woodstock of recent past where bottled water was $4 a bottle. This was the original shag carpet in the back of VW buses and the peace sign.

One more quick side-note: I tend to travel quite a bit, and as I went through the many airports I saw Obama T-shirts with a peace sign on them, reflective of the hope and peace that the president promises. So one morning during preliminary voting, I emerged from the poll location to a middle-aged gentleman, balding on the top, holding an Obama sign. I couldn't help myself. I looked right at him and gave a peace sign. He smiled from ear to ear and promptly gave me back a peace sign. For whatever reason, I felt this nostalgic coolness come over me, like we were part of something in common, something real, something big. And as it turned out, we were and are today.

Heroes to this generation include the following.

- Gandhi
- Martin Luther King, Jr.
- John and Jacqueline Kennedy
- John Glenn

Baby Boomer cultural memorabilia include the following:

- The Ed Sullivan Show
- Quonset huts
- Fallout shelters
- Poodle skirts and pop beads
- Slinkies
- TV dinners
- The Laugh-In
- Hula hoops
- The Mod Squad
- The peace sign

A poodle skirt quite literally was a mid-calf bloused skirt with a poodle stitched into it. Usually, it was worn with what were termed bobby socks—white socks folded over with lace at the tops. And, of course, no ensemble would have been complete with saddle shoes. In fact, I still wear a saddle shoe-type of footwear today, only mine have light brown sides and dark brown saddles. Another cultural remembrance of this time is the peace sign, especially as we remember Richard Nixon looking back from his plane and flashing the sign. *The Ed Sullivan Show* brings memories of, "We're going to have a really big show tonight."

This generation, as briefly eluded to earlier, believed wholeheartedly in growth and expansion. They were very optimistic and trusted in infinite possibilities. Their sheer numbers required they understand and deal effectively with teamwork. This group of individuals was basically raised with a traditional perspective of family—in other words, they had a working dad and a stay-at-home mom. Because of the size of this group, they experienced new everything, from hospitals to elementary and high schools (Dychtwald, 1999, p. 68). This whole scenario caused this group to think of themselves as stars of the show. They basically experienced it all: endless growth, prosperity, new everything, and only good times.

This group was also the first to pursue their own gratification, uncompromisingly. If their marriages didn't work out, then they divorced and found another spouse. If they didn't like their jobs, then they found another one. If they got caught in a shady deal, then they apologized, shed a tear, blamed circumstances, and moved on—and this not a slam against Bill Clinton, although he comes to mind as one of the most prominent past examples.

Baby Boomer core values can be summarized as:

*   Optimism
*   Team orientation
*   Personal gratification
*   Health and wellness
*   Personal growth
*   Youthfulness
*   Solid work ethic
*   Extreme involvement in everything

How does this group differ from their parents?

*   Their parents followed traditional roles (male/female ethic)—this group redefined roles and promoted equality.
*   Their parents were loyal to their marriages and companies—this group left unfulfilling relationships for more fulfilling ones.
*   Their parents were disciplined and patient, waiting for their rewards—this group sought immediate gratification.
*   Their parents played by the rules—this group manipulated the rules to meet their own needs.

About halfway through the Baby Boomer period were born what is sometimes referred to as the Late Boomers (Goldberg, 2000, p. 87). These individuals represent about 3 million more babies than in the first half of the Boomer period. In fact, this group of Late Boomers represents the single largest Boomer segment.

Where the older Boomers drive BMWs, the Late Boomers drive Accords. These two groups also see parenting entirely differently. Earlier Boomers were basically workaholics, whereas this later group of Boomers see parenting as being involved and emotional. This later group is predominantly made up of college-educated individuals, as compared to their earlier Boomer group. This later group is the Reagan-era of Boomers. They also were the first group to see the largest corporate downsizings since the Great Depression.

All of this makes the Late Boomers more cynical and less gung ho about management than their earlier siblings. They recognize that economics are blind, and they firmly believe that hard work and a positive attitude may not always be rewarded. They sometimes feel, "Here comes another management fad, consultant, reform, reorganization, vision, or plan." They would be the first to suggest "this too will pass."

The Late Boomers look at life a little differently than their older siblings. They recognize justice is blind to endless hours, so, since they cannot control their work environment to their liking, they turn their attention to something they can control, their children. This latter group of Boomers has become known as "helicopter parents." If they are militant about controlling their young, they are sometimes called "Black Hawks"; otherwise, you might hear them referred to as "traffic control helicopter" parents.

On the job, earlier Boomers are tremendous assets:

*   They are service-oriented.
*   They are driven.
*   They are willing to go the extra mile.
*   They are good at relationships.
*   They want to please.
*   They are good team players.

Their liabilities may include:

- Not naturally budget-minded
- Uncomfortable with conflict
- Reluctant to go against peers
- May put process ahead of result
- Overly sensitive to feedback
- Judgmental of those who see things differently
- Self-centered

Messages that motivate this group of individuals include: "you're important to us," "you're valued here," "your contribution is unique and important," "we need you," and "you're worthy." All of these will stroke this group in accordance with their being the stars of the show.

The Late Boomer leadership style is not much different from that of their parents. Late Boomers grew up in command and control environment, and, as such, have difficulty with listening, understanding another's perspective, communicating, motivating, and delegating. They tend to preach participatory management, but they find it hard to do.

When recruiting these individuals, let them know their experience is valued. Challenge them to make a difference in your organization. Stress your organization as a warm and humane place to work. Show them where they can excel; after all, this is the group that built this country after the war years. Additionally, promote the leading-edge nature of your company.

When orienting these individuals to your company, discuss the near future of the company. Late Boomers tend to be future-oriented. Focus on the challenges; this group wants to solve problems and turn things around.

The key items to focus on when thinking about developing this group are:

- Strategic planning, budgeting, coaching, and soft skills
- Providing development exercises, as opposed to simple book teaching
- Give lots of "atta boys" and "atta girls"; remember, they like attention
- Encourage them to read business books; they tend to constantly look for ways to get ahead.

When considering motivating techniques for this group, consider giving them lots of public recognition and providing them with material items such as cars, expense accounts, first-class travel, and the like. Help this group to gain name recognition, and most important, reward their long hours and solid work ethic.

Current and future issues associated with group:

- They are the biggest buyers of everything from toothpaste to financial services (Wallace, 1999, p. 82).
- Many of the Late Boomers have a poor savings record. We can expect them to work, therefore, longer into their senior years.
- This group is the group that instituted most of the policies, procedures, and structures that govern organizations today.
- Beginning back in January 2006, someone turns 60 at a rate of roughly 10 thousand a day, 4 million a year, for the next 18 years.
- Work, especially for the Late Boomers, is slowly slipping down their list of priorities.

In general, markings of a Late Boomer might include designer glasses, cell phones, whatever's trendy, BMWs, designer suits, and/or bodies and vintage wines. Their spending style is generally buy now and pay later—usually with credit cards. They tend to read *BusinessWeek* and *People Magazine,* and their humor is indicative of *Doonesbury.*

When discussing the Boomers, Veterans would say, "they talk about things they ought to keep private—like the details of their personal lives" and "they are self-absorbed." Generation Xers would say, "they're self-righteous," "they're workaholics," "they're too political, always trying to figure out just what to say, to whom, and when," "they do a great job of talking the talk, but don't walk the walk," "get outta my face," "lighten up, it's only a job," "what's the management fad this week," and "they're clueless." The Nexters would say, "they're up on the music we like" and "they work too much." Keep in mind that the Nexters are the children of the Late Boomers, and as discussed in the Nexters section, these children were very much wanted and coddled by their Boomer parents.

Myth and facts related to this group:

- Myth: They're on their way out. Fact: Not necessarily so. The average age for men and women is currently at 78 and 82, respectively.
- Myth: They'll grow up. Fact: Harley-Davidson sales doubled in the early 1990s, and a majority of buyers were Boomers.
- Myth: They've always had it easy; they're assured of a comfortable retirement. Fact: Not necessarily so again. Boomers have the largest credit card debt of any working current generation. They have on average 20 years left on their mortgages, and they have the largest gap between what they should be saving and what they are saving.
- Myth: They've quit learning. Fact: Enrollment in continuing education programs is up significantly, primarily due to this age group.
- Myth: Boomers are workaholics Fact: For the past 30 years, Boomers worked grueling hours; today, Boomers are working fewer hours and are committed to a slower pace, especially as they approach their mid-50s.

In a survey from 2006, of the Boomer population surveyed, 76 percent said they felt the best years of their life were still ahead of them. When asked when they planned to retire (see figure 11.2), 34 percent said they do not ever plan to retire and 51 percent said if they retire it would at age 66 or older. Although there are lots of surveys with varying findings, figures 12.3 and 12.4 reflect surveys on why they wanted to work longer pointed to liking to work, money, and concerns about health benefits in older age.

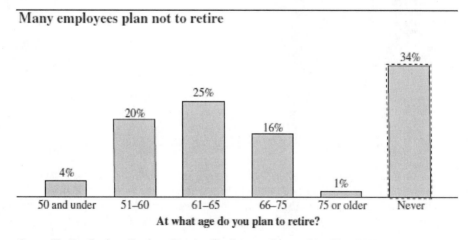

Many employees plan not to retire

At what age do you plan to retire?

Source: *The New Employee/Employer Equation,* The Concours Group and Age Wave, 2004.

Figure 11.2. At What Age Do You Plan To Retire—Survey Report, Age Wave

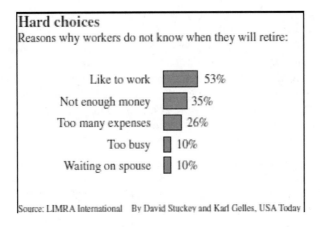

Figure 11.3. Reasons for Wanting to Work Later in Life—Survey Report, HSBC, *USA Today*

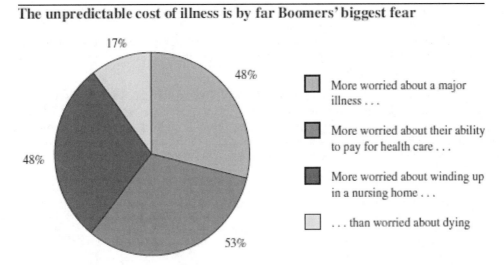

Source: Shannon O'Brien, *How Baby Boomers Will Change Retirement*, http://seniorliving.about.com/od/retirement/newboomerretire.htm, August 2006.

Figure 11.4. Biggest Fear is Cost of Illness—Survey Report

If we look at the forty years from 1970 to 2010, and then from 2010 to 2050, we see an internationally accepted slower growth in the working age population (see figure 11.5). In fact, some authors have predicted an 18 million worker shortfall by 2014. Ironically, however, in looking at the same data forecast for 2014, there will be 14 million people available to work between the ages of 65 and 74.

Percent increase during the forty-year period

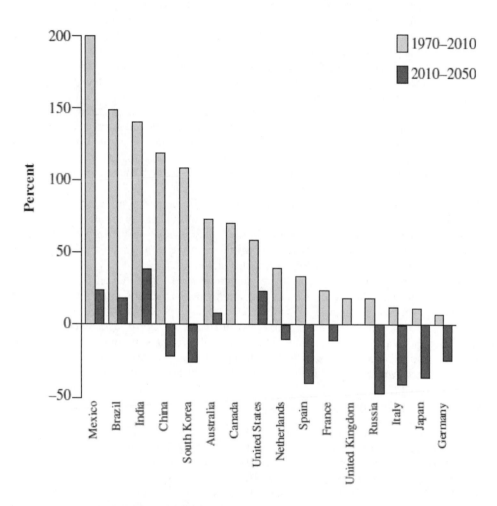

Source: Deloitte Research/UN Population Division, "It's 2008: Do You Know Where Your Talent Is? Why Acquisitions and Retention Strategies Don't Work," 2004, p. 6, http://esa.un.org/unpp/.

Figure 11.5. International Reduction in Working Age Population

Gerontological Phases (Early Adulthood)

This age group of 20- to 40-year-olds begins to experience what is referred to as senescence. Senescence is the state of physical decline in which the body gradually becomes less strong and less efficient with age.

In males, boys typically reach their maximum height by age 18, whereas girls may reach their maximum height by age 16. Body systems are at optimum levels of efficiency in early adulthood. The digestive, respiratory, circulatory, and sexual reproductive systems are all functioning at optimum capacity. During this period, however, collagen, connective tissue in the body, begins to decrease, the result of which is more wrinkles and generally thinner skin. Lung capacity tends to begin to drop at the rate of about 5 percent per year beginning around age 20. The eyes and hearing also begin to change.

Homeostasis refers to the adjustment of the body's systems to keep physiological functions in a state of equilibrium. As the body ages, it takes longer for these homeostatic adjustments to occur, making it harder for older bodies to adapt to stresses. For example, when we are active, our breathing and heart rates increase to bring more oxygen to our cells. As we age, these systems become strained to reach comparable levels as when we were younger. As we age, we are also less capable of recovering from a poor night's sleep, and it's more difficult to bounce back from a previous day's heavy exertion.

In terms of the sexual reproductive systems, one study found that sexual intercourse generally occurs about 12 times per month at age 20; about 7 times per month at age 40; and about 1 time per month at age 70. As men age, they require more explicit and prolonged stimulation to initiate sexual excitement. As women age, they are more likely to become aroused and experience orgasm during love-making. This may very well be contributed to the male's slowing responses, which create a longer period of female stimulation, which many women need to reach orgasmic plateaus.

Relative to cognitive development, with age comes experience and opportunity for advanced education. Experience and advanced education provide the framework for making more informed decisions. In general, college-educated people tend to be less threatened by conflicting views. Maturity also decreases the requirement for absolute truths and acknowledges the relativity of each situation. Continued learning heightens cognitive development, especially during this phase.

In terms of psychosocial development, there is a strong need for affiliation during this generational phase. Friendships are important, especially to single individuals. Worth noting is that marriage success is directly related to age on first marriage. Between 20 and 30 years of age, 60 percent of the men and 46 percent of the women have never been married. Between 20 and 30 years of age, 3 percent of the men and 5 percent of the women are divorced and not yet remarried. There is a strong need for achievement in this age group. Their achievement may be satisfied by either parenthood or work. This age group expects several job changes over their working lifetime, and they recognizes the need for continual learning.

Cohort Group (Generation Xers)

Generation Xers are those individuals generally, today, who range from 27 to 44 years of age and are the children of the older Boomers or the younger siblings of the Boomers whose parents were the Veterans cohort group. The parents of these children were the movers and shakers who helped our nation to evolve economically, socially, and in every other manner. These children, therefore, grew up in their shadow. There are considerably fewer Generation Xers than Boomers, 78 million versus 62 million. This group received many economic luxuries, but they also have seen many negative events in their time. Their circumstances caused this group to develop a "survivor mentality"—in other words, "just tell me if it's going to be on the test." This was the first group of young people whose parents could have taken the birth control pill to avoid having them. When surveyed on this, one might have expected them to generally have said "*Wow! That's great! I must have been really wanted.*" But the actual majority response was more along the lines of, "Great—they forgot to take the pill."

Defining moments for this group include a few positive events, but on the whole, a lot of negative events, leaving an impression quite different from that with which their Boomer parents grew up.:

- • 1970—Women's liberation protests and demonstrations
- • 1972—Arab terrorists at Munich Olympics
- • 1973—Watergate scandal
- • 1973—Energy crisis began
- • 1976—Tandy and Apple market PCs

- 1978—Mass suicide in Jonestown
- 1979—Three Mile Island nuclear reactor melted down
- 1979—U.S. corporations began massive layoffs
- 1979—Iran held 66 Americans hostage
- 1980—John Lennon was shot and killed
- 1980—Ronald Reagan inaugurated
- 1986—*Challenger* disaster
- 1987—Stock market plummeted
- 1988—Terrorists bomb blew up Flight 103 over Lockerbie
- 1989—*Exxon Valdez* oil tanker spill
- 1989—Fall of Berlin Wall
- 1991—Operation Desert Storm
- 1992—Rodney King beating videotaped, Los Angeles riots

In determining how to tell a Generation Xer from a Boomer, ask the question, "Where were you when John F. Kennedy was shot?" If they can remember, then they are probably Boomers; if not, then they are most likely in the Generation X age group.

The Generation Xer's heroes list is short, namely, none. To be more specific, their heroes are those individuals, parents, ministers, coaches, or teachers who exude integrity—in other words, they do, what they say, or who walk the talk.

Cultural memorabilia indicative of this age group includes:

- The Brady Bunch
- Pet rocks
- Platform shoes
- *The Simpsons*
- *Dynasty*
- ET
- Cabbage Patch dolls

Their core values include:

- Diversity
- Thinking globally
- Balance—as they have seen their parents working endless hours, only to be, perhaps, downsized
- Technoliteracy—this group has seen it all, technologically speaking
- Fun
- Informality
- Self-reliance
- Pragmatism

In terms of generational personality, this group is very self-reliant. Remember, nearly half of their parents' marriages ended in divorce (Santrock, 1999, p. 407). This group, therefore, grew up with joint custody, visitation rights, and weekend parents. With this self-reliance and independence came maturity. The earlier we assume responsibilities, the sooner we are required to learn about things that we might not normally get an opportunity to learn, and therefore, the sooner we must mature. Those that do not mature as required to handle this new level of independence usually end up in some form of trouble.

This was the first generation with a predominance of two-income families. A derivative of this is what has been coined "latchkey kids." These are children who come home after school, let themselves in the house, and begin doing whatever they need to do until their parents return from work. They are accustomed to being alone. The result of their parents coming home late from work and pulling dinner together at the last minute is less time is available for quality time.

According to the Bureau of Labor Statistics, the percent of women entering the workforce in 2000 was at an all-time high of 62 percent. During this same period, the divorce rate peaked at nearly 51 percent. Psychologists and sociologists are not sure whether the increase in the number of working women caused the increase in the divorce rate, or vice versa. Figure 11.6 depicts this phenomenon.

This group is seeking a sense of family. They tend to have a close group of friends in lieu of a close supportive family. They also would like a sense of balance in their lives. They have seen their workaholic parents bring work home and expend vast amounts of energy on work-related issues, only to not be fully appreciated by their companies, and perhaps even laid off. Where their parents lived to work, this generation would prefer to work to live.

This generation also appears to have a nontraditional orientation to time and space, meaning, it doesn't matter how and when work gets done, as long as it gets done. They may even show up late to work or leave early, still getting the work done but lacking in focus. This has caused some to label this generation as slackers. More specifically, this group places a greater emphasis on efficiency than having to demonstrate face time. They feel that if they can get the job done during normal or less working hours, then why should they be the first one in and the last to leave at night if it isn't necessary?

This generation prefers informality. They believe their parents are too serious and need to lighten up. They prefer to wear jeans and T-shirts to work—they feel more comfortable and productive. Anything that makes work less "corporate" is good.

The Generation Xer approach to authority is very casual. They're not against authority; they are simply not impressed with it. In their lifetimes, they have seen presidents, politicians, and reverends all fall from their respective graces. A story in a book I read talked about a new young Generation Xer who was walking into work with the corporate CEO. On inquiring into where the CEO lived, the new young Generation Xer suggested that perhaps the two of them could carpool to work.

Generation Xers tend to be skeptical. They are careful with their loyalties and commitments. They've seen individuals fall from grace and social contracts change. With all of this, they recognize that there are no guarantees, that perhaps the only constant in life is change.

Generation Xers tend to be attracted to the edge. At work, their job is just their job, but in their personal lives, they are attracted to higher-risk activities. In fact, on television there are "sporting" events under the nomenclature of *The X-Games*. I was watching one such exhibition the other day. Individuals would ride their bicycles down a ski slope and (while airborne) would perform death-defying tricks, just prior to landing on the snow below. This was so new to me that I couldn't help but watch for a while. I also couldn't help but wonder why anyone would do such a thing. A common trick appeared to be removing their hands at the peak of their jump and ultimately landing with no hands on their handlebars. Those that survived and landed successfully were applauded endlessly. Those that crashed and ended up in a pile at the bottom of the snow slope still got rounds of applause, but also received some level of pain. One individual, according to the announcer, had broken more than 360 bones in his body, as if this were something to be proud of.

This group is also very technologically savvy. They generally have excellent computer skills, are familiar with high-tech games, and can easily program their phones, DVD players, and other electronics.

On the job, their assets are that they are adaptable, technoliterate, independent, unintimidated by authority, and creative. Their liabilities are that they are impatient, may have poor people skills, are inexperienced, and tend to be cynical. Worth noting, however, is that 80 percent of all new businesses over the last three years were started by this generation of individuals.

The Generation Xer leadership style is one of being skilled at supporting and developing a competent team that can change direction quickly. They are used to being challenged. They tend to ask "why" frequently. They are fair, competent, and straightforward. In fact, sometimes they are too honest, especially on performance reviews of others, suggesting that perhaps they could show a little more empathy.

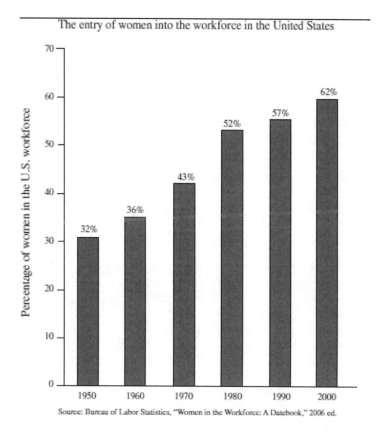

The entry of women into the workforce in the United States

Source: Bureau of Labor Statistics, "Women in the Workforce: A Databook," 2006 ed.

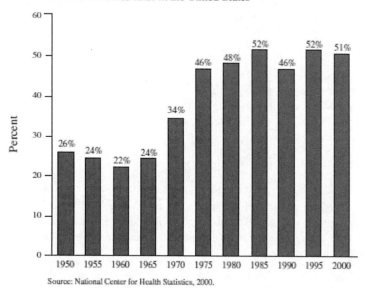

Growth in divorce rates in the United States

Source: National Center for Health Statistics, 2000.

Figure 11.6. Predominance of Working Mothers and Peaked Divorce Rate, BLS/NCHS

In terms of recruiting this generation:

- Let them know that your company has fun.
- Let them know that their ideas are evaluated on their merit and not their seniority.
- If the organization is undergoing change, let them know; they tend to see opportunity in change.
- They prefer a relaxed environment, not necessarily a warm or humane one.
- Stress technological innovation as being important.
- Stress hands-off management, that is, let them know you do not micromanage.

In terms of orienting this generation as new hires, show them your website and let them take it for a spin. Provide a list of people they may call if they have any questions. Let them know you want them to have fun.

Relative to opportunities, this generation tends to look out for themselves and realize that nothing is forever. They are self-reliant, which implies you should give them plenty of freedom. They tend to find satisfaction in moving horizontally as opposed to vertically. They like to be trained, and they perceive their value to be in their skills, not their politics.

In terms of developing this generation, training and development is absolutely essential from their perspective. They are self-learners and prefer brief and multiple input stimuli. As an employer, always promote the value of learning to this group. They tend to like leaving every day knowing more than when they arrived.

When mentoring this group, suggest that office politics are a way of getting around the rules, not an essential element of moving in the organization. Generation Xers like mentors. Mentors are sort of like surrogate parents to this group. Additionally, they like to be challenged to find alternative solutions to a given problem. Use them in this capacity whenever possible.

What others have to say about this generation:

Veterans:

- They're not educated.
- They don't respect experience.
- They don't follow procedures.
- They don't know what hard work is.

Boomers:

- They're slackers.
- They're rude and lack social skills.
- They're always doing things their own way.
- They spend too much time on the Internet and e-mail.
- They won't wait their turn.

Nexters:

- Cheer up! It's not so bad.

Markings of this generation include nose rings, naval rings, functional clothing, tattoos, and Japanese cars. Their spending style is generally cautious and conservative. They read such material as *Spin* and *Wired* and spend time in chat room dialogue. This generation's humor is typical of *Dilbert*.

Myth and facts related to this group:

- Myth: They're materialistic. Fact: Many are struggling to make ends meet. This is the first generation that may not be able to improve on their parents' lifestyle. Many simply want to get out of debt.

- Myth: They're whiners. Fact: They face real challenges: college loans, health care costs, and the like.
- Myth: They have a "you owe me" attitude. Fact: No more so than other generations.
- Myth: They're not willing to work hard. Fact: This group is willing to work very hard. They are simply not willing to work 70 hours for 40 hours of pay. They want a life outside of work.
- Myth: They're living on easy street. Fact: In 1950, the average monthly mortgage payment was 14 percent of adjusted household income. Today, it is 40 percent of adjusted household income. If you are over 60 years of age you will get back $200 for every $100 put into Social Security; Generation Xers will lose more than $100 for every $450 contributed.

Gerontological Phases (Adolescence)

This phase of the maturing female and male adolescent is probably the most pronounced phase of physical maturation, short of the noticeable declines in late adulthood. Everything changes, from physical appearance to social habits and perception of oneself as a human being. During this period, both females and males will experience rapid physical growth and associated sexual changes that make reproduction possible.

Many teenagers will commit their time, dollars, and well-being to attain that ideal model appeal or male hunk physique. Even those who already have relatively attractive physical appearances will strive for that one physique better than their own. Those that are so blessed may become very self-critical, while those who inherit a shape or size far from the culturally acceptable ideal may suffer excessive self-consciousness or even depression.

There is a noticeable difference in this age group's cognitive development. Having a conversation with a 14- or 15-year-old is quite different from having a conversation with a 7- or 8-year-old. Because of advances in their cognitive abilities, adolescents are increasingly aware of both external concerns and their own internal needs. Adolescents are also considerably more capable of reasoning, logic, and rational thinking (Santrock, 1999, p. 406).

For many developmentalists, the single most important distinguishing feature of adolescent thought is the capacity to think in terms of possibility rather than only in terms of reality. This allows adolescents to fantasize, speculate, and hypothesize on a much grander scale than in their preadolescent earlier years. Preadolescent thinking tends to tie children to the here and now (Berger & Thompson, 1998, p. 412).

The physical changes of puberty initiate biosocial changes by transforming the childish body into an adult one. Cognitive changes enable the young person to begin to transcend the realm of concrete thought and to think abstractly and hypothetically. However, it's the psychosocial growth—relating to parents with new independence, to friends with new intimacy, to society with a new commitment, and to oneself with new understanding—that eventually brings the young person adult status and maturity. Taken as a whole, psychosocial development during adolescence can best be understood as a quest for self-understanding and for a new identity. That is, the adolescent searches for answers to questions that seldom arise in younger years, such as, "Who am I?"

Indicative of this search for oneself is such things as body markings of one form or another, such as piercing or tattoos. It is also not uncommon for individuals of this developmental stage to wear what others might consider unusual clothing or clothing only made for this age group. Hair is yet another identifying characteristic of this transitional age group. Colored hair, spiked hair, shaved heads, and the like are all indicative of this aspect of finding oneself.

Cohort Group (Nexters)

Nexters, at this writing, are roughly between 7 and 27 years of age. They have been called Generation Y, the Internet generation, the Net generation, the Nintendo generation, and the Millennials.

The Nexters are those children born to the Late Boomers and early Generation Xers. These parents are the ones who demand that they provide nothing but the best for their children and exercise perfection in their childrearing process. The parents of this generation insist on only the best early childhood care facilities, elementary, middle, and high schools, and on being intimately involved in almost every aspect of their children's lives.

The parents of this generation planned to have these kids, sometimes elaborately decorating their newborn rooms and cuddling them endlessly. These kids were wanted, to say the least.

It is not uncommon, at a very early age, that these kids might have televisions and DVD players in their rooms, computers, CD players, iPods, and/or PlayStations of one type or another. Technology, which to some of us might seem difficult to manage at first, is second nature to this generation.

In a 1995 survey, an unprecedented 93 percent of 10- to 13-year-olds queried said they felt loved by their parents. In a repeat survey in 2008, nearly 90 percent reported being "very close" to their parents. This generation is also more trusting of authority than either Generation X or the Boomers. In a recent survey, 86 percent said they trust their parents and teachers, and 83 percent said they trust the police.

This generation has had increasingly involved parents. This has led one author to write, "Gen Ys have been blessed with an almost cocoon level of parental attention—immersed in a very pro-child culture" (Tulgan, 2009, p. 16). Nexters have experienced an unequivocal level of father-child and mother-child contact, peaking at 83 percent of the fathers spending one hour or more daily with their children, and 71 percent of mothers spending up to two hours per day. This generation is astonishingly family-centric. They authentically love their parents. Nexters describe their parents as role models and are most likely to consult with their parents on major decisions, including employment. More than 50 percent of families with children eat dinner together seven days a week. Eight in 10 children who live away from home have talked to their parents in the past day; three in four say they see their parents at least once a week; and 50 percent say they see their parents daily. Additionally, in a recent survey, more than 61 percent of college seniors say they expect to move back home after graduation. Again, an unprecedented 78 percent of high school students say family ranks higher in describing success than money or fame.

Whereas Generation Xers ran into a stagnant economy and tight job market, Nexters are wanted in most every job market, with openings on all shifts and an ever-growing demand for their skills. The parents of this group want their children to experience the job market but are not afraid to pull them out of work in a heartbeat if the parent feels there is nearly any reasonable reason to do so. For example: Sally's mother says, "Sally, you need to get off early tonight so we can go to your grandmother's birthday party." Sally replies, "But I can't, Mom. I have to work until 9:00 p.m. this evening." "No, you need to tell your boss you have to leave at 7:30 because we have a birthday party to go to," says her mother. "I can't!" exclaims Sally. "Sally, if you want me to, I'll go in with you and explain to your boss that you will be leaving at 7:30 tonight," her mother replies firmly, to which Sally replies, "Fine! I'll tell them. You don't need to go in."

In an article written by Danielle Sacks (*Fast Company,* January/February 2006) entitled "Scenes from the Culture Clash," Sacks says:

A 22-year-old pharmaceutical employee learned that he was not getting the promotion he had been eyeing. His boss told him he needed to work on his weaknesses first. The Harvard grad had excelled at everything he had ever done, so he was crushed by the news. He told his parents about the review, and they were convinced there was some misunderstanding, some way they could fix it, as they'd been able to fix everything before. His mother called the human-resources department the next day. Seventeen times. She left increasingly frustrating messages: "You're purposely ignoring us"; "you fudged the evaluation"; "you have it in for my son." She demanded a mediation session with her, her son, his boss, and HR—and she got it. At one point, the 22-year-old reprimanded the HR rep for being "rude to my mom."

The patients on Sophy's couch aren't the twentysomethings dealing with their first taste of failure. Nor are they the "helicopter parents." They're the traumatized bosses, as well as the 47-year-old woman from HR who has been hassled time and again by her youngest workers and their parents. Now the pharmaceutical company that employs her has her in therapy, and she's on six-month stress leave. (p. 74)

Joan Ryan, *San Francisco Chronicle* columnist (Zemke, Raines, & Filipczak, 2000), says,

We Mappies (Middle-Aged Professional Parents) have elevated child-rearing to a sacrament. We arrange our schedules around our children's soccer games, volunteer as much as we can put in the classroom, hover over every science project and book report, and take our kids with us to restaurants and on outings with a frequency that makes our own parents snort and roll their eyes.

We're told we will produce a generation of coddled, center-of-the-universe adults who will expect the world to be as delighted with them as we are. And even as we laugh at their knock-knock jokes and exclaim over the refrigerator drawings, we secretly fear the same thing. (p. 130)

One of the things I find interesting comes from Marston (2007, p. 92), who talks about things this generation doesn't remember:

- They study the 1960s as history with no nostalgia.
- They have no memory of the Cold War.
- *Leave it to Beaver* is a Discovery Channel show.
- Landing on the Moon was what they did in the olden days.
- AIDS has always existed.
- If you tell them they sound like a broken record, they'll ask, "What's a record?"
- They don't remember Pac Man.
- They've never seen a TV without cable.
- *The Tonight Show* has always been hosted by Jay Leno.
- Popcorn eaten at home has always been cooked in a microwave.
- They don't know Mork or "De plane! De plane!"
- They cannot answer the question, "Where's the beef?"

And, a few years back, AARP provided an interesting comparison.

THEN	NOW
Eating wild berries in the woods	Eating Lunchables on a play date
Climbing trees	Allergy tests
Walking with pals along train tracks	Walking with parents on a leash
Stickball	Xbox
"Be home by dark"	"Answer your cell phone when I call"
Summer camp	Fat camp
Doing cannonballs off the high dive	Wearing floaties in the shallow end
Skinned knees	Carpal tunnel
Jumping on a trampoline	What's a trampoline?

Figure 11.7. Then and Now—AARP 2008

Major events that have, and continue, to form this young group include:

- A cultural focus on childrearing—everything from cartoons, to toys, to movies
- Violence; Oklahoma City bombing and schoolyard shootings
- Technology
- Busy, over-planned lives
- Stress
- Clinton/Lewinsky
- Columbine High School massacre

Their cultural memorabilia include such items as:

- Barney
- Teenage Mutant Ninja Turtles
- Tamagotchi and other virtual pets
- Beanie Babies
- Pogs
- American Girl dolls
- Oprah and Rosie
- The Spice Girls
- The X Games

Anyone remember the Teenage Mutant Ninja Turtles? They are a group of, well, quite literally, mutant turtles. They wear headbands, know karate, and generally fight the bad guys. Their leader is nothing less than a rat, literally. I remember when my older sons were young; I swear they must have had all the turtle figurines. And recently, in trying to appeal to the next generation and play on the heartstrings of the Boomers, the movie industry released a full-screen movie entitled *TMNT*.

Unlike the previous generation, the Generation Xers, this age group has a lot of heroes:

- Michael Jordan
- Princess Diana
- Mark McGwire, Sammy Sosa
- Mother Teresa
- Bill Gates
- Kerri Strugg
- Mia Hamm
- Tiger Woods
- Christopher Reeves

Perhaps one of the best attributes about this generation, having two teenage children myself, is that they believe their parents may actually be cool. Parents of this generation wear similar clothing—small logos on T-shirts and jeans, as an example. This generation also shares common music with their parents, for example, "Mambo #5," "Leaving on a Jet Plane," "Thong Song," "Who Let the Dogs Out," and "Oar's Revolution." I recall my oldest son and I in the car going somewhere when the song "Leaving on a Jet Plane" came on. He was floored when I began singing the song along with him. He said, "I didn't know you listened to [whoever]" ([whoever] in his opinion had created the song). He was equally floored when I told him the song had been around for forty years, remade a dozen or more times, and who the original person was that first sang it.

Aside from music, this generation shares with their parents the same taste in movies, again to name only a few, *The Matrix, The Rock, James Bond, Austin Powers, Toy Story II, Con Air,* and *The Bee Movie*. What's interesting is how the movie production companies have caught on to the idea that a movie must appeal to the parents to be successful. So today, when attending a youth movie, parents laugh at some of the lines that simply slide right over the tops of the younger heads. The humor is embedded and sometimes makes reference to the dark side of some of the childhood characters, an example being some of the lines in the *Shrek* movies.

At work, this generation has significant assets. They form collective action, are optimistic, have tenacity, possess a heroic spirit, have significant multitasking capabilities, and are technologically savvy. Their liabilities, which might be expected given their age, include their need for supervision and structure, and their inexperience, particularly with handling difficult people issues. Ron Alsop, in his book *The Trophy Kids Grow Up,* says, "This generation is . . . bred for achievement by success-driven parents, and most will work hard as long as the task at hand is engaging and promises a tangible payoff" (2008, p. 37).

In terms of messages that motivate this group, sayings such as, "you'll be working with other bright, creative people," "your boss is in his or her 60s," "you and your coworkers can help turn this company around," and "you can be a hero here."

Identifying characteristics include polyester and retro clothing and cell phones. Their spending style can typically be described as spend their parents' money as fast as they can, and of course, their parents let them. In their earlier years, they may have read *Goosebumps, The Baby-sitter's Club, Matt Christopher,* and *American Girls* and engaged in chat room conversation. Their humor is typically on the order of *Calvin and Hobbes.*

Myth and facts related to this group:

- Myth: The youth of this country is going to hell in a handbasket. Fact: Experts believe this is a fine new crop of young people who could quite easily make heroes of themselves.
- Myth: Today's kids are getting a good education. Fact: There is a widening gap between the haves and the have-nots.
- Myth: Kids need to spend more time reading and less time watching TV or playing video games. Fact: Kids are spending more time reading. Video games are cutting into TV, not reading time.

Figure 11.8 summarizes the four generations discussed in the above paragraphs (Strauss & Howe, 1991, p. 56).

	Veterans	Boomers	Xers	Nexters
Outlook	Practical	Optimistic	Skeptical	Hopeful
Work Ethic	Dedicated	Driven	Balanced	Determined
View of Authority	Respectful	Love/hate	Unimpressed	Polite
Leadership by	Hierarchy	Consensus	Competence	Pulling Together
Relationships	Personal Sacrifice	Personal Gratification	Reluctant to Commit	Inclusive
Turnoffs	Vulgarity	Political incorrectness	Cliché, hype	Promiscuity

Figure 11.8. Comparison of Perspectives

Before we leave this section, you may have read my use of the word cool a few times. You may have recognized this slang term and then speculated on my age. Well, as an aside, the slang term cool has been around since the tracking of slang terms. It is the only slang term to withstand the test of time and is still used today. Other "wannabe" slang terms (figure 11.9) have come and gone, as most fads tend to do, but cool remains as a staple in our slang terminology.

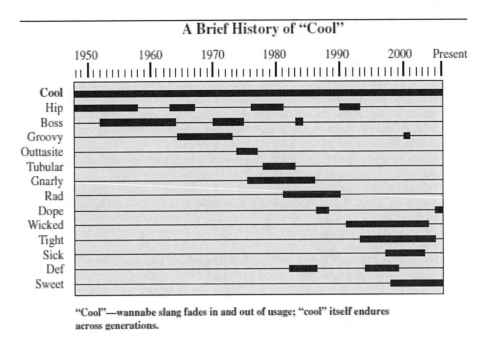

"Cool"—wannabe slang fades in and out of usage; "cool" itself endures across generations.

Figure 11.9. A Brief History of "Cool" and Other Slang Terms, *Fast Company*

Concluding Remarks on the Nurture Side

Traditional arguments of nature versus nurture hinge on whether an individual's behavior is essentially predetermined at birth, or is the result of environmental factors. Although one might reasonably argue that our behavior is the result of both, there are some who argue endlessly for either end of the spectrum. This section focused on behavior that is predominantly determined by the environment in which we developed, that is, the "nurture" perspective.

Harvard zoologist Edward O. Wilson claims the study of human behavior is not the sole province of social scientists, whose perspective of human development is that it is generally environmentally based. Human beings are not born a blank slate, argues Wilson, with their behavior totally a response to their environment. Wilson views a large part of our behavior,—why we organize ourselves as we do, act as we do, and even behave as we do—to be part of our genetic makeup. Genetic makeup helps to guide and create culture, and culture, in turn, operates directly on the genes.

Wilson believes that by selecting and controlling our genetic makeup, we could significantly increase SAT scores and produce employees with higher internal motivation. The study of topics like stress, perception, learning, and creativity would be analyzed in physiological terms. Stress would be evaluated in terms of neurophysiological perturbations and their relaxation times. Perception would be translated into brain circuitry. Learning and creativity would be defined as the alteration of specific portions of the cognitive machinery regulated by input from the motive centers (Robbins, 1998, p. 24).

Chapter 12

Connecting Generational Cohorts to Associative Thinking

Many times it has been asked which of the four predominate generational cohorts (Veterans, Boomers, Generation Xers, and Nexters) in the workforce today are more able to perform that which is required for producing disruptive technologies? In thinking through this question, it appears one must consider disruptive technologies and the underlying ability to break free of associative thinking as a set of related topics, namely:

- Understanding the breadth and depth of a discipline
- "Seeing" across disciplines
- Practical experience and ability to recognize the bigger picture
- Ability to recognize cultural realities
- Understanding of current technologies
- Unbounded by hierarchical pressures
- Propensity for "just trying it"

Understanding the Breadth and Depth of a Discipline

In the first of the topics, to fully appreciate the entirety of the breadth and depth of a discipline would require a significant level of knowledge and experience. In addition to knowledge and experience of a given discipline, there is the exposure to:

- Working on programs
- Working across programs
- Working on proposals

Which cohort, then, possesses the opportunity to have the greatest level of knowledge and experience in a given discipline? The answer would appear to be the Veteran and Boomer cohorts. These two cohorts have clearly been around the longest and have had the opportunity to work across many disciplines, therefore collecting numerous experiences.

"Seeing" across Disciplines

Which cohorts would be best suited to see across disciplines? Again, the ability to see across disciplines implies some level of understanding of the many other disciplines involved in the program/project. The logic seems rather straightforward, that being, if an individual has worked on programs of any complexity, then that individual most likely has been exposed to the complexities of cross-discipline challenges and opportunities. There is an element of unknown unknowns here. Meaning, if we have not yet had the opportunity to work across disciplines, then we most likely may not know what we don't know. To this end, it would again appear the Veteran and Boomer generational cohorts are probably best suited to see across disciplines.

Practical Experience and Ability to Recognize the Bigger Picture

When we discuss which cohorts would have the greatest practical experience and ability to recognize the bigger picture, the immediate response might again be the more senior Veteran and Boomer generational cohorts. However, if we are not necessarily talking about cross-discipline activities, then in this instance, we may be addressing a bigger question related to individuals more so than generational cohorts—that being the individual personal characteristic for detailed versus big-picture thinking preference. If this latter is a consideration, then the question quickly turns to the discussion put forth in the chapter on "Building Teams—Understanding Ourselves and Others through MBTI." If, from the original premise, we are talking about the bigger picture from a program/project perspective, then our original suspicion would most likely fit—that being the Veteran and Boomer generational cohorts would appear to possess the greater opportunity to recognize the bigger picture.

Ability to Recognize Cultural Realities

Which generational cohort might be best suited to recognize cultural realities? This question directly relates to the business case for diversity that may be stated as: corporate growth is predominately from innovation; innovation comes from ideas, and lots of them; ideas come from all kinds of people. To this end, the more inclusive an organization is in welcoming people to share their ideas, the more ideas are available to select from to be innovative, and the more innovative an organization, the greater the chance for business growth (i.e., inclusivity spawns growth). This, too, supports our thinking outside of the box.

Recognizing cultural realities, then, begs the question which generational cohort is most open-minded when viewing cross-cultural interactions. Given the significant intercultural exchanges of the last fifteen years, directly related to social and economic globalization, it would stand to reason the latter generational cohorts would be, seemingly, more open and perhaps best read as "used to" intercultural exchanges. As justification for suggesting the relatively recent increase in intercultural exchanges, we could look at education and the number of degrees awarded to international students on U.S. campuses, the increase of H-1B visas issued, the transfer of skilled labor across borders, the growth in the international science and engineering workforce, the increase in the world's research workforce, the number of worldwide first university degrees awarded, how corporations are now employing a worldwide model for teaming to advance new technologies and advanced research, and on a more personal note, the increase in intercultural marriages from previous years. Clearly, given the relative newness of all of these many changes, the latter Generation X and Nexters cohorts would appear to be most open to recognizing and valuing cultural realities.

Understanding of Current Technologies

Understanding current technologies directly implies:

- A natural understanding and comfort with the Internet
- Familiarity and comfort with social communication networks (social networking sites), such as Facebook, Google+, Twitter, MySpace, and LinkedIn
- Comfort with handling multiple simultaneous activities (multitasking)
- Lack of technology-oriented fear

Which, then, of the generational cohorts might feel most a home with these many current technologies? Given the significant increase in these technologies over relatively few years would lead us to suggest the Generation Xers, and perhaps Nexters even more so, would be the most applicable generational cohorts.

While it is true the Boomer generation has adapted well to these technologies, they are new to this cohort, and not all have equally adapted. Meanwhile, Generation Xers and Nexters grew up with these technologies and have never been without them. It could easily be argued Nexters in particular find these many technologies as their only real acknowledged source of communication.

Unbounded by Hierarchical Pressures

Which cohort might feel less bound to hierarchical pressure? It seemingly would not be the Veteran and Boomer generations. They both grew up in a very structured environment. The Veteran generation experienced successive war years. Because of the period in which they matured, Veterans have been subjected to significant struggle and strife. The fathers of this age group were most likely impacted in some way by World War I, and this age group themselves may have impacted by World War II. The personality of those individuals in this age group is reflective of the events of this period, namely, World War I, World War II, the industrial economy in general, and the type of command and control management style prevalent of the time. The most enduring workplace legacy of this particular group is likely to be their older command and control style of management. This is something most familiar to them and what they learned from their war year experiences. Boomers, as well as the Veterans, grew up in families that espoused the command and control mind-set. This generation believed wholeheartedly in growth and expansion. They were very optimistic and believed in infinite possibilities. Their sheer numbers required they understand and deal effectively with teamwork. This group of individuals was basically raised with a traditional perspective of family—in other words, they had a working dad and a stay-at-home mom. It could readily be argued that both the Veteran and Boomer cohorts would favor and fully appreciate hierarchical pressure, and subsequently, conform to it.

Generation Xers are the children of the older Boomers or the younger siblings of the Boomers whose parents were the Veterans cohort group. The parents of these children were the movers and shakers who helped our nation to evolve economically, socially, and in every other manner. These children, therefore, grew up in their shadow. This group received many economic luxuries, but also they have seen many negative events in their time. Their circumstances caused this group to develop a "survivor mentality"—in other words, "just tell me if it's going to be on the test." This group is very self-reliant. Nearly half of their parents' marriages ended in divorce (Santrock, 1999, 407). This group, therefore, grew up with joint custody, visitation rights, and weekend parents. With this self-reliance and independence came maturity. Generation Xers were the first generation with a predominance of two-income families. A derivative of this is what has been coined "latchkey kids." They are accustomed to being alone. The Generation Xers approach to authority is very casual. They're not against authority; they are simply not impressed with it. Given this overall persona, it would seem most likely that the Generation Xers would less bound by hierarchical pressure.

Propensity for "Just Trying It"

Which generational cohort might say, "Let's just do it"? given the Generation X and Nexter focus on freedom, independence, and not having a strong sense of fear, it could readily be argued that both Generation X and Nexter cohorts would adhere to this mind-set. It does not reason at all that the Veteran and Boomer cohorts would pursue this approach. Both the Veteran and Boomer cohorts would prefer a much more structured approach to moving forward, given their command and control historical impact.

While the above is simply a narrative on which generational cohorts might best fit the identified topics, it certainly isn't the final thought. Generational cohorts, in general, are very broad groupings of stereotyped individuals. Given this, not everyone fits well into these compartmentalized chronological groupings. To this end, those in the gaps of these cohorts may very well go one way or the other; however, given the purity of these cohorts based on historical events that shaped each, the above could easily be argued to be generally true.

Chapter 13

Leadership and Gender—A Science-Based Understanding

Remembering program/project management is both an art and a science, it is important to continue to examine those qualitative areas that help us to better understand ourselves and others. Leadership and gender (females) is one of those areas most worthy of understanding better.

It used to be, when discussing gender in senior leadership positions, that we made reference to psychological and sociological perspectives. Historically, we would suggest females should behave more like men. Many books were written on this subject with this mind-set, in particular the recent books titled *Don't Think Pink* by Johnson and Learned (2004) and *The Feminine Warrior* by Marrewa (1998). The underlying idea was if you wanted to get ahead in a man's world, you should look at the behaviors and skills exhibited by men and behave in a similar fashion. Some experts still espouse this theory.

Now, however, we have significant science-based research that helps us to better understand the similarities and differences in the way males and females behave and act in varying situations. This new look into the minds of males and females provides us with a fresh appreciation for what each gender is most capable of doing, in what circumstances one may excel over the other, and generally why both genders may behave the way they do in a business environment.

The bulk of this topic stems from Gurian and Annis in their book *Leadership and the Sexes*. The information in this chapter is premised on research conducted over all continents covering 30 unique cultures. The findings from this research, that males and females have consistent brain wiring, are consistent regardless of the continent or culture.

We now have the science-based opportunities to examine brain differences through the use of three basic technologies:

- positron emission tomography (PET)
- magnetic resonance imaging (MRI)
- single-photon emission computed tomography (SPECT)

PET scans look at areas of brain activity. Scientists can locate active regions while a person speaks, works, relates, loves, and performs tasks. MRI uses magnets to detect positive electrical charge impacted by blood flow due to increased activity-related changes. SPECT, similar to PET, provides higher resolution images. The below Gurian and Annis figure is a depiction of this technology's capability. Figure 13.1 represents a male and female brain at deep rest. Notice how the male brain has essentially closed down, except for the area predominantly used for maintaining bodily functioning. The female brain, on the other hand, is not at all closed down. In fact, the female brain is just the opposite; it appears to be very much stimulated in multiple brain centers throughout the brain.

As is the case whenever we group individuals into a category, we need to be aware that stereotyping in this manner is not always accurate. As much as we might imply an individual is of one mind or another, the truth is that there is always tremendous latitude of gray area for interpretation. So, to the extent this discussion fits each of us as individuals, or not, should be received in this light.

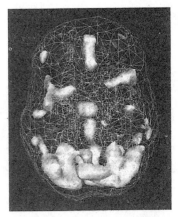 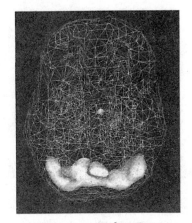

Figure 1.1. *Female at Rest.*   **Figure 1.2.** *Male at Rest.*

Source: Brain scans courtesy of Dr. Daniel Amen. Used by permission

Figure 13.1. Male and Female Brains at Rest

In a science-based paradigm, gender and gender roles are required to be differentiated. Perhaps the best way to emphasize this difference is by example. In numerous management and leadership texts, as well as presented by Gurian and Annis, is the following example:

Canadian Authorities (CA) versus a U.S. Navy Aircraft Carrier

CA: Please divert your course 15 degrees to the south to avoid collision.

U.S. Carrier: Recommend you divert your course 15 degrees to avoid collision.

CA: Negative, you divert your course 15 degrees to avoid collision.

U.S. Carrier: This is the Captain of a U.S. Navy ship. Change your course now or countermeasures will be taken to ensure the safety of this ship! Over!

CA: This is the lighthouse mate. It's your call . . .

This simple and widely used example is an easy way to see the differences between gender roles (U.S. Navy aircraft) and genetically endowed gender. In a science-based paradigm, gender is something we are born with, whereas gender roles are defined by society and are subject to change as societies evolve in normative behaviors.

Male and female brains have an equal but different intelligence, as depicted below.

- How and what we remember:
  - women take in more through each of their five senses than men do, and they store more of this material for later use
- How we process words:
  - women use more words than men, including reading and writing; both may speak the same amount in a week, but not generally read and write the same amount
- How we experience the world:
  - female eye retinas see more color and fine detail, whereas male retinas see more physical motion of objects
- Midbrain (limbic system) and emotional processing:
  - women link more of the emotional activity in the middle of the brain with brain center thoughts and words in the top of the brain

- men might need more time to process a major emotionally laden experience
- women can process it quicker
- White and gray matter in the brain—this is one of the major differences in brain structure. The more white matter we have, the more neural connections we have. Gray matter has less dense neural connectivity. The more neural connectivity exists, the more capable we are of running information through the many brain centers. The less neural connectivity we have, the less capable we are of moving information across brain processing centers. One is better or worse; everything is entirely contextual:
  - women have more white matter; men have more gray matter, as related to cognitive functioning
  - white matter connects brain centers in the neural networks
  - gray matter tends to localize brain activity to a single active brain center
  - women often are able to make crucial connections between widely disparate elements of thoughts
  - men tend to task focus on one element or pattern without distraction

There are three major areas to focus attention on relative brain differences (Gurian & Annis, 2008, p. 27):

- Differences in neural blood flow patterns
- Differences in particular structures in the brain
- Differences in brain chemistry

Differences in Neural Blood Flow Patterns

Relative to neural blood flow patterns, simply stated, where electricity is present among the cells of the brain, there is blood flow. Blood flow creates electrical impulse.

- Female brain: more neural activity in parts that think in and create words and in the parts that connect those words to memories, emotions, and sensory cues
- Male brain: more neural activity occurs in parts that use physical and kinesthetic intelligence as well as spatial mechanics and abstraction (Gurian & Annis, 2008, p. 9)

An example of males being more physical and kinesthetic-oriented has been reported in most psychology books for years. If dolls are provided to male and female infants and toddlers, boys see physical objects as physical and mechanical toys to be explored through spatial manipulation. When provided two dolls, the male is more likely than the female to throw dolls into the air or bang them together, making a crashing sound, only then to watch them fall to the ground. Girls, on the other hand, see dolls as relational, emotional, and verbal objects. They may integrate dolls into a hospital, house, or other relational environment.

Men often want to do something spatial in order to feel at home in the world and to work off stress (e.g., tossing a physical object in the air). How many times have males tossed a football or basketball in the air as they lay on the couch watching a football or basketball game? What typically happens, then, is our significant other will vocalize a reminder that we are going to break something. To which we reply, "No, I'm not." Then, without warning, what happens? The ball gets loose from our clutch.

Females, on the other hand, often bond, build cohesion, succeed against challenge, and focus their energy by other means. For example it is not uncommon for a female to suggest, "Let's talk—I just want to get this off my chest."

Relative to gray and white matter:

- Males have 6.5 times more gray matter than females
  - Gray matter processes information locally in the brain

- • Males tend to localize information in one or two centers
  - • Males tend to excel at tasks one at a time ("Don't bother me right now, I'm busy")
  - • May hear someone say, "Males are more direct and to the point"
- • Females have 10 times more white matter than males, and thus more neural connectivity
  - • White matter processes and connects information between brain processing centers
  - • Females tend to move information among different brain centers
  - • Females tend to excel at integrating and assimilating information from multiple regions, such as required for greater language facility and multitasking
  - • May hear someone say, "Women are quite creative, but in their own way"

Continuing to look at implications of blood flow, the cingulate gyrus is part of the midbrain, inside the limbic system, responsible for circulating life experiences.

- • Females have a more active cingulate gyrus than males
- • At any given point, females are running sentences, tones of voice, gestures, facial expressions, meetings, TV commercials, or arguments with a colleague through this part of the brain
- • Males don't remember as much—spend less time internally processing and can be less contextual than females
- • Females can be more sensitive in general to situational contexts because they are processing information more frequently and completely then males
- • Males are more likely to zoom in on what they perceive to be the "facts"

In further examining rest states in the brain between males and females:

- • Male brains go into a rest state more often than female brains—sort of a starry-eyed daydreaming mode
  - • Female brains don't rest or deactivate the way male brains do—remember the earlier picture of the female brain in total rest still showed activity
  - • More neural activity in a female's brain at any given point in time (again, the earlier picture)
  - • 15–20 percent more blood flow in the female brain at rest than the male brain at rest—this creates the electrical imagery detected through science tools
  - • Male brains are more prone to "zone out" during times of conversation, exhaustion, or stress
  - • Males may tap a pencil, move their feet, or swivel in their chair in an attempt to keep themselves from zoning out or allowing their brain to go into a rest state—generally an unconscious act
  - • Easy for females to interpret men as not paying attention to them or not caring

Differences in Structures of the Brain

Relative to differences in structures in the brain (Howard, 2006), the hippocampus is a significant memory center of the brain.

- • Females test better than males routinely in remembering specific and minute details (eyes sense more incoming stimulus)
- • Females have more neural pathways between hippocampus and other brain centers (white space and attendant neural connectivity)
- • Gender intelligent men will often trust what women "see" during contract negotiations—this being a combination of increased processing capability and female senses collecting more information than male senses

The amygdala is another structure in the brain. Its primary role is in the processing of memory and emotional reactions. Males and females may deal differently in emotionally charged situations. The amygdala is larger in males than females and performs a different function. In males, the amygdala pushes signals downward through the brainstem and into the physical body. In females, the amygdala pushes signals upward into talking centers. What this implies, then, is that males will potentially behave differently under emotionally charged situations than females. This conversation is tied directly to the following conversation on brain neurochemicals—namely, oxytocin, serotonin, testosterone, and vasopressin.

Differences in Brain Chemistry

Males secrete more testosterone and vasopressin (aggression and territorial chemicals) than females. Males have 10 to 20 times more testosterone than females. Females secrete more serotonin (calms impulses, reduces stress) and oxytocin (bonding chemical). Serotonin, in particular, might require some additional explanation. If an individual goes the doctor because of a depressed emotional state, doctors will frequently prescribe something called a SSRI (selective serotonin reuptake inhibitor). SSRIs allow more of our "happy" neural chemicals to pass between the synapses of our brain neurons, therefore creating a happier emotional state.

When humans feel connected to someone or something, this bonding is from oxytocin; it's what biologists call the "tend and befriend" instinct, versus testosterone's "fight or flight" instinct. Higher levels of oxytocin yield lesser levels of physical aggression.

Male testosterone cycles throughout the day. It peaks in morning hours. Between 3:00 p.m. and 5:00 pm, it is at its lowest, yielding more agreement, less aggression, and offense, leaving males more open to calming conversation. After 8:00 pm, testosterone cycles down again and oxytocin increases, allowing for more expression of feelings and conflict resolution. Given this, one might ask what time of day an individual should approach a male supervisor in hopes of having a more calm and peaceful conversation? That answer would clearly be between 3:00 p.m. and 5:00 p.m.

Stress creates increased levels of cortisol. Cortisol is our stress hormone. Meetings and other situations raise our levels of stress, and therefore cortisol. In females, increases in cortisol raises levels of oxytocin; the brain directs to reduce stress by tending and befriending, therefore protecting rational cohesion, keeping tension down, and securing social connections. In males, increases in cortisol raises levels of testosterone; the brain causes the male to assert himself independently, become aggressively known, interrupt, mark his territory, take risks, and challenge social cohesion. Cortisol, then, behaves very differently in males than it does in females. It isn't hard to visualize this situation in the many meetings we've experienced over the years, whether personally or professionally.

Leadership—Interpersonal Relationships

Females tend to be more interactive. They tend toward participative teams; the more support generated, the less stress and the more effective leaders they become. Females tend to see possible connections between each person's ideas. They are more likely to enjoy solving problems with others. They tend to be more inductive in their reasoning and more reluctant to "toot" their own horn, believing their actions speak for themselves.

Males, on the other hand, tend to be more transactional: "I'm in this to give and get something." They tend toward hierarchy and see colleagues as potential competition. Males want to move more quickly toward end goals and spend less time on each underlying piece. They tend to be more deductive in problem solving and tend to define themselves by their accomplishments and performance.

Leadership—Management Styles

Females tend to be more descriptive. They describe what they are looking for and spend more time detailing it. Females tend to not seek out conflict. They are more forgiving of others, especially men who fail. In meetings, females seek more verbal opinions. They allow people to speak longer. Females are less direct and more consensus-oriented. They tend to have longer memories of conflicts and emotional stresses; this is due to the more active cingulate gyrus and more time spent in the limbic system for processing of emotions.

Males, on the other hand, tend to be more prescriptive and direct, telling people what to do. They tend to seek out more direct conflict than women; their hierarchy and power are the direct result of testosterone levels. Males may perceive females to be holding a grudge, this because females remember more interactions. In meetings, males tend to interrupt more. They are more right-brained (i.e., spatial); therefore, they find lots of words to be frustrating. Males are more directive and direct in their input requests. They have shorter memories of conflicts; this in part because of a less active cingulate gyrus and less time spent in the limbic system for processing of emotions.

Leadership—Things We Might See

Males tend to bond through short exchanges—a pat on the back or words of praise. Their goal achievement is tied to action more than words or emotions. It is not uncommon for fathers to promote risk-taking and independence of others (e.g., fathers push children away from caregivers and encourage them to "grow up" more so than females). This is manifested in the example of a father suggesting, "Let him ride the bike. He'll be all right." The mother replies, "He'll fall at the end of the driveway and get hurt," to which the father might reply, "That's all right. It will only happen once, and then he will learn."

Females tend to bond by extending conversations in exploratory ways; they tend to interconnect data and share common experiences. Females try to ascertain the needs of a person, sensing how morale impacts productivity. They seek a multitude of possibilities for a product as well as another's untapped capabilities. Females work toward helping others express emotions through words, not simply actions. They express empathy when someone's feelings are hurt ("How are you feeling?") and may relinquish personal independence to be cognizant of another person's needs.

Leadership—In Meetings

Male brains rest more often and may keep awake by fidgeting, tapping, clicking a pen, or looking away. Male brains are not necessarily wired for multitasking. This may cause frustration when others are having conversations that don't seem focused (remember the brain picture at rest). Male brains process fewer words and are more likely to zone out if discussions become lengthy or wordy. Male brains are wired for aggression (testosterone), and may sometimes dominate the meeting. When meetings become stressful, cortisol increases testosterone, creating increased male competitiveness and aggression.

Female brains are wired to cross-connect information from both sides of brain. They may appear to move from one topic to another seemingly unrelated topic, though they may be connecting dots. Female brains are wired for less competitiveness, therefore, if their opinions are not heard, they may feel left out. If meetings become stressful, the stress hormone cortisol increases oxytocin, causing females to more readily seek social cohesion. It is not uncommon; males may interrupt females when they feel the "word limit" has been met.

Relative to return on equity and total return to shareholders, Gurian and Annis (2008) report companies with the highest representation of females in top management teams have 35.1 percent higher return on equity and 34 percent higher total return to shareholders.

In inquiring into leadership traits, the Pew Research Center (2008) performed a survey and found the following in figure 13.2:

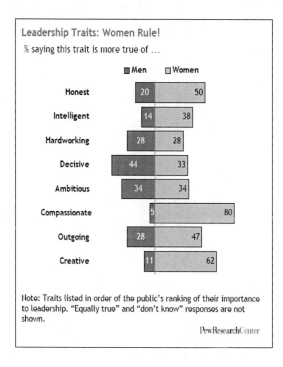

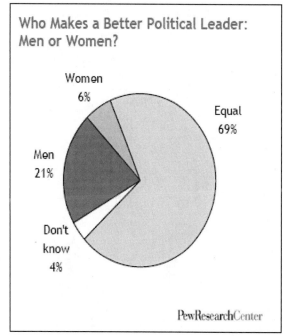

Figure 13.2. Leadership Traits More True of . . . , Survey Results, Pew Research Center

Dan Abrams, in his 2011 book *Man Down,* makes observations on which fields females are better at than males. Three fields of study that seem to make some level of immediate sense relative to brain neuro-chemicals and structure are:

- Women are better doctors: Females spend more time with patients. This could be the direct result of the brain neural chemicals oxytocin and serotonin. These two chemicals create the "tend and befriend" impulse, coupled with serotonin being our "happy" neural chemical.
- Women are better at faking attraction: Females seem tougher to read. Again, this isn't all that difficult to envision. Females possessing greater levels of oxytocin and serotonin may simply be trying to carry on a conversation with their male counterpart. Males, however, don't always view it that way. It is not uncommon for males to view this interaction as being more than a casual conversation, and in fact, perhaps being some form of communication based on attraction (hence the faking attraction play).
- Women have better memories: Everyday events, words, objects, and pictures are all moving through the female brain at a greater rate than their male counterparts, predominately due to the increased white matter, which comes with increased neural connections. This, coupled with female eyes and other senses picking up more environmental information, makes this suggestion feasible.

Chapter 14

Motivation and Leadership—Why We Do What We Do

What motivates individuals to produce? Why is it that what seems to motivate one person does not necessarily motivate another? I remember many times in my career where I said, "Man, if I made that amount of money, I'd work all the hours anyone ever asked." Then I did make that amount of money, and it didn't seem enough after a period of time. I remember thinking, "If they would pay me $10 per hour for every hour of overtime worked, I'd work all the hours I could get." But then, after a few weeks of making that kind of money, the money didn't seem so important to me anymore, and I didn't want the hours.

The field of motivation seeks to understand the causation of specific actions. Motivation theorists do not necessarily agree with each other about the cause. For example, take a shooting incident: there may be three different perspectives on the cause for the incident.

- The shooter had a bursting loose of furious anger, perhaps pent up for many years and originally directed at the parents.
- The shooter had a history of reinforcement for violent actions. The incident was probably caused by a lack, or absence, of reinforcement at the present time.
- The shooting incident was a result of reasoned, if not rational decision making. The individual simply decided that people were the cause for his or her misery.

Motivation may be defined as: "The willingness to exert high levels of energy toward organizational goals, conditioned by the effort's ability to satisfy some individual need" (Robbins, 1999, p. 50).

In this chapter we are going to discuss the top motivation theories. Namely:

- Need theories
- Goal-setting theory
- Reinforcement theory
- Equity theory
- Expectancy theory

Need Theories

Need theories are designed to explain and predict job satisfaction. There are three theories that we will examine, in this category:

- Maslow's hierarchy of needs theory
- Herzberg's motivation-hygiene theory
- McClelland and Atkinson's need theory

Abraham Maslow (1908–1970) was a humanistic psychologist. Maslow's hierarchy of needs is perhaps the most widely recognized theory of motivation. The hierarchy is depicted in figure 14.1.

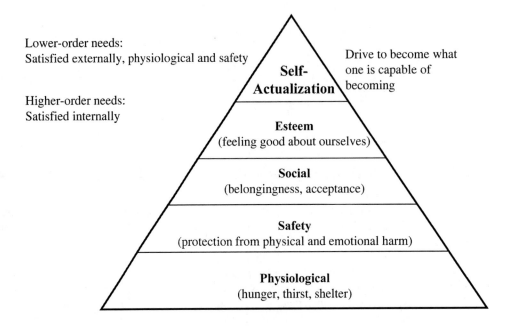

Figure 14.1. Maslow's Hierarchy of Needs

Maslow's hierarchy assumes that we must pass through each phase before we can begin the next. At any point in time we may fall back to a previous phase, but we must satisfy that phase before we can continue. The theory further says that as each lower-level need is satisfied, it ceases to be a need, and the next higher-level need is active.

An excellent example of this is the story of a company president who was trying desperately to build morale and a sense of family in his organization. He had just initiated two kinder and gentler policies, namely, casual dress and 9/80. 9/80 meant that the employee could work 80 hours in nine days and take the tenth day (Friday) off.

The organization however, was on their third owner in as many years and had seen a reduction in workforce from 8,600 people ten years earlier to about 2,000 people. At that rate, the reduction averaged 660 people per year. In this type of climate, the employees were terribly concerned about their jobs and ultimately their long-term well-being.

During this time, an employee entered into a discussion with a member of the human resources organization. The employee had bachelor's and master's degrees in engineering and ten years of experience. The employee was nearly in tears when he explained that he was afraid to purchase a new lawn mower for fear he would lose his job and be unable to make the payments.

Aside from the obvious concern this individual was experiencing, he was basically at the physiological level in Maslow's hierarchy. That is, he was concerned about being able to pay the bills and provide basic shelter for his family. The organization's president, on the other hand, was trying to satisfy a need at the social level, that is, he was trying to create a sense of belonging and acceptance.

The organization's president, on hearing this from the human resources organization, decided to change his upcoming presentation to the employees, to now address the brighter future that he saw by way of the opening up of key markets, and how the organization was going to invest in the technology to allow entry into these markets. The employees unanimously applauded this newly revealed direction, and then the 9/80 and casual dress program had meaning and value.

The motivation-hygiene theory was proposed by psychologist Frederick Herzberg (1923–2000) in the late 1950s. Believing that an individual's relation to his or her work is a basic one, and his or her attitude toward work determines success or failure, Herzberg investigated the question, "What do people want from their jobs?"

Herzberg, after significant research, determined that there existed two categories: motivators, which were factors that increased job satisfaction, and hygiene, which were factors that eliminated job dissatisfaction. These are depicted as follows:

Motivators	Hygiene Factors
achievement	supervision
recognition	work conditions
work itself	salary
responsibility	relationship with peers
advancement	status
growth	security

Motivators contribute to job satisfaction or no satisfaction. Hygiene factors contribute to job dissatisfaction or no dissatisfaction. Removing dissatisfaction factors does not necessarily make the job satisfying (i.e., making a hygiene factor better does not make us more motivated, it simply makes us less dissatisfied).

According to Dessler (2000, p. 408), David McClelland and John Atkinson agree with Herzberg that higher-level needs are most important at work. They have studied three needs that they believe are especially important: affiliation, power, and achievement.

People with strong need for achievement have a predisposition to strive for success. They are highly motivated to obtain the satisfaction that comes from accomplishing a challenging task or goal. They prefer tasks that they have a reasonable chance of accomplishing, and they avoid tasks that are either mundane or too difficult.

People with strong need for power desire to influence others directly by making suggestions, giving their opinions and evaluations, and trying to talk others into things. They enjoy roles requiring persuasion, such as teaching or public speaking, as well as positions such as leaders or clergymen.

An individual's need for power is manifested and visible through an understanding of their other needs. For example, a person with a high need for power but a low need for warm and supportive relationships might become dictatorial, while one with a high need for relationships might become a clergymen or a social worker.

People with a strong need for affiliation are highly motivated to maintain strong, warm relationships with friends and relatives. In meetings they try to establish friendly relationships, often by being agreeable or giving emotional support.

Goal-Setting Theory

Goal-setting theory purports that specific and difficult goals lead to higher levels of performance. Research shows:

- Specific goals increase performance
- Difficult goals, when accepted, result in higher performance than do easy goals
- Feedback leads to higher performance than does no feedback

Goal-setting theory proposes that an individual's purpose directs his or her actions. An example of this theory is, "Do your best" versus "strive for 85 percent or higher." The more quantifiable the goal, the more specific the goal, and the more likely the motivation to perform to higher levels.

Reinforcement Theory

Where goal-setting theory proposes that an individual's purpose directs his or her actions, Reinforcement theory purports that behavior is externally caused. That is, if an act is positively reinforced within a reasonable period of time, then the behavior is more likely to reoccur. In other words, behavior is a function of its consequences.

Reinforcement theory has an impressive record of predicting factors, such as quality and quantity of work, persistence of effort, absenteeism, tardiness, and accident rates. It does offer much insight into employee satisfaction or the decision to quit.

Summarizing reinforcement theory:

- Behavior is a function of its consequences
- Behavior is environmentally caused
- Ignores the inner state of individual and focuses solely on the consequences of the action.

Equity Theory

Equity theory was developed by J. Stacy Adams. It proposes that employees perceive what they get from a job as outcomes, in relation to what they put into it (inputs). The employees then compare their input-outcome ratio to other applicable parties.

Equity theory purports that the employee can make four referent comparisons:

- Self inside—an employee's experience in a different position inside his or her current organization
- Self outside—an employee's experiences outside his or her current organization
- Other inside—an employee's experience to an individual or group inside the organization
- Other outside—an employee's experience to an individual or group outside the organization

Figure 14.2 depicts this relationship and summarizes this theory.

$$O/Ia < O/Ib \quad \text{Inequity: under rewarded}$$
$$O/Ia = O/Ib \quad \text{Equity}$$
$$O/Ia > O/Ib \quad \text{Inequity: over rewarded}$$

Figure 14.2. Perception of Equity

Expectancy Theory

Expectancy theory offers the most comprehensive explanation of motivation to date. It was created by Victor Vroom. The theory basically states that the strength of an individual to act in a certain way depends on the strength of an expectation that the act will be followed by a given outcome, and on the attractiveness of that outcome to the individual.

Basically it focuses on three relationships:

- Effort—Performance: probability that exerting a given amount of effort will lead to performance
- Performance—Reward: performing at a particular level will lead to a desired outcome
- Reward—Personal goals: degree to which a reward satisfies a personal goal

Figure 14.3 depicts this relationship.

Individual Effort $\xrightarrow{\quad 1 \quad}$ Individual Performance $\xrightarrow{\quad 2 \quad}$ Organizational Rewards $\xrightarrow{\quad 3 \quad}$ Personal Goals

1. Effort-Performance Relationship
2. Performance-Reward Relationship
3. Reward-Personal Goals Relationship

$$\text{Performance} = f\,(A \times M \times O)$$

where, A = ability
M = motivation
O = opportunity

Figure 14.3. Expectancy Theory

Again, the concept is that individual effort will lead to individual performance, which will lead to organizational goals, and ultimately to personal goals. Performance, however, is a function of the individual's ability, motivation, and opportunity. If either one of the three is insufficient, then the individual may not be able to perform satisfactorily enough to merit organizational rewards perceived necessary to achieve personal goals.

A good example of this is where there is a set of identified and documented abilities, skills, and knowledge necessary to move into the next higher job grade. However, there is not the opportunity to fill a job that requires this level of job grade. The individual, therefore, may have all of the necessary personal tools to move up, but he or she simply lacks opportunity. If this condition lasts for a prolonged period of time, the individual may seek other employment because he or she cannot satisfy his or her personal goals. This is a very real challenge in today's flatter organizational models. The solution to this is to provide peer-level, horizontal opportunities that will allow the individual the opportunity for personal growth and financial gain, without having to move vertically in the organization.

Chapter 15

Organization Design Models—Not Right or Wrong, More or Less Applicable

Theorists have devised many ways to partition an organization into subunits, with the intent of improving efficiency. Additionally, the intent of partitioning an organization is to decentralize authority, responsibility, and accountability. The mechanism through which partitioning is accomplished is called "departmentalization." In all cases, the objective is to arrive at an orderly arrangement of interdependent components.

Many basic management courses refer to the three-variable formula below:

- Accountability = Authority + Responsibility

Authority is the power granted to individuals (possibly) by their position in the company, so they can make decisions for other individuals to follow.

Responsibility is the obligation incurred by individuals in their roles in the formal organization in order to effectively perform assignments.

Accountability is being totally answerable for the satisfactory completion of a given assignment.

In the above formula, they teach us in management school that if you are given any two variables without the third, there is a high probability of some form of failure. Certainly, this seems most obvious when we are given responsibility and held accountable, but have no formal authority to execute. Likewise, authority and responsibility, without accountability, seems to promote subjectivity in decision making.

Traditional

In the traditional organizational structure, organizational units are based on distinct common specialties, such as engineering, manufacturing, and finance. Figure 15.1 depicts an example of a traditional organization structure.

There are many advantages to the traditional (functional) structure. Below are listed some of the more pertinent ones:

- Easier budgeting and cost control is possible. This is true, for example, because all costs related to the above finance organization are rolled up to a single functional manager.
- Efficient use of collective experience and facilities.
- Institutional framework for planning and control. Under this type of organizational structure, planning as well as control is administered from a single functional stovepipe at the division level.
- All activities receive benefit from the most advanced technology. In this type of structure, great strength comes from focusing at the top the most state-of-the-art methodologies, technologies, and practices, and then disseminating these throughout all organizations utilizing functional resources.

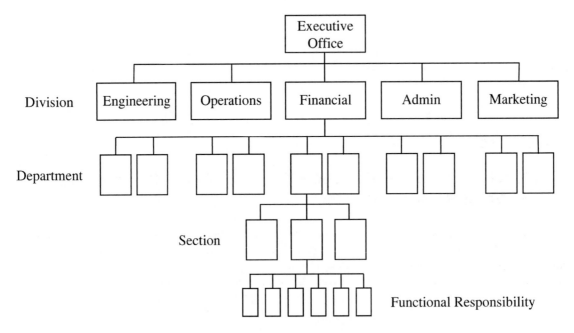

Figure 15.1. Traditional Organizational Design Model

- Allocates resources in anticipation of future business. When using a functional organization structure, the functional manager has responsibility for allocating resources based on immediate needs as well as future needs.
- Effective use of production elements.
- Career continuity and growth for personnel. Under a single functional umbrella, the functional manager can assure that all personnel under that umbrella receive like education and can assure that, for example, more senior personnel are assigned projects with increasingly greater responsibility or visibility, thus aiding in career opportunities and development.
- Well suited for mass production of items.
- Communication channels are vertical and well established.

The traditional (functional) organization has many disadvantages as well. Again, the more predominant ones are discussed below:

- There is no central project authority. With this type of organizational structure, the many functions simply come together, usually centered around the type of program, and contribute to the accomplishment of the program's goals.
- Little or no project planning or reporting. Without a single program manager to be held accountable for the program's overall tasks, the functional managers simply concern themselves with their functional responsibility, therefore causing potential programmatic concerns.
- Weak interface with the customer, no single focal point. While this may not always be true, the absence of a program manager may cause multiple interfaces through functional managers.
- Poor horizontal communication across functions. Employees whose care and feeding comes from a functional stovepipe will generally take great care to nurture those individuals in that

stovepipe who have supervisory control. Naturally, a stronger bond with functional management will occur over interfaces with horizontal functions.

- Difficult to integrate multidisciplinary tasks.
- Tendency of decisions to favor strongest functional group. This is true especially if the functional group is taking the lead on a given program.
- Response to customer needs is slow, primarily because functions are more concerned with functional activities than program activities.
- Ideas tend to be functionally oriented.
- Projects have a tendency to fall behind schedule. This stems from a lack of a single program manager tending to programmatic concerns.

Product

In a product organizational structure, distinct operating units are organized around, and given responsibility for, a major product or product line. Figure 15.2 depicts a typical product-oriented structure.

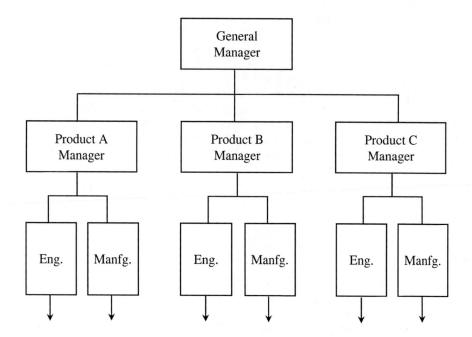

Figure 15.2. Product Organizational Design Model

Product organizational structures are centered on major product or brand lines. For example, if an organization produced dish soaps, toothpaste, facial tissue, and so on, each might become a product structure and have its own product manager. Worth noting in the above is that other functions are replicated within each product organization. This is discussed further below.

Advantages and disadvantages of this type of organizational structure are as follows:
Advantages:

- Strong control by a single product authority.

- Rapid reaction time. The product manager has all of the resources he or she needs to be successful, and can command these resources in any way required to satisfy the customer's changing needs.
- Encourages performance, schedule, and cost tradeoffs.
- Personnel are loyal to a single individual. Where that individual was the functional manager in the traditional structure, it is the product manager in this type of structure.
- Interfaces well with outside units. Here a single product manager is given primary responsibility for interfacing with other units, both externally and internally.
- Good interface with customer.
- Strong communication channels. It helps in this type of structure that all employees have a common goal: to produce a single product or brand of product. This builds a unified allegiance to a single cause.

Disadvantages:

- Inefficient use of resources; duplication of effort. This may be the single greatest argument against this type of organizational structure. The fact that, in the above example, engineering, finance, and so on are duplicated for every product line implies full-time employees are being used where part-time employees may only be required.
- Does not develop strong functional technology. Single individuals performing a single function on the product do not have the time or the breadth of exposure to see what the latest and greatest methodologies, techniques, and practices may be.
- Does not prepare for future business. Without functional oversight, the entire product organization is focused on design, development, and delivery of a single product or brand. If greater vision does exist, it typically is limited to similar, or like, products.
- Less opportunity for technical interchange among projects.
- Minimal career opportunity and continuity for project personnel. In other words, there may be limited growth potential.
- Difficulty in balancing workloads as projects phase in and out. Individuals may not have work in a particular time frame, but must be kept busy doing something until that specific type of function is again in demand.

Matrix

The matrix structure is a hybrid organization that attempts to balance the use of human resources as people are shifted from one project to another. It can be viewed as a project organization superimposed over a functional organization. Figure 15.3 is an example of a typical matrix organizational structure.

The matrix structure is more complex than either the traditional or product-oriented structures. To this end, it requires some basic ground rules to be successful:

- Participants must spend committed time on a project; this ensures a degree of loyalty.
- Horizontal as well as vertical channels must exist for making decisions.
- There must be quick and effective methods for conflict resolutions.
- There must be good communication channels between managers.
- All managers must have input into the planning process.
- Both horizontal and vertical managers must be willing to negotiate for resources.
- Horizontal line must be willing to operate as a separate entity except for administrative purposes.

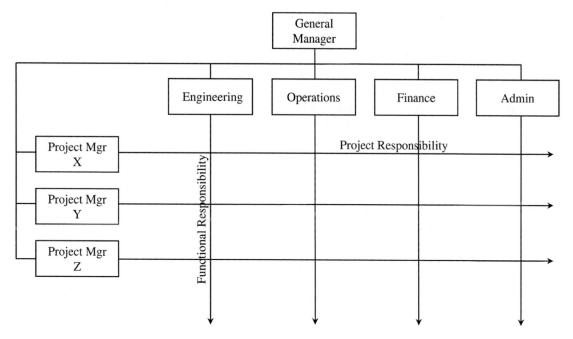

Figure 15.3. Matrix Organizational Design Model

Project management is more behavioral than quantitative. Interpersonal and communicative skills are extremely important attributes of the project manager.

In a matrix organizational structure:

- There should, ideally, be no disruption due to dual accountability.
- A difference in functional management judgment should not delay work in progress.

Advantages of this type of organizational structure are:

- Combines the strengths of both project and functional organizations.
- Provides a good interface with the outside customer.
- Promotes effective interdisciplinary task integration.
- Promotes an efficient use of production resources.
- Promotes effective project control, as programmatic concerns are assigned to a single individual.
- Promotes career continuity and professional growth, as each functional individual has a home after project completion.
- Perpetuates technology. By this, functional resources gain the benefit of a functional strength, which can be transferred to the program of the day.
- Functional knowledge is available for all projects on an equal basis.

Disadvantages of this type of organizational structure include:

- Dual accountability of personnel. This is perhaps the biggest threat to this type of structure. Personnel will generally favor whoever it is that completes their performance review and subsequently has control over their income adjustments. Confusion here can derail a unified effort.

- Conflicts between project and functional managers. This issue will be discussed in more detail below.
- Profit and loss accountability is more difficult.
- There are continuously changing priorities, especially on the part of the functional managers, who control the resources.
- The balance of power between functional and project managers must be watched. Later we discuss their respective perspectives of what is important.
- Functional managers might be biased toward their own priorities.
- Because of the duality of authority, employees may not feel a strong commitment to a single source.
- Employees may feel confused about loyalty.

Project managers have different concerns than do functional managers. A project manager is concerned with:

- What is to be done?
- When will the task be done?
- What is the importance of the task?
- How much money is available to do the task?
- How well has the total project been done?

The functional manager has a more hands-on concern, as listed below.

- How will the task be done?
- Where will the task be done?
- Who will do the task?
- How well has the functional input been integrated into the project?

Project Management

The project management structure attempts to further organize the project/functional (matrix) structure by providing a single point of authority, responsibility, and accountability for all projects, in much the same manner as a functional manager.

Figure 15.4 depicts the typical project management structure.

The advantages and disadvantages of this form of organizational structure are as follows.

Advantages:

- Better overall control of projects. A single director of projects can work with the numerous project managers to ensure uniformity in execution.
- More consistent customer relations.
- Better overall project visibility. The director of projects can ensure that all programs report the same information in the same manner.
- Improved coordination among company divisions.
- Accelerated development of managers due to breadth of project responsibility.

Disadvantages:

- May be too much shifting of personnel from one project to another.
- May be potential conflict with functional managers. The conflict should be less between the individual functional managers and the director of projects than between the individual functional managers and the individual program managers.

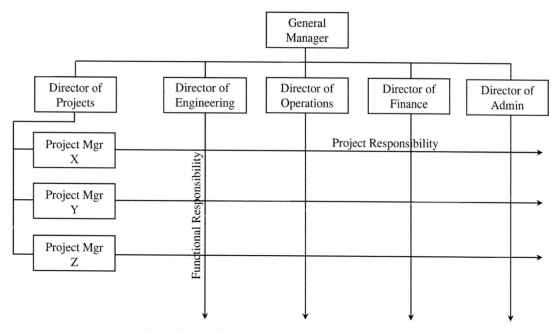

Figure 15.4. Project Management Organizational Design Model

- Functional managers may resist taking direction from a director of projects because to do so would imply an admission that the project manager might be next in line to the division manager.

Criteria for Selecting an Organizational Structure

When looking the reasons why an organization might select one form of organization versus another, three points are applicable.

- Technology—Functional organizations tend to have greater process and technology focuses.
- Communications—Traditional and product organizational structures tend to provide clearer communication paths.
- Responsibility—Product structures very clearly identify the responsible party; matrix structures are not as clear.

Summary Remarks

Just to summarize in hopes of providing additional guidance:

- No single structure is optimal for all organizations.
- Organizational structure may, and will, change to meet changing requirements.
- There is no such thing as a good or bad organizational structure; there are only appropriate and inappropriate ones.

Chapter 16

Building Teams—Understanding Ourselves and Others through MBTI

Have you ever been in a meeting where you or a coworker might have suggested an idea, only to have it abruptly shot down by someone else? Her or his reason for shooting it down may have been that the budget just didn't exist, or the resources weren't available, or even that it simply did not compute given other considerations. Perhaps, during this same meeting, you sailed another test balloon, only to have it shot down by the same person. Then, continuing in this vein, you floated another idea, and again it, too, was popped. After a number of these failed attempts to spur support for your bigger idea, you may have looked over at the individual and thought they had exhibited a great deal of negativity. Further, you may have thought that there was something about this other person that sort of rubbed you the wrong way, and perhaps, you began to not like that other individual for so quickly shooting down your ideas. Maybe you even began to think that the other individual was intentionally deflating your ideas.

What this section deals with is attempting to understand ourselves and (subsequently) others better. In doing so, we begin to realize that others may not be doing things out of spite, but instead are doing what comes naturally to them, which is thinking differently than ourselves. They collect, organize, and present data in a manner different than, perhaps, we do. That does not make their methods less right; to the contrary, it brings to the table a potentially different perspective that, when combined with our own way of doing things, creates a significant synergy.

Sensing (S) and Intuition (N)

From a sensing, "S," perspective, people who prefer to gather information through sensing:

- Focus on what is actual; they tend to focus on the present, the here and now
- Focus on data available to the senses: sight, smell, touch, feel, hearing

From an intuition, "N," perspective, people who prefer to gather data through intuition:

- Focus on connections between data
- Focus on patterns, meanings, or theoretical explanations

What's interesting to do at this point as an exercise, is to break the "S" group out from the "N" group. Show both groups a brightly colored leaf and ask each group to talk about it. The sensing group will invariably describe the physical characteristics of the leaf, such as its size, shape, color, and other things they see with their eyes. The intuitive group, on the other hand, will jot down phrases of things such as "football games," "the smell of leaves burning," "Charlie Brown and Lucy," and "hot apple cider with cinnamon sticks." Their descriptions are indicative of their preferred way of gathering and thinking about the data. The sensing group is much more focused on detail, while the intuitive group is more pattern or "blue-sky-oriented."

Thinking (T) and Feeling (F)

When we talk about ways of making decisions, the opposites here are "thinking" and "feeling":

- People who make decisions using a "thinking" perspective tend to apply logical principles to their decision making.
- People who make decisions using a "feeling" perspective tend to make decisions through a process of valuing their own feelings, others' feelings, and organizations to which they feel a commitment.

One can usually tell the difference between someone who prefers thinking to feeling in decision making by asking a very simple question, "Tell me about . . ." The individuals with a thinking preference will generally respond with something on the order of, "I think . . . ," where those with a feeling preference will say, "I feel . . ." Thinkers, as well, will be more object- and activity-oriented, whereas feelers will generally be more people-oriented.

Extraversion (E) and Introversion (I)

Aside from the way in which we gather information, "S" or "N," and the way in which we structure, prioritize, and make decisions, "T" or "F," there are differences in our orientation to the outside world and direction of energy. These differences are identified as extraversion, "E," and introversion, "I."

People exhibiting a strong preference for extraversion focus their energy and attention primarily on the outside world, while people with a strong preference for introversion focus their energy and attention on the inner world of ideas, values, and experience.

Have you ever tried to leave a party of some type, and the other person in the car began a series unending questions before you even had a chance to respond? The other person may have said, "What did you think of the party? Do you like it? How about that garden in the back? Wasn't it really cool? I thought the party went pretty well. I couldn't believe . . ." Perhaps at this point you may have said, "Enough already! Will you just shut up for a while?"

Extraverted people tend to think out of their heads in the area just above, sort of like a cartoon caption. Introverted people, however, like to internalize and reflect on what was said. Whereas extraverts tend to live by the sequence ready, fire, aim, introverts tend to collect, assimilate, reflect, and when ready, speak. This very sequence causes me to listen when an introvert wishes to say something. I know when my introverted friends have something to say that they generally have thought it through well beforehand.

Extraverts, on the other hand, formulate their final opinions as a matter of verbal discussion outside of their heads. So when an extraverted individual says something, he or she is most probably waiting to formalize the thought once a series of exchanges has taken place between the sender and the receiver. If the receiver is an introverted individual, the extraverted individual saying something she or he may not mean causes confusion unnecessarily. For example:

Extraverted individual: "Blah, blah, blah, blah blah."
Introverted individual: "What did you just say?"
Extraverted individual: "I don't know, what?"
Introverted individual: "You just said, 'Blah, blah, blah, blah.'"
Extraverted individual: "I did? I didn't mean it."
Introverted individual: "Well, if you said it, you must certainly feel that way."
Extraverted individual: "No. Not really. I was just talking out loud."
Introverted individual: "Well, if you didn't mean it, why did you say it?"
Extraverted individual "I don't know! I guess I was just talking. I really didn't mean it."
Introverted individual "Well, if you are going to be saying things just to be saying things, how will I know when you mean what you're saying and when you don't?"
Extraverted individual: "I don't know. Just ask me, I guess."

Judging (J) and Perceiving (P)

Some individuals direct their decision-making process (thinking or feeling) toward the outside world (regardless of their extraversion or introversion). The Myers-Briggs Type Indicator (MBTI) terms these individuals as judging, "J." Individuals with a judging preference prefer their outside world to be orderly, clear, planned, and scheduled.

Other individuals direct their process for information gathering (sensing or intuition) toward the external world (regardless of their extraversion or introversion). MBTI terms these individuals as perceiving, "P." Individuals with a perceiving preference direct their information gathering from the outside world. Because of this, they like to keep their external environment as open and unstructured as possible.

Type Combinations

The MBTI personality inventory has four sets of opposites that result in sixteen possible combinations. The number identified through participating in the assessment depicts the strength the individual favors a particular opposite. A table can be drawn that depicts the sixteen possible combinations of types. Figure 16.1 reflects these combinations.

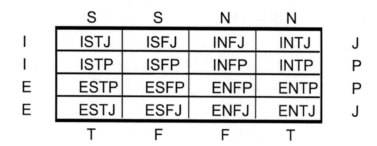

	S	S	N	N	
I	ISTJ	ISFJ	INFJ	INTJ	J
I	ISTP	ISFP	INFP	INTP	P
E	ESTP	ESFP	ENFP	ENTP	P
E	ESTJ	ESFJ	ENFJ	ENTJ	J
	T	F	F	T	

Figure 16.1. Type Combinations

The types share a preference for ways of gathering information (sensing/intuition) and ways of making decisions (thinking/feeling).

Type and Organizational Change

In discussing organizational change, Fitzgerald and Kirby (1997, p. 12) provide the following:

- In the top left-hand quadrant of a type table are four types that share preferences for introversion and sensing. The quick phrase to describe the IS reaction to proposals for change is, "Let's keep what we have."
- The types in the top right-hand quadrant of the type table share preferences for introversion and intuition. The quick phrase to describe the IN proposal for change is, "Let me go away and think about it—I'll get back to you."
- In the bottom left-hand quadrant of the type table are types that share preferences for extraversion and sensing; these types respond to change proposals by saying, "Let's just do it."
- The types in the bottom right-hand quadrant of the type table share preferences for EN and typically respond to change by saying, "Whatever there is, let's change it."

The four types in the corner squares of the type table share a preference for thinking and judging; these types have been referred to as "tough-minded." The combination of thinking and judging means that these types extravert their thinking, using it to plan, structure, and systemize their external environment. They rationally analyze likely consequences of various alternatives and make quick decisions based on logic.

Type Dynamics

The synergy that evolves from summing the individual preferences is referred to as type dynamics. MBTI provides relative preferences on four scales:

- Extraversion (E)/Introversion (I)
- Sensing (S)/Intuition (N)
- Thinking (T)/Feeling (F)
- Judging (J)/Perceiving (P)

It is natural to conclude that each combination is simply a summation of each individual type preference. This, however, is not the case.

Using MBTI's type theory, the order in which we favor these preferences is inborn. The four-letter type formula is a shorthand mechanism for telling us the order in which an individual prefers to use the four mental functions. Figure 16.2 depicts the order of preferences for each of the sixteen type combinations.

ISTJ	**ISFJ**	**INFJ**	**INTJ**
Sensing	Sensing	Intuition	Intuition
Thinking	Feeling	Feeling	Thinking
Feeling	Thinking	Thinking	Feeling
Intuition	Intuition	Sensing	Sensing
ISTP	**ISFP**	**INFP**	**INTP**
Thinking	Feeling	Feeling	Thinking
Sensing	Sensing	Intuition	Intuition
Intuition	Intuition	Sensing	Sensing
Feeling	Thinking	Thinking	Feeling
ESTP	**ESFP**	**ENFP**	**ENTP**
Sensing	Sensing	Intuition	Intuition
Thinking	Feeling	Feeling	Thinking
Feeling	Thinking	Thinking	Feeling
Intuition	Intuition	Sensing	Sensing
ESTJ	**ESFJ**	**ENFJ**	**ENTJ**
Thinking	Feeling	Feeling	Thinking
Sensing	Sensing	Intuition	Intuition
Intuition	Intuition	Sensing	Sensing
Feeling	Thinking	Thinking	Feeling

Figure 16.2. Order of Preferences by Type

Having an understanding of our order of preferences allows us to more readily see the potential reasons for conflict in an organization, team, or even our personal lives. Figure 16.3 depicts two types indicative of this potential problem.

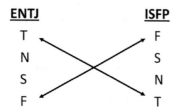

ENTJ   **ISFP**

T   F

N   S

S   N

F   T

Figure 16.3. Type Preference Order Potential for Conflict

In this example, the greatest strength of, or most preferred function for, an ENTJ is thinking. The least preferred function is feeling. For an ISFP, however, the most preferred function is feeling, whereas the least preferred function is thinking. This type of combination poses many situations for potential conflict. For example, between two spouses, one might suggest that they should buy a new home because it feels like the right time to do so. While the ENTJ spouse might suggest that the budget, being reviewed over time, does not support the additional expense of the new home, the ISFP, on the other hand, might argue that money is not everything, and that sometimes you simply have to proceed based on what feels like the right thing to do. The ISFP spouse might continue the discussion by reminding the ENTJ that everything has worked out in the past and it will be all right.

This type of conflict between the ENTJ's logical, rational, and methodical position is in stark contrast to the ISFP's spontaneous, heartfelt, value-laden approach.

Summary Thoughts by Type

The following types appear in Fitzgerald and Kirby's *Developing Leaders* (1997, pp. 68–69):

ISTJ

Serious, quiet, earn success by concentration and thoroughness. Practical, orderly, matter-of-fact, logical, realistic, and dependable. See to it that everything is well organized. Take responsibility. Make up their own minds as to what should be accomplished and work toward it steadily, regardless of protests or distractions.

ISFJ

Quiet, friendly, responsible, and conscientious. Work devotedly to meet obligations. Lend stability to any project or group. Thorough, painstaking, accurate. Their interests are usually not technical. Can be patient with necessary details. Loyal, considerate, perceptive, concerned with how other people feel.

INTJ

Have original minds and great drive for their own ideas and purposes. Have long-range vision and quickly find meaningful patterns in external events. In fields that appeal to them, they have a fine power to organize a job and carry it through. Skeptical, critical, independent, determined, have high standards of competence and performance.

ESFP

Outgoing, accepting, friendly, enjoy everything, and make things more fun for others by their enjoyment. Like action and making things happen. Know what's going on and join in eagerly. Find remembering facts easier than mastering theories. Are best in situations that need sound common sense and practical ability with people.

ISTP

Cool onlookers—quiet, reserved, observing and analyzing life with detached curiosity and unexpected flashes of original humor. Usually interested in cause and effect, how and why mechanical things work, and in organizing facts using logical principles. Excel at getting to the core of a practical problem and finding the solution.

ESTP

Good at on-the-spot problem solving. Like action, enjoy whatever comes along. Tend to like mechanical things and sports, with friends on the side. Adaptable, tolerant, pragmatic; focused on getting results. Dislike long explanations. Are best with real things that can be worked, handled, taken apart, or put together.

INFJ

Succeed by perseverance, originality, and desire to do whatever is needed or wanted. Put their best efforts into their work. Quietly forceful, conscientious, concerned for others. Respected for their firm principles. Likely to be honored and followed for their clear visions as to how best to serve the common good.

ISFP

Retiring, quietly friendly, sensitive, kind, modest about their abilities. Shun disagreements, do not force their opinions or values on others. Usually do not care to lead but are often loyal followers. Often relaxed about getting things done because they enjoy the present moment and do not want to spoil it by undue haste or exertion.

ESTJ

Practical, realistic, matter-of-fact, with a natural head for business or mechanics. Not interested in abstract theories; want learning to have direct and immediate application. Like to organize and run activities. Often make good administrators; are decisive, quickly move to implement decisions, take care of routine details.

INFP

Quiet observers, idealistic, loyal. Important that outer life be congruent with inner values. Curious, quick to see possibilities, often serve as catalysts to implement ideas. Adaptable, flexible, and accepting unless a value is threatened. Want to understand people and ways of fulfilling human potential. Little concern with possessions or surroundings.

ENFP

Warmly enthusiastic, high-spirited, ingenious, imaginative. Able to do almost anything that interests them. Quick with a solution for any difficulty and ready to help anyone with a problem. Often rely on their ability to improvise instead of preparing in advance. Can usually find compelling reasons for whatever they want.

INTP

Quiet and reserved. Especially enjoy theoretical or scientific pursuits. Like solving problems with logic and analysis. Interested mainly in ideas, with little liking for parties or small talk. Tend to have sharply defined interests. Need careers where some strong interest can be used and useful.

ENTJ

Frank, decisive, leaders in activities. Develop and implement comprehensive systems to solve organizational problems. Good in anything that requires reasoning and intelligent talk, such as public speaking. Are usually well informed and enjoy adding to their fund of knowledge.

ESFJ

Warm-hearted, talkative, popular, conscientious, born cooperators, active committee members. Need harmony and may be good at creating it. Always doing something nice for someone. Work best with encouragement and praise. Main interest is in things that directly and visibly affect people's lives.

ENFJ

Responsive and responsible. Feel real concern for what others think or want, and try to handle things with due regard for the other's feelings. Can present a proposal or lead a group discussion with ease and tact. Sociable, popular, sympathetic. Responsive to praise and criticism.

ENTP

Quick, ingenious, good at many things. ENTPs make for stimulating company, are alert and outspoken. They may argue for fun on either side of a question. Resourceful in solving new and challenging problems, but may neglect routine assignments. ENTPs are apt to turn to one new interest after another. They are skillful in finding logical reasons for what they want.

Chapter 17

Capitalizing on the Collective Knowledge of the World

To discuss capitalizing on the world's collective intelligence/knowledge is to recognize the discussion is not singular in nature and, in fact, is stitched with multiple threads, each with its own story. To fully understand and appreciate the complexity of the topic requires attendant discussions on the prevailing major issues associated with the shortfall of skilled labor and the international influence. In many regards, the word "intelligence" is probably too narrow and specific a term—better might be the word "knowledge." For purposes of this chapter, we will use the terms somewhat interchangeably.

The number of books and articles discussing the rising level of world intelligence is proliferating at a brisk pace. This coincides with the ever-increasing awareness that a country's intelligence and attendant opportunities are directly related to its world social economic ranking and standing. Although intelligence, at a macro level, is hard to singularly measure, there are a number of key indicators that aid in the ability to make generalizations, namely, government funding for research, education of a country's populace, governmental policies on taxes, and the like (Zakaria, 2011).

Perhaps one of the biggest issues worth addressing is the basic definition of innovation—this given the acceptance knowledge promotes innovation. Zakaria (2011) writes, "What is innovation? We don't really have a good fix on the concept. We know it when we see it. But this much is clear: it encompasses more than just scientific or technological breakthroughs." (p. 30) This, perhaps more than anything else, can be argued as the manifestation of an intelligent society and the underlying premise for social economic prosperity. These many concepts, seemingly unrelated, are in fact tremendously intertwined: world intelligence/ knowledge, innovation, and technology. These are the topics of this chapter.

Availability of Skilled Labor

"We are entering the era of unparalleled talent scarcity, which if left unaddressed, will put a brake on economic growth around the world, and will fundamentally change the way we approach workforce challenges" (World Economic Forum, 2011, p. 1).

There is probably nothing more confusing at the moment than the magnitude of research-based articles telling us we are going to have a skills shortfall on the one hand, and then, we are not on the other. These forecasts are being made by extremely reputable sources—people and organizations whose reputations are solidly founded on being in the know. Is there now, or is there going to be, a shortfall of skilled labor in the U.S. and/or the world? In many regards, it is time- and situation-specific and interviewee dependent, and the factors contributing to their representative perspectives.

Skilled Labor Shortage Forecasts

As early as 2000, it was forecasted we would have a shortfall of skilled labor by 2010, roughly 14 million people, 7 million of which were skilled labor. In 2003, Herman, Olivo, and Gioia (2003, p. 49) forecasted a shortage of over 10 million skilled workers by 2010. Dychtwald, Erickson, and Morison (2006, p. 11) forecasted a shortfall of 6 million skilled people, and then made reference to other estimates of skilled labor shortfall, namely, the National Association of Colleges and Employers estimate shortfall of 4 million by 2010, Watson Wyatt's (Herman et al., 2003) shortfall estimate of 8.9 million by 2010, and The Employment Policy Foundation's estimate of several million by 2010, 10 million by 2015, and 35 million by 2030. More recently it was forecasted that there will be a 20 million skilled labor job shortage by 2021 (Krell, 2011). Krell projects the need for 22 million new college graduates by 2018, with a projected graduating target of only 19 million, therefore producing an increasing shortfall. The World Economic Forum, in collaboration with the Boston Consulting Group, generated a 2011 report entitled "Global Talent Risk—Seven Responses." This report is based on international research data from 22 countries and 12 industries. In the report, the authors forecast:

- By 2030, the U.S. will have to add more than 25 million additional workers, and Western Europe will need to add more than 45 million employees
- 300 million new jobs will be needed between now and 2015 throughout the world (this is essentially the total population of the U.S. at 311 million)
- In 2050, most G7 and all BRIC (Brazil, Russia, India, China) countries will have more than doubled age 65 and older dependency ratios, and all except India will have more aged societies than today's most aged society, which is Japan
- In China, by 2050, the 10 workers now supporting each senior citizen will fall to 2.5

According to Woolhouse (2011), "the national Association of Manufacturers surveyed 779 industrial companies last year [2010] and found 32 percent already reported 'moderate to serious' skills shortages . . . 63 percent of life science companies and 45 percent of energy firms cited similar shortages" (para. 15). Memmott (2011) states we have 2 million open jobs, which is "an eye-catching claim at a time when the unemployment rate is 9.1 percent, 13.9 million people are officially unemployed and another 8.5 million are working part-time but would like to have full-time jobs" (para. 1). The crux of the argument for a skills shortage, perhaps most generally, resides in the word itself—"skills." It appears on the surface; it isn't that there are not jobs available, but a lack of people with appropriate skills to fill those jobs; this as reported most famously in the report entitled "America's Perfect Storm" (Kirsch, Braun, Yamamoto, & Sum, 2007). Memmott, in interviewing Anthony Carnevale, Director of Georgetown University's Center on Education and the Workforce, says, "[we have a] mismatch problem . . . even though there are not enough jobs to go around, there are a lot of jobs that people don't have the skills to fill . . . the industries we are talking about are fairly broad-based, the ones we call orphan jobs . . . manufacturing, utilities, transportation, mining and a whole set of agriculture jobs . . . [these industries] are dying because so many Baby Boomers will be retiring in the next decade" (paras. 3–5).

Over the last 10 or more years there has been absolutely no lack of skilled labor shortage forecasts. Inevitably, the argument for a shortfall of skilled labor worldwide is premised on an aging Baby Boomer population and slower birth rates, therefore creating the perceived shortfall (Woolhouse, 2011).

Aging World Population

In discussing the imminent retirement age population, we naturally, and most simplistically, look at the current cultural definitions of general cohorts in the workforce based on age demographics.

A "cohort" is a group of people born in a similar time period who have experienced similar major events. Names associated with these major events have been "defining moments" (Zemke, Raines, & Filipczak, 2000, p. 16) and "signposts" (Johnson & Johnson, 2010, p. 4).

Demographics form the underlying premise of further discussions and have been the topic of authors since the major seminal works beginning in 1991. There really have been five major books that formed the premise for most subsequent writings: *Generations* (1991), *Age Power* (1999), *Age Quake* (1999), *Age Works* (2000), and *Generations at Work* (2000). The proliferation of articles and books on the topic of demographics and understanding the many cohort groups in our workforce has been substantial.

Defining the Age Demographic Cohorts

Although we have documented as many as eight individual cohort groups (Strauss and Howe, 1991, p. 36), in practicality, we have four primary age demographic groups in our workforce today (Smith and Clurman, 1997, p. 9; Zemke et al., 2000, p. 3):

- Veterans (1922–1946; 52 million population)
- Boomers (1946–1964; 76 million population)
  Began turning 65 in January 1, 2011
- Generation X (1964–1980; 44 million population)
- Generation Y (1980–2000; 69.7 million population)

Worth noting, some authors have changed the years associated with the cohort groups, therefore altering the cohort populations. Although THE U.S. Census Bureau provides the basic information on live births and birth rates, aside from the Veteran and Boomer cohorts, it is not wholly agreed to exactly which years should be counted in post-Boomer groups, although very few years fluctuate between definitions. Some of the alternative views are premised not as much on number of live births, as they are on seminal events and the age of individuals at the time of those events—keeping in mind a cohort group is typically defined by age and major life-changing and remembered events. Examples of these varying definitions are depicted in the following alternative cohort perspectives:

- Veterans (Traditionalist; 1922–1946; 52 million people who were born prior to WWII)
- Baby Boomers (1946–1964; 76 million people who were born during or after WWII and raised during a period of extreme optimism, opportunity, and progress)
- Generation Xers (1965–1976; 44 million people who came of age in the shadow of the Boomers; children of older Boomers)
- Generation Y/Nexters (1977–1990; 69.7 million people who are currently the most high-tech and neo-optimistic; most loved)
- Generation Z (1991–present)

Johnson and Johnson (2010, p. 7):

- Veterans (1922–1946; 52 million population)
- Boomers (1946–1964; 76 million population)
- Generation X (1965–1980; 49 million population)
- Generation Y (1981–1995; 70.4 million population)
- Facebook Generation (1995–present)

Plunkett (2010, p. 200):

- The Elderly (pre-1935; 18 million population)
- Pre-Boomers (1935–1945; 23 million population)
- Baby Boomers (1946–1964; 76 million population)
- Generation X (1965–1980; 66 million population)
- Generation Y (1981–2002; 91 million population)
- Diversity Generation (2003+; 32 million population)

In any case, regardless of the definition used above, most of the Veteran cohort group has already retired or are on the verge of doing so. Looking at the year span of this group, 1964 and earlier, we see that the youngest of this group turned 65 in 2011. Behind this group of 52 million are 76 million Boomers, whose oldest just began to turn 60 in 2006 and 65 in January 2011. Clearly, we want to retain the knowledge of the Veteran cohort group, but their exiting the workforce does not form a trough given the 76 million Boomer backfills.

The trough exists at the next generation down, Generation X, where we move from a population of 76 million Boomers to a 42 percent reduction of 44 million Generation Xers, and the gap of scientists and engineers are even greater than the 42 percent decline in the general population. All speculation concerning the shortage of skilled labor in the United States is premised on these numbers and the attendant reduction in working age population.

The Nexters cohort group, even though large in numbers (69.7 million, or 91 million per Plunkett), is not yet fully available or ready to fill the requirements gap left by the reduction of Boomers. And, beyond Nexters, in comparison to the previous decade, males are marrying later in life from their previous age of 22 to today's age 27, while females are experiencing a comparable move to the right from age 20 to 25 years of age. The average age for first-time mothers in 2001 was 30, whereas the average age for first-time fathers was 32. Some male Nexters even nominate 40 as a good age to become a father (Huntley, 2006, p. 182), suggesting another reduction in population may manifest itself in our next documented generation.

Defining the Aging World Population

Since 1996, every 8.5 seconds someone turned age 50 (Dychtwald, 2003, p. 27). Since January 2006, someone turned 60 years of age at a rate of nearly 10,000 per day, approximately 4 million per year, for the subsequent 18 years (Dychtwald, Erickson, & Morison, 2006). In and of itself, without further information, we don't know if this is good or bad. In a Pew Research Center (Taylor et al., 2009) report titled "America's Changing Workforce: Recession Turns a Graying Office Grayer," the authors make a number of observations:

- 93 percent of the growth in the U.S. labor force from 2006–2016 will be among workers 55 and older
- 54 percent of workers say the main reason they work is because they want to; just 17 percent say the main reason is that they need the paycheck
- Older workers emphasize psychological and social factors "to feel useful," "to give myself something to do," and "to be with other people" for working
- Younger workers are much more inclined to site classic pocketbook considerations: "to support myself and my family," "to live independently"
- Four in ten adults who have worked past the median retirement age of 62 say they have delayed their retirement because of the recession
- A rising share of Americans ages 16–24 are in school and a declining share are in the labor force—57 percent in 2009 versus 66 percent in 2000
- The labor force participation of women has flattened out at 59 percent in 2009 versus a 60 percent peak in 2000
- Older workers are the happiest workers; 54 percent of workers ages 55 and older say they are "completely satisfied" with their job, compared with just 29 percent of workers ages 16–64

Continuing, current revisions to the mortality tables used by insurance companies reflect a reduced risk of dying at all ages. The average life expectancy is currently 78 for males and 82 for females (Arias, 2006, p. 1). Under the old mortality tables, the ultimate life expectancy was just over 99 years. Now that figure has been lengthened to 120.5 years (Hankin 2005, p. 11).

Data from the National Science Foundation and the U.S. Census Bureau clearly reflects an aging world population, coupled with a substantial existing decrease in the U.S. population after 1960. From 1900 to 2000, the U.S. population increased 3 times, while the number of individuals age 65 and older increased 11

65 or older		16-64	
Feel useful/productive	68	Support myself/family	88
Live independently	59	Live independently	78
Give myself something to do	57	Feel useful/productive	69
To be with other people	56	Qualify for pension/ Social Security	65
Support myself/family	53	Receive health benefits	57
Help improve society	40	Help improve society	48
Qualify for pension/ Social Security	35	Give myself something to do	40
Receive health benefits	24	To be with other people	35

Note: Based on those who work full time or part time; n=1,140.

**Figure 17.1. Reasons for Working by Age—
Percent Who Say This is a "Big Reason" They Work, Pew**

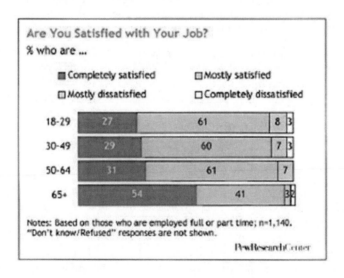

Figure 17.2. Job Satisfaction by Age, Pew

times. Within the U.S. population, 1 in 8 people were age 65 and above in 2005, 1 in 6 by 2020, and 1 in 5 by 2030; in the year 2100, the number of individuals age 65 and above will be greater than the entire U.S. population in 1940 of 131.2 million. Hence, there are fewer people to support those that require Social Security benefits. Women, it could be argued, are the secret heroines of Social Security. If they had not joined the labor force in droves, the financial condition of the Social Security system would be significantly worse than it is today (Kotlikoff, 2004, p. 21).

The year was 1940 when the first monthly Social Security check was issued (Social Security Administration, 2005, p. 6) to Ida May Fuller, a retired paralegal. In 1940, there was no early Social Security benefit, so an individual had to be 65 years of age to begin drawing the funds. The average life expectancy in 1940 was around 63 for females, which, as the system was designed, meant if you lived to 65, you might collect from Social Security for a couple of years before death. Fuller, however, lived to the age of 100 and ended up collecting Social Security for some 35 years before dying in 1975. This conversation lends itself to discussion on the current Social Security situation, that being, life expectancy is currently at 78 for males and 82 for females, while Social Security retirement still hovers around 65–67 years of age. Following the original plan for Social Security, by today's life expectancy tables, the average eligibility age should be around 84. Lang, Alfonso, and Dawkins (2009) anticipate a healthier scenario, stating, "why the rosy forecast for Social Security? You can thank the 1965 immigration reform for that outlook. Just as the Baby Boom ended, the U.S. reopened to immigrants. The numbers were small at first, but in the last 20 years they equaled the immigrant boom of the late 19th and early 20th centuries" (p. 13). Relaxed immigration policies and subsequent increases in immigration have been cited before as an alternative solution to current U.S. economic problems, and now they are being cited as an alternative solution to the reported ailing Social Security fund (Plunkett, 2010, p. 13).

The "dependency ratio" is that portion of the population not likely to be working (65+) compared to the number of people of working age (15–64). In the U.S., for every person 65 and older, there were 12 people age 15–64 in 1950. By the year 2045, for every person age 65 and older, there will be 4 people age 15–64 to support them. In comparing the years 2000 to 2030, we see an increase in the dependency ratio of 21.1 percent to 37.0 percent of people age 65 to those aged 20–64 (Kinsella & Velkoff, 2001, p. 154). According to the Organisation for Economic Co-operation and Development (OECD) Factbook 2009, member nations reflected an increase in the overall OECD dependency ratio (measured as 65+ and under 15 years of age) from 27.2 percent to 31.3 percent from 2000 to 2010. According to the OECD as reported by Plunkett:

> by 2050, [many nations] estimates paint a dark picture, with an average DR [dependency ratio] of 62.3% in these nations. In other words, there will 6.2 people of 65+ years for every 10 people likely to be in the workforce. Among nations forecast to suffer the most devastating DRs in 2050 are Germany at 73.9%, Spain at 91.3%, Poland at 83.1%, Korea at 91.4%, and Japan at 94.9%. Italy tops the chart at 98.5%; which means there will be only slightly more than one member of the labor force for each senior in Italy. (2010, p. 31)

According to Saunders

> A closer look at the 2004–14 labor force shows that certain demographic groups are projected to grow more rapidly than others. The labor force will continue to age, with a projected 4.1 percent annual growth of the 55 and older age group, more than four times the rate of growth of the overall labor force. Baby boomers entered the labor market beginning in the late 1960s as a huge wave of workers who swelled the level and growth of the labor force. During the decade of the 1990s, baby boomers were in the prime-age working group of 25- to 54-year-olds, still contributing to a relatively high annual growth of the workforce. They will be concentrated in the 50- to 68-year-old workforce in 2014. Because older workers tend to have significantly lower participation rates, the baby boomer exit from the workforce, as with their entrance, will have significant impacts on the growth of the labor force. (2005, p. 5)

We are not alone. Every major developed or undeveloped nation, from Germany to China, Japan, Russia, and Brazil, is experiencing this phenomenon. We are all seeing a major aging of our world populations (Wallace, 1999, p. 9).

Retirement and the Working Senior Population

Contributing to the reduction of the available workforce, by age 62, 50 percent of both science and engineering bachelor's and master's degree holders will no longer work full time; however, science and engineering doctorate holders do not reach the 50 percent mark until age 66 (NSF, 2006, p. 30). According to the "Science and Engineering Indicators 2004," by age 65, more than half of the science and engineering

Table 2. Civilian labor force by sex, age, race, and Hispanic origin, 1984, 1994, 2004, and projected 2014											
[Numbers in thousands]											
Group	Level				Percent distribution				Annual growth rate (percent)		
	1984	1994	2004	2014	1984	1994	1004	2014	1984–94	1994–2004	2004–14
Total, 16 years and older	113,544	131,056	147,401	162,100	100.0	100.0	100.0	100.0	1.4	1.2	1.0
16–24	23,989	21,612	22,268	22,158	21.1	16.5	16.5	13.7	-1.0	.3	.0
25–54	74,661	93,898	102,122	105,627	65.8	71.6	71.6	65.2	2.3	.8	.3
55 and older	14,894	15,547	23,011	34,316	13.1	11.9	11.9	21.2	.4	4.0	4.1

Note: Age of baby boomers is 20–38 in 1984, 30–48 in 1994, 40–58 in 2004, and 50–68 in 2014.

Figure 17.3. Projected Growth of Baby Boomer Segment of Population through 2014, CDC

bachelor's and master's degree holders will leave the workforce entirely, but a similar proportion of Ph.D. holders do not do so until age 68 (NSF, 2006, p. 31). Overall, ignoring education level, Americans are choosing not to wait to reach 65 to retire, but 60 percent of workers currently retire at age 62, a pattern that shows little sign of changing (Goldberg, 2000, p. 2). More specifically, working individuals with bachelor's degrees will generally not work full time by age 62; master's degree holders by age 62; and doctorate degree holders by age 66. This means, from January 1, 2008, the age Boomers first started to turn 62, and then January 1, 2011, the age Boomers first started to turn age 65, we would expect to experience a significant exiting of skilled labor. This clearly represents a trough in the available workforce when compared to the available backfill of Generation Xers.

Retirement ages, depicted in the below figures (Chomik and Whitehouse, 2010), coupled with the gains in life expectancy, means adults are spending more of their life in retirement. The below figure depicts this relationship through life stages broken into four states: years before entry into the labor market (primarily spent in school); years not in work due to unemployment or economic uncertainty; years in the labor force; and years in retirement. According to Kinsella and Velkoff (2001), in 1960, men on average could expect to spend 46 years in the labor force and a little more than 1 year in retirement. By 1995, the number of years in the labor force had decreased to 37 while the number of years in retirement had jumped to 12. Given today's average retirement age of 62–63, and life expectancy for males of 78, this yields roughly 15 years in retirement, and for women, 20 years in retirement (OECD, 2011). Unlike the trend for men, the average number of years in employment for women has been increasing. At the same time, the number of years that women live after reaching retirement age has increased significantly, from 9 years in 1960 to more than 21 years in 1995 (Kinsella & Velkoff, 2001, p. 111). Clearly, we will have to change our mind-set about how to live our extra years of retired life (Dychtwald, 1999, p. 1).

Recent historical data would have proven to have been sufficient for a discussion on senior retiree availability. Today, however, given the many economic uncertainties and the most recent economic downturn, current senior retiree sentiment needs to be addressed.

It is reported (Collins, 2011; Dugas, 2011; Ellis, 2011; Helman, Copeland, & VanDerhei, 2011) that retirement confidence is at record lows. More than a quarter of those surveyed say they are not at all confident about retirement. A reported 56 percent of those surveyed have less than $25,000 saved in preparation for retirement, which includes savings and investments. A reported 29 percent have less than $1,000 saved. Although 59 percent of respondents said they are saving for retirement, 34 percent of workers and 33 percent of retirees were forced to tap into their retirement savings last year to cover basic expenses.

Some of the top reasons people are reported to be delaying retirement include:

- Perceptions of a poor economy
- High unemployment rates
- Rising health care costs
- Lower investment returns
- Lack of faith in Social Security or government
- Change in their employment situation
- Simply can't afford it

The result of this very real or perceived reality is:

- 74 percent of workers now plan to hold paying jobs in retirement
- 89 percent report their expected retirement age has increased
- 70 percent now report they expect to remain employed until at least age 65
- 11 percent report predicting their retirement between the ages of 66 and 69
- 25 percent report working until age 70 or above
- 8 percent report they will never retire

In a Pew Research Center study (Taylor et al., 2009, p. 2), 63 percent of both men and women age 50–61 report delaying their retirement because of the recession that began in 2008. In this same study, 54 percent of males and 72 percent of females report delaying their retirement. Of those males and females aged 62 and above, 38 percent reported having delayed their retirement due to the recession.

Hiring Senior Retired Workers—A Workforce Multiplier for Success

This section describes the synergistic effects of hiring senior retired workers. It discusses the many hidden values predominately stemming from the significant breadth and depth of knowledge, both theoretical and experiential. Senior retired workers want to remain actively involved in, and a part of, the greater social construct while transitioning from one life phase to the next. Their motivation is slanted toward self-actualization. There is a natural conversational flow when discussing the aging of the world's population, proposed shortfall of skilled workers in the United States, mind-set of senior retired workers, and the attendant cost implications.

Based on cohort characteristics, there are four primary areas where senior retired workers bring advantages to a work environment: work ethic, financial awareness, experience, and emotional intelligence.

Work Ethic

Studies show retired senior workers have lower absenteeism and lower turnover than their younger counterparts (Finn, 2008). Some of this evolves from having fewer family obligations, such as children at home. Other reasons may be because senior retired workers have more of a commitment to their work and use work as their social construct. Other individuals report (Rathe, 2010) that "older workers' productivity does not fall but rises because of greater dependability, better judgment and accuracy" (para. 1). Rathe goes on to say, "studies show older workers actually miss less work than younger workers and can learn new techniques and technologies effectively" (para. 1).

In a 2004 study reported by the Concours Group and Age Wave (Erickson, 2008, p. 90), the retired senior cohort group felt most energized by their work, thought time passed quickly when they were at work, and felt a great deal of their pride came from their work and career.

Financially Frugal

Perhaps because of the stock market crash of 1929 or the Great Depression of 1930, or perhaps because of the many economic cycles of recent years, retired senior workers, on the whole, tend to be more frugal than non-retired workers. Another reason for their frugality may very well stem from the recognition that their ageing cohort will live longer than previous cohorts and that financial means may not carry forward to those

	1949	1958	1971	1983	1989	1993	1999	2002	2010	2020	2030	2040	2050
Australia	65.0	65.0	65.0	65.0	65.0	65.0	65.0	65.0	65.0	65.0	66.0	67.0	67.0
Austria	65.0	65.0	65.0	65.0	65.0	65.0	65.0	65.0	65.0	65.0	65.0	65.0	65.0
Belgium	60.0	60.0	60.0	60.0	60.0	60.0	60.0	60.0	60.0	60.0	60.0	60.0	60.0
Canada	70.0	69.0	68.0	67.0	66.0	65.0	65.0	65.0	65.0	65.0	65.0	65.0	65.0
Czech Republic		60.0	60.0	60.0	60.0	60.0	60.0	60.5	61.0	62.2	63.5	65.0	65.0
Denmark	65.0	65.0	67.0	67.0	67.0	67.0	67.0	67.0	65.0	65.0	67.0	67.0	67.0
Finland		65.0	65.0	65.0	65.0	65.0	65.0	65.0	65.0	65.0	65.0	65.0	65.0
France		65.0	65.0	65.0	60.0	60.0	60.0	60.0	60.5	61.0	61.0	61.0	61.0
Germany	63.0	63.0	63.0	63.0	63.0	63.0	63.0	63.5	65.0	65.0	65.0	65.0	65.0
Greece	55.0	57.0	57.0	57.0	57.0	57.0	57.0	57.0	57.0	60.0	60.0	60.0	60.0
Hungary	60.0	60.0	60.0	60.0	60.0	60.0	60.0	60.0	60.0	64.5	65.0	65.0	65.0
Iceland		67.0	67.0	67.0	67.0	67.0	67.0	67.0	67.0	67.0	67.0	67.0	67.0
Ireland	70.0	70.0	70.0	70.0	65.0	65.0	65.0	65.0	65.0	65.0	65.0	65.0	65.0
Italy	60.0	60.0	60.0	55.0	55.0	55.0	55.0	57.0	59.0	61.0	65.0	65.0	65.0
Japan		60.0	65.0	65.0	65.0	65.0	65.0	65.0	65.0	65.0	65.0	65.0	65.0
Korea							60.0	60.0	60.0	60.0	60.0	62.0	64.0	65.0
Luxembourg	65.0	65.0	65.0	65.0	65.0	60.0	60.0	60.0	60.0	60.0	60.0	60.0	60.0
Mexico		65.0	65.0	65.0	65.0	65.0	65.0	65.0	65.0	65.0	65.0	65.0	65.0
Netherlands	65.0	65.0	65.0	65.0	65.0	65.0	65.0	65.0	65.0	65.0	65.0	65.0	65.0
New Zealand	65.0	60.0	60.0	60.0	60.0	60.0	61.1	64.1	65.0	65.0	65.0	65.0	65.0
Norway	70.0	70.0	70.0	70.0	67.0	67.0	67.0	67.0	67.0	67.0	67.0	67.0	67.0
Poland	60.0	60.0	60.0	60.0	65.0	65.0	65.0	65.0	65.0	65.0	65.0	65.0	65.0
Portugal	65.0	65.0	65.0	65.0	65.0	65.0	65.0	65.0	65.0	65.0	65.0	65.0	65.0
Slovak Republic		60.0	60.0	60.0	60.0	60.0	60.0	60.0	62.0	62.0	62.0	62.0	62.0
Spain	65.0	65.0	65.0	65.0	65.0	65.0	65.0	65.0	65.0	65.0	65.0	65.0	65.0
Sweden	67.0	67.0	67.0	67.0	65.0	65.0	65.0	65.0	65.0	65.0	65.0	65.0	65.0
Switzerland		65.0	65.0	65.0	65.0	65.0	65.0	65.0	65.0	65.0	65.0	65.0	65.0
Turkey			60.0	45.0	45.0	45.0	45.0	44.0	44.9	48.6	53.1	57.7	62.3
United Kingdom	65.0	65.0	65.0	65.0	65.0	65.0	65.0	65.0	65.0	65.0	66.0	67.0	68.0
United States	65.0	65.0	65.0	65.0	65.0	65.0	65.0	65.0	66.0	66.0	67.0	67.0	67.0
Average	*64.3*	*63.9*	*63.9*	*63.2*	*62.8*	*62.5*	*62.6*	*62.7*	*63.0*	*63.5*	*64.1*	*64.4*	*64.6*

Source: National officials, OECD calculations and Turner (2007).

Note: Germany refers to West Germany for the period 1949-2002. Czechoslovakian data are used for the Czech and Slovak Republics where appropriate. Where there is more than one value per calendar year, these have been averaged.

Figure 17.4. Men's Pensionable Age in OECD Countries, 1949–2050

extra years. Social Security plays a role in allowing seniors to live a continuing lifestyle. The recognition, however, that Social Security is under constant attack from lawmakers seeking to balance federal budgets never strays far from the minds of this cohort.

From an employer's perspective, hiring senior retired workers can be a financial windfall, in that numerous members of this cohort are receiving income from other sources, including Social Security, pensions, and a lifetime of savings. Additionally, this cohort may already have medical coverage from previous employment or through Medicare. In these scenarios, this cohort demands less and will cost less to employ than their non-retired younger counterparts.

It is important to note, in many cases, that this cohort reported not working for the money as their primary reason for employment. In reporting why workers do not know when they will retire, 53 percent said they like to work and only 35 percent said not enough money.

Lifetime of Experiences
Senior retired workers bring a lifetime of experience to bear on each problem. In many situations, they have experienced very similar or perhaps a specific instantiation of a similar situation before. It is not uncommon, in the many years leading up to their retirement, that they would have had numerous jobs, perhaps spanning multiple companies or even industries.

	1949	1958	1971	1983	1989	1993	1999	2002	2010	2020	2030	2040	2050
Australia	60.0	60.0	60.0	60.0	60.0	60.0	60.0	61.0	62.0	64.0	66.0	67.0	67.0
Austria	65.0	60.0	60.0	60.0	60.0	60.0	60.0	60.0	60.0	60.0	63.0	65.0	65.0
Belgium	55.0	60.0	60.0	60.0	60.0	60.0	60.0	60.0	60.0	60.0	60.0	60.0	60.0
Canada	70.0	69.0	68.0	67.0	66.0	65.0	65.0	65.0	65.0	65.0	65.0	65.0	65.0
Czech Republic		60.0	55.0	57.0	57.0	57.0	57.0	58.0	58.7	60.7	63.3	65.0	65.0
Denmark	65.0	60.0	62.0	62.0	62.0	67.0	67.0	67.0	65.0	65.0	67.0	67.0	67.0
Finland		65.0	65.0	65.0	65.0	65.0	65.0	65.0	65.0	65.0	65.0	65.0	65.0
France		65.0	65.0	65.0	60.0	60.0	60.0	60.0	60.5	61.0	61.0	61.0	61.0
Germany	60.0	60.0	60.0	60.0	60.0	60.0	60.0	60.5	65.0	65.0	65.0	65.0	65.0
Greece	55.0	57.0	57.0	57.0	57.0	57.0	57.0	57.0	57.0	60.0	60.0	60.0	60.0
Hungary	55.0	55.0	55.0	55.0	55.0	55.0	55.0	55.0	59.0	64.5	65.0	65.0	65.0
Iceland		67.0	67.0	67.0	67.0	67.0	67.0	67.0	67.0	67.0	67.0	67.0	67.0
Ireland	70.0	70.0	70.0	70.0	65.0	65.0	65.0	65.0	65.0	65.0	65.0	65.0	65.0
Italy	55.0	55.0	55.0	55.0	55.0	55.0	55.0	57.0	59.0	61.0	65.0	65.0	65.0
Japan		60.0	60.0	60.0	60.0	61.0	63.0	65.0	65.0	65.0	65.0	65.0	65.0
Korea						60.0	60.0	60.0	60.0	60.0	62.0	64.0	65.0
Luxembourg	65.0	65.0	65.0	65.0	65.0	60.0	60.0	60.0	60.0	60.0	60.0	60.0	60.0
Mexico		65.0	65.0	65.0	65.0	65.0	65.0	65.0	65.0	65.0	65.0	65.0	65.0
Netherlands	65.0	65.0	65.0	65.0	65.0	65.0	65.0	65.0	65.0	65.0	65.0	65.0	65.0
New Zealand	65.0	60.0	60.0	60.0	60.0	60.0	61.1	64.1	65.0	65.0	65.0	65.0	65.0
Norway	70.0	70.0	70.0	70.0	67.0	67.0	67.0	67.0	67.0	67.0	67.0	67.0	67.0
Poland	60.0	60.0	60.0	60.0	60.0	60.0	60.0	60.0	60.0	60.0	60.0	60.0	60.0
Portugal	65.0	65.0	65.0	65.0	62.0	62.0	62.0	65.0	65.0	65.0	65.0	65.0	65.0
Slovak Republic		60.0	55.0	57.0	57.0	57.0	57.0	57.0	57.0	62.0	62.0	62.0	62.0
Spain	65.0	65.0	65.0	65.0	65.0	65.0	65.0	65.0	65.0	65.0	65.0	65.0	65.0
Sweden	67.0	67.0	67.0	67.0	65.0	65.0	65.0	65.0	65.0	65.0	65.0	65.0	65.0
Switzerland		60.0	60.0	60.0	62.0	62.0	62.0	62.0	63.0	64.0	64.0	64.0	64.0
Turkey			60.0	45.0	45.0	45.0	45.0	40.0	41.0	45.2	50.4	55.6	60.8
United Kingdom	60.0	60.0	60.0	60.0	60.0	60.0	60.0	60.0	60.0	65.0	66.0	67.0	68.0
United States	65.0	65.0	65.0	65.0	65.0	65.0	65.0	65.0	66.0	66.0	67.0	67.0	67.0
Average	62.9	62.5	62.1	61.7	61.1	61.1	61.2	61.4	61.9	62.9	63.7	64.1	64.4

Source: National officials, OECD calculations and Turner (2007).

Note: Data shown in bold type indicates that pension ages are different for women than men. Germany refers to West Germany for the period 1949-2002. Czechoslovakian data are used for the Czech and Slovak Republics where appropriate. Where there is more than one value per calendar year, these have been averaged.

Figure 17.5. Women's Pensionable Age in OECD Countries, 1949–2050

As humans, we form associations or memory maps of each situation we encounter. These associations allow us to quickly make decisions when a situation arises. The more experiences we encounter, the more we make associations or memory maps.

It is not uncommon for senior retired workers to gain great joy from being able to share their learned experiences, and in fact, to take great pride in calmly addressing situations as they occur. Where younger workers may experience anxiety from not knowing how to address a problem, or may react with a level of immaturity, senior workers can pull from their many experiences to quickly suggest potential alternative solutions.

Senior retired workers recognize and value their contributions and have come to understand that they are not destined for the CEO chair. The National Federation of Independent Business (2011) reports, "semi-retired workers are seldom trying to climb the corporate ladder or establish a corporate reputation, as many have already done so. These men and women leave their egos at the door and are typically thankful to have a post-career job" (p. 1). In fact, CEO is not where they wish to be if such an opportunity presented itself. This age-specific cohort values their ability to do what they feel comfortable doing. In many ways, they are realizing their full potential at this point in their life and are self-actualizing. They enjoy what they do, feel a part of a bigger social construct, feel valued, and for these many reasons they tremendously enjoy their employment opportunities.

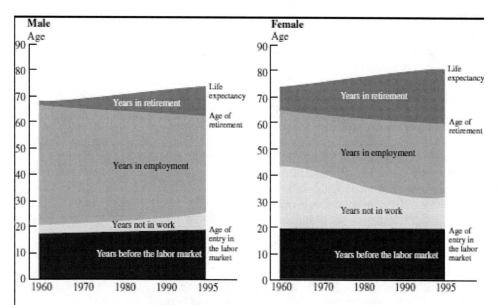

Note: Based on an unweighted average of data for 15 member countries, using average life expectancies and labor force patterns as they existed for the years shown. These graphs are illustrative of overall trends, and should not be construed as representing the experience of any particular age cohort.
Source: Organization for Economic Co-Operation and Development, 1998b.

Figure 17.6. Decomposition of the Life Course, OECD

Emotional Intelligence

As stated in the book *Promoting Emotional Intelligence in Organizations* (Cherniss & Adler, 2000), "emotional intelligence is the ability to accurately identify and understand one's own emotional reactions and those of others. It also involves the ability to regulate one's own emotions, to use them to make good decisions and to act effectively" (p. 34).

Cherniss and Adler go on to discuss how purely cognitive ability does not represent the whole picture, stating, "emotional intelligence and cognitive ability actually work together for effective action in organizations" (p. 5). In addressing numerous studies, the authors suggest that the difference between exceptional performance and average performance is almost entirely based on emotional intelligence.

In discussing the relationship between leadership and the brain's design, Goleman, Boyatzis, and McKee recognize:

New findings in brain research show that the neural systems responsible for intellect and or emotions are separate, but have intimately interwoven connections. This brain circuitry provides the neural basis for [leadership]. Although our business culture places great value on an intellect devoid of emotion, our emotions are more powerful than our intellect. In emergencies, the limbic system, our emotional center, commandeers the rest of our brain. There is a good reason for this. Emotions are crucial for survival, being the brain's way of alerting us to something urgent and offering an immediate plan for action—fight, flee, freeze. The thinking brain evolved from the limbic brain, and continues to take orders from it when it perceives a threat. The trigger point is the amygdale, a limbic brain structure that scans what is happening to us moment by moment, always on the alert for an emergency. It commandeers other parts of the brain, including the rational cortex for immediate action if it perceives an emergency. (2002, p. 24)

Aside from structural implications in the brain, there are other commanding factors—brain neural chemicals. It used to be, when discussing leadership and gender, we relied heavily on our understanding of psychological and philosophical studies and implications. While this is true today for the most part, there is a growing portion of scientific study based on brain imaging, using such tools as positron emission tomography (PET), magnetic resonance imaging (MRI) and single-photon emission computed tomography (SPECT). These tools have allowed us unparalleled insight into how male and female brains function during any number of acts. Results of these findings are organized around neural blood flow patterns, brain structures, and brain chemistry (Gurian & Annis, 2008).

Relative to brain chemistry, males have roughly 10 to 20 times more testosterone than females. Testosterone in males is known as the "fight or flight" neural chemical. Males also produce more vasopressin, the male territorial chemical. Females secrete more serotonin (calms impulses, reduces stress) and oxytocin (bonding chemical). When humans feel connected to someone or something, this bonding is from oxytocin; it's what biologists call the "tend and befriend" instinct. Higher levels of oxytocin yield lesser levels of physical aggression. Testosterone can be implied to have a link to our inability to remain calm in crisis, and it can inductively be tied to a level of emotional intelligence (EI). EI has been defined along four dimensions with a total of 23 competencies (Cherniss & Adler, 2000, p. 10):

- Self-awareness
- Emotional self-awareness: recognizing one's emotions and their effects
- Accurate self-assessment: knowing one's strengths and limits
- Self-confidence: a strong sense of one's self worth and capabilities
- Self-management
- Adaptability: flexibility in handling change
- Self-control: keeping disruptive emotions and impulses in check
- Conscientiousness and reliability: taking responsibility for personal performance; maintaining standards of integrity and honesty
- Initiative and innovation: readiness to act on opportunities; being comfortable with novel ideas, approaches, and new information
- Achievement drive: striving to improve or meet a standard of excellence; persistence in pursuing goals despite obstacles or setbacks
- Social awareness
- Empathy: seeing others' feelings and perspectives and taking an active interest in their concerns
- Service orientation: anticipating, recognizing, and meeting customers' needs
- Organizational awareness: reading a group's emotional currents and power relationships
- Developing others: sensing others' developmental needs and bolstering their abilities
- Social skills
- Leadership: inspiring and guiding individuals and groups; aligning with the goals of the group or organization
- Influence: wielding effective tactics for persuasion
- Change catalyst: initiating or managing change
- Communication: listening openly and sending convincing messages
- Conflict management: negotiating and resolving disagreements
- Collaboration and building bonds: working with others toward shared goals; nurturing instrumental relationships
- Team capabilities: creating group synergy in pursuing collective goals

Given this basic understanding of emotional intelligence, it becomes relatively straightforward to align senior retired worker characteristics to an opportunity for advanced emotional intelligence. Beginning with the discussion on brain neural chemicals, as males chronologically age, beginning at age 30, their relative levels of testosterone to oxytocin change. Over time, males tend to become kinder and gentler human beings. This supports an argument for a more steady state emotional reaction in times of crisis as well as a lessening of a need to be confrontational if challenged.

Additionally, in examining the above 23 competencies, along the four dimensions of EI, most suggest a level of maturity commonly exhibited in chronologically aged individuals. This is not to suggest all chronologically aged individuals are equally emotionally mature; consideration of life experience plays a critical role in this more advanced state. This does imply, however, that senior retired workers bring a lifetime of experiences to bear on each situation and can therefore, ideally, make a more informed decision; this is especially true given the previous discussion on memory mapping.

Concluding Thoughts on Hiring Senior Retired Workers

The senior population in the U.S. is living longer and experiencing a healthier longevity. Although the average retirement age is just over 62 years of age, this cohort of individuals wants to remain active and productive members of society. Today's individuals nearing retirement are reporting they don't expect to retire until at least age 66, with a full 34 percent saying they don't ever expect to retire. With the projected shortfall in skilled labor by 2014, the senior retired workforce can play a significant role in bridging the potential gap. Senior retired workers bring a wealth of synergistic effects to the workforce, premised on their breadth and depth of theoretical and practical experience. These individuals, through these many experiences as well as documented changes in brain neural chemicals, bring another calming effect frequently referred to as emotional intelligence. The hiring of senior retired workers can truly create a workforce multiplier for organizational growth.

Science and Engineering Demographics

In the 2010 updated report from the National Academy of Science (2010, p. 4) titled *Rising Above the Gathering Storm, Revisited: Rapidly Approaching Category 5*, the authors state, "a primary driver of the future economy and concomitant creation of jobs in the 21st century will be innovation, largely derived from advances in science and engineering. While only 4 percent of the nation's workforce is composed of scientists and engineers, this group disproportionately creates jobs for the other 96 percent" (p. 4).

Growth of Science and Engineering Workforce

We have a disturbance in the time and space continuum, modified in this scenario to say we have a disturbance in the supply and demand continuum. There are roughly 311 million people in the U.S., of which, depending on whether you research the Bureau of Labor Statistics or the National Science Foundation (NSF), 1 to 2 percent are classified as scientists and engineers. It had been forecasted that by the year 2010, science and engineering would grow three times faster than any other occupation, reflecting a 47 percent increase in personnel needs. That's a 47 percent increase in skilled labor, which by 2010 was forecasted to experience a 10 million person shortfall. This, seemingly, would have a compounding effect on available talent. From 182,000 in 1950 to 5.5 million in 2007, the average annual growth rate in the science and engineering workforce was 6.2 percent, which was nearly four times the annual growth rate of the remainder of the U.S. workforce population at 1.6 percent (NSF, 2010, pp. 3–11).

Understanding the supply of those with science and engineering credentials is only part of the equation. The other side is the demand. According to the NSF, "S&E occupations are projected to grow by 21.4% between 2006 and 2016, while employment in all occupations is expected to grow 10.4% over the same period" (2010, pp. 3–14). Given, then, the projected growth rate of the science and engineering workforce of 6.2 percent, and the projected demand of those educated in science and engineering of 21.4 percent, one can clearly see the potential, given all things equal, of a forecasted shortfall of science and engineering educated individuals.

Science and Engineering Graduation Rates

To understand the growth portion of the equation, the incoming, or more accurately, the graduating college population, is required to fully appreciate the science and engineering dilemma. Relative to undergraduate education, less than 40 percent of those entering college who are pursuing bachelor's degrees in science and engineering actually graduate (Business-Higher Education Forum, 2005, p. 6). To put this another way, more than 60 percent of those entering college in science and engineering do not graduate in science and engineering, meaning they either switch majors or leave college altogether. According to the American Society of Engineering Education (ASEE), from 1999 to 2004, and the NSF (2006, pp. 2–11), which reflects recent data, the full-time undergraduate enrollment in science and engineering has increased only slightly, flattening from 2003 to 2004 (ASEE, 2004, p. 35). More alarming, and quite revealing, is the depiction of the rate of change in enrollment numbers, which looks like a downward roller coaster ride or a falling rock.

According to the NSF (Ladika, 2006, p. 69), the ratio of science and engineering degrees per 100 24-year-olds across numerous nations are:

- Finland—13
- France—11
- Taiwan—10.9
- South Korea—10.7
- United Kingdom—10.5
- Sweden—9.8
- Ireland—8.5
- Spain—8.1
- Japan—8.0
- Canada—6.6
- Germany—6.4
- United States—5.7

Ladika, in the article "The Brain Race," claims post-9/11, "more red tape and increased competition are driving top foreign students away from the U.S., and leaving a potential skills gap in science and technology fields" (2006, p. 30).

At one point, it was reported that China's undergraduate science and engineering enrollment was expanding at a rate ten times faster than that in the United States. As reported, a full 75 percent of all Chinese Bachelor of Science degrees were in science and engineering, compared to 30 percent in the United States. In looking at the decade from 1994 to 2004, we see U.S. undergraduates with bachelor's degrees have decreased from 73,000 to 65,000, while at the same time, China's graduates with bachelor's degrees increased in number from 60,000 to 325,000—that's five times the 2004 U.S. number of graduates (BHEF, 2005, p. 7).

According to Geri Smith:

For years the Mexican workforce has meant one thing to multinationals: cheap, reliable labor, perfect for assembling cars, refrigerators, and other goods in the maquiladoras lining the border with America. More complex design work was better done elsewhere in the global economy—usually at company headquarters in the U.S., Europe and Japan. But, as maquila-style assembly work migrated to cheaper locales, and India and China grabbed more sophisticated design and engineering assignments, Mexican officials knew they had to do something to stay in the global race . . . Over the past 10 years, the country's policymakers have been building up enrollment in four year degree programs in engineering . . . The result is a bumper crop of 451,000 Mexican students enrolled in full-time undergraduate engineering programs. (2006, p. 42)

Adding to this discrepancy, of the 868,000 Bachelor of Science degrees in science and engineering, the U.S. graduated only 7 percent. Said another way, 93 percent of the 868,000 bachelor's degrees in science and engineering were from other, non-U.S. countries (BHEF, 2005, p. 7).

- 1994 (United States 73,000; China 60,000)
- 2004 (United States 65,000; China 325,000; 5 times)

According to the National Academy of Sciences, "over two-thirds of the engineers who receive PhD's from United States Universities were not United States citizens" (2010, p. 4).

To summarize, we have a slower growing science and engineering labor force, coupled with an increasingly older science and engineering U.S. labor force. To emphasize the latter, a majority of individuals in science and engineering in the U.S. are 45 years of age or older, and, 25.6 percent of those individuals in the science and engineering labor force are 55 years of age or older (NSF, 2006, p. 30; updated 2011). By age 61, nearly half of all science and engineering workers are no longer working in a full-time capacity (NSF, 2010, pp. 3–6). We clearly have a pending gap in supply and demand, and on the surface, looking at the data, it would appear to be widening.

International Impact

The NSF's "Science and Engineering Indicators 2010" discusses the increasing importance of science and engineering to advancing a society:

> Governments in many parts of the developing world have come to view science and technology (S&T) as integral to economic growth and development, and they have set out to build more knowledge-intensive economies in which research, its commercial exploitation, and intellectual work would play a greater role. (p. O–3)

To further express this proposition, "Science and Engineering Indicators 2010" discusses the global expansion of research and development, noting:

> the steady and large upward trend illustrates the rapidly growing global focus on innovation. . . . A U.S. goal in the 1950s was to achieve an R&D investment of 1% of GDP by 1957. More recently, many governments set their sights at 3% of GDP in pursuit of developing knowledge-based economies; the EU formally embraced the 3% goal as its long-term planning target. (p. O-4)

On the global science and engineering labor force:

> Science is a global enterprise. The common laws of nature cross political boundaries, and the international movement of people and knowledge made science global long before "globalization" became a label for the increasing interconnections now forming among the world's economies. . . . technical innovations is creating a new competitive environment. New ways of doing business and performing R&D take advantage of gains in new knowledge discovered anywhere in the world, from increases in foreign economic development, and from the expending international migration of highly trained scientists and engineers. (p. 3-47–3-48)

The world is evolving socially, politically, economically, and in nearly every other conceivable manner. Plunkett (2010) writes, "three powerful platforms have tremendous synergy that will boost the world of business while bringing stunning world challenges during the 2011-2025 period. These vital building blocks include: a soaring global population; sweeping changes in consumers, demographics and education; emerging technologies centered on healthcare, wireless communications, biotechnology, nanotechnology and energy" (p. 1).

Zakaria, in his 2012 book *The Post-American World: Release 2.0*, writes:

We are now living in the third great power shift of the modern era. It could be called the "rise of the rest." . . . over the past few decades, countries all over the world have been experiencing rates of economic growth that were once unthinkable. While there have been booms and busts, the overall trend has been unambiguously upward. Even the economic rupture of 2008–2009 could not halt or reverse this trend; in fact the recession has accelerated it. While many of the world's wealthy, industrialized economies continued to struggle with slow growth, high unemployment, and overwhelming indebtedness through 2010 and beyond, the countries that constitute "the rest" rebounded quickly." (p. 2)

Zakaria goes on to say that 85 countries grew at a rate of 4 percent or more during the 2008–2009 recession; 50 countries are the poorest and need help, but in the other 142—to include China, India, Brazil, Russia, Indonesia, Turkey, Kenya, and South Africa—the poor are slowly being absorbed into productive and growing economies. Zakaria continues, "for the first time ever, we are witnessing genuinely global growth" (p. 4). Zakaria goes on to briefly identify those aspects of American icons that are now largely held by other countries:

- The tallest building in the world is now in Dubai
- The world's richest man is Mexican
- Largest publicly traded corporation is Chinese
- World's biggest palace is built in Russia and Ukraine
- World's leading refinery is in India
- World's largest factories are all in China
- Hong Kong now rivals London and New York as the leading financial center
- United Arab Emirates is now the home of the most richly endowed investment fund

While these items are somewhat selective in nature, they begin to illuminate the point that there is a growing list of countries who are striving for world economic recognition and realize that the wealth of their nation as well as the well-being of their population is dependent upon being a key player in the new world order—economically, politically, and socially.

We would be remiss not to include alternative perspectives to the previously and current forecasted shortfall of skilled labor in the U.S. and abroad. Alternative perspectives are premised on three foundational elements: (1) the expected growth in the world's population (discussed later), (2) rise of the youngest generations, including Generation Y (91 million by some counts) and Generation Z (81 million, 2003–2020), and (3) the increase in world knowledge through improved educational opportunities and increased enrollments. Those suggesting there may not be a long-term shortfall of skilled workers generally concede the short term in some cases; worth noting however, is that the recession of 2008 has not created the previously envisioned shortfall referenced by those above and many others.

The solution to the many forecasted shortfalls of skilled labor may very well be to capitalize on the world's collective intelligence.

Woolhouse (2011) states, "labor shortages ignore a large and growing number of college graduates who work in low-skill, low-paying occupations. These are the legions of overeducated waiters and waitresses, retail clerks, and receptionists who hold college degrees, a problem known as 'malemployment'" (para. 4). In referencing Andrew Sum, director of the Center for Labor Market Studies at Northeastern University, Woolhouse writes, "25 percent of all employed, college-educated adults in the nation work in jobs that don't require a college degree. That number increases to nearly 40 percent for recent college graduates" (para. 6).

The world's collective intelligence is greater than ever before and continues to increase. We could have used India for our next piece of the puzzle, but China's data has been in the forefront recently and is possibly more familiar to us.

The issue is not about the fall of the U.S. so much as it is about the rise of the rest of the world. The below figure from the National Academy of Sciences (2010, p. 6) reflects current U.S. world standings.

Current innovation-based competitiveness[a]	6th	(in the world)
Percentage of young adults who have graduated from high school[b]	11th	(in the OECD)*
Science literacy among top students[c]	15th	(of 65 countries/regions tested)
College completion rate[b]	16th	(in the OECD)*
High school completion rate[b]	20th	(in the OECD)*
Density of broadband Internet penetration[d]	22nd	(in the world)
Science proficiency of 15-year-olds[c]	23rd	(of 65 countries/regions tested)
Proportion of college students receiving S&E degree[b]	27th	(in the OECD)*
Mathematics literacy among top students[c]	28th	(of 65 countries/regions tested)
Mathematics proficiency of 15-year-olds[c]	31st	(of 65 countries/regions tested)
Improvement in innovation-based competitiveness in the past decade[a]	40th	(in the world)
Quality of mathematics and science education[e]	48th	(in the world)
Density of mobile telephony subscriptions[d]	72nd	(in the world)

*The Organization of Economic Cooperation, and Development (OECD) currently has 34 members.

[a] Information Technology and Innovation Foundation, *The Atlantic Century: Benchmarking EU & U.S. Innovation and Competitiveness*, February 2009. See: *http://www.itif.org/files/2009-atlantic-century.pdf*.

[b] OECD, 2009. Rankings include OECD members and partners, and college graduation ranking is based on Tertiary-A institutions. See: Tables A1.2.a, A2.1, A3.1, and A3.5 at *http://www.oecd.org/document/24/0,3343,en_2649_39263238_43586328_1_1_1_1,00.html*.

[c] National Center for Education Statistics, PISA 2009 Data Tables, Figures and Exhibits, Tables S1, S3, M1, and M3. See *http://nces.ed.gov/pubs2011/2011004_1.pdf*.

[d] S. Dutta and I. Mia, *Global Information Technology Report 2009-2010: ICT for Sustainability*, World Economic Forum, 2010.

[e] World Economic Forum, *The Global Information Technology Report 2009-2010*, Available at: *http://www.weforum.org/node/48197*.

Figure 17.7. Current U.S. World Standings, OECD 2010

To further drive home this point, the National Academy of Sciences "Executive Summary" (2010) reports:

- China is now second in the world in publication of biomedical research articles
- In 2009, 51 percent of United States patents were awarded to non-United States companies
- The World Economic Forum ranks the United States 48th in quality of mathematics science and education
- Of Wal-Mart's 6,000 suppliers, 5,000 are in China
- The legendary Bell Laboratories is now owned by a French company
- Only four of the top ten companies receiving United States patents last year were United States companies
- The world's largest airport is now in China

- In 2000, the number of foreign students studying the physical sciences and engineering in United States graduate schools for the first time surpassed the number of United States students
- China has now replaced the Unites States as the world's number one high-technology exporter
- During a recent period during which two high-rise buildings were constructed in Los Angeles, over 5,000 were built in Shanghai
- In a survey of global firms planning to build new R&D facilities, 77 percent say they will build in China or India
- The United States ranks 27th among developed nations in the proportion of college students receiving undergraduate degrees in science or engineering
- According to OECD data the United States ranks 24th among thirty wealthy countries in life expectancy at birth
- 68 percent of U.S. state prison inmates are high school dropouts
- The United States has fallen from first to eleventh place in the OECD in the fraction 25–34 year olds that has graduated high school
- When MIT put its course materials on the worldwide web, over half of its users were outside the United States
- Roughly half of America's outstanding public debt is now foreign-owned—with China the largest holder
- In 2008, 770,000 people worked in the United States correction sector. . . . During the same year, there were 880,000 workers in the entire United States automobile manufacturing sector
- In January 2010, China's BGI made the biggest purchase of genome sequencing equipment ever (pp. 6–9)

The full impact of this availability of international resources is currently unknown, but we know for sure that other major world economies are now realizing the potential financial impact of global outsourcing and the role an intelligent and skilled workforce plays in capturing a piece of this growing knowledge market.

Growing World Population

At this writing, there are approximately 312 million people in the U.S. The population increases at a projected rate of one birth every eight seconds, one death every 13 seconds, and one international migrant every 43 seconds, yielding a net gain of one person every 13 seconds. Calculating this out in time yields a U.S. projected population of roughly 350 million people in the year 2025, and 400 million by 2043 (Plunkett, 2010, p. 13). From the world's perspective, extrapolating in the same manner yields a world population of roughly 7 billion by 2012, and 8 billion by 2025—this compared to today's world population of roughly 6.9 billion. Some forecast a world population of 10 billion by 2100 (United Nations, 2011). All of this means, from 2011 to 2025, a 14-year period, that we will experience a 40 million—or 13 percent—increase in the U.S. population and a potential 1 billion—or 13 percent—increase in the world population. One billion new people worldwide, simply stated, is a lot of new people. Some may believe 14 years is a long time, but is it? Still memorable is the original 1984 Macintosh, which is well over a quarter century old. Those of any reasonable chronological age will attest that 14 years is a relatively short amount of time. One billion new people seems like a lot, but to think about the impact on required resources really stimulates thought—education, health care, housing, and food.

The U.S. Census Bureau regularly makes forecasts for the U.S. population. They typically use three estimates: low, medium, and high. Reality reflects that the actual numbers are usually between the medium and the high estimates. The underlying premise for the estimates is typically hinged on assumptions in the following (Lang et al., 2009):

- There will not be another world war
- There will not be a devastating global pandemic
- Any current or forthcoming recession will not become another equivalent to the Great Depression of the 1930s
- The U.S. remains attractive to immigrants
- U.S. fertility rates remain stable

Lang and colleagues go on to state, "predicting population growth is also like forecasting the weather, the further into the future one estimates, the less accurate the forecast" (p. 12).

Immigration is frequently looked at from a protectionist perspective—limiting access to the United States. Many, however, point to the benefit of increasing visa availability and creating reforms to not block access to the U.S., but, more palatably, to reform laws to capitalize on the potential for an increased tax base, therefore boosting the U.S. economy (Plunkett, 2010; Overly, 2011).

In the U.S., Plunkett (2010) writes:

Sometime during the second half of 2010, a special person, a portent of the future, arrived in the United States of America. Statistically speaking, this arrival was probably a newborn female. She became the 310 millionth resident of the U.S. . . . overwhelmingly, the odds show she was likely Hispanic, a ballooning sector that will account for one out of four Americans by the time she is 27 years old. Born too late to be part of Gen Y, she is a member of the new cohort, the Diversity Generation, which by 2020 will be 81 million young people. (p. 11)

In 2008, Arthur Nelson, demographer and speaker at the American Planning Association's conference in Las Vegas, forecasted the U.S. population would grow to as much as 1–1.2 billion people between 2100 and 2120, citing high fertility rates, continuing incoming streams of immigrants, and the much anticipated longer life spans of the future (Lang et al., 2009).

Discussing growing the world's population requires a fundamental understanding of fertility rates, which is sometimes referred to as replacement rates. There are numerous considerations that need to be taken into account when discussing the potential for a country to grow—birth rates and death rates to name two. Taking into consideration these and other factors, used is a common term "total fertility rate" or TFR (Plunkett, 2010, p. 26). TFR is the estimated average number of births per female. A TFR of 2.0 would account for the replacement of one man and one woman, and in a general sense would create a breakeven replacement rate. In actuality, "because of other considerations, a TFR of 2.0 or 2.1 is more likely the minimum required to avoid a declining population in a highly developed economy, where good nutrition and postnatal care lead to high survival rates among infants" (Plunkett, 2010, p. 27).

World's Education

Another positive development is the worldwide growth of our collective international intelligence. Although there are no comprehensive measures, according to the NSF's "Science and Engineering Indicators 2010," the number of individuals 15 years and older with a tertiary education, broadly comparable to at least a U.S. technical school or associate's degree, can serve as a proxy measure for the expansion of highly educated populations. Figure 17.8 clearly depicts this reality, as one after another of the major economic powers have increased the education level of their respective populations. "Science and Engineering Indicators 2010" states:

In recent decades, the increasing number of new S&E degrees, including degrees in natural sciences and engineering, awarded in developing countries has diminished the advantage that mature countries had held in advanced education. . . . Worldwide, the number of persons with tertiary education continues to grow. . . . The completion of tertiary education expanded most rapidly in developing

Asian economies, where the combined shares of China, India, South Korea, the Philippines, and Thailand increased from 14% to 25% of the world's total. . . . In the developing world, the number of first university NS&E [natural science and engineering] degrees, broadly comparable to a U.S. baccalaureate, is rising, led by large increases in China, from about 239,000 in 1998 to 807,000 in 2006. New NS&E degrees earned by Japanese and South Korean students combined in 2006 (about 235,000) approximated the number earned by U.S. students in that year, even though the U.S. population was considerably larger (300 million versus 175 million) (pp. O-6,O-7).

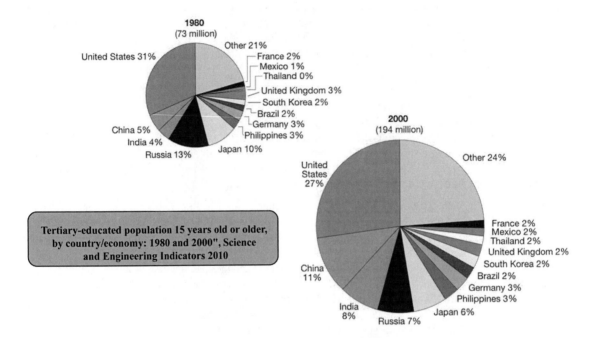

**Figure 17.8. Tertiary-Educated Population 15 years Old or Older,
by Country/Economy: 1980 and 2000, NSF, 2010**

World's Research Workforce

Another indicator of an increasing worldwide educational attainment can be found in the research workforce. The size of the research workforce is another indicator of the economic importance of efforts to develop new knowledge and innovative products and processes. The data in the below figure shows a robust 43 percent growth from 1995 to 2007, depicting an increase in the number of researchers from nearly 4 million in 1995 to about 5.7 million in 2007 (NSF, 2010, p. O-8). The U.S. and the 27 members of the European Union accounted for nearly 1.4 million researchers, 49 percent of the total worldwide, below the 51 percent held 10 years earlier. China's researchers doubled in numbers from roughly 500,000 to more than 1.4 million, increasing its worldwide share from 13 to 25 percent over the same period.

First University Degrees Awarded

The number of first university degrees a nation awards in natural sciences and engineering (NS&E) is a workforce indicator that is more specifically focused on a nation's capacity to innovate in science and technology (S&T). The rising number of Chinese-trained engineers is similarly striking, especially in contrast with declining numbers of U.S. engineering graduates, again, according to the "Science and Engineering Indicators 2010."

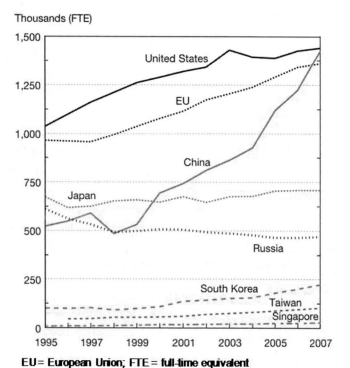

EU = European Union; FTE = full-time equivalent

NOTES: U.S. data for 2007 estimated based on 2004–06 growth rate. EU includes all 27 member states.

Figure 17.9. Researchers in Selected Regions/Countries/Economies: 1995–2007, NSF, 2010

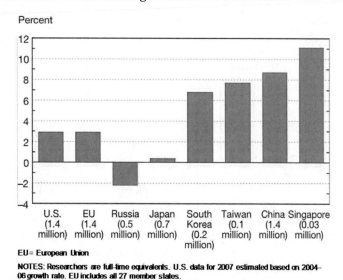

EU = European Union

NOTES: Researchers are full-time equivalents. U.S. data for 2007 estimated based on 2004–06 growth rate. EU includes all 27 member states.

Figure 17.10. Average Annual Growth in Number of Researchers in Selected Regions/Countries/Economies: 1995–2007, NSF, 2010

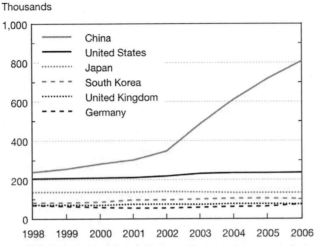

Thousands

The number of first university degrees a nation awards in natural sciences and engineering (NS&E) is a workforce indicator that is more specifically focused on a nation's capacity to innovate in S&T.

NOTE: Natural sciences include physical, biological, earth, atmospheric, ocean, agricultural, and computer sciences and mathematics.

Figure 17.11. First University Degrees in Natural Sciences and Engineering, Selected Countries: 1998–2006, NSF, 2010

Corporate Research and Development

We are also seeing a change in our corporate research and development (R&D) laboratory structure. We are tapping the collective intelligence of leading academics around the world. Historically, R&D labs at IBM, General Electric, Hewlett-Packard, and others were rooted in the industrial era, where communications traveled slowly and information was exchanged in lunchrooms and conferences. Organizations are now moving toward an external model, capitalizing on universities, start-ups, business partners, and government labs.

To this point, IBM has now created what are termed "collaboratories," where IBM is matched with researchers with governments, industries, and universities. IBM is currently working with Saudi Arabia, Switzerland, China, Ireland, Taiwan, and India on these collaboratories. Additionally, according to IBM, there is enough demand for 100 more collaboratories in a multitude of countries.

In summary, we are capitalizing on the collective intelligence of the world for the betterment of humankind.

Value of Education

Education provides opportunities that would not otherwise be available. The more formal education one earns, as degree completions, the more opportunities present themselves. Figure 17.12 depicts most recent data released from the U.S. Bureau of Labor Statistics "Current Population Survey." The data reflects the unemployment rates and median weekly earnings of increasingly greater levels of educated individuals. In 2009, the early stage of the 2008–2009 recession, U.S. unemployment was running 7.9 percent on average, well short of the maximum unemployment during this recession of over 10 percent. Those individuals with less than a high school diploma experienced 14.6 percent unemployment, while those with bachelor's degrees were at 5.2 percent, master's degree holders at 3.9 percent, and doctorate degree holders at 2.5 percent. This data clearly supports the "education pays" proposition.

As to median weekly earnings, using the same categories as above, less than a high school diploma was $454, bachelor's degree holders at $1,025, master's degree holders at $1,257, and doctorate degree holders at $1,532. Annualizing this data suggests individuals with less than a high school diploma earned $23,608, bachelor's degree holders earned $53,300, master's degree holders earned $65,364, and doctorate degree holders earned $79,664. If one were to extrapolate this data for a lifetime, assuming a 45-year uninterrupted work experience (not accounting for inflation or earning increases), the total earnings across the same levels of education would be: individuals holding less than high school diploma at $1,062 million, bachelor's degree holders at $2.4 million, master's degree holders at $2.94 million, and doctorate degree holders at $3.58 million. In looking strictly at science and engineering as a demographic, roughly half of those in science and engineering occupations earned nearly $71,000 more than those not in science and engineering in 2007, which was more than double the median earnings of the total U.S. workforce of $31,400 in the same year (NSF, 2010, pp. 3–7).

Overall wages of college graduates in the U.S. were 74 percent higher than high school graduates in 2008 (Woolhouse, 2011). The wage advantage was just 30 percent in 1979. Clearly, given this data, the more you academically achieve through formal education and credentialing, the more opportunities for employment are available, and the more you earn throughout your lifetime.

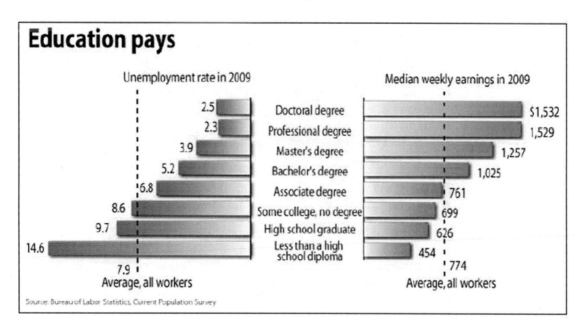

Figure 17.12. Education Pays, Bureau of Labor Statistics, 2011

Outsourcing of Goods and Services

We live in a world economy where outsourcing is demanded by our populace. China, as an example, sews more clothes, stitches more shoes, and assembles more toys than any other nation in the world. It receives more foreign investment than any other nation in the world, and half of China's trade is controlled by foreign firms (Fishman, 2005, p. 70). China makes 40 percent of all furniture sold in the United States. It has already been stated that the country graduates significantly more engineers than the U.S. Additionally, Wal-Mart is the sixth largest importer from China ahead of France, the United Kingdom, and Canada (Shenkar, 2005, p. 150). This is especially interesting, given that the largest importers from a particular country are usually other countries. But in the end, we demand lower prices, which generally requires outsourcing. This is not a bad thing; it's actually quite good when viewed from the overall benefits to a world population, recognizing, however, the more immediate local impacts. The top reasons companies outsource are depicted in figure 17.13.

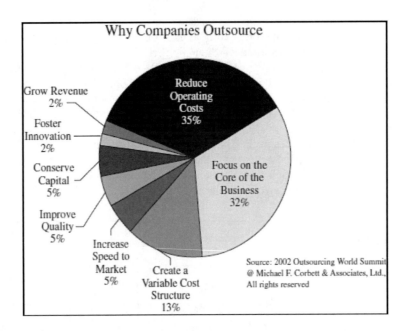

Figure 17.13. Top Reasons Companies Outsource, Outsourcing World Summit, 2002

India is now experiencing an interesting phenomenon. It has so much work from outsourcing that the number of companies providing such services has increased significantly. This means that workers have more options for employment, which directly means, by concepts of supply and demand, that the cost for the shortage of skilled labor has gone up (Puliyenthuruthel & Kripalani, 2005, p. 52). However, even with annual wage inflation of 15 to 20 percent, U.S. companies can hire well-educated Indians for $10,000 or less a year, one-fourth the cost of an entry-level worker in the United States (Dolan, 2006, p. 76). According to Hewitt Associates, salary increases (in percentages) for 2006 in Asian-Pacific countries are as follows:

- India 13.9
- Philippines 8.2
- China 8.1
- Thailand 6.3
- Malaysia 5.4–6.1
- Australia 4.4–4.5
- Singapore 3.4–4.3
- Taiwan 3.9–4.6
- Japan 3.3–3.5
- Hong Kong 2.3–2.8

There are competing Indian companies, to the point that India is now outsourcing their overflow work to other nations with more available talent and lower costs. In fact, outsourcing has become more than simply call centers or backroom operations. Outsourcing has moved up the food chain to design and development of sophisticated hardware and software systems. According to Dolan:

In the 1980s outsourcers in India did low-rung jobs such as data entry and some software development. In the 1990s, they expanded by doing some larger software projects and by taking over whole IT systems and taking over backroom functions such as accounting for European and U.S.

corporations. Now they draw a bead on more sophisticated services—engineering, research and development, and designing auto parts, sections of aircraft wings and chips for wireless services. (2006, p. 75)

In April 2006, Mikhail Gorbachev took the stage at a packed Boston hotel ballroom to address the Massachusetts Software & Internet Council. Company presidents and other high-level members of the consortium thought they might hear about perestroika, the organizational restructuring of the Soviet economy and bureaucracy that began in the 1980s. What they heard instead was a discussion of Russia's world-class software engineering skills. Gorbachev urged the audience of seven hundred executives to send software engineering work to highly talented Russian software shops (Reinhardt, 2006, p. 62).

In a 2011 article, Powell (2011) discusses the end of cheap labor in China, saying, "the Chinese Government, worried about an ever widening gap between the rich and the poor, has raised the minimum wage 14% to 21% in the past year" (p. 2). In quoting Harley Seyedin, president of the American Chamber of Commerce in South China, "the era of cheap labor in China is over . . . that doesn't mean that labor costs in China, even in the most expensive parts of the country, are higher than in most other places, particularly in the developed world, they aren't. The average manufacturing wage in China is still only about $3.10 per hour, compared with $22.30 in the U.S." (p. 2). To combat the rising wages near sea borders, many multinationals and Chinese companies are expanding and relocating inland, where labor is still very cheap. Powell continues, writing, "the changing economics of made in China will benefit both the rich and the poor world. Countries like Cambodia, Laos, India and Vietnam are picking up some of the cheapest labor manufacturing left by the Chinese" (p. 4).

Countries are moving in a direction to increase their respective socioeconomic status relative to the rest of the world. Other major players hoping to capitalize on this growing trend in world economics include Central and Eastern Europe, China and Southeast Asia, Latin America, the Caribbean, and the Middle East and Africa.

According to the National Science Foundation's 2010 report:

The global expansion of high-technology trade has made China the largest single high-technology exporter and has changed the relative positions of the developed and developing countries. China's share of world high-technology exports increased from 6% in 1995 to 20% in 2008, while the Asia-9 [India, Indonesia, Malaysia, Philippines, Singapore, South Korea, Taiwan, Thailand, and Vietnam] maintained a 26%–29% share. . . . the U.S. share dropped from 21% to 14%, and the EU maintained a 16%–18% share. (p. O-16)

Figure 17.14 reflects the relative share of high-technology exports.

Concluding Thoughts on the International Impact

Countries are more inclined now than ever before to build into their long-term strategies a science and technology plan for continued growth and economic prosperity. Science and technology is no longer, singularly, the domain of a few well-developed nations; it is now on the radar screen of every major developed and developing nation, recognized as an essential element of an ever more globalized world. The National Science Foundation's 2010 report includes:

The quest for international talent, once largely limited to major Western nations, is now pursued by many, and "brain drain" has evolved into cross-national flows of highly trained specialists. . . .

The globalization of the world economy has brought unprecedented levels of growth to many countries, demonstrating that benefits can accrue to all. But the structural changes that are part and parcel of rapid growth bring with them painful dislocations, amplified by the uncertainties and potential changes fostered by the world-wide recession. . . .

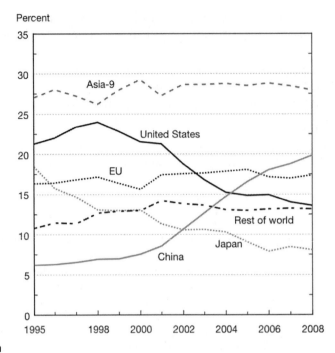

Percent

EU = European Union

NOTES: Excludes intra-EU trade. Asia-9 includes India, Indonesia, Malaysia, Philippines, Singapore, South Korea, Taiwan, Thailand, and Vietnam. China includes Hong Kong. EU excludes Cyprus, Estonia, Latvia, Lithuania, Luxembourg, Malta, and Slovenia.

Figure 17.14. Share of Global High-Technology Exports, by Region/Country: 1995–2008, NSF, 2010

Growth of the U.S. S&E workforce continues to exceed that of the overall workforce. However, the 2000–07 period showed the smallest growth rate (2.2%) in S&E occupations since NSF began tracking these data in the 1950s. Although the U.S. recession that began in 2007 affected workers across all occupations, S&E occupations appear to be less severely impacted. The unemployment rate in April 2009 was 9.0% for all workers, but, 4.3% for those working in S&E occupations. The influence of the recession on longer-term S&E labor force behavior . . . remains to be seen. . . .

The globalization of the S&E labor force continues to increase. The number of people with S&E is skills rising, especially in developing nations, and the location of S&E employment is becoming more internationally diverse. S&E workers are becoming more internationally mobile. These trends reinforce each other: as R&D spending and business investment cross national borders in search of available talent, talented people cross borders in search of interesting and lucrative work, and employers recruit and move employees internationally. (p. O-20, 3-58)

Innovation, Technology, and the Systems Integrator

Credit for introducing and advancing this section is premised on the seminal work of Gary R. Bertoline, dean of the College of Technology at Purdue University. Bertoline penned an unpublished work titled "Future College of Technology." This document formed the underlying vision and detailed plan for creating preeminence in defining and developing the twenty-first century technologist—this, through reinvention of the Purdue University College of Technology, a tier 1 research-intensive university. Subsequent conversations to advance this objective yielded the collection of thought reflected in the following paragraphs.

In one day, on July 26, 2011, three major announcements were reported on major technological advances. First, it was reported (Ackerman, 2011; Dillow, 2011) that Boeing and BAE Systems, two large defense contractors, had created a shipboard defense solid-state laser machine gun combination, affectionately reported in the press as a "Death Ray" (think *Star Wars*). This gun has the ability to lock onto a target and deliver machine gun lead ammunition or, alternatively, a high-powered laser beam; either will cause serious damage to the intended target. Second, Sorrel (2011) reported IBM had applied for a new patent that trains the device to recognize the fatness or thinness of an individual's fingers, and then reformat the keyboard to accommodate the specific user. Third, a German company (Hennigan, 2011) created a flying seagull so life-like that it flew around and convinced a flock of seagulls it was part of their flock. The implications of this type of drone are significant. Nearly every day, something of similar significance is reported on.

Technology and the process of creating it—innovation—is moving at a thunderous pace throughout world societies. Our rate of technological advancements dwarfs any previous period in our world history. It is nearly inconceivable what will be created next, as organizations small and large are busily working to produce the next iPhone, robotic lifelike animal, electric car, cloned DNA structure, or death ray.

There, again, is no shortfall of innovation and innovation as a sense of governmental urgency. Zakaria (2012) states, "Innovation is as American as apple pie. It seems to accord with so many elements of our national character—ingenuity, freedom, flexibility, the willingness to question conventional wisdom and defy authority. But politicians are pinning their hopes for innovation on more urgent reasons. America's future growth will have to come from new industries that create new products and processes" (p. 10).

Innovation is not only the underlying basis for the United States, as a national strategy, but additionally, China is betting on transitioning their economy from one built on imitation to one built on innovation (Lohr, 2011). According to Lohr, China's goal for annual invention patent filings is one million by 2015, this up from 300,000 in 2010. In contrast, the U.S. filed 480,000 ending September 2011. The Chinese expect to have 9000 patent examiners by 2015, compared with 6,300 U.S. examiners today.

The National Science Foundation's "2008 Business R&D and Innovation Survey" (Boroush, 2010) reviewed innovation practices from over 1.5 million U.S. companies active in the U.S. Their findings reveal 9 percent of the reviewed 1.5 million companies were active innovators. Of that, 22 percent were product and process innovations from manufacturing companies, 8 percent were process innovators from non-manufacturing sectors, and 8 percent of those total innovative companies were product innovators. Higher innovation occurred in manufacturing subsectors of chemicals, computer and electronic parts, and electrical equipment/appliances/components.

For purposes of this discussion, innovation has been addressed from multiple perspectives:

- The number of first university degrees a nation awards in natural sciences and engineering is a workforce indicator that is more specifically focused on a nation's capacity to innovate in science and technology.
- Organizations are now moving toward an external model capitalizing on universities, start-ups, business partners, and government labs.
  - Foreign nationals are authors of the majority of patent applications filed by many U.S. companies: 65 percent at Merck, 64 percent at GE, and 60 percent at Cisco.
- The size of the research workforce is another indicator of the economic importance of efforts to develop new knowledge and innovative products and processes.
- One after another of the major economic powers have increased the education level of their respective populations.

What is innovation? Is there a process to follow for innovation? How do you measure the success of following an innovation process? If innovation is a process, then it has to have multiple activities with attendant products as output of the process. Are there corollary concepts to the innovation process? All of these questions, and a dozen more, are valid and predictable discussion topics addressed in numerous business books, texts, and articles.

To a large extent, innovation and the manifestation of the innovation process is intrinsically interconnected to the role of the systems integrator. Systems integration is the higher level of cognitive understanding of the many separate, yet highly related disciplines/functions of a product or service. Those practicing systems integration are capable of "seeing" whole system connections. Be able to "see" connectivity between seemingly unrelated architectures has been recently characterized as "associational thinking." Given this, if systems integrators are capable of "seeing" the interrelatedness of whole systems, and those who can "see" the interrelatedness of whole systems are considered individuals with an innovator's DNA, then it stands to reason that systems integrators are prone to be classified as having the characteristically defined DNA of successful innovators, yielding the connection between innovators, innovation, and systems integrators.

The basic element of successful systems integration is the vision of interrelatedness of these many attendant knowledge domains—vision, which acts as the common thread through the innovation process. The evolution of this concept resides between the philosophical underpinnings of leadership and innovation, and the tactical realities of curriculum design, development, and implementation.

Understanding Technology as a Discipline

This section focuses on the worldwide growth of our collective international intelligence and the direct applicability it has to technological innovation in the United States. While there has been much attention to the proposed shortfall of science and engineering skilled labor, technology and its attendant innovation process is a natural derivative of both science (the study of the natural world: physical, biological, and chemical) and engineering (the design of the human-made world: artifacts, systems, and processes). To adequately address the educational imperative to create technological innovation is to recognize the value international intelligence brings to this tightly integrated and intrinsically intertwined third discipline.

To fully appreciate the value of our world's collective knowledge in advancing US innovation, we must first accept a definition of technology and innovation, one that stands aside from that of science and engineering. Once we accept the underlying premise that the study of technology is a discipline and technological innovation a process, then it becomes quite obvious why the world's collective knowledge actually promotes technological innovation here and abroad.

To fully appreciate the breadth of this proposition, this overall section has addressed the proposed shortfall in science and engineering through reduced graduates and senior workers soon to retire. Further discussion of technology as a discipline, its practitioners as technologists, and attendant innovation as a process is explored below.

As discussed by Bertoline (2011), technology is a pervasive feature of our contemporary culture, but it is more than that; it is a defining feature of the human condition. Bertoline writes:

> We know a great deal about technologies in an individual sense, but much less about technology in the way of general understanding. We have detailed studies about the history of individual technologies, analysis of the design process, economic impacts of technology, and the societal impacts of technology. However, we have no agreement on the meaning of the word "technology". We also have no overall theory of how technologies are accepted and integrated into society, no deep understanding of innovation, and no theory of evolution for technology. Unlike other disciplines or knowledge areas, there is no set of overall principles that would give technology, as a subject, a logical structure. We need to develop a Body of Knowledge for technology and the [Purdue

University] College of Technology can serve a leadership role for the nation and the world by undertaking this. . . .

Technology is used to create the human-made world. Technologists apply human and physical resources to design, produce, and assess artifacts and systems that control and modify the natural and human-made environments. Developing and using technology impacts people, society, and the environment. Therefore, technology is the practices used to develop, produce, and use artifacts and the impacts these actions have on humans and the natural world. . . .

Technology has a process for the way new artifacts are developed and used. It, also, has an accumulated body of knowledge that explains existing technologies and provides the foundation for new technological advancements. Technology educators need to look at these foci so students can study (1) the processes used by practitioners to innovate, develop, maintain, commercialize, and manage existing or new technology, (2) the areas of technology that represent the accumulated knowledge of practice, and (3) the impacts of technology on people, society, and the environment.

The discipline of Technology has established a way to structure the knowledge of technology, which includes the productive human activities of communication, construction, manufacturing, and transportation as well as energy, information and material processing.

The third focus of a complete technology education program has received the least attention and may well be the most important. It requires identifying the relationship and interaction among technology, people, society, the environment and other disciplines. Technology is not a natural phenomenon. It is a product of human choice. People saw its development, production, and use as necessary or economically profitable. However, reaching this human vision has positive and negative impacts on people, societies, and the environment.

Likewise, technology is not an isolated body of knowledge. It has strong connections with all other areas of knowledge. Science explains the natural laws that are applied by technology. Engineering is used to design systems, processes, and the artifacts that comprise our technological world. Mathematics and mathematical models explain the operation of technological systems. Language and art can be used to describe technology and its impacts. The social studies can describe how technology has, is, and may well impact and be impacted by people and society.

The engineered human-made world (to distinguish from the human managed world; human doing) is designed, created, operated, and maintained through a continuum of highly skilled and highly educated professionals. Engineers work with nature and its laws as revealed by science. Technologists work with tools, process, systems, and artifacts. The engineer makes with the mind, the technologist works with the mind and with the hand.

The essence of engineering is the design process; planning in the mind a device, process, or system that will solve a problem or meet a human need. The engineer usually does not make or construct but more commonly directs, plans, or designs.

The essence of a technologist is the mastery of a whole field with a broad and deep understanding of the technology; the processes, systems, tools, and techniques necessary to construct, modify, innovate, operate, and maintain the engineering design.

There is a continuum in technology that moves from vocationally trained skilled craftsmen at one end, to technicians narrowly focused on one aspect of technology, to technologists . . . who have mastered a whole field of technology, to the engineer who have mastered whole technological systems. There is a clear distinction between a technician and a technologist. The technologist is a highly skilled professional that is positioned in the "sweet spot" between the engineer and the technician and skilled craftsmen. Technologists serve an important and unique role as the "integrators" in business and industry. Technologists have a deep understanding of the human-made world and use a problem solving methodology that can lead to innovation through the development of new and improved artifacts, systems, and processes.

Clearly defining and describing technological knowledge while seeking its integration with other disciplines will lead the technology profession, as a whole, to a recognition that (1) technology studies is the study of the human-made world, (2) technologists use the technological method (problem solving, innovation and commercialization cycle) to develop new and improved artifacts and systems, (3) technology is used to help people meet their communication, product, and transportation needs and, (4) technology impacts and is impacted by people, society, and the environment (p. 10).

This four-point philosophy leads us to believe that, like science, there is a general way to approach a technological problem or opportunity; there are unique practices used to produce, operate, and maintain each device or system; there is a unique body of knowledge that through use-inspired and applied research methodologies will produce new knowledge, and these actions are operated in historical, personal, and societal contexts.

The above makes the connection between the evolving discipline of technology, the technologist, and the systems integrator. The neural thread through all three entities is the ability to "see" the interrelatedness of the contextual differences. The "seeing" of the interrelatedness again resides as a common characteristic of successful innovators. Continuing to define and differentiate, recently published work reviews the working titles assumed by technology and engineering graduating Bachelor of Science majors entering business and industry. The article makes the association of equality between the two disciplines (Land, 2012).

Defining the Systems Integrator

To truly have a discipline, there must be a body of knowledge. Technology leadership is no different. There is significant literature detailing leadership theories—trait, behavioral, situational, and the like. But what does it mean to have a discipline in technology leadership? What would the basic body of knowledge in technology leadership look like? This section examines technology leadership and proposes the basic knowledge and skill set required to function in the discipline of technology leadership. The resultant individual, educated in the discipline of technology leadership, may be categorically defined as a systems integrator.

Overview of the Systems Integration Concept

Systems integration, as a discipline, is well founded in industry and exists at many levels. Within a given discipline (e.g., software engineering or hardware engineering), systems integration involves bringing together those many aspects of sub-knowledge within the specific discipline. At the lowest level, integrating two components of a given discipline within a larger system serves as an example of an integration function to be performed; this given the increasingly complex hierarchy of components, sub-assemblies, assemblies, systems, and platforms. At each level in our overall system, there exists a level-specific integration function. For our purposes, we are defining and differentiating between two different systems integration functions: (1) the integration of a given discipline and its components, and (2) the integration function that brings together multiple disciplines within a given system. Our interest in systems integration does not extend to the lowest component integration level.

To illustrate our areas of interest, assume a system made up of software and hardware with mechanical operational requirements. An iPhone serves this purpose, wherein the placement of the buttons the user employs is orchestrated by the mechanical discipline, the physical internal hardware chips and accessories are the domain of the hardware discipline, and the software that allows the iPhone to operate being the domain of the software discipline. Within the software of the system, to be designed, developed, *integrated*, and tested are the following components: an operating system, database management system, and user applications. Within the operating system there exists lower-level modules to be designed, developed, *integrated*, and tested, namely, the central processing unit, memory management unit, input/output interface, and others. At the lowest level, we will integrate and test, from the bottom-up, the modules within the operating system; then, we will integrate the operating system with the database management system and the user applications. Our first level of interest in systems integration is at the entire software discipline level—something commonly referred to as a *software systems integrator/engineer*. Our second level of interest in systems integration is at the systems level, where we bring together the software discipline, hardware discipline, and mechanical discipline; this level is commonly referred to as a *systems integrator/engineer*.

To this end, the tactical implementation with courses and curriculum implications is hinged on a strategic decision of which level of systems integration one is most interested in pursuing, namely, discipline-specific systems integration (e.g., software systems integration) or the higher-level systems integration function (e.g., systems integration). The implication of this strategic decision is critical to further evolution of a tactical decision on curriculum. Figure 17.15 depicts these two levels of hierarchical integration.

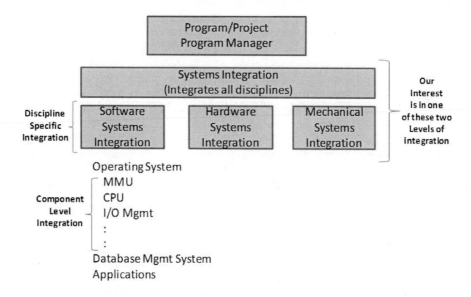

Figure 17.15. Levels of Integration

Discipline-Specific Systems Integration/Integrator

If one chooses the path of a discipline-specific systems integrator, then the core curriculum will be domain-specific and offer courses as an umbrella that provides systems integration knowledge. This given that systems integration is, in fact, a process with multiple activities and attendant products.

For example, a student would enroll in Computer Graphics Technology, and made room for in the curriculum would be perhaps as many as four courses that would provide the body of knowledge for systems integration as it relates to Computer Graphics Technology. Now, the immediate implication is that the systems integration courses are tailored to a given discipline; however, this is not necessarily required in that systems integration, as mentioned above, is a process in and of itself with activities and attendant products. The systems integration body of knowledge assumes that if you follow the process, perform the activities, and generate the attendant products along the way, a systems integrator can help to ensure a consistent and coherent output from the process.

While it may be easy to visualize disciplines such as computer graphics, information technology, building construction, and others as possessing a body of knowledge and serving as a discipline-specific knowledge domain to underlie core knowledge of the systems integration process, it is equally possible to bring together the many aspects of technology leadership in such a manner to also benefit from a higher-level understanding of systems integration. Should one pursue this level of discipline-specific systems integration, each of the above many disciplines would be reviewed with an eye to tailoring the umbrella systems integration process core curriculum.

Systems Integration/Integrator

If, on the other hand, the strategic interest is to educate graduates in whole systems integration, then we would want to pull together into a single curriculum those related disciplines within the college or university, and then offer the same four or more core courses in the systems integration process as we proposed in the above discipline-specific systems integration alternative. This creates an eclectic collection of seemingly unrelated disciplines, but in reality, it brings together a sufficient overview of disciplines that may play together in future innovative or disruptive systems. An example of this may be a curriculum composed of courses from computer graphics, information technology, and technology leadership, with courses on the systems integration body of knowledge and others as deemed to complete a whole curriculum. Point being, we have introduced into this level of curriculum other discipline-specific bodies of knowledge.

In some regards, we are deciding between advancing directional knowledge versus intersectional knowledge (Johansson, 2004), where directional knowledge and ideas are those ideas that evolve through the recognized and accepted "normal" process of advancing the basic body of a given discipline. Directional ideas are generally identified as improvements of a given product or service in a fairly predictable way along defined measures and dimensions. Intersectional knowledge and ideas evolve through the combining of knowledge between and across multiple "pure" fields of study or disciplines. Intersectional ideas are those ideas that change the way we perceive the world.

In the end, subsequent tactical discussions related to curriculum are contingent upon our strategic intent—systems integration or discipline-specific systems integration?

General Model of the Systems Integrator

Looking at systems integration as either discipline-specific or the more general systems integrator aligns with commonly accepted understanding and practice in industry. Another way, however, to view the systems integrator role is to define a basic body of general knowledge that can be applied across any number of industrially based disciplines. Figure 17.16 (Springer, 1995; Robbins, 1999; Vandeveer, 2011) below depicts a general model forming the basic body of knowledge for the systems integrator.

The above model proposes the ideal systems integrator is one who possesses a basic body of knowledge in three primary areas: technical skills, human skills, and conceptual skills. The entire three-pronged skill set is embedded within discipline-specific knowledge. In other words, once the basic skill set defined by the above model is learned, then the learned skill set forms a toolbox with general applicability across unlimited industrial disciplines.

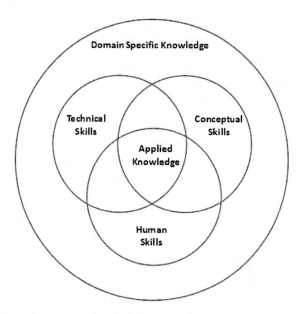

Figure 17.16. Systems Integrator Framework

Technical Skills

Technical skills are not domain-specific skills. Instead, they represent knowledge focused on better under-standing past and present processes as well as having a basic knowledge of technology and its implications on society, cultures, and economic prosperities.

Process knowledge, both past and present, encompasses heightened awareness of such initiatives as:

- ISO (9000) Standards
- Quality Function Deployment (QFD)
- Continuous Improvement (Japanese termed Kaizen)
- Zero Defect Programs—based on statistical process control
- PDCA—plan, do check, act, cycle
- Quality Circles
- Department Quality Teams (DQTs)
- Taguchi Methods
- Total Quality Management (TQM)
- Business Process Reengineering (BPR)
- Deming (14 points)
- Object-Oriented Quality Management (OQD)
- Lean Thinking
- Six Sigma

Additionally, technical skills include technology awareness, meaning:

- The history of technology
- Technology policy and economics
- The philosophy of technology
- Technology from a global perspective
- Technology and society

Human Skills

Human skills are those skills required to "lead" or "manage" a group of individuals within or across multiple disciplines. Human skills include skills typically conceived as critical to individuals that transition from an individual contributor role to an increasingly higher role with superior-subordinate relationships. Underlying this skill set are skills depicted below:

- Human resources
- Motivational
- Conflict management
- Negotiation
- Ethics
- Change management
- Group dynamics
- Interpersonal

Some of the skills defined as "leadership" may be more appropriately categorized as "management" skills. It is not the intent of this chapter to debate or differentiate the definition of leadership versus management, as others have long since discovered this as an effort in futility given the current and continuing controversy (Yukl, 2002, p. 5). It is more important in defining the body of knowledge for technology leadership to identify those skills that organizations would like their individual contributors to have as they transition into first-line or subsequent leadership/management roles with attendant responsibilities. To this end, the above list is indicative of those skills and not all encompassing.

Conceptual Skills

Conceptual skills are premised on a general analytical ability. Conceptual skills may be thought of as:

- Logical thinking
- Proficiency in concept formation
- Conceptualization of complex and ambiguous relationships
- Creativity in idea generation and problem solving
- Ability to analyze events and perceive trends
- Ability to anticipate changes
- Ability to recognize opportunities and potential problems (both inductively and deductively)
- Possessing an understanding of entrepreneurship and intrapreneurship
- Broad-based knowledge of innovation and commercialization

The body of knowledge, relative to conceptual skills, would be those educational entities contributing to the above. Additional areas of study would include:

- Strategic planning
- Critical thinking
- Problem-solving techniques
- Effectiveness and efficiency understanding

In some regards, it is expected that all participants with an awareness of the technology leadership body of knowledge would be equally educated in these conceptual skills and possess the ability to function in a conceptual capacity. In reality, however, varying levels of leadership, relative to management, are expected to demonstrate an increased conceptual capability with a declining expectation in technical skills. Figure 17.17 below depicts this understanding.

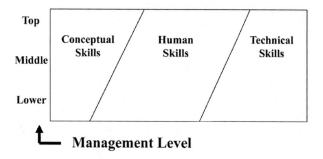

Figure 17.17. Management Level versus Expected Skill Sets

Technical skills are those that support the knowledge of, or actual doing of, the tasks to be performed. This is especially true of middle management, or better yet, first-line supervisors. These individuals are more involved with the day-to-day operations of the organization.

For example, assume an individual spent many years in the discipline of software engineering. Because of this, he/she would be versed in the many forms of programming languages, design methodologies, and terminology in general. This would more readily allow the individual to provide valuable insight into this discipline. As time progresses, however, technical skills begin to become obsolete and somewhat antiquated. For this reason, continuous lifelong learning is required if we wish to stay abreast of our technical disciplines.

As well, as an individual moves into higher and higher levels of management, it is not expected that individual will maintain such sharp skills. In fact, as individuals progress into higher levels of management, they are expected to contribute in a different manner and to apply a different set of skills, such as human or conceptual.

Next Steps toward Curriculum Development

If we were to accept the above definition of what constitutes the basic body of knowledge for technology leadership, then the next step would be to further evolve the requirements into a curriculum—clearly not a small undertaking. Each of the courses forming the underlying premise of the curriculum would have to have an empirically conceptual as well as procedural foundation. Meaning, for each module defined and developed there would be underlying evidence characterized by observation or experiment versus being based solely on theory. This combination of empirically based and procedurally based education would provide a basis for application and individual theory formulation based on a deeper and richer understanding of observable phenomena. This, then, would work toward advancing the agreed to technology leadership body of knowledge through directional ideas and their subsequent formalization, which directly supports the continuation and advancement of the technology leadership body of knowledge and survival and growth of the discipline.

Integrating Intersectional Ideas

The above examples cut to the root of the concept of having multiple disciplines come together to create a disruptive technology, or in this case, disruptive process. Each of the above discussed products required a unique set of discipline-specific skills and knowledge, and only together could they have orchestrated such an amazing and prime example of a disruptive technology capitalizing on the collective intelligence of "pure" disciplines. Again, if someone were to look at the entire product development process and all its attendant disciplines, they could, conceivably, take this intersectional idea and advance it, creating yet another intersectional idea and improvement, and therefore, advancing the basic body of new knowledge brought about by the combinatorial effects of multiple pure disciplines.

So, given the above, if there are directional ideas and intersectional ideas, then would advancing intersectional ideas be more intersectional ideas, even though we were really only advancing the existing intersectional idea? Or is there yet another, higher-level body of knowledge originating from intersectional ideas that creates a sub-assembly type of idea hierarchy. And if so, what would it be called? Are ideas like systems, where we have component-level, sub-assembly-level, system-level, and ultimately, platform-level ideas?

In approaching the dean of an engineering college with the question of how we intend to teach our youth to think in the gaps, at the intersection of the pure disciplines, came the reply that we already do teach at the intersection. We have many degrees entitled:

- Biogerontology
  - Evolutionary biologists, calorie restriction researchers, nanotechnologists, medical professionals
- Bioterials or biomaterials (human tissues)
  - Biology, materials sciences
- Biomechanics
- Biomedical
- Biomolecular
- Bioinformatics
- Biometrics and pattern recognition
- Genomics—emerging science of understanding the human genome
- Proteomics—what proteins do in the human body
- Bioengineering—integrates physics, mathematics, chemistry, biology, and life sciences
- Mechatronics—mechanical electronics

It becomes more and more obvious that we are coming to understand the power of integrating disciplines. The climate change work being done has produced multiple volumes. Volume I, produced by the International Panel for Climate Change (IPCC), used 152 coordinating lead authors from over 30 countries, reviewed by over 600 experts.

Tom Friedman has written a number of books, including *The Lexus and the Olive Tree* as well as *The World is Flat*. In this latter book, he points out that politics, culture, technology, finance, national security, and ecology are no longer single nation based. He adds that any one nation is tightly intertwined with another. He identifies three forces behind the rise of these intersections (Johansson, 2004, p. 22):

- Convergence of science. The work of the IPCC mentioned above is indicative of this. Oceanographers, meteorologists, geologists, physicists, chemists, and biologists all working collaboratively to better understand the effects of global warming.
- Leap in computational capabilities. If you have ever been to Disney World in Orlando Florida, there is the opportunity to stand and watch as animators draw the next Disney movie to be produced. They draw frame after frame, one at a time, which when quickly turned create an image moving ever so gently across a screen. It takes roughly 24 hand drawn frames per second. For a 75-minute typical Disney movie, that equals over 100,000 hand drawn frames. Steve Jobs on leaving Apple Computer assumed a position at Pixar. Pixar, as you may recall is the creator of *Shrek, Monsters, Inc.,* and other like movies. Jobs wanted to disrupt the old hand-drawn process so he advocated the creation of software which promoted, what appears to be real-time images, moving across the screen. While some thought it would be the end of the animators, it was not. The animators simply assumed a higher-level cognitive function, where they were now used to look closely at the changing images on the computer screens and offer suggestions as to how exactly the hair on the images should move and blow to direc-

tional changes and wind effects, and, how facial expressions might change as one experiences changing emotional states.

- Movement of people. There are many books and articles written about the growth of our collective world intelligence. Everything from number of individuals, by country, who are attending post-secondary school, to the number of patents being filed. We are unequivocally growing our world's collective intelligence, and most individuals, although perhaps partial to their home country, are not all thinking their home country is the only place to work.

Creating an Integrative Mind-set

So how do you create an integrative effect? The answer resides in understanding the concept of associative barriers. Associative barriers are those associations we create over time and with experience allow us to quickly follow a chain reaction of activities, events, or conclusions, based on a specific stimulus. In other words, we see something happening and can quickly jump to the end result or what we believe to be correct answer. Associative barriers are also what somewhat prohibit us from the proverbial "thinking outside of the box."

As an example, for anyone who has ever seen the television show *Iron Chef*, you realize it pits two chefs against each other to create a five-course meal out of a single item, for example, codfish. The Iron Chef and his/her wannabe Iron Chef competitor feverishly cook a meal that is then judged by a panel who determine and crown a winner. If an Iron Chef and a fisherman are strolling through a fish market and happen on codfish, each would most likely view the fish from a different lens. The Iron Chef would most likely be thinking cod salad, cod appetizer, cod main course, cod dessert, and so forth, while the fisherman might very well be thinking, "Ah, yes. Cod is best caught in the Pacific, or perhaps the Gulf." Point being, each "sees" the codfish from his or her own mental associations, and these associations are exactly what prohibit the individual from immediately "seeing" the other's perspective. On introduction to another's perspective, the individual might then grow his or her own associations to include such alternate perspectives, but, in general, we form our associations from our own personal experiences or those of others we hold dear.

What's a joke? A joke is a story that takes us down an associative path and then introduces an integrative idea—one we didn't see coming. A few Sunday mornings ago, I was watching Joel Osteen on television. He opened with the following:

> There was a cul-de-sac on which many Catholics and one Protestant lived. Every first day of Lent, while the Catholics were preparing and eating fish, the Protestant would be grilling a big, juicy steak. All of the Catholics could smell that steak throughout the cul-de-sac, so the Catholics got together and decided they would convert the Protestant to Catholicism. After a period of time, the Protestant decided to become Catholic, and the priest sprinkled holy water on him, saying, "You were born Baptist, raised Baptist, and today you are Catholic." So the following Lent season, on the first day, once again the Catholics on the cul-de-sac were preparing their fish, and again, they smelled the tantalizing smell of a steak. They all walked over to the Protestant's home only to find him again grilling this big, juicy steak. Only this time, he was sprinkling water on the steak and heard saying, "You were born a cow, raised a cow, and today you are a fish."

So again, while associations yield quick conclusions to problems through focus, they can be prohibitive when trying to think outside of the box.

The business case for diversity may be stated as: corporate growth is predominately from innovation; innovation comes from ideas, and lots of them; ideas come from people, all kinds of people. To this end, the more inclusive an organization is in welcoming people to share their ideas, the more ideas are available to select from to be innovative, and the more innovative an organization, the greater the chance for business growth (i.e., inclusivity spawns growth, simple as that). This, too, supports our thinking outside of the box.

These many thoughts, although separate, are surgically integrated into the essence of the creation of disruptive technologies.

Systems Engineering—The Cross-Discipline Eclectic Nature of Knowledge

A man-made system is a collection of objects that interact in accordance with a set of rules to achieve some purpose or function (Grady, 2010, p. 3). A technological system, then, is a collection of technology-based entities, brought together to achieve a specific purpose, where technology-based entities may be anything natural or assembled. Technological systems may be simple or complex, but they will always be entities joined together through some type of interface, or relationship, to satisfy a common or intended purpose. Systems development is an organized problem-solving process for transforming needs into preferred solutions (p. 5).

Within the realm of technology, technology formation, and technology development, there are individuals tasked to perform in a technology-oriented integration capacity. These individuals are typically referred to as systems engineers. According to Grady (2010):

> Systems engineers are specialists in dealing with complexity. Many people think of systems engineers as being a mile wide and an inch deep in knowledge, and this is true except for the fact that every systems engineer must come to the job through some path seldom involving a university degree in system engineering followed immediately by work in that field in industry. So, most systems engineers have some particular domain knowledge acquired during their years in college and early career work in electrical, mechanical or other engineering domains. (p. 7)

In other words, systems engineers are seldom made through undergraduate work. Systems engineers are typically created within a specific company and have some level of product domain knowledge. Their domain knowledge is evolved through defined systems engineering processes composed of multiple activities and attendant products. A given systems engineer can transfer systems engineering process knowledge from one product to another across companies, as the systems engineer comes to understand the product-specific operational domains.

From an industrial perspective, systems engineers are, therefore, made, not hired directly out of undergraduate university programs. Systems engineers typically possess a unique overarching umbrella of knowledge representing an eclectic collection from related disciplines. Meaning, systems engineers have a basic understanding of many disciplines, but they are not considered experts in any specific discipline except the one from which they evolved, most likely as a result of undergraduate study.

From an industrial perspective, then, to build or create a good systems engineer means to take an individual from a given generally applicable discipline, provide him or her with additional breadth of other discipline-specific knowledge from program-related experiences, and then promote the individual to the hierarchically higher-level systems engineer where he or she can express their collective knowledge of multiple disciplines through systems engineering practices.

Closing the loop, then, relative to innovation and disruptive technologies, the systems engineer is the type of industrial individual to work between the gaps of the "pure" disciplines. How then, to pose a question, do we create the integrative knowledge curriculum sufficient to support current industrial demand for these very unique individuals? The answer may not be as elusive as first suggested, given the previously discussed many already available integrated disciplines currently being taught in major universities.

Diversify Our Knowledge through Multiple Job Experiences

Clearly, another way to gain a breadth of knowledge is through multiple work-related experiences. Each experience supports its own policies, processes, methodologies, and practices. As one moves across disciplines, there is a core set of non-discipline-specific cross-fertilization that occurs. For example, engineering processes associated with change management support comparable tasks in human resources (HR). The discipline of HR, however, does not readily recognize the formality of change management as a process where changes are identified, brought before a change management board, tracked, and verified as to their efficient and effective implementation. That is not to say HR doesn't deal with change or change management. On the contrary, HR deals extensively with damage assessment and damage control, and the subsequent change required. What HR doesn't necessarily have is an exhaustive, documented, validated change management process. Why not? The answer generally resides in massive efforts to define and document processes that provide consistent, predictable outcomes. Organizations generate and promote quality engineering initiatives such as Carnegie Mellon University's Software Engineering Institute, which is responsible for the Capability Maturity Model Integration (CMMI), or the International Organization for Standardization 9000 (ISO 9000). These and many other standards are devised for engineering and related disciplines and are not imposed or routinely discussed in HR, as an example.

With that said, there are many qualities of the above referenced standards and guidelines that have direct applicability to non-engineering disciplines. For example, CMMI makes reference to institutional processes, one of which is organization training. While this section is somewhat tangential to the primary disciplines of design, development, and implementation, it is nonetheless important. In fact, the HR department, in any organization pursuing CMMI certification, will be required to address this HR section of the process standards. Unfortunately, this section is sufficiently light in requirements and generally easily satisfied, therefore, not requiring significant processes or subsequent adherence to process standards. This example serves to demonstrate the breadth of general applicability, however unintentional. From software engineering, to software systems engineering, systems engineering, program/project management, HR, and back to engineering operations, there is significant testimony to the large number of applicable cross-discipline processes.

Summary Thoughts

To this point, this section has explored the following:

- A case for understanding the look of disruptive technologies through innovation
- The integrative mind-set and minimal means to achieve it
- The cross-discipline nature of knowledge through systems engineering
- The cross-fertilization of multiple, seemingly unrelated disciplines

Given this, how do we prepare graduates in the processes, methodologies, and practices of technology leadership and innovation with an underlying breadth of understanding in technology to create the disruptive technologies of the twenty-first century and beyond?

The answer may reside in two threads of thought: (1) prepare graduates in the processes of innovation and (2) prepare graduates in the higher cognitive function of systems integration.

Technology from a Worldwide Perspective

Technology has been intentionally differentiated from engineering and science because of its uniqueness. Technology, on the surface, could be defined by the discipline-specific instantiations evident in many programs (construction management, computer graphics technology, technology leadership and innovation, etc.). Most individuals would find little difficulty in identifying a technological invention or product; a mechanical pencil, a desk, and even a coffee cup are all examples of technology and the utilization of technological processes. It is easy to identify the end product, or artifact, of technology at work. The higher-level cognitive function, however, is to define technology, not as an artifact, but as an entity and, more specifically, as a discipline.

Technology as a discipline has to possess a body of knowledge. Without a body of knowledge there is not an organized manner in which to evolve the theoretical and practical underpinnings. Some might argue the body of knowledge for technology is nothing more than the eclectic collection of discipline-specific bodies of knowledge. In other words, that knowledge required to build and construct, as in construction management, or the many software applications and their interrelatedness and subsequent application, as in computer graphics. From a higher cognitive level, however, we need to be able to define technology, the very nature of what technology is (ontology of technology), and the attendant nature of our knowledge about technology (epistemology of technology). Without this basic philosophical ontological and epistemological understanding of technology, we will never be able to fully appreciate and subsequently document a technology body of knowledge to advance technology as a discipline. Perhaps, as has been documented, we begin with a philosophical definition of technology as humanity at work. From here, we can begin to deduct the very essence and our understanding of technology.

This requirement to define and evolve technology as a body of knowledge is not well understood. Technology, however, is not an isolated body of knowledge. It is intricately intertwined with all other areas of knowledge. Science explains the natural laws that are applied by technology. Engineering is used to design systems, processes, and the artifacts that comprise our technological world. Mathematics and mathematical models explain the operation of technological systems. Language and art can be used to describe technology and its impacts. The social studies can describe how technology has, is, and may well impact and be impacted by people and society.

The essence of a technologist is the mastery of a whole field with a broad and deep understanding of the technology—the processes, systems, tools, and techniques necessary to construct, modify, innovate, operate, and maintain the engineering design.

There is a continuum in technology that moves from vocationally trained skilled craftsmen at one end, to technicians narrowly focused on one aspect of technology, to technologists who have mastered a whole field of technology, to the engineers who have mastered whole technological systems. There is a clear distinction between a *technician* and a *technologist*. The technologist is a highly skilled professional who is positioned in the "sweet spot" between the engineer and the technician/skilled craftsmen. Technologists serve an important and unique role as the "integrators" in business and industry.

Clearly defining and describing technological knowledge while seeking its integration with other disciplines will lead the technology profession, as a whole, to a recognition that (1) technology studies is the study of the human-made world, (2) technologists use the technological method (problem solving, innovation, and commercialization cycle) to develop new and improved artifacts and systems, (3) technology is used to help people meet their communication, product, and transportation needs, and (4) technology impacts and is impacted by people, society, and the environment (Bertoline, 2011).

According to Bertoline:

> This four-point philosophy leads us to believe that, like science, there is a general way to approach a technological problem or opportunity; there are unique practices used to produce, operate, and maintain each device or system; there is a unique body of knowledge that through use-inspired and applied research methodologies will produce new knowledge, and these actions are operated in historical, personal, and societal contexts. (p. 9)

Further, if innovation has at its core a consistent or semi-consistent series of interrelated activities over time, then those series of time-phased, interrelated activities form a process. This proposition, then, is that innovation is a process with a series of time-phased, interrelated activities, where each activity produces an attendant product. As such, innovation can be researched, taught, assimilated, and subsequently reapplied.

If, as defined, innovation is a process, then technological innovation may be dependent on the underlying foundations of engineering and science, but not necessarily those evolved entirely from the U.S. Inductively, advancing the U.S. position in technological innovation can most generally occur through world advancements in our understanding of underlying disciplines, regardless of country origin. Our grand challenge, then, is to adequately prepare our citizens for technological innovation, not necessarily through predominance in science and engineering education, but more applicably, through studies in technology and the technological innovation process. Creating a more understanding and intelligent workforce in technological innovation that is premised on use-inspired and applied findings would promote the creation and maintenance of a technologically advanced nation.

This does *not* imply science and engineering is less important to the advancement of a society. This does imply technology is a discipline with an attendant innovation process that is not dependent on where the underlying body of science and engineering comes from. And, if properly trained as technologists, any society will be poised for economic growth as products and services become more pronounced. To this end, we should welcome the growing world collective intelligence, while at the same time train our future technology leaders on how to capitalize on our internationally available collective knowledge through the study of technology as a discipline and the study of innovation as a process.

The Bio-Economy—A Truly Worldwide Experience

There may not be any better subject that represents a truly international participation and evolution than discussing the deciphering of the human genome. The deciphering of the human genome has such potential for all of humankind that its full realization is beyond our immediate comprehension, but very much locked into our visionary sights. To fully appreciate the breadth and interrelatedness of the many tangential topics, we need to briefly discuss the relationships between genetics, DNA, stem cells, and cloning.

Genetics, at the simplest level, is the scientific study of how traits, or all kinds, are passed from one generation to the next. There are four generally accepted categories of genetics: classical genetics, molecular genetics, population genetics, and quantitative genetics.

Classical genetics is the study of how physical characteristics are passed from one generation to the next: grandparent, to parent, to child, and so on. Molecular genetics is the study of chemical and the physical structure of genes, deoxyribonucleic acid (DNA), ribonucleic acid (RNA), and proteins. DNA was discovered in 1869 by the Swiss physician Friedrich Miescher.

As humans, we have one human genome, made up of approximately 21,000 genes, with roughly 100 trillion cells, where each cell contains 23 pairs of chromosomes. Stated another way, for every cell with a nucleus, there are 23 pairs of chromosomes, where the pairs contain the 3.2 billion base pairs of "T," "A," "C," and "G." Combinations of these base pairs form our roughly 21,000 genes. Genes (DNA) transmit information to our cells through RNA to tell them which proteins to create. Proteins, then, are what keep us functioning. Understanding the makeup of each gene is an enormous first step. Successful application of that knowledge, however, will come from a better understanding of how the genes play together and what each gene is responsible for doing in harmony with other intertwined genes (NHGRI, 2007, p. 14).

Population genetics looks at the genetic content of large groups of seemingly homogeneous people. The intent is to see the similarities and differences of this group over time. Quantitative genetics is the study of varying traits from a complex statistical perspective. The intent is to look at the expression of a trait, compare it to the underlying overall genetics of the organism, and subsequently view it through the lens of nurture versus nature evolution. In other words, which trait expressions are due to the environment and which are due to genetics and genetic permutations?

Interestingly, we actually share 51 percent of our genes with yeast, the stuff used to make bread rise. We share 98 percent of our genes with monkeys. And, most impressively, we share 99.9 percent of our entire genome with other human beings. That means the only thing that separates my brown hair from your blond hair, my five-foot-nine-inch stature from your six-foot-tall stature, and my blue eyes from your hazel eyes are 0.1 percent of the entire human genome. That's one-tenth of one percent that differentiates each of us. In other words, we are more alike than different—at least from a chemical composition perspective. The thought of that is so profound that it reverberates and should simultaneously resonate the historical significance of our biases and prejudices, or more precisely, perhaps the insignificance they should have been and why they should not have existed at all.

The role this plays in this discussion is that it provides a perspective, a glimpse, of yet another great opportunity for our and other nations to turn unknown unknowns into known knowns. It's an exciting, entirely new frontier yet to be realized, and its impact on what knowledge we might need or the number of workers it might employ is not clear. We don't know entirely how this new discipline will integrate with other science and engineering disciplines. Its overall impact is not yet realizable, but all the same its potential is very pronounced.

The Potential in Understanding DNA Makeup

Nearly every day something is written about the potential of better understanding the genetic makeup of our human or animal DNA. The Holy Grail, if you will, resides in truly understanding not only the pure state of the four composite chemicals of each gene, but more specifically, what role each gene plays in our growth, development, and survival. Sequencing the genes in a lung tumor, for example, exposes the unnatural permutation in the cancer gene and can subsequently guide doctors to gene treatments to correct the malformed gene (Park, 2011). A better understanding of the many permutations of a given gene can also help prevent the extinction of an entire species. Recently, in an attempt to better understand a transmittable cancer found in the Tasmanian devil, which has killed roughly 60 percent of the population, scientists have dedicated efforts to look at population genetics in various parts of the animal's habitats (Schuster, 2011).

According to the National Institutes of Health (n.d.), already the Human Genome Project:

- Fueled the discovery of more than 1,800 disease genes.
- Helped researchers find the genetic cause of inherited diseases in a matter of days, versus the years it took before the human genome was deciphered.
- Allowed for the development of more than 2,000 tests for human conditions.
- Created more than 350 biotechnology-based products.
- Spawned the HapMap Project, which is a catalog of common genetic variation in the human genome. The project contains data from 11 global populations, the largest global survey of human genetic variation performed to date.
- Spawned pharmacogenomics, a field that looks at how genetic variation affects an individual's response to drugs.

Going forward:

- The cancer genome atlas aims to identify all the genetic abnormalities seen in 50 major types of cancer.
- Based on a better understanding of diseases, we'll see a whole new generation of targeted interventions.
- The cost to sequence an individual's genome should drop to $1,000 or less, making it easier to diagnose, manage, and treat many diseases.
- Individualized analysis based on an individual's genome will lead to a powerful form of preventive, personalized, and preemptive medicines.

Difficulty with Mapping a Genome and Pharmaceutical Sales

Somewhat needless to say is the complexity of sequencing the gene and the organism's genome (the entire sequence of all genes of the organism). Sequencing the gene is not an easy task. Scientists have successfully mapped genomes for many organisms, including mice, horses, cattle, pigs, chickens, sheep, apes, and humans, as well as crops like rice and certain types of moss, fungus, and bacteria (Goldstein & Schneider,

2010, p. 44). We've also cloned some animals for reasons some felt were not desirable; namely, we've cloned a rabbit with a phosphorescent jellyfish, the result of which is a rabbit that glows in the dark. On the surface this seems interesting, but the controversy came about when it was disclosed as the creation of a Chicago artist named Eduardo Kac and a team of French genetic researchers. The artistic effort met with public debate (Marcel, 2000).

In the end, however, mapping a genome is an expensive and difficult process. Makers of targeted drugs rely entirely on having the genome mapped of the individuals being targeted. To this end, drugmakers are buying companies that sequence genetic DNA. Waters (2011) writes:

> On Feb. 28, Japanese pharmaceutical maker Daiichi Sankyo agreed to pay $935 million for Plexxikon, a Berkley (Calif.) biotech startup that has a new treatment for melanoma. Plexxikon's drug stops cancer cells [from replicating]. . . . Plexxikon was able to develop the drug because researchers using the gene sequencing machine had mapped the genomes of melanoma cells and found a key mutation. (p. 58)

On April 28, 2011, a U.S.-based company named Pacific Biosciences (PacBio) created a gene sequencing machine that reportedly can map an entire genome in minutes. The machine sells for roughly $700,000 (Vance, 2011) and has been the result of nearly $600 million in investment. The company owners believe the machine can change the current understanding of life itself by deciphering the DNA of millions of organisms around the globe. From a pharmaceutical perspective, this speed is a tremendous boost for further identifying, developing, and rushing drug products to market.

Pharmaceutical sales grew an average of 24 percent a year in China from 2006–2010 and will expand at a 19–22 percent annual clip over the next five years (Loo, 2011a) to an estimated $115–$125 billion by 2015. To help market these drugs overseas, pharmaceutical companies are using hefty salaries to hire Chinese doctors away from their patient practice. China is concerned with this move as the population of China continues to age and the need for rural doctors increases.

Given the tremendous opportunity for financial success, other companies around the world are beginning to take notice and follow in the U.S. predecessor footsteps. BeiGene, a Chinese biotech company, has launched a world-class biotech industry focusing on cancer drugs (Loo, 2011b). BeiGene is also wooing top medical talent to develop and market its drugs. Spending on pharmaceuticals in China is expected to grow significantly due to its primary focus on these and other cancer inhibitor drugs.

Stem Cells and Their Potential

Every living organism has billions of cells. These numerous cells live and replicate within the many parts of our body. For the most part, each cell is preprogrammed to replicate as the type of cell its parent was; in other words, lung cells replicate to become more lung cells, skin cells replicate to become more skin cells, and so forth. There is one special type of cell, however, that has the ability to become any type of cell it wishes to become; these cells are known as stem cells.

Stem cells are unique cells in that they are not predetermined to become a specific type of cell. Instead, they are free to become the type of cell they are encouraged to become. Stem cells go by a few names: pluripotent (meaning "many potential"), omnipotent (which generally means the same thing as pluripotent), and totipotent (usually only the first eight cells of humans).

In theory, when a part of a human organism is damaged (internal organ, bone, muscles), the injection of stem cells into that damaged part of the human body will create a scenario where the stem cells replicate as the required organ it is injected into, therefore repairing the damage in the original human organism. Sternberg (2011) writes:

> Before New York Yankees pitcher Bartolo Colon pulled his hamstring while running from the mound to first base on June 11, fans would have been forgiven for thinking he had chugged from the Fountain of Youth. Colon had not completed a full season since 2005 and sat out 2010 to rest

his injured and aging right arm. But this season, his fastball is back. His ERA, 3.10, was among the tops in the league. On May 30, six days after his 39th birthday, he pitched his first shutout in five years, hurling his final pitch at 95 mph. What lit the fuse on his fastball? An infusion of stem cells. . . . Experts liken stem cells to the seeds from which many body tissues grow. If scientists can harness stem cells in healing, researchers say, they can revolutionize medicine. (para. 1–3)

Cloning—Once a Boilermaker, Always a Boilermaker

Cloning is a fascinating and highly controversial scientific phenomenon. In short, it involves making an exact replica of a living organism, or, for that matter, a dead organism. Cloning does not necessarily require an understanding of the genome of the parent organism to be cloned. Although there are many ways to clone something, the most discussed is a process where the DNA of one cell is extracted and placed in another cell without a nucleus (denucleated egg). The new cell is then placed in a female recipient for eventual delivery of the replicated entity. This process results in an identical, or cloned, replica of the original. The first cloned living organism was Dolly the sheep on February 22, 1997, at the Roslin Institute in Scotland. Dolly only lived until 2003, a short six years. On examination, it was determined that Dolly had prematurely aged. This phenomenon was later attributed to telomeres found at the end of each strand of chromosome composing DNA.

Every year after Dolly, from 1997–2007, something new was successfully cloned (Begley, 2007):

- Mice, 1998—50 clones of a single mouse
- Bull, 1999—leads to a debate on the safety of meat and milk from cloned cows
- Pig, 2000—five cloned piglets opens the way to clone animals for growing organs to be used in humans
- Goat, 2000—first goat clone died of an abnormal lung development
- Guar, 2001—first clone of an endangered species
- Mouflon, 2001—first endangered species cloned, who survives infancy
- Rabbit, 2002—clones a rabbit that could model human diseases
- Cat, 2002—a company formed to reproduce cherished pets clones the first cat
- Mule, 2003—offspring of a horse and a donkey yields the first hybrid clone
- Rat, 2003—a challenge to researchers, its eggs begin dividing almost instantly
- African wildcat, 2004—scientists use a domestic cat as the surrogate mother
- Dog, 2005—researches in South Korea clone an Afghan puppy named Snuppy
- Water buffalo, 2005—cloned in China, it opened interest in improving the animal and its milk
- Horse, 2005—first clone whose surrogate mother is also a genetic donor
- Ferret, 2006—researchers in Iowa hope to use it to study human respiratory diseases
- Wolf, 2007—South Korean scientists clone two gray wolves, an endangered species

Today, there are companies capitalizing on a potentially lucrative market. These companies successfully clone and sell animals to those who have lost their beloved pets (Veale, 2009). BIO, a South Korean company, cloned a pit bull terrier and sold the animal to an American for $50,000. In another instance, a Labrador was cloned and sold to a Florida couple for $150,000. In 2009, South Korea was the only country cloning and selling pets.

Telomeres and the Fountain of Youth

If ever there was a fountain of youth, telomeres may very well be it. Every cell in our body has DNA. DNA is composed of two long twisted strands called chromosomes. There are 23 pairs of chromosomes, where the pairs contain the 3.2 billion base pairs of "T," "A," "C," and "G." The chromosomes are paired in twos, with one from the mother and one from the father. The DNA contained in chromosomes contains everything about us and constitutes what is required to quite literally replicate us. This is one reason why it is critical, when our cells replicate, that these chromosomes remain intact. Should a chromosome not remain intact, then a permutation of our DNA has materialized and the subsequent cell behavior is defective.

At the end of each chromosome are "junk" DNA, that without meaning, called telomeres. Telomeres may be thought of as the plastic tips on our shoelaces that keep the shoestring from unraveling. As our cells replicate, a small part of each telomere is lost. On each subsequent replication, the telomere gets shorter and shorter. When the telomere can no longer shorten, the cell quits dividing and dies. We know at conception that an embryo has about fifteen thousand base pairs in each telomere. By the time we are born, we have roughly ten thousand base pairs in each telomere. This means we lost five thousand base pairs in each telomere while being formed in the womb. From this perspective, we actually begin to die the minute we are conceived (Fossel, Blackburn, & Woynarowski, 2011, p. 5).

Given this, we can measure the length of a cell's telomere and subsequently use that information to compare biological age from chronological age (Pollack, 2011). What this information does not tell us, however, is how long we will live. Infants and small children have longer telomeres and subsequent life spans, while adults have shorter telomeres and shorter remaining life spans. When Dolly the sheep was cloned, she was actually cloned with aged cells, those that already had a shortened life span. As a result of being cloned with these aged cells, Dolly never lived a normal sheep lifetime, but instead, she died after having lived a shortened life; the reason was that the cells quit replicating, and ultimately, the living organism died.

Fossel and colleagues (2011) report:

In his April 2010 column in Forbes magazine, Peter Huber pointed out the insanity of the Food and Drug Administration (FDA) regulations that currently block consideration of potential drugs to treat (that is, prevent or reverse) aging:

For the most part, the FDA still operates under the medical mind-set that prevailed when the federal drug law was amended in 1962. The go/no-go regulatory calls are decided by clinical trials. The key metrics are clinical, like the survival time for a cancer patient. A clear reduction in mortality from a serious disease gets the drug licensed on the double. So far, so good—this panel sounds diligently anti-death. But it's interested only in brinkmanship, at the back end.

The "aging" drugs that the agency deals with reasonably well are the ones that beat back a single specific disease long after the microscopic seeds of the problem have blossomed into big symptoms. Aging is an incremental, whole-body problem. All cells, tissues and organs age—and in different ways, at different rates, in different people. As defined by their late-stage clinical symptoms, the diseases of old age are legion. At the FDA they will have to be beaten one at a time or not at all. Which means that nobody is ever going to get "antiaging" drugs through the FDA as it currently operates. (p. 7)

There are many studies that correlate the length of telomeres to diseases and to the eventual death of living organisms. The diseases of cancer, atherosclerosis, Alzheimer's disease, osteoarthritis, osteoporosis, macular degeneration, cirrhosis of the liver, AIDS, and even skin aging (Fossel et al., 2011, p. 8) are all related to shortened telomeres.

From above, when the telomeres can no longer shorten, the cell does one of two things: it either enters into a state of senescence, a continual downward change in a biological system, or it dies by committing a sort of cell suicide called apoptosis. In short, cells die when telomeres become too short (Fossel et al., 2011, p. 8). In 1961, Leonard Hayflick, while working at the Wistar Institute in Philadelphia, demonstrated each cell can replicate between 40 and 60 times before dying, presumably because of exhausted telomeres, those that can't shorten any longer.

An article in the January 16, 1988, issue of *Science* first documented the potential to extend the life of a cell through the lengthening of the telomere after replication (Bodnar et al., 1998). In this seminal work, the authors identified the enzyme telomerase as the agent capable of slowing the deterioration of the telomere during replication, and in some cases reversing the shortening process and actually lengthening the telomere. In describing the events leading to this article, Fossel and colleagues (2011) write:

> On Christmas day 1984, Greider developed an audioradiogram of their latest batch of DNA. Holding the X-ray image up to the light, she could see a clear pattern of recurring bands that extended like a ladder all the way up the gel. When Blackburn took a look, she noticed right away that evenly spaced bands were too far apart to represent a random mix of DNA molecules. It was the proof they had been looking for: an enzyme that added telomeric DNA to the ends of the chromosomes.
>
> Blackburn says about this moment, "Thoughts rushed through my mind that this discovery of a new enzymatic activity was as important as the discovery of DNA polymerase. DNA polymerase had garnered a Nobel Prize for its discoverer. I said nothing about this [to Greider], not wanting to raise unrealistic hopes. But we both knew what it was."
>
> Blackburn and Greider had discovered the little enzyme that could. Many months later, they finally came up with a name for their discovery. They called the enzyme telomerase. (p. 9)

We now know, years later, that telomerase is one of the reasons cancer cells never die when left unattended. Overactivity of telomerase in cancer cells is why these cells replicate uninterrupted. Overactivation of telomerase is one of the few constants between almost all types of cancers; it is present in almost 85 percent of all cancer cells (Fossel et al., 2011, p. 10). We have also discovered that the introduction of telomerase inhibitors has the ability to stop cancer cell replication. Telomerase inhibitors are a whole new class of drugs being developed. What, then, does this say about increasing telomerase to normal cells and their chance of becoming cancerous? Fossel and colleagues (2011) write:

> Lest anyone be confused, however, it is important to point out that stimulating the growth of telomeres on normal chromosomes does not cause them to become cancerous. A cancer begins when something else goes wrong with the cell, causing it to lose control of its growth. However, the telomeres continue to shorten in these cells, and very soon these fast dividing cancer cells will die.
>
> Very occasionally however, they will find ways to turn on the telomerase gene and relengthen their telomeres. When this happens, a cancer begins to divide not only uncontrollably but also indefinitely. The cancer becomes truly dangerous.
>
> So, turning on the telomerase of normal cells must be highly dangerous, right?
>
> The answer to this question is a resounding no. Although telomerase is necessary for cancers to extend their life span, it does not cause cancer. This fact has been repeatedly demonstrated by performing many different types of genetic tests for cancer on telomerase-positive human cells. Scientists have turned on the telomerase of normal cells in attempts to turn these cells into cancer cells, and it just hasn't happened.
>
> Generally speaking, bad things happen when telomeres become short. As cells approach senescence, the short telomeres stimulate chromosome instability, which can cause the mutations that can cause cancer. . . .

Paradoxically, even though cells require telomerase to become dangerous cancers, turning on telomerase may actually prevent cancer. . . . because telomerase can extend the life span of our immune cells, improving their ability to seek and destroy cancer cells. (p. 10)

In the final analysis, normal cells do not express telomerase because the cells suppress the enzyme. The key to immortality is turning the telomerase gene on (Fossel et al., 2011, p. 11).

In a recent reported study (Centro Nacional de Investigaciones Oncologicas, 2012) researchers have proven it is possible to develop a telomerase-based antiaging gene therapy without increasing the incidence of cancer. The authors state, "Aged organisms accumulate damage in their DNA due to telomere shortening, [this study] finds that a gene therapy based on telomerase production can repair or delay this kind of damage" (para. 6). In the study, mice treated at the age of one lived longer by 24 percent on average, and those treated at the age of two by 13 percent. The authors say, "The therapy, furthermore, produced an appreciable improvement in the animals' health, delaying the onset of age-related diseases—like osteoporosis and insulin resistance—and achieving improved readings on aging indicators like neuromuscular coordination" (para. 4). The authors conclude, "This study is viewed primarily as 'a proof-of-principle that telomerase gene therapy is a feasible and generally safe approach to improve healthspan and treat disorders associated with shortened telomeres'" (para. 13).

Chapter 18

Establishing Program/Project Management as a Discipline

Over the years I have been asked many times how one might leave the classroom and establish some organized form of program/project management within one's own organization. To this end, I have been sharing my personal experiences in how I have seen this done. What follows is a discussion of some of the basic products of the program management process that can be used to establish program/project management as a discipline.

Stated requirements are "will" statements in some form of contractual document. In this case, stated requirements must be satisfied. The stated requirements are as indicated:

- Creation of a common and consistent program management process for our programs to follow
- Creation of a common set of activities to perform
- Creation of common products to produce
- Creation of common templates to utilize
- Creation of a quality program plan to execute
- Program personnel identified and adequately trained

Derived requirements include:

- Creation of a core program management office
- Definition and development of process, product, and notation standards
- Identification of program management office personnel
- Provision for an administrative functional stovepipe
- Auditing ongoing programs for adherence to the defined process
- Establishing program metrics based on company/organizational thresholds

An organization chart depicting the basic core program office personnel might look like that in figure 18.1.

In figure 18.1, notice that the program office is led by a manager, whose name is S. T. Pang. We have labeled this bloc with the nomenclature "A01." This makes referencing easier when we create the next product, which is the program office responsibility assignment matrix.

In figure 18.1, note that there are three managers. The first manager, "B01," is responsible for the generation of the program management process and the assurance that programs are adhering to this process. Manager "C01" is responsible for the identification and training of program management office personnel, as well as their career development. Manager "D01" is responsible for the creation of standard tools and information systems for collecting of the program data, analysis of said data, and consistent reporting of the same.

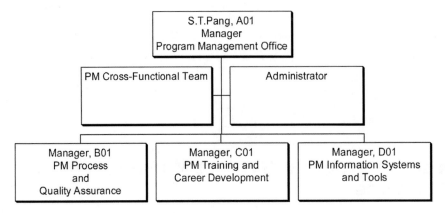

Figure 18.1. Corporate Program Office

The PM cross-functional team is a steering committee designed to offer input on what current practices are and how the new process should be designed to incorporate the varying functional requirements, and to basically aid in the ultimate acceptance of the new process. In the ideal sense, steering committee members feel a sense of ownership and can help to sell the new concept.

Figure 18.2 depicts the work assignments of each of the corporate program management office personnel.

WBS ID			Task Description	A01	B01	C01	D01
A			Program Management Discipline	P			
	AA		Define PM Process		P	S	S
		AAA	Generate Process Plan		P	S	S
		AAB	Generate Stds and Guides		P	S	S
		AAC	Define Training		S	P	S
		AAD	Define PM Information System		S	S	P
	AB		Implement PM Process				
		ABA	Generate Process Implementation Plan		P	S	S
		ABB	Train Personnel		S	P	S
		ABC	Implement PM Information System		S	S	P
		ABD	Incorporate Process		P		
	AC		Perform PM Quality Assurance		P	S	S
		ACA	Monitor/Audit PM Process		P	S	S
		ACB	Implement Corrective Action		P	S	S
		ACC	Support Customer Audits/Reviews		P	S	S
	AD		Obtain ISO9000 Certification	P			
	AE		Manage PM Personnel	P			
		AEA	Establish and Maintain PM Career Paths			P	
		AEB	Provide PM Resources to Programs	P			

Figure 18.2. Corporate PM Office Responsibility Assignment Matrix

The work defined in figure 18.2 is further detailed in the work breakdown structure (WBS) depicted in figure 18.3.

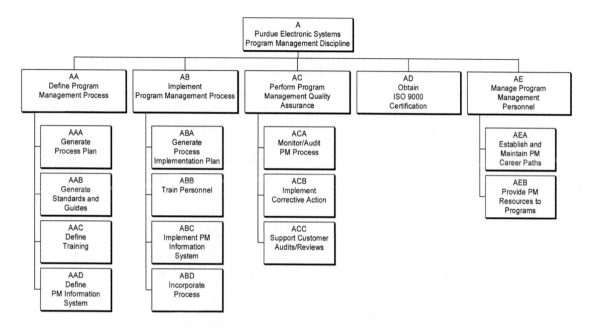

Figure 18.3. Level Three Work Breakdown Structure

In figure 18.3, under the WBS element "AA," we see that defining the program management process involves generating the process plan. This is essentially what this whole chapter is about. Next we see that under this element we will need to generate standards and guides, define the training for the program management office personnel, and define the program management information system. The program management information system will, again, be created to provide a consistent and coherent mechanism to collect, analyze, and report program data to the varying levels of applicable management in the organization's hierarchy.

The other level-two phases include the implementation of the process, quality assurance, obtaining (optionally) some form of certification (perhaps International Organization for Standardization (ISO) 9000), and the management of program management personnel. Note that program management personnel does not necessarily include only program managers, but may, and should, include all program management office personnel, that is, schedulers, cost controllers, support personnel, and administrative assistants.

WBS elements "AA," "AB," "AC," and "AE" are further detailed in subsequent figures 19.4, 19.5, 19.6, and 19.7.

WBS element "AAAC" basically suggests that after all program management activities and their attendant products have been identified, sequenced, and properly depicted in some form of network flow diagram (figure 18.8), then this approved process becomes a functional baseline. The functional baseline then becomes the foundation for developing those required standards and guides represented under WBS element "AAB."

WBS element "AABF" describes the generation of any corporate standard operating procedures. Typically, there exists some form of corporate mandate that requires the use of a corporate process.

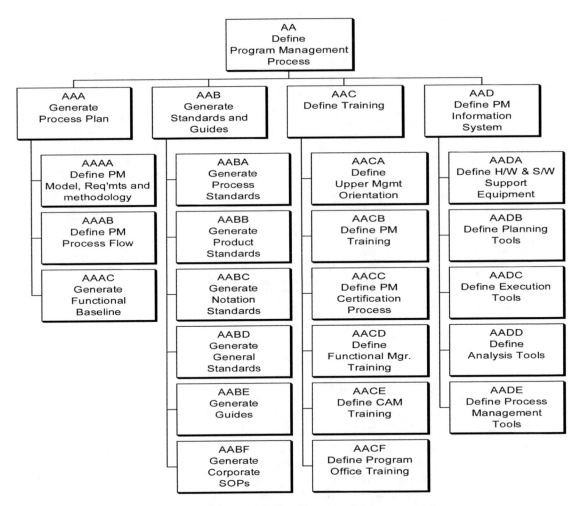

Figure 18.4. Breakdown of Define Program Management Process

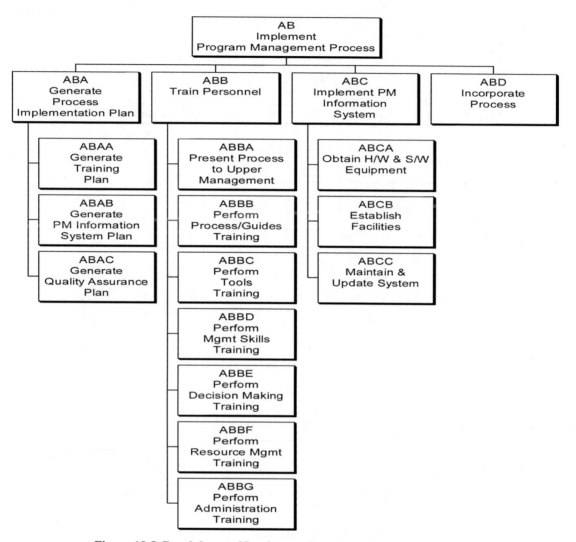

Figure 18.5. Breakdown of Implement Program Management Process

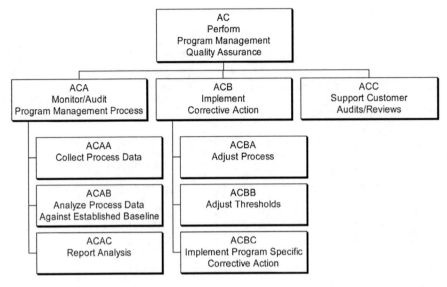

Figure 18.6. Breakdown of Perform Program Management Quality Assurance

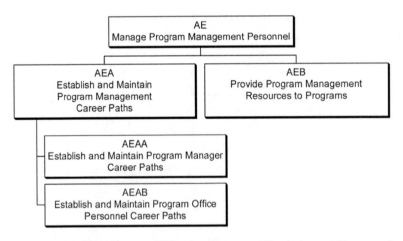

Figure 18.7. Breakdown of Manage Program Management Personnel

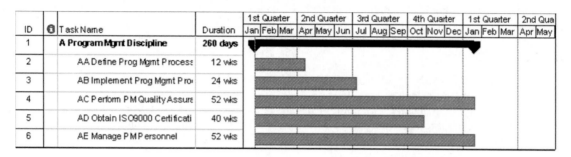

ID	ⓘ	Task Name	Duration	1st Quarter			2nd Quarter			3rd Quarter			4th Quarter			1st Quarter			2nd Qua	
				Jan	Feb	Mar	Apr	May	Jun	Jul	Aug	Sep	Oct	Nov	Dec	Jan	Feb	Mar	Apr	May
1		**A Program Mgmt Discipline**	**260 days**																	
2		AA Define Prog Mgmt Process	12 wks																	
3		AB Implement Prog Mgmt Pro	24 wks																	
4		AC Perform PM Quality Assure	52 wks																	
5		AD Obtain ISO9000 Certificati	40 wks																	
6		AE Manage PM Personnel	52 wks																	

Figure 18.8. Program Management Process Master Schedule

WBS "AACC" holds a slot for those activities associated with certifying a program manager. Some companies want to create a series of training and education requirements, coupled with real-world experience that qualifies a program manager for the next level of responsibility. In some cases, a test or small program is required to certify that an individual as a program manager is ready for greater responsibility.

In my experience, however, if certification is required, it should be a recognized outside organization that provides it. Internal certifications are generally limited in significance to the organization that the employee currently resides in. An external certification, however, such as the Program Management Institute's Project Management Professional (PMP) certification, is recognized around the world. The PMP certification not only provides the employee with additional verbiage for his or her résumé, but also attests that the individual understands a basic body of accepted knowledge associated with the discipline of program/ project management.

WBS element "ABCA" involves the acquisition of required hardware and software in support of the information system being designed and developed. This hardware may involve some form of common shared server with distributed workstations on a local area network for each program.

WBS "ACB" involves implementing corrective actions on the program after a variance from the program's plan has been detected. Under this element is "ACBA," which is adjusting the corporation's program management process. Adjusting thresholds, "ACBB," is also applicable to the corporation's program management process.

WBS element "AEB" is perhaps one of the more controversial elements of the program management functional stovepipe. One aspect of functional management is to take care of the feeding and nurturing of its membership. This also entails moving people from one program to another as the requirements of a given program change. Program managers responsible for a program do not want their people moved until the program manager says it is time to move them. This is in contradiction, sometimes, to the actual requirements that might mandate that someone of lesser or greater experience be assigned at a particular time. As well, a start-up program might require the services of the more knowledgeable individual.

But remember, the program management functional stovepipe should function in much the same manner as the other functional stovepipes (engineering, manufacturing, purchasing, information technology, contracts, etc.).

How long should it take to design, develop, and implement a program management process in an organization? The answer will obviously vary based on level of management commitment, number of individuals assigned to work the process, funding, and the like, but six months is not out of the question. More expectedly, up to 24 months might be more realistic. The above schedule was simply provided to illustrate how the various major activities might align in a time series.

What education should the three managers have within the corporate program management office? Below identifies some potential qualifications for those three individuals.

For the manager of the program management process and subsequent adherence, qualifications might look like the following:

- Education: B.S.C.S., B.S.E.E., or equivalent; master's in business administration or equivalent business master's degree.
- Experience: may include a minimum ten years of experience with emphasis on technical management/program management. Must be versed in management techniques, tools, and methodologies, and must have an understanding of PM responsibilities. Must have advanced written and oral communication skills.
- Duties and responsibilities of the position: generation and management of program management process, product and notation standards, and guides. Implementation plans must be defined and implemented. Program audits to assure adherence to process are required. Must analyze performance data. Position involves intense interaction with program managers and corporate personnel.

For the manager of training and career development, qualifications might look like the following:

- Education: bachelor's degree in education or equivalent. Master's degree preferred but not required.
- Experience: minimum ten years of experience. Must be versed in educational techniques, tools, and methodologies, and must have an understanding of PM responsibilities. Must have advanced written and oral communication skills.
- Duties and responsibilities of the position: position requires definition and coordination of training plans and course content. Must define and coordinate career development profiles and overall training for discipline.

And lastly, for the manager of the information systems and tools, qualifications might look like the following:

- Education: B.S.C.S., B.S.E.E., or equivalent; master's in business administration or equivalent business master's degree.
- Experience: minimum ten years of experience with emphasis on management information systems. Must be versed in information management techniques, tools, and methodologies, and must have an understanding of PM responsibilities. Must have advanced written and oral communication skills.
- Duties and responsibilities of the position: position includes the definition and implementation of the program management information system. Tasks include evaluating, selecting, and implementing hardware and software for the system. Responsibilities include determining data needs within the PM process and possibly writing software in support of this task.

In all cases, it is absolutely mandatory that the individuals who make up the corporate program management office be senior-level and well-respected individuals in their own disciplines. If this is not the case, they will not be as effective as possible.

Remembering an earlier experience, I was once assigned to teach our newly developed program management process to a group of existing program managers. Now, keep in mind that I was relatively young, and these program managers were some of the first to go through the training. Looking back, I swear that not one of them was less than 75 million years old with 50 million years of service, and possessed all of the gruff of their age and experience. Before I was ten minutes into my first multi-hour training session, one of the oldest and gruffest stood up, walked over to the coffee pot, and said, "I have forgotten more about program management than you will ever know!" To say the least, I could feel some tension in the room. Having been trained in how to teach adults, I simply responded that by the end of this session I hoped that all of the rest of us might gain some additional knowledge because of this individual's wealth of experience. Point being, you do not want a young person in your corporate program management office trying to sell senior, seasoned program managers on how to do their job better.

Chapter 19

Managers, Leaders, and Entrepreneurs

Leadership has been written and talked about nearly forever. In fact, even discussing it at this time seems somewhat antiquated. However, there is value in understanding the relative roles and responsibilities of leaders, especially as they relate to roles of managers or even entrepreneurs. While there are many overlapping characteristics, each does have some unique attributes.

Over the many years I have been involved with teaching, instructing, and facilitating courses and sessions on management and management methodologies and practices, there had always been an interest in discussing the differences between managers, leaders, and entrepreneurs. Perhaps it's a natural curiosity to better understand these individuals, their roles and responsibilities, and the like, in an attempt to compare ourselves to which, if not more than one, we would like to be.

Given these many discussions, I thought it might be interesting to look at the research and body of accumulated knowledge on what each of the above are and how they are similar or not.

The following discussion, therefore, is merely meant to heighten our awareness of what exists in the way of material from research and practice, such that each of us can make our own conclusions and subsequently draw parallels of similarities and differences.

Defining Management

Management refers to the process of getting activities completed efficiently and effectively with and through other people.

- Efficiency is defined as getting more output from the given input yields, and getting more output from the given input yields an increase in efficiency.
- Effectiveness is defined as achieving organizational goals—in other words, doing the right things.

Efficiency is concerned with the means, while effectiveness is concerned with the ends. Is it possible, then, to be efficient, but not effective? Sure. An individual can be highly efficient, can do a great deal of work, and can do it with minimal resources. But that does not mean that what got done was what was intended to be done. On the other hand, one can do what is intended to be done, but do it with considerably more resources (money, people, equipment, etc.) than another, thus the inefficiency.

Pictorially, one could create a chart, then, which depicts this relationship based on resources used versus goal attained. Figure 19.1 reflects such a relationship.

From figure 19.1, it can be seen that as goal attainment increases, we move from ineffective to effective. As resource usage increases, that is, we waste more resources to accomplish the same objective; we move from being efficient to being less efficient. The result, then, when looking at the extremes: low goal attainment with low resource utilization yields an efficient/ineffective rating, while in high goal attainment and high resource utilization yields an inefficient/effective rating.

Figure 19.1. Resource Utilization versus Goal Attainment

Is there an ideal? High goal attainment with low resource utilization would be ideal. This combination would yield an efficient/effective rating.

Management Functions

In the early part of the twentieth century, a French industrialist by the name of Henri Fayol proposed that all managers perform five management functions: plan, organize, command, coordinate, and control. In the mid-1950s, two professors at the University of California, Los Angeles, drew upon Fayol's work and used the functions of planning, organizing, staffing, directing, and controlling as the framework for a management textbook that for 20 years was the most widely sold text on the subject (Robbins, 1999, p. 11).

In the context of program/project management, we frequently do not include the management function of staffing. Staffing, from a matrix or project management organizational design perspective, is performed by the functional managers. The program manager simply provides the requirements to the functional managers, who then provide the required resources.

For example, as a contractor responsible for the overall construction of a new home, I might provide the blueprints to the electricians for pricing and performing the work. As the program manager, I am interested, of course, in the quality, timeliness, and cost of the work, but I have little interest in the labor grade of the individuals performing the work. Neither do I care about how many individuals it takes to perform the required tasks, so long as it does not affect the overall quality, schedule, or price of the effort.

Ironically, each of the management functions listed below are performed during both the planning and execution phases of the program life cycle. In other words, during the planning of a program, we perform all of the functions of planning, organizing, leading, and controlling. During the planning phase, we are applying these basic functions to the planning team for purposes of planning the program. During execution, we perform these basic management functions again, only this time it's for the ever-changing aspects of execution.

Planning

The planning function involves the process of identifying the work to be performed, determining which of the requirements of the job are required by the customer (stated requirements) and which are required by internal processes or required in support of the customer's stated requirements (derived requirements). The basic premise is to identify what is required to satisfy the program's overall goal and objectives.

In traditional management terminology, planning is defining goals, establishing strategy, developing plans, and coordinating activities.

Organizing

Organizing, from a program management perspective, involves grouping like work together into some form of work breakdown structure (WBS). The work is then described in a dictionary of some form and subsequently assigned to an individual or organization to be performed. Organizing the work is based a sound definition of what the requirements are to accomplish the overall objectives of the program. These requirements were identified in the planning function.

Again, in a traditional management sense, organizing is determining what needs to be done, how it will be done, and who is to do it.

Leading

Leading is used, generally, when we're talking about oversight of program personnel. The terms *leading, managing, directing, influencing, motivating,* and the like are all synonyms to the term *leading*. A large but less discussed part of leading is conflict resolution.

Controlling

Controlling is concerned with establishing, collecting, and reviewing metrics. The purpose for metric collection and review is to be able to better determine the overall health of the program during the execution phase. Identification of applicable, reflective metrics will significantly aid in the management by exception or management through thresholds, types of management control mechanisms.

Management Roles

In the late 1960s, Henry Mintzberg performed a detailed study of five top managers at work. What he discovered challenged several long-held notions about the manager's job. In contrast to the predominant view at the time that managers were reflective thinkers who carefully and systematically processed information before making decisions, Mintzberg found that his managers engaged in a large number of varied, unpatterned, and short-duration activities. There was little time for reflective thinking because the managers were constantly interrupted. Half of these managers' activities lasted less than nine minutes each. In addition to the insight on what managers did, Mintzberg separated their activities into three broad categories, representing a total of ten different but highly interrelated roles (Robbins, 1999, p. 13). The three categories are interpersonal, informational, and decisional.

Interpersonal

All managers are required to perform duties that involve people who are subordinates as well as those who are outside of the organization. These duties can be categorized as interpersonal, ceremonial, or symbolic in nature. They can basically be broken into three subcategories: figurehead, leader, and liaison.

A figurehead is a symbolic head. In this capacity the manager performs routine duties of a social nature, such as greeting guests, signing documents, and the like.

As a leader, the manager is tasked to motivate and move people toward a common goal. This might involve performing a staffing function as well as ensuring adequate training for subordinates.

As a liaison, the manager acts as a go-between for the organization and the outside world. In the case of a manager being a liaison between the company as a whole and the outside world, the manager might sit on other companies' boards of directors or on university committees.

Informational

The informational role that a manager plays is involved with the monitoring and disseminating of information as well as acting as the organization's spokesperson.

As a monitor of information, the manager acts as the nerve center for the collection of related and applicable information. This information may come from many sources, including magazines, books, seminars, conferences, and the like. The manager must then disseminate this information to the appropriate individuals within the organization.

As the spokesperson for the organization, the manager must communicate information to outsiders on the organization's plans, actions, intent, and positions as appropriate and applicable.

Decisional

In the decisional role, the manager must act as an entrepreneur, disturbance handler, resource allocator, and negotiator.

As an entrepreneur, the manager is responsible for visualizing and bringing to reality visions of greater opportunities. Identifying, seeking out, and acting upon potential opportunities typify this activity.

As a disturbance handler, the manager must maintain a level of harmony among the organization's participants. Disturbances may take on many forms, including problems with personnel as well as impacts from outside forces, such as competitive forces. Another form of disturbance, which is not readily discussed, is that which originates from a parent organization manifested through short-term demands and, ultimately, crises. The adage "a lack of planning on your part does not constitute a crises on my part" is not applicable when the lack of planning originates from a parent organizational authority.

As a resource handler, the manager must allocate sufficient resources, such as people, facilities, and equipment, to perform the many activities of the organization or program.

And finally, as a negotiator, the manager may be called on to represent the organization's interest in some form of contract negotiation. An example could be a union negotiation.

Management Skills

Generally, a manager requires certain skills that may be categorized into three broad groupings: technical, human, and conceptual.

Technical Skills

Technical skills are those that support the knowledge of, or actual doing of, the tasks to be performed. This is especially true of middle management, or better yet, first-line supervisors. These individuals are more involved with the day-to-day operations of the organization.

For example, I have spent many years in the discipline of software engineering. Because of this, I am well versed in the many forms of programming languages, design methodologies, and terminology in general. This would more readily allow me to provide valuable insight into this discipline. As time progresses, however, our technical skills begin to become obsolete and somewhat antiquated. For this reason, continuous lifelong learning is required if we wish to stay abreast of our technical disciplines.

As well, as we move into higher and higher levels of management, it is not expected that we maintain such sharp skills. In fact, as we progress into higher levels of management, we are expected to contribute in a different manner and to apply a different set of skills, such as human or conceptual.

Human Skills

Human skills are those skills that allow us to work harmoniously with others inside and outside of our organization. These skills not only help us to work with individuals, but with groups. There is a significant body of training and education available to help managers to develop these skills. Aside from the obvious and readily available training associated with effective listening and communicating, group problem solving, and motivation, I have a particular fondness for personality instruments, which allow managers to better understand their personality preferences and those of their teams.

Conceptual Skills

Conceptual skills are those that we would use to think and conceptualize about abstract situations. The popular phrase "thinking outside of the box" is more likely to materialize when the manager has strong conceptual skills.

Conceptual skills allow individuals (1) to focus on connections between data and (2) to focus on patterns, meanings, or theoretical explanations of the data. Managers with strong conceptual skills tend to be visionary and imaginative, have an accurate feeling for what is going on, and make decisions based on theoretical projection of future possibilities of what they "see."

Figure 19.2 depicts the relationship between conceptual, human, and technical skills as an individual moves through the lower, middle, and top layers of management.

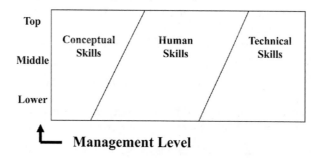

Figure 19.2. Management Levels versus Required Skills

Leaders

Managers are appointed. Their ability to influence is based on their formal authority inherent in their positions. Leaders, on the other hand, may be appointed or may emerge from within a group. Leaders influence others to perform beyond what might normally be expected.

All managers should ideally be leaders. This enhanced capacity can increase the efficiency of performing their tasks.

Not all leaders necessarily have skills in other management functions, such as planning, organizing, and controlling.

Numerous studies and detailed works have addressed leaders and leadership. Basically, these efforts fall into three categories of efforts: trait theories, behavioral theories, and contingency theories.

Theories of Leadership

During the 1920s and 1930s, trait theories of leadership evolved. These theories focused on those characteristics of leaders that might be used to differentiate a leader from a non-leader. The process was really quite simple: select recognizable leaders, isolate traits, and make recognizable generalizations.

Traits thought to be indicative a good leader included the following:

- Drive—leaders have a high effort level
- Desire—leaders have a strong desire to influence others
- Honesty and integrity—leaders build trusting relationships; they are truthful and not deceitful
- Self-confident—leaders seem to lack self-doubt
- Intelligence—leaders are sufficiently intelligent to gather, synthesize, interpret, and apply large amounts of data

When all was said and done, it became obvious that traits alone could not adequately define who might make a good leader and who might not. Therefore, researchers refocused their attention on behaviors.

Note that had trait theorists been successful, it would have created a basis for selecting the right people to assume formal leadership positions in organizations. In contrast, if behavioral studies would have turned up key behavioral determinants of leadership, people could be trained to be leaders.

There are four primary behavioral studies in this category of leadership studies: University of Iowa, Ohio State University, University of Michigan, and the Blake and Mouton Managerial Grid.

The University of Iowa identified three behavioral dimensions:

- Autocratic—a leader who centralizes authority, dictates work methods, makes unilateral decisions, and limits subordinate participation
- Democratic—a leader who involves subordinates in decision making, delegates authority, encourages participation in deciding work methods and goals, and believes firmly in feedback as an opportunity for coaching
- Laissez-faire—a leader who gives groups complete freedom to make decisions and complete work in whatever way it sees fit

Results from the University of Iowa studies were mixed, although it was expected that the democratic style of leadership was most effective.

The Ohio State University studies sought to identify independent dimensions of a leader's behavior. They began with more than a thousand dimensions and ultimately settled on two:.

- Initiating structure—the extent to which roles are structured to attain goals. Initiating structure organizes work, relationships, and goals. It assigns tasks and expects standards of performance and the meeting of deadlines.
- Consideration—the extent to which a person has job relationships characterized by mutual trust and respect for subordinates' ideas. It also provides for a high regard for subordinates' feelings.

In the Ohio State University studies, a high-high leader, that is, high in initiating structure and high in consideration, achieved high subordinate performance and high satisfaction. But, like the University of Iowa studies, the results were mixed and therefore inconclusive.

About the same time as the Ohio State University studies, the studies of the University of Michigan took place. These studies attempted to measure leaders along two axes:.

- Employee-orientedness is premised on interpersonal relationships.
- Production-orientedness focuses on task or technical aspects of the job.

The University of Michigan studies found that employee-oriented leaders were generally associated with high group productivity and higher group satisfaction. But, like studies before it, they were unable to provide consistent results to make conclusive findings.

The behavioral findings of these earlier studies formed the basis for the Blake and Mouton Managerial Grid. The managerial grid uses "concern for people" and "concern for production" as the X and Y axes. It uses nine possible positions along each axis, creating 81 different categories of styles. The five key positions include:

- Impoverished management—low concern for people and low concern for production. Leader exertion of minimal effort to attain organizational goals is all that is required to maintain a successful workforce.
- Task management—high concern for production and a low concern for people.
- Country club management—high concern for people with a low concern for production. In this scenario, the focus is on the people to the exclusion of the tasks.

- Middle-of-the-road management—this scenario maintains adequate task efficiency and employee morale.
- Team management—typified by a high concern for people and a high concern for production.

The managerial grid generally indicated that managers performed best with a high concern for people and a high concern for production. Figure 19.3 reflects the relative positions of these management positions.

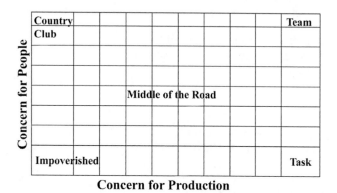

Figure 19.3. Managerial Grid

In general, the behavioral theories of leadership:

- Were not very successful in identifying patterns of leadership behavior
- Failed to create consistent generalizations
- Had varied results based on circumstances
- Created a sense that the problem was more complex than isolating traits or preferred behaviors

The next wave, and the current thinking, is referred to as contingency theories of leadership.

Contingency theories focus on the leader's ability to change leadership styles based on situational specifics.

One contingency theorist was Fred Fiedler. Fiedler believed that we should not attempt to change the leader's style, but instead we should attempt to match the leader to a more compatible organizational situation. According to Fiedler, leader-member relations, task structure, and the position power of the leader are the three primary factors that should be used for moving leaders into situations more appropriate for their leadership style.

Leader-member relations is the degree to which a leader feels accepted by his or her followers. Task structure is the degree to which the goals and tasks to be performed are outlined clearly. Position power is the degree to which the leader has control over the rewards and punishments the followers will receive.

Hersey-Blanchard was another model premised on situational theory. The Hersey-Blanchard model focuses on task and relationship behaviors with an implication as to the maturity of the followers. This model identifies four basic quadrants representing four leadership styles:

- Telling—representative of a high-task and low-relationship situation. In this quadrant, the leader defines roles and tells people what, how, when, and where to perform the various identified tasks.
- Selling—representative of a high-task and high-relationship situation. The leader provides both directive and supportive behaviors.

- Participating—representative of a low-task and high-relationship situation. In this scenario, the leader and the followers share in the decision making.
- Delegating—representative of a low-task and low-relationship situation. In this scenario, the leader provides basic direction.

Another contingency theory was Robert House's path-goal theory. This leadership theory assumes four leadership styles:

Directive

- leader tells subordinates what is expected of them
- leader schedules work to be done
- leader tells how to do it
- similar to the initiating structure of the Ohio State University studies

Supportive

- leader is friendly and shows concern for the needs of the subordinates
- synonymous with the Ohio State University dimension of "consideration"

Participative

- leader consults with his or her subordinates
- leader uses subordinates suggestions when making decisions

Achievement-Oriented

- leader sets challenging goals
- leader expects subordinates to perform at their highest level

In conclusion, relative to contingency theories, in deciding the best leadership style, contingency theory recognizes the three key elements of any leadership situation:

- Leader's style—stems from trait theories
- Leader's behavior—how the leader interacts with subordinates; stems from behavioral theories
- Leader's situation—stems from work of contingency theorists

Power

A discussion of managers and leaders would not be complete without some reference to power and its implications. There are five generally accepted sources of power.

- Legitimate power—legitimate power is the result of a position of formal authority in the organizational hierarchy.
- Coercive power—coercive power is based on fear and negative results that might occur if the subordinate does not obey.
- Reward power—reward power is the opposite of coercive power. Reward power is the ability to distribute fair and equitable rewards for positive performance that the receiver views as valuable.
- Expert power—expert power is influence possessed as a result of an individual's expertise. It is special skills or knowledge. Expert power is earned, not awarded.
- Referent power—referent power arises from identifying with a person with desirable resources or personal traits. For example, "If I admire and identify with you, you can exercise power over me because I want to please you."

Military Leadership Fundamentals

I have spent nearly my entire professional career servicing the defense industry. It is only natural that many of my acquaintances and friends have a military background. To this end, I asked them for information on how the military trains and prepares leaders for command. One of the books, which I found to be a wonderful source of information, is entitled *Taking Charge: A Practical Guide for Leaders,* by Perry Smith (1986).

In his book, Smith refers to 20 military fundamentals identified below (p. 20):

- A leader must trust his or her subordinates.
- A leader must be a good teacher.
- A leader should rarely be a problem solver; a leader should facilitate problem solving, but let subordinates solve the problem.
- A leader must be a good communicator.
- A leader must manage time well and use it effectively.
- A leader should trust her or his intuition.
- A leader must be willing to remove people for cause.
- A leader must take care of his or her people. He who receives a benefit should never forget it, he who bestows should never remember it.
- A leader must provide vision.
- A leader must subordinate her or his ambitions and egos to the goals of the unit or institution for which she or he serves.
- A leader must know how to run meetings.
- A leader must understand the decision-making and implementation process.
- A leader must be visible and approachable.
- A leader should have a sense of humor.
- A leader must be decisive, but patiently decisive.
- A leader should be introspective.
- A leader should be reliable.
- A leader should be open-minded.
- A leader should establish and maintain high standards of dignity. Dressing well, being well-mannered, avoiding profanity, helping subordinates, conducting ceremonies, welcoming newcomers with a personal letter—all help to keep performance and morale high.
- A leader should exude integrity. Of all qualities, integrity is the most important.

To further help these potential military leaders, there are checklists that quickly summarize those things to think about in a given situation. For example, the checklist for when you are looking at yourself as a leader is depicted below (p. 27):

- Do you allocate time to visit areas you control?
- Does everyone know what your priorities are?
- Are you reliable?
- Who tells you all the news? Good and bad?
- How well do you listen?
- Do people fear you, like you, distrust you, love you?
- What is your body language like?
- Are you considered a communicator?
- Are you considered to be a disciplinarian?
- Do you enjoy your job?
- Are you an innovator?
- Are you flexible?

- Do you maintain physical and intellectual fitness?
- Are you a deflector of pressure from above or a magnifier of pressure?
- Are you tuned in, or are you out of touch?
- Are you a delegator?
- Are you a non-drinker, a drinker, or an alcoholic?
- Are you an optimist or a pessimist?
- Are you religious?
- What are your ethics and values?
- Are you a writer?
- Are you ambitious?
- Are you secure, or are you insecure?
- Are you a philanderer?
- What is your integrity level?
- Are you intense, or are you relaxed?
- Are you decisive, or are you a decision ducker?
- Are you conceptually oriented?

The military also provides a number of operational checklists for leaders. Some of these are outlined below:

- Transition checklist
- Communications checklist
- Integrity checklist
- Hiring checklist
- Counseling checklist
- Hang-up checklist
- Firing checklist
- Thank-you checklist
- Planning checklist
- Divestiture checklist
- Decision-making checklist
- Executive skills checklist
- Meeting checklist
- Introspection checklist
- Promotion board checklist
- Antenna checklist
- Phrases to avoid checklist
- Congressional visit checklist

Relative to the transition checklist, the following are useful questions to ask when you have been selected to assume a leadership position.

- What is the mission?
- What are the organization's goals, priorities, plans, programs, and budgets?
- What is the size and structure of the organization?
- What means of communication will I have (newspaper, radio, television, social gatherings, etc.)?
- Who reports directly to me? How many? Why? Why not others?
- Who is my boss? What is his or her leadership/management style? What is his or her means of communication to me?

- Am I responsible for geographically separated units? Do they report directly to me? Do they report indirectly to me?
- Which organizations, staff agencies, or individuals should I visit? In what order? How often for subsequent visits?
- What is the standard of integrity? Have there been recent violations of these standards? How frequent and what was the outcome?
- What are the standards of performance? How are they measured? What are the results of recent outside inspections, self-inspections, or audits?
- What documents should I read? In what order? Is there an annual organizational history? If not, why not?
- Are there procedures and regulations? What are the most important plans? Is there a long-range plan? If not, why not?
- What skeletons are in the closet?
- Where are the personnel shortages/weaknesses?
- What are the toughest problems I should expect to encounter during the first few months?
- How often do the top leaders and their subordinates go to off-site seminars together?

Entrepreneurs

Entrepreneurs can be defined as individuals who recognize and pursue opportunities where others see chaos or confusion.

Entrepreneurship is a process by which individuals recognize and pursue opportunities.

Entrepreneurs are typically associated with forming external new ventures. Intrepreneurs possess the same basic characteristics, but apply their knowledge and drive to internal opportunities to the company for which they work.

The most frequently reported characteristics of an entrepreneur are listed below:

- High need for achievement
- Believe they control their own destiny
- Frequently take only calculated risks
- Independent
- Prefer to be personally responsible for solving problems
- Not afraid to take chances
- They have a willingness to work hard
- Self-confident
- Optimistic
- Determined
- High energy levels
- Are not likely to be content in typical large bureaucracies

Managers versus Entrepreneurs

Not all small business owners or managers are entrepreneurs. Some small business managers simply operate their business; they don't necessarily innovate.

A few noted, theoretically accepted, differences between managers and entrepreneurs are detailed below:

- Entrepreneurs actively seek change. Managers tend to be more custodial.
- Entrepreneurs often put their own personal financial security at risk. Managers tend to be more conservative and assume only conservative risks.
- Entrepreneurs accept risks. Managers tend to avoid risks.

- Entrepreneurs are motivated by independence and the opportunity to create financial gain. Managers tend to be more motivated by career promotions and corporate rewards such as office location, size, staff, and power.
- Entrepreneurs look at business growth over the longer term. Managers tend to be more oriented to the achievement of short-term goals.
- Entrepreneurs tend to be directly involved in all phases of their organization's operational activities. Managers tend to delegate tasks and supervise those performing the tasks.
- Entrepreneurs tend to accept mistakes as the normal part of doing business. Managers tend to avoid putting themselves in situations where they may fail or make a mistake.

How Do Entrepreneurs Get Their Ideas?

In a survey of a hundred highly successful entrepreneurs:

- 71 percent replicated or modified an idea gained from previous employment
- 20 percent built temporary or casual jobs into a business
- 5 percent benefited from the PC revolution
- 4 percent benefited from systematic research for opportunities

Entrepreneurial Strategic Planning

The entrepreneur is driven by the perception of opportunity, rather than by the availability of resources. Managers ask a different set of questions with different priorities than does the entrepreneur.

The manager might ask:

- What resources do I control?
- What structure do we have or need to compete?
- How can I minimize the impact of others on my ability to perform?
- What opportunity is appropriate?

The entrepreneur might ask:

- Where is the opportunity?
- How do I capitalize on it?
- What resources do I need?
- How do I gain control over them?
- What structure is best?

Note the difference in order and emphasis! Entrepreneurs tend to be more concerned with what and where the opportunity is, then how they can capitalize on it, and lastly, how they can accomplish the work. The manager, being more attuned to performance, would naturally be more concerned with how to do it.

Continuing with entrepreneurial strategic planning, entrepreneurs tend to:

- Risk financial security
- Bypass career opportunities
- Risk family relations
- Believe hard facts about new business start-ups are not applicable to them:
  - 40 percent of the new businesses fail in the first year
  - 60 percent fail by the end of the second year
  - 90 percent fail by the end of the tenth year
- Entrepreneurs believe they will be in the top 10 percent that do not fail

Evolution of the Entrepreneurial Firm

The entrepreneurial firm evolves through a natural evolution based on size.

- The firm becomes bigger than one person can handle.
- The entrepreneur hires people to perform functions (accounting, marketing, human relations (HR), etc.). Notice here the introduction of the traditional functional organizational design.
- The entrepreneur learns to delegate and manage people, or not.
- The entrepreneur tries to maintain the original small company atmosphere as the firm continues to grow.

Ethics at All Levels

Regardless of description—manager, leader, or entrepreneur—a basic understanding of the premise of ethics is in order.

Ethics refers to the principles of conduct governing an individual or group and specifically the standards used to govern conduct. Ethical decisions involve normative judgments.

A normative judgment implies that something is good or bad, right or wrong, better or worse. For example: "I see you wrote a report," is non-normative. To say, "the report you wrote is really good" is normative.

Ethical decisions involve morality. Morality is society's accepted norms of behavior. A few basic definitions, therefore:

- Ethics—the rules or standards governing the conduct of a profession.
- Morals—being or acting in accordance with the standards of good behavior.
- Values—a principle, standard, or quality considered inherently worthwhile or desirable.

Criteria that shape ethical decisions include: utility, rights, and justice.

The goal of utilitarianism is to provide the greatest good for the greatest number. Using this criterion, decisions are made solely on the basis of their outcome and consequences. This criterion is consistent with like goals of efficiency, high productivity, and high profits.

Using utilitarianism, one would make the argument that laying off 100 people is for the good of all who remain. But, while this criterion promotes efficiency and productivity, it can ignore the rights of some individuals.

Rights as a criterion means respecting and protecting the basic rights of individuals to privacy, free speech, due process, and the like.

Under this criterion, rights protects, as an example, whistleblowers who report unethical or illegal acts or practices. It also protects individuals from injury and is consistent with freedom and privacy, but it can create overly legalistic work environments that hinder productivity and efficiency.

Justice imposes and enforces rules fairly and impartially so there is an equitable distribution of benefits and costs. Unions favor this criterion. It justifies paying the same wage for a given job regardless of performance. It also justifies using seniority to make layoff decisions. Justice protects the interests of the underrepresented or less powerful. Justice can, however, create a sense of entitlement that reduces risk taking, innovation, and productivity.

In summary:

- Ethics refers to the principles of conduct governing an individual or group. Ethical decisions always include both normative and moral judgments.
- Being legal and ethical are not the same thing. One does not imply the other.
- Organizational leaders shape our work ethics: published codes, compliance mechanisms, hotlines, training, culture, and accountability.

Concluding Thoughts

The purpose of this chapter was to provide insight into some the most recent thinking, theory, methodologies, and practices as they relate to managers, leaders, and entrepreneurs. The purpose was not to make definitive generalizations.

To this end, it would appear on the surface that every one of us has performed as a manager, leader, or entrepreneur at one point in our lives or another. It could be suggested the traits and behaviors that make one versus the other are present in all of us, and further, are more or less prevalent as we each enter into, and out of, different situations. This would suggest that sometimes, given the situation, we might behave as a manager, a leader, or an entrepreneur. It would further suggest that rather than looking at our traits or behaviors, it might be more helpful to look at our personality preferences—which is exactly what we do in other chapters.

Chapter 20

The American Social Economic Context

The purpose of this chapter is to bring a broader perspective to the American social economic context and the relationship between management philosophies and organizational design models. To fold in the people aspect, attention will be given to the attendant relationships of gerontological life phases and generational cohort groups. Organizational design models, gerontological life phases, and cohort groups are each addressed in other chapters in this text.

Simply stated, management philosophies, since the late nineteenth century, have been dominated by four basic categories of thinking: (1) classical/scientific management, (2) behavioral sciences, (3) contingency approaches, and (4) systems theory. While each differs from the other in basic philosophy, they are actually intuitive when viewed from the bigger picture of the economic circumstances from which they evolved.

Organizational designs are those many ways in which we organize our workforce to gain the greatest productivity given the product or service we produce. Although on the surface one might guess that our organizational designs actually evolve from well thought-out strategic planning based on our current management philosophies, the reality is quite opposite. We will discuss, again, how economic circumstances force successful organizations to permute themselves into more efficient and effective entities.

When we talk about gerontological phases of human life, we are actually talking about changes to our biosocial, cognitive, and psychosocial development as we chronologically mature over time. These three perspectives can be thought of as domains of human development.

Biosocial changes are those changes having to do with physical growth and development, as well as the family, community, and cultural factors that affect that growth and development.

Cognitive changes addresses the mental processes through which the individual thinks, learns, and communicates.

Psychosocial changes include emotions, personality characteristics, and relationships with other people.

Our discussion of like groups within the workforce centers on groups having similar ages, therefore sharing similar experiences and defining moments (Levinson, 1978, p. 56). Defining moments are those instances where something catches the attention and hearts of hundreds, if not thousands, of individuals at the same basic time in their formative lives.

The list below combines life phases (gerontology) with similar age-related cohort groups in the workforce:

- Late adulthood (60+ years old); Veterans
- Middle adulthood (40–60 years old); Baby Boomers
- Early adulthood (20–40 years old); Generation Xers
- Adolescence (10–20 years old); Nexters
- The school years (7–11 years old)
- Early childhood or preschool (2–6 years old)
- Infants or toddlers (0–2 years old)

Note that our discussion will focus on adolescence (Nexters) through late adulthood (Veterans).

The discussion of similar age groups within the workforce is in and of itself quite interesting, but it is even more enlightening when coupled with the basic phases of human development. When the two similar age groups and basic developmental phases of human development are placed in the context of organizational designs and management philosophies, and then nestled in the overall picture of American economic circumstances, the whole picture evolves nicely into a single cohesive and coherent discussion.

Figure 20.1 forms the premise for all subsequent discussion.

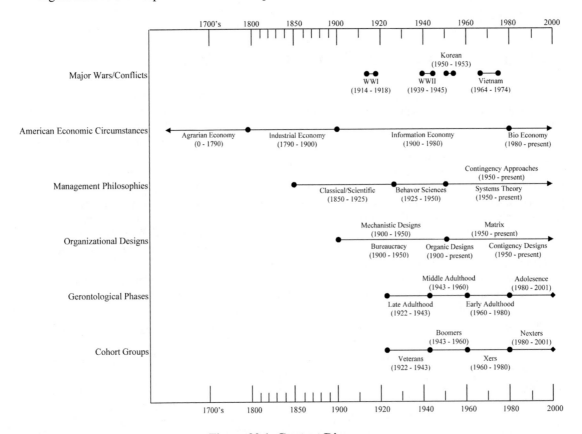

Figure 20.1. Context Diagram

The following sections are organized by time period. This strategy provides the easiest mechanism for discussing the many facets we wish to address. The sections are:

- Prior to 1920
- 1920 to 1945
- 1945 to 1960
- 1960 to 1980
- 1980 to Present

Not all sections equally discuss management philosophies, organizational designs, gerontological phases, or cohort groups. The reason for this is quite simply that not all of these factors have applicability to each of the economic circumstances being discussed. For example, it wasn't until the industrial economy or industrial period in time that management philosophies and organizational designs became a documented intentional focus of attention. As well, when talking about gerontological phases or cohort groups in the workplace, it generally does not add value to our discussion to go beyond 80 years. This is because the primary focus of this text is on those individuals who still have an impact on our workplaces. Late adulthood, therefore, ranges back to about 1922, which picks up just after our discussion on the Industrial Revolution.

Again, it should be stated that the intent of this chapter is to advance the basic body of knowledge of the collective dimensions being discussed. To this end, the various aspects being discussed originate from numerous sources and will be referenced so that the readers may formulate their own interpretations of the data. The information on core values, seminal events, cultural memorabilia, heroes, and generational personality of the age groups in the workforce, while discussed in many articles and those applicable texts as referenced herein, comes predominantly from the work of Zemke, Raines and Filipczak in *Generations at Work* (2000). Worth noting is that the seminal work on developmental phases most likely is Levinson's 1978 book *The Seasons of a Man's Life.*

The sections that follow, then, will discuss in chronological order the American economic circumstances. Invidiuals, in those attendant time periods, in terms of gerontological life phases and cohort similarities and differences, management philosophies, and organizational design models attendant to the time period of the section are best discussed as a block. Therefore, these latter discussions will reside in their own chapters of this text.

Prior to 1920

American Economic Circumstances

Agrarian Economy
Agriculture is the systematic raising of useful plants through human oversight and intervention. The production of food is the main reason for agriculture, but cultivated plants also furnish substances useful as textile fibers, dyestuffs, medicines, and ornaments. Gathering wild plants for food or other purposes is not agriculture. The crucial innovation that separated wild plant gathering from true agriculture was the deliberate planting of seeds and other plant material. Cultivation, harvesting, and processing were byproducts of this innovation.

In a broad sense, agriculture can include animal husbandry, which is closely associated with plant raising. On the other hand, agriculture can be used in a limited technical sense to refer only to raising field crops; in this usage it is differentiated from horticulture (gardening) and arboriculture (orcharding).

Humans have lived by farming for only a short time. For most of their existence, now believed to extend to forms as much as two million years old, human beings lived as wild plant gatherers and as hunters. Deliberate plant raising began only about ten thousand years ago. In this relatively brief period, farming has made possible revolutionary changes in human life. Human population has greatly increased, partly because more people could be fed. Moreover, agriculture has been a major factor in transforming human societies from small, primitive local bands into huge, technologically advanced nations. Agriculture does not by itself create civilization, but without agriculture early civilization would not have developed.

Hunting and wild plant gathering were sufficient for the world's small human population until twelve thousand to ten thousand years ago. The melting of the continental ice sheets of the last glaciation brought a return of milder climates and led to rises in sea level and major shifts in both plant and animal life. Several important game animals became extinct, and the growing scarcity of game appears to have caused a shift to more intensive harvesting of wild seeds and roots. Improved seed-collecting methods, storage baskets, and seed grinders developed near the beginning of what archaeologists call the Neolithic, or New Stone Age. Evidence of a stage between wild plant gathering and systematic agriculture comes from Owens Valley in eastern California, occupied by the Paiute Native Americans. The Paiutes increased the yield of wild grasses by building rock and soil checkdams to slow the runoff of water and by harvesting seeds. The fundamental difference between this and true agriculture is that the grass was not planted, but seeded itself.

The first real cultivation was probably incidental and casual, begun by people having no notion that they were embarking on a momentous phase of cultural evolution. It was during the Neolithic period that the actual change from hunting and gathering to food production, the so-called Neolithic revolution, occurred. This "food-producing revolution," the incipient phase and the interval between the achievement of agriculture and the advent of urban life, lasted almost four thousand years. The establishment of permanent agricultural villages had (and still has) certain disadvantages:

- Farming peoples who are overly dependent on a single starch staple often suffer from nutritional deficiencies.
- Closely built villages promote communicable diseases.
- Stored surpluses invite enemy attack, and growing crops are subject to destruction by storms, floods, or insect ravages in ways that wild resources are not.
- Cleared tropical forests spread malaria.
- Irrigation farming in tropical areas favors transmission of liver flukes from snails to barefoot farmers.

Because of such factors it is probable that the development of agriculture brought about significant biological changes in human beings, apart from its effect in promoting population expansion.

Wild plant gathering did not cease with the advent of farming. Nuts, berries, various greens, fruit, and mushrooms are still gathered wild even in the most advanced agricultural countries. Moreover, most of the world's wood products still come from wild forest growth, although replanting (or "tree farming") is increasing.

There are no written records of the actual beginnings of agriculture, but it is clear from archaeological findings that the earliest agriculture, in the Middle East and in the New World, preceded pottery making, one of humankind's ancient crafts. The carbonized remains of clearly domesticated plant forms have been unearthed in early sites. Finds of farming tools are another line of evidence, although early stone or wooden implements may also have been used by non-farming food collectors. In later times, hoe blades were made of polished stone, bone, or shell. Plows, unambiguous evidence of farming, appeared no earlier than about 3,000 BC in the Middle East. In some areas, traces of old field patterns exist, but the best evidence of farming is found around the buildings where crops were stored and processed.

Botanical evidence, based on studies of the distribution range of plants, indicated fairly conclusively that wheat, barley, and rice originated in the Old World and that maize, potatoes, and manioc (large, starchy root plant) came from the Americas. With the advent of writing, records became important evidence. Certain ancient peoples left well-illustrated documents, the earliest of which come from Egypt and Mesopotamia. Human beings, crops, and farming methods are described in the Old Testament. The ancient Greeks and later Romans compiled treatises on plant life.

Despite the variety of archaeological and historical evidence, however, it is difficult to trace the geographical diffusion of early cultivated plants. Conclusions about dates and routes by which plants were spread in ancient times remain conjectural. Only in recent times have precise records become available. For example, a recent instance of plant diffusion involving the Brazilian rubber plant is well documented. The seeds of the rubber plant were smuggled from Brazil to the Royal Botanical Gardens at Kew, near London, in the 1870s. From there they were taken to Ceylon and the East Indies.

The first immigrants to America in the seventeenth century went not to set themselves up in farming, but to trade to the natives, fish, and search for gold. Trading and fishing from the outset absorbed the attention of some, but most immigrants were soon forced to turn to agriculture, which continued to be the mainstay of colonial life thereafter. The agriculture they practiced was very different from that found anywhere in the Old World. English practices influenced colonial agricultural everywhere, particularly in New England, but in the middle colonies the Dutch, Germans, Welsh, Scotch-Irish, and Swedes and in the southern colonies the French contributed to the developing agricultural pattern. All these groups brought with them agricultural practices, seeds, crude farm tools, livestock, cuttings, and plants that varied widely, assuring a diverse mixture of methods, techniques, plants and livestock. More important in shaping the growth of agriculture in the New World was the great abundance of land, its cheapness and ease of acquisition, the dissimilarities of soil and climate, the freedom of enterprise, the initiative of the settlers, and finally the heritage of new commodities acquired by the Indians.

Agricultural education trains people to produce, process, and distribute food or fiber, and spreads scientific and technical information related to all phases of such work. It strives to help the people of the world improve the quantity and quality of products indispensable to human life.

Agricultural education is concerned with one of the oldest and largest areas of work. In many countries of Latin America, Asia, and Africa, from 50 to 80 percent of the working force is employed in farming. These countries face the need to multiply the productivity of their farms if their increasing populations are to escape undernourishment or outright famine. In the highly industrialized nations the proportion of the labor force engaged in farming may be relatively small, perhaps 10 percent, but agriculture continues to be a major industry. In such countries it takes in far more than the work done on the traditional family farm, not only raising crops and livestock, processing the crops, and marketing them, but also providing many of the goods and services that farmers use. Agriculture must continually increase its productivity in industrial countries also, so that industrial countries can feed their own expanding populations, provide raw materials for the textile, plastics, and other industries, and ship surpluses abroad.

Agricultural education takes many forms, from children's classes in village schools to graduate study in university laboratories. Much of it goes on outside of school. Some of the most useful training is given by men and women who work directly with farmers to demonstrate new crops, techniques, and machines. All forms of agricultural education can be illustrated by descriptions of programs in the United States.

The United States is one of the highly industrialized nations in which farmers are a relatively small group. The comparatively small number of farmers in the nation represents a great change from the middle of the nineteenth century, when about eighty-five persons lived on the land for every fifteen who lived in cities. In the course of a century these figures were reversed, and only about one-seventh of the total labor force remained in agriculture. But while people moved away from the farms, the productivity of agricultural labors increased by more than 600 percent between 1870 and the mid-1960s. Four-fifths of the increase occurred after 1945.

The number of farmers in the United States has decreased at each census, while the total population has increased. For these reasons, agricultural workers have needed to acquire the technical skills and scientific knowledge that would enable them to meet the rapidly expanding demand for their products. Agricultural education has grown rapidly to meet this need.

In the United States, organized agricultural education began toward the end of the eighteenth century. The Philadelphia Society for Promoting Agriculture was organized in 1785, with George Washington and Benjamin Franking as members. Similar societies were established in South Carolina (1785), Maine (1787), New York (1791), Massachusetts (1792), and Connecticut (1794). In addition to publishing bulletins and encouraging the establishment of agricultural fairs and exhibitions, these societies furthered agricultural instruction in the common schools. The Philadelphia Society, for example, in 1794 prepared a plan to promote agricultural instruction through the University of Pennsylvania and, at a lower level, through the common school system of that state.

The earliest specialized school of agriculture in the United States was the Gardiner Lyceum, founded at Gardiner, Maine, in 1821. In 1823, the state legislature appropriated $1,000 for the maintenance of the school, in what was probably the first instance of state aid for agricultural education. By 1840, agricultural instruction in the schools was being encouraged in Maine, Massachusetts, Connecticut, New York, and Michigan. In the domain of higher education there was considerable agitation early in the nineteenth century for the establishment of state colleges of agriculture. In 1818, Governor DeWitt Clinton of New York recommended that the state legislature take steps "by which means a complete course of agricultural education would be taught." By the time of the American Civil War, some states had created colleges of agriculture. The state constitution adopted in 1850 by Michigan required that a college of agriculture be established and maintained. The Michigan Agricultural College (now Michigan State University) was dedicated on May 13, 1857. In Pennsylvania, the Farmers' High School was founded in 1855 and became, in 1862, the Agricultural College of Pennsylvania (now Pennsylvania State University). The Maryland Agricultural College was chartered in 1856 and became part of the University of Maryland in 1920.

The year 1862 was a milestone in the development of agricultural education in the United States. On May 15, 1862, Congress created the Department of Agriculture. Among other functions, the department was "to acquire and diffuse among the people of the United States useful information on subjects connected with agriculture." On July 2, 1862, President Abraham Lincoln signed the Land-Grant College Act, called the Morrill Act after its original sponsor, Justin S. Morrill. Under the provisions of the act, each state was offered thirty thousand acres of public land (or its equivalent in scrip) for each of its senators and representatives who were then in Congress. Proceeds from the sale of these lands were to be used for the establishment of at least one college "where the leading objects will be . . . to teach such branches of learning as are related to agriculture and the mechanic arts." By this act, higher education was placed within the reach of the growing number of youths from all walks of life who sought training in scientific, agricultural, and industrial pursuits.

Purdue University, founded May 6, 1869, was one such university to be created as a direct result of the Morrill Act. Purdue, entangled in the political struggles of Indiana and the actual implementation of the Morrill Act, opened its doors for its first class on September 16, 1874, a full five years after its founding and twelve years after the Morrill Act was signed into law.

The land-grant colleges and universities created with the help of the Morrill Act are in a central position in agricultural education. They offer a threefold program of resident instruction, research, and extension education service. Moreover, the curricula of these institutions have greatly influenced the development of farming in the 50 states. Federal aid for land-grant colleges and universities is administered, for resident instruction, by the U.S. Office of Education and, for research and extension, by the U.S. Department of Agriculture. This aid, however, represents only a small proportion of the total institutional expenditures. State and local governments contribute more than twice as much as the federal government.

Industrial Economy

This period in time is characterized by scientific management theories, mechanistic models of organizational design, and orientation toward production efficiency and effectiveness.

The Industrial Revolution in the United States appears to have been the catalyst for the earliest forms of organizational design and management philosophies. Three advances in technology launched the period: the steam engine (1790–1810), the railroads (1830–1850), and the telegraph (1844). These technologies are thought to have been responsible for the proliferation of U.S. entrepreneurship by 1860. Along with these technologies came increasing demand for manufactured goods and industrial markets. During the last half of the 19th century, the United States underwent an explosive transition from an agricultural nation to an industrial nation.

With the transition to an industrial society came demand for more efficient and effective production techniques. The goal of this period was to meet demand.

World War I (1914–1918)

World War I, the name commonly given to the war of 1914–1918, began in Europe and was fought principally on that continent, but eventually involved all of the continents of the world. While the wars between

Great Britain and France from 1689 to 1815 had been extended to North America, Africa, and Asia, they remained wars between European governments. The term *World War* is properly applied to the conflict of 1914–1918 because the various parts of the British Empire on all continents as well as many countries in Asia, North America, and South America participated in it. For the first time, all of the great powers of the world were engaged: Austria-Hungary, France, Germany, Great Britain, Italy, and Russia in Europe; Japan in Asia; and the United States in North America. It is estimated that by the end of the war about 93 percent of the population of the world was in greater or lesser degree involved.

War costs are of two kinds, direct and indirect. Direct costs embrace all expenditures made by belligerents in carrying on hostilities. Indirect costs include the economic losses resulting from deaths due directly or indirectly to the war, the value of property damaged or destroyed, the loss of production arising from the transfer of civilians to military pursuits, expenditures from war relief work, the costs of war to neutral nations, and the like. The direct costs of World War I, based on the most reliable statistics, were $186,333,637,000; the indirect costs have been estimated at $151,646,942,560, making the total war bill $337,980,579,560. It has been possible to appraise the direct costs fairly accurately, but the indirect costs can only be estimated, for there is no unit of measurement by which they may be definitely fixed, notwithstanding the many figures purporting to show how much money was spent to carry on the war. The fact is that it was fought mainly on credit, since the gold available at the outbreak of hostilities was not sufficient to have kept it going for more than 40 to 50 days. During the first three years of the war, the average daily cost was $123 million, and in 1918, it rose to $225 million.

The number of casualties in World War I exceeded by far those of any other war before World War II, in which almost 17 million men of the armed forces perished. Civilian deaths from military action, massacre, starvation, and exposure in the war between 1914 and 1918 are estimated at 12,618,000 (*Encyclopedia Americana*, 1996, vol. 29, p. 258).

Management Philosophies

In this period, quality and price frequently gave way to availability. During this time, scientific management unfolded through the efforts of Frederick W. Taylor (1856–1915). Taylor was credited with the scientific management philosophy, which sought to increase productivity and make work easier by scientifically studying work methods and establishing standards.

Taylor did most of his work at the Midvale and Bethlehem Steel Companies in Pennsylvania. As a mechanical engineer with a Quaker and Puritan background, he was continually appalled by workers' inefficiencies. Employees used vastly different techniques to do the same job. They were inclined to "take it easy" on the job, and Taylor believed that worker output was only about one-third what was possible. Therefore, he set out to correct the situation by applying the scientific method to shop floor jobs. He spent more than two decades passionately pursuing the "one best way" for each job to be done (Robbins, 1999).

Scientific management, as developed by Taylor, was based upon four main principles (Rue & Byars, 1989):

- The development of a scientific method of designing jobs. This involved gathering, classifying, and tabulating data to arrive at the "one best way" to perform a task or series of tasks. This "best way" was to replace the old rule-of-thumb.
- The scientific selection and progressive teaching of employees. This was not a generalist perspective, but instead a matching of the job or single task to a single worker. Taylor also emphasized the need to study worker strengths and weaknesses and to provide training to improve employee performance. Previously, workers chose their own work and trained themselves as best they could.
- The bringing together of scientifically selected employees and scientifically developed methods for designing jobs. Taylor believed that new and scientific methods of job design should not merely be put before an employee; they should also be fully explained by management.

He believed that employees would show little resistance to changes in methods if they understood the reasons for the change and they saw a chance for greater earnings for themselves.
- A division of work resulting in an interdependence between management and the workers. If they were truly dependent on one another, Taylor felt, then cooperation would naturally follow.

The scientific study of work also emphasized specialization and division of labor. In time, the need for an organizational framework became more and more apparent. The concepts of line and staff were developed. In an effort to motivate workers, most scientific management programs developed wage incentives. Once standards were set, managers began to monitor actual performance and compare it with the standards. Thus, the management function of control was launched.

Summarizing scientific management as a managerial philosophy, Taylor saw equal benefits for both management and workers: management could achieve more work in a given amount of time, and workers could produce more and earn more, with little or no additional effort (Rue & Byars, 1989, p. 38). Taylor believed that economic rewards could motivate employees, provided that those rewards were linked to individual performance.

Other scientific management pioneers followed in Taylor's footsteps. Morris Cooke applied scientific management principles to educational and municipal organizations. Henry Gantt created a scheduling technique for production control that utilized a bar chart, coined the "Gantt chart." The Gantt chart is still widely used today. Frank and Lillian Gilbreth combined the study of motion and work methods with psychology. The Gilbreths' work contributed significantly to research in the areas of fatigue, micromotion, and morale.

Frank Gilbreth, a construction worker by trade, gave up his contracting career in 1912 to study scientific management after hearing Taylor speak at a professional meeting. Gilbreth is probably best known for his experiments in reducing the number of motions in bricklaying. By carefully analyzing the bricklayer's job, he reduced the number of motions in laying of exterior brick from eighteen to five. On interior brick, the eighteen motions were reduced to two. Using Gilbreth's techniques, the bricklayer could be more productive and less fatigued at the end of the day.

The Gilbreths also created a microchronometer that recorded time to one-two-thousandths of a second. They placed it in a field of study being photographed and were therefore able to determine how long each hand motion took. Wasted motions missed by the naked eye could be identified and eliminated. The Gilbreths also devised a basic classification scheme to label seventeen different hand motions, including, among others, search, select, grasp, and hold, which they called "therbligs." This scheme allowed the Gilbreths a more precise way of analyzing the exact elements of any worker's hand movements.

It was Henri Fayol who first issued a complete statement on a theory of general management. In Fayol's primary work, he introduced fourteen principles of management:

- Division of work—specialization increases output by making employees more efficient.
- Formal positional authority—managers must be able to give orders. Authority gives them this right. Along with authority, however, goes responsibility.
- Discipline based on obedience and respect—employees must respect and obey the rules that govern the organization. Good discipline is the result of good leadership, a clear understanding between management and workers regarding the organization's rules, and the judicious use of penalties for infractions of the rules.
- Unity of command—every employee should receive orders from only one supervisor.
- Unity of direction—each group of organizational activities that have the same objective should be directed by one manager using one plan.
- Subordination of the individual interests to the general interests—the interest of any one employee or group of employees should not take precedence over the organization as a whole.
- Dependence of wages on many factors—workers must be paid a fair wage for their services.

- Centralization of authority—refers to the degree to which subordinates are involved in decision making; whether decision making is centralized (to management) or decentralized (to subordinates) is a question of proper proportion. The task is to find the optimum degree of centralization for each situation.
- Scalar chain (line) of authority—the line of authority from top management to the lowest ranks is the scalar chain. Communications should follow this chain. However, if following the chain creates delays, cross-communications can be allowed if agreed to by all parties and superiors are kept informed.
- An ordered and ensured place for everything—people and materials should be in the right place at the right time.
- Equity—managers should be kind and fair to their subordinates.
- Stability of tenured personnel—high employee turnover is inefficient. Management should provide orderly personnel planning and ensure that replacements are available to fill vacancies.
- Initiative—employees who are allowed to originate and carry out plans will exert high levels of effort.
- The building of harmony and unity within the organization—esprit de corps promoting team spirit will build harmony and unity within the organization.

Organizational Designs

During the early 20th century—a time of fairly rapid industrialization that encouraged public and private organizations to emphasize production and efficiency as criteria of effectiveness—mechanistic design evolved. Mechanistic design is informed by the hierarchically structured management philosophies of the time. Mechanistic organizational design promotes an effective organizational structure characterized by highly specialized jobs, homogeneous departments, narrow spans of control, and relatively centralized authority. Classical design theory presupposes a single best way to structure an organization to achieve these ends (Gibson, Ivancevich, Donnelly, & Konopaske, 2011).

Max Weber, in describing applications of the mechanistic model, coined the term *bureaucracy*. Because authority involves the legitimate right to exact obedience from others, organizational design involves domination. Weber's search for the forms of domination that evolve in society led him to the study of bureaucratic structure (Gibson et al., 2011, p. 497). Gibson and colleagues (2011) write, "According to Weber, the bureaucratic structure is superior to any other form in precision, stability, stringency of its discipline and its reliability. It thus makes possible a high degree of calculability of results for the heads of the organization and for those acting in relation to it. The bureaucracy compares to other forms of organizations as does the machine to other non-mechanical modes of production" (p. 498).

Weber's description of bureaucratic organizational design has the following characteristics:

- Division of labor—jobs are broken down into simple, routine, and well-defined tasks.
- Authority hierarchy—offices or positions are organized in a hierarchy, each lower one being controlled and supervised by a higher one.
- Formal selection—all organizational members are to be selected on the basis of technical qualifications demonstrated by training, education, or formal examination.
- Formal rules and regulations—to ensure uniformity and to regulate actions of employees, managers must depend heavily on formal organizational rules.
- Impersonality—rules and controls are applied uniformly, avoiding involvement with personalities and personal preferences of employees.
- Career orientation—managers are professional officials rather than owners of the units they manage. They work for fixed salaries and pursue their careers within the organization.

The nature of Weber's characteristics of an organizational bureaucracy is identical to Fayol's management theory principles. Both describe an organization that functions mechanically to accomplish the organization's goals in a highly efficient manner.

1920 to 1945

American Economic Circumstances

The Great Depression of 1929 saw unemployment in excess of 25 percent. Afterward, unions sought and gained major advantages for the working class. In this period, known as the golden age of unionism, legislatures and courts actively supported organized labor and the worker. Graff and Krout (1971) described this event:

> The collapse of the stock market was the initial stage of the long and bleak great depression. Unemployment which had been growing since the previous July, continued to increase at an alarming rate following the crash on Wall Street. Spending by consumers, which had been declining since July, continued to slacken. As businessmen stopped building new plants, the number of jobs available decreased. Income was not distributed well enough to keep people employed through an increase in spending by consumers. Farmers found prices lower than ever; millions of working people could neither buy factory goods nor find employment. Middle-class people everywhere could not meet the time payments on their cars, refrigerators or houses. The "prosperity decade" had ended with a sickening thud. (p. 631)

During these times of greater employee supply and lesser demand, employers easily solicited efforts from employees. As was the case when quality and price frequently gave way to availability in production decisions during the industrialization period, so too did employers sacrifice the human aspects of the employer-employee relationship during the lean years of the Great Depression.

Recognizing this problem, emphasis during this time shifted to attempts at understanding the needs of workers.

World War II (1939–1945)

World War II is the name commonly given to the global conflict of 1939–1945. It was the greatest and most destructive war in history. Whereas military operations in World War I were conducted primarily on the European continent, World War II included gigantic struggles not only in Europe, but in Asia, Africa, and the far-reaching islands of the Pacific as well. More than 17 million members of the armed forces and the belligerents perished during the conflict. Its conduct strained the economic capabilities of the major nations and left many countries on the edge of collapse.

World War II spread death and devastation throughout most of the world to an extent never before experienced. The loss of life can only be generally summarized; an attempt to express the value of property and livelihoods destroyed in terms of money is futile. The resulting sums reach astronomical figures that have little if any practical meaning. The U.S. armed forces total numbers in World War II were estimated at: 292,131 battle deaths, 115,187 deaths from other causes, 671,801 wounded, and 139,709 captured or missing. In terms of civilian casualties, 146,777 were killed or seriously injured from bombs or artillery fire.

The U.S. budget expenditures from 1940 to 1945 were $336.7 billion (*Encyclopedia Americana*, 1996, vol. 29, p. 530).

Management Philosophies

The human relations movement arose in the early 1930s, and no activity better exemplifies this philosophy than the famous Hawthorne studies (1924–1932) conducted by Harvard University psychologist Elton

Mayo. The Hawthorne studies led to an increased interest in the human problems in the workplace and a refocusing on the human factor of production.

Without question, the most important contribution to the developing field of understanding human behavior in the workplace came out of the Hawthorne studies conducted at the Western Electric Company Works in Cicero, Illinois. The studies started in 1924 but expanded and carried on through the early 1930s. The studies were initially created by Western Electric industrial engineers as a scientific management experiment. They wanted to examine the effect of various illumination levels on worker productivity. Control and experimental groups were established, in accordance with scientific practices. The experimental group was exposed to various lighting intensities, while the control group worked under a constant lighting intensity. Engineers had expected individual output to be directly related to the varying intensities of the light. They found, however, that as the intensity of the light increased for the experimental group, the level of output for both groups increased. To the surprise of the engineers, as the light level was decreased in the experimental group, productivity continued to increase in both groups. In fact, productivity decrease in the experimental group was observed only when the light was decreased to that of a moonlit night. The engineers concluded that illumination intensity was not directly related to productivity, but they could not explain the results they had observed.

In 1927, the Western Electric engineers asked Harvard professor Elton Mayo and his associates to join the study as consultants. This began a relationship that would last through 1932 and encompass numerous experiments in the redesign of jobs, changes in workday and workweek length, introduction of rest periods, and individual versus group wage plans.

The Hawthorn studies did receive criticism. Attacks were made on procedures, analyses of findings, and the conclusions (Robbins, 1999, p. 49). From a historical standpoint, however, it's of little importance whether the studies were scientifically sound or their conclusions justified. What is important is that they stimulated an interest in human behavior in organizations. The Hawthorne studies played a dominant role at the time of changing the perspective that humans were no different from machines, whose sole purpose was to help the organization meet its production goals.

Again, as was the case with the efforts of Frederick Taylor, many followed in Mayo's humanistic footsteps to better understand, describe, and document the intangible human relations of the time. One such person was Mary Parker Follett, who from 1920 to 1933 espoused a basic theory that the fundamental challenge for any organization was to build and maintain dynamic, yet harmonious, human relations within the organization. In 1938, Chester Barnard, another follower of Mayo, effectively integrated traditional management and the behavioral sciences. Barnard viewed the organization as a social structure and stressed the psychosocial aspects of organizations.

This whole period, coupled with the many studies and examinations into human performance in the workplace, spurred the efforts of great thinkers to attempt to capture what motivates humans to perform more efficiently and effectively in the workplace.

A discussion of applicable motivational theories may be found in a previous chapter.

Organizational Designs

During the human-relations era, an alternative to mechanistic design theory developed and was sustained by the growing interest of behavioral scientists in the study of management and organization. This alternative theory, termed "organic design," proposed that the more effective organization has relatively unspecialized jobs, heterogeneous departments, wide spans of control, and decentralized authority. Such organizational structures, Gibson and colleagues argue, achieve not only high levels of production and efficiency, but also satisfaction, adaptiveness, and development (2011, p. 526).

The two organizational models, mechanistic and organic, are probably best characterized by their orientations to organizational complexity and their degrees of centralization and formalization. The mechanistic organizational design tends toward highly complex organizations because of its emphasis on the specialization of labor. It is centralized because of its emphasis on authority and accountability, and it is formal because of its emphasis on function as the basis for departments. In contrast, the organic organizational design is relatively simple because of its de-emphasis on specialization and its emphasis on increasing job range. It is relatively decentralized because of its emphasis on delegation, authority, and increasing job depth, and it is relatively informal because of its emphasis on product and customer as its basis for departments. The mechanistic and organic organizational models prevailed until the late 1960s.

1945 to 1960

American Economic Circumstances

What do foreign trade zones, free ports, in-bond arrangements, and economic trade zones have in common? What do the European Community, the European Free Trade Association, the Andean Common Market, and the Afro-Malagasy Economic Union have in common? Each of these phenomena represents an attempt to organize individual countries to take positive steps to reduce trade and tariff barriers among the participating countries.

As Norman M. Scarborough points out:

> Agriculture, manufacturing and services account for the majority of jobs in our economy. [As pointed out above], early in American history the United States relied primarily on an agricultural economy. Then, at the turn of the twentieth century, our economic base moved towards manufacturing. Heavy industry, steel, automobiles, railroads and others became the foundation for our growing nation. But beginning around 1970 the U.S. economy had begun another shift, away from manufacturing and towards services. The U.S. Department of Labor predicts that, of the new jobs created by 1995, 90% will be in the service industry. Roughly seventy-seven million people are service industry related workers. Examples of service providers are banks, consulting firms, hotel chains, restaurants and airlines. One challenge for firms in declining industries is to find growth opportunities in the service industries. The shift towards services means that fewer manufacturing jobs are being created. While the number of service jobs are growing rapidly, they tend to be lower paying positions. Having difficulty competing on a global basis, many American firms are becoming "hollow corporations"—farming out the actual manufacturing of their goods to low-cost foreign producers. In addition to losing manufacturing jobs, this trend poses a danger to creating even higher standards of living. Improving productivity, the ratio of output of goods and services to the inputs . . . required to produce them, is essential to reaching higher living standards. The problem is that significant productivity gains are harder to achieve in a service economy. (1992, p. 27)

N. Jonas (1986) states that "the idea that a post-industrial America can become increasingly prosperous as a service-based economy appears to be a dangerous myth" (p. 42). This position of an increasingly lower standard of living, from what we know today, as we shift from an industrial economy to a service-based economy is readily supported by many noted authors. C. Jackson Grayson, Jr., and Carla O'Dell, in their book *American Business: A Two-Minute Warning* (1988), make a series of alarming revelations: "(1) U.S. competitiveness is seriously eroding, (2) the international competitive challenges are far greater than most realize, (3) the U.S. response to-date is inadequate to meet the challenges, and (4) not only can the United States lose its world economic leadership, but at the moment it is losing" (p. 4). Nathan Rosenberg and L. E. Birdzell (1986) also address the wealth of a nation being primarily derived by the value-added to its output products, something generally accepted as being only possible in an industrial society.

It should be noted, however, that not everyone agrees that the United States is tending toward a lower standard of living as a result of our reductions in industrialization. John Naisbitt and Patricia Aburdene propose that the United States is not in a decline, and that while it is true we are moving away from an industrial economy, we are moving toward an information economy, not a service economy. Naisbitt and Aburdene suggest that the myth of United States' decline and the attendant low-wage thesis were promoted by pro-labor attempts to unionize industrial workers in 1986 (1991, p. 26). The authors go on to suggest that while the middle class is indeed diminishing, it is moving upward, not downward, as many suggest. Further, the poor are not getting poorer; in fact, there are fewer poor today than in 1959.

Whether or not the United States will suffer an increasingly lower standard of living, or whether the United States is capable of capitalizing on Naisbitt and Aburdene's proposed information society, is an interesting topic that is, however, not within the scope of this account. Our point is that never before have American businesses been so deeply involved in, and affected by, international trade. Philip Cateora (1990) states that "four long term trends are affecting U.S. businesses, small or large, domestic or international. The first trend is the internationalization of U.S. markets; second, interdependence of world economies; third, the emergence of international competitors all over the world; and fourth, the globalization of world markets" (p. 2).

Korean War (1950–1953)

The Korean War was an armed conflict that began on June 25, 1950, when the forces of the Democratic People's Republic of Korea (North Korea) invaded the Republic of Korea (South Korea). Two days later, on June 27, the United States introduced a resolution in the Security Council of the United Nations, urging UN members to contribute such assistance that might be needed to repel the aggressors of Korea. Because the Soviet Union was boycotting the world organization, and hence its delegate was not present to exercise the Soviet Union's right to veto resolutions in the Security Council, the resolution passed. Later that day President Harry Truman announced that he had ordered American air and naval forces to provide combat support to the South Koreans. Three days after that, as the rout of the South Korea army continued, he committed American ground forces to the Korean battle zone.

The Korean conflict had exacted a heavy toll. The Koreans and the Chinese had absorbed the most substantial losses. It was estimated that 520,000 North Koreans, 900,000 Chinese, and 1,300,000 South Koreans had been killed or wounded in combat or died of injuries and diseases related to the war. About 1 million South Koreans who died or suffered wounds were South Korean civilians. American dead in the war totaled 54,246 (*Encyclopedia Americana*, 1996, vol. 16, p. 553).

Management Philosophies

In this changing context, organizational design and management philosophies are attempting to combat these newly perceived international opportunities or threats. The predominant management philosophies of this period are the systems, contingency, and total quality management (TQM) approaches.

The systems approach (late 1960s to early 1970s) to management analyzes how the different elements of a corporation function and operate. This model is based on a simple concept: inputs get processed, which in turn results in outputs. The inputs are from the environment: human, physical, financial, and informational resources. The organization's technology processes these inputs, resulting in products/services, behaviors, and profits/losses. The systems approach provides five useful contributions (Van Fleet & Peterson, 1994):

- Interaction with the environment is a concept based on the open systems concept.
- Subsystem interdependency is the realization that systems exist within larger (or outer) systems. A change in the inner system most likely will result in a change to the outer system.
- Synergy suggests that two people or units can achieve more working together than separately.
- Entropy, the steady degradation of a system, happens when organizations take a closed system perspective in today's tougher economic times.
- Equifinality is the idea that two or more paths may lead to the same place.

James Higgins (1994) describes the early evolution of the contingency approach: "Fayol and other early theorists searched for general principles of management that might be applied to all situations. However, while many of these principles worked in most situations, none could be applied to all situations. In the 1970s, it became evident that a manager's actions should be contingent on the various key elements of a given situation. This led to the development of the contingency approach" (p. 62).

The contingency theory of management is closely tied to the numerous works on leadership styles. Fred E. Fiedler, an early leadership theorist, in 1967 was the first to undertake major research on the contingency approach to management. Until this time, leadership styles had been characterized as either production oriented or people oriented. Fiedler found that managers and leaders should exhibit varying degrees of concern for both production and people, depending on three things: the quality of the leader-member relations, the degree to which a task is defined, and the degree of the managers'/leaders' power.

The contingency approach to management argues that the appropriate managerial actions in a situation depend on, or are contingent on, certain major elements of that situation. Proponents believe that there is no one best way to manage; the best way depends on the specific circumstances. Leslie Rue and Lloyd Byars (1989) state that "contingency theorists have often gone much further than simply to say 'it all depends.' Many contingency theorists outline in detail the style or approach that works best under certain conditions and circumstances" (p. 50).

Contingency theory in its purest form would attempt to define all factors in a given situation and prescribe appropriate behaviors. As one might guess, however, there are numerous potential factors in any given situation. Thus the contingency theory of management has evolved into yet another management philosophy, situational management. Situational management involves reviewing the key factors in a situation before determining what action to take.

TQM encompasses the entire spectrum of quality initiatives used in business today. TQM origins actually date back to statistical quality control in the United States in the 1920s and 1930s. Its real emphasis came only after the Japanese implemented its concepts after World War II under the leadership of a statistician at the Massachusetts Institute of Technology named W. Edwards Deming.

TQM relies on a strategic commitment to quality and on employee involvement, materials, methods (processes), and technology to achieve improvements in quality. The starting point for any real TQM effort is a strategic commitment by top management to quality improvements in all aspects of the corporation. A superficial attempt to promote a quality initiative usually leads to unsatisfactory results and can cause more damage to the firm's reputation than if the firm had not initiated the attempt at all.

Employee involvement is also a key characteristic of TQM. Numerous concepts flow from this aspect, including, but not limited to, employee participation, employee empowerment, operational work teams, department quality teams, and quality circles. Regardless of which concepts or terms are employed, the general underlying principles are to give the employees more information regarding the applicable operations and to support their autonomy in making informed decisions.

Materials are also a part of TQM initiatives, and efforts are made to secure a limited number of highly dependable suppliers of critical components. These suppliers are required to support the daily operations of the firm with materials of superior quality. Quality can also be enhanced through the use of more efficient and effective methods of operation. The concept associated with this effort is to identify the steps in a given process and then reduce or eliminate any unnecessary steps or combine steps. In addition to improvements in material and processes, there are also improvements to be gained from advances in technology. Buying new equipment and investing in automation can provide a higher degree of standardization with fewer defective units.

Organizational Designs
Organizational design during this period evolved through various levels of organic design. Characteristics of organizations in this period are outlined by Rensis Likert (1967, pp. 197–211).

- Leadership process includes perceived confidence and trust between superiors and subordinates. Subordinates feel free to discuss job problems with their superiors, who in turn solicit their ideas and opinions.
- Motivational process taps a full range of motives through participatory practices. Attitudes are favorable toward the organization and its goals.
- Information flows freely throughout the organization—upward, downward, and laterally. The information is accurate and undistorted.
- Interaction process is open and extensive; both superiors and subordinates are able to affect organizational goals, processes, and activities.
- Decision process occurs at all levels through group processing and is basically decentralized.
- Goal-setting process encourages group involvement in setting high, yet realistic, goals.
- Control process is dispersed throughout the organization and emphasizes self-control and problem solving.
- Performance goals are high and are actively sought by superiors, who recognize the necessity of making a full commitment to developing and training the human resources of the organization.

Contingency organizational design theories simply ask questions as to which of the two primary organizational designs, mechanistic or organic, are suited to a given situation. To answer these questions corporate officials must specify the factors in a situation influencing the relative effectiveness of a particular design (Gibson et al., 2011, p. 503).

Matrix organizational designs overlay product or project departments on existing functional organizations or departments. Matrix organization designs attempt to minimize the weaknesses of both the mechanistic and organic designs. Matrix structures are found in organizations that require responses to rapid change in two or more environments, such as technology or markets; face uncertainties that generate high information-processing requirements; and must deal with financial and human resource constraints (Gibson et al., 2011, pp. 518–19).

There are many advantages to the matrix organization: efficient use of resources, flexibility in conditions of change and uncertainty, technical expertise, freeing top management for long-range planning, improving motivation and commitment, and providing opportunities for personal development (Gibson et al., 2011, p. 520). The differing forms of increasingly greater matrix organizational design include task forces, product teams, product managers, and product management departments.

Gibson and colleagues state, "Organizational design remains an important issue in the management of organizational behavior and effectiveness. . . . Organizational design will become even more important . . . strategies that have been effective in the past will prove ineffective in the face of new international competition, technological change, and shifting patterns of industrial development. As organizations experiment with new management theories they will be forced to experiment with new organizational design" (2011, p. 525).

Process management, as a management philosophy, has evolved most notably in this era of internationalization. Process management crosses over both management philosophy and organizational design concepts, as discussed below.

Process management is discussed in greater detail in a previous chapter.

1960 to 1980

American Economic Circumstances

Richard Oliver, in his 2000 book *The Coming Biotech Age,* probably best describes the information economy that prevailed most noticeably during this and the following period in American economic history. He presents the following from the perspective of the next economic era, the bio age.

During the last three decades of the 20th century (although this text shows the information age actually stretching back as far as 1900), it was commonplace to refer to our economy as the information age, and to a whole set of companies in computer, telecommunications, digital electronics, software industries, and the like as "hi-tech." As the value and availability of information grew, it became rather fashionable for commentators to extol the glorious future of these technologies and argue that we are "at the dawn of a new era of information."

They were right for this period. But, in the new millennium, it is becoming more evident daily that we are at the end, not the beginning, of the information age. Information is important, and it always will be. However, in the coming era, information will be like electricity—cheap and ubiquitous. In this new era, information will be a valuable tool, but only a tool, and one that has receded into the background. Again, like electricity, it will be conspicuous only by its rare absence.

There are three overarching technologies at the heart of today's rapidly maturing information economy. The first is digitalization, or the converting of content, whether voice, data, video, or image, into a common digital form that can be sent individually or collectively over a common set of transmission media. The second is software, to manipulate, control, and direct the flow of this information. The third is a microprocessor or computer chip, the core driver and storage device for the other two. Essentially, these three technologies rapidly drove down the cost of information, while simultaneously driving up its functionality and ease of use at an equally accelerating pace. Each of these technologies is maturing rapidly. We have the Internet, for example, because each of these technologies is maturing, not new.

The basic product life cycle goes through fixed periods generally referred to as introduction, growth, maturity, and decline. To say that a product has a life cycle is to assert four things:

- Products have a limited life.
- Product sales pass through distinct stages, each posing different challenges, opportunities, and problems to the seller.
- Profits rise and fall at different stages of the product life cycle.
- Products require different marketing, financial, manufacturing, purchasing, and human resource strategies in each stage of their cycle.

Most discussions of product life cycle portray the sales history of a typical product as following a bell-shaped curve. This curve is typically divided into four stages: introduction, growth, maturity, and decline.

- Introduction—a period of slow sales growth as the product is introduced into the market. Profits are nonexistent at this stage because of the heavy expenses incurred with product introduction.
- Growth—a period of rapid market acceptance and substantial profit improvement.
- Maturity—a period of a slowdown in sales growth because the product has achieved acceptance by most potential buyers. Profits stabilize or decline because of increased marketing outlays to defend the product against competition.
- Decline—the period where sales show a downward drift and profits erode.

It is often difficult to identify where each stage begins or ends. Usually the stages are marked where the rates of sales growth or decline become pronounced.

Given that the above product life cycle is applicable to technology, then at the end of the technology or product life cycle, the reverse is true. The product is inexpensive and widely available from many suppliers, and advertising messages are about its many uses. Competition among suppliers is on the basis of brand image, typically describing the differences or new varied uses for the same product.

Despite being only about fifty strong years old, it is obvious that the core product of the information age, the computer chip, is aging. Everywhere around us the signs of a maturing computer/information economy are flagrantly obvious. In 1999, the number of chips made for devices other than computers (cell phones, appliances, etc.) exceeded those going into computers. Even, now, as computer sales seem to have slumped, every part of life, economic and noneconomic, is alive with an abundance of computer power.

The cost of information has also declined rapidly, and is so widely available, that many have been heard to complain that they are drowning in information. Classes, seminars, and books can help individuals to better deal with the significant information influx. Computers, once scarce and very expensive, are now found in nearly every office and distributed widely across manufacturing floors, controlling functions such as reordering to process flow. The next-generation computer is expected to drop well below $800 while the software continues to perform increasingly greater functionality. In fact, even as much as I use my Microsoft Suite of software, I realize that I only really utilize a small fraction of its total capabilities. The capabilities of each software product so much overlap that they are beginning to blur in distinction to each other.

Rather than being hard to find, the microprocessor, and indeed the computer, has become ubiquitous, that is, available from nearly every vendor. And many information services have become nearly free, in that for a nominal fee (about $20 per month) one can gain unlimited access to the wealth of information available through the Internet. Along these same lines, long-distance telephone connections are now available for about ten cents a minute anywhere in the country. It will probably not be long before a call to anywhere in the world will be considered a local call; after all, I can already communicate anywhere in the world for free through the Internet. We will continue to make basic advances in microchip design, making them smaller, lighter in weight, and more powerful in capability and capacity, but all in all, this is simply advancing the basic frontier that has already been discovered. As new science goes, we are building an existing body of knowledge. We have moved from the unknown unknowns, where it was inconceivable to us that such things even existed, through the known unknowns, where we knew about it, but didn't know much about it, to our current state of known knowns, where we not only know about it, but know nearly every aspect of it and how to make it better.

By virtually every definition, then, information technologies and the companies that spawned them are rapidly maturing. Information technologies will continue to be important to the maturing of our society, similar to cars, steel, oil, and electricity. But on the basis of availability, cost, use, further development, and potential, these technologies and their permutations are not going to be considered what we use to refer to as "hi-tech." Although still very exciting and their applications increasing, with their importance to our lives unquestioned, information technology is being upstaged by the next economic era, coined bioeconomics.

Vietnam War (1964–1974)

The Vietnam War, also called the Indochina War or Second Indochina War, may be said to have started in 1957, when Communist-led rebels began mounting terrorist attacks against the government of the Republic of Vietnam (South Vietnam). The rebel forces, commonly called Vietcong, were later aided by troops of the Democratic Republic of Vietnam (North Vietnam). American combat personnel were formally committed to the defense of the south in 1965.

An agreement calling for the cease-fire was signed in January 1973, and by March, the few remaining military personnel were withdrawn. However, the war between the two sides persisted inconclusively for two additional years before South Vietnamese resistance suddenly and unexpectedly collapsed. Saigon, the capital of South Vietnam, fell to the Communists on April 30, 1975.

By the time of their completed withdrawal in 1973, U.S. forces had participated in the Vietnam conflict longer than any other war. A total of 57,605 Americans had lost their lives in combat, compared with 33,629 in the Korean War. An additional 303,700 U.S. military personnel were wounded in battle. The U.S. spent an officially acknowledged $165 billion on the Vietnam War. Only in World War II were U.S. direct military expenditures higher (*Encyclopedia Americana*, 1996, vol. 28, p. 112).

Management Philosophies and Organizational Designs

The contingency managerial approach as well as the systems managerial approach continued to prevail and evolve through this period.

The contingency organizational model and the matrix model also continued to evolve through this period from the last. In looking at matrix models, however, we can examine permutations of the pure matrix model.

A detailed discussion of organizational design models may be found in a previous chapter.

1980 to Present

American Economic Circumstances

While it is quite clear that information technologies increasingly became the major economic engine of the past five decades, a whole new set of technologies, biology, and advanced materials is poised to become the new engine expanding and driving our economy.

Regardless of terminology, it is becoming increasingly obvious that the next few decades are going to be tremendously exciting as we continue to explore the known unknowns. There isn't a week that goes by that some magazine or text isn't documenting our increasingly greater knowledge in this amazing new world of science that forms this period in time and our current economic circumstance.

The article "Of Transgenic Mice and Men" from the May 25, 1999 issue of *USA Today* states:

In 1980 genetics in general and mouse genetics in particular took a leap forward when researchers at Yale transplanted foreign genes into mice. Jon Gordon, Mount Sinai School of Medicine, injected genetic material from two viruses into freshly fertilized mouse embryos fixed under a microscope. The genes he inserted originally took root only in a small percentage of mice. But, scientist have perfected the process with new tricks, chiefly including "promoters" to tell the new genes to turn on. (p. 11D)

An article titled "Biotech (Innovators in the Biotechnology Industry)" from the November 1, 1999 issue of *Technology Review* includes:

Talk to the young innovators named to the [Technology Review] 100 for their contributions to biotechnology and biomedicine, and you may begin to wonder whether Lewis Carroll has been tinkering with their world. Surely, only the creators of Alice could have dreamed up the strange new cast of characters that is turning out for biotech's tea party these days. Being a mathematician, Carroll might well have spiked the guest list with others of his ilk, and also numerically minded computer scientists, engineers, physicists and businesspeople, who of course keep their eyes on the numbers as well. That's exactly what's going on in biology today, and the winners in this category reflect the field's increasingly eclectic makeup: Indeed, only half of them have degrees in biology or medicine at all. (p. 92)

Many of *Technology Review*'s 100 bio-innovators stressed their belief that the growing fluidity between fields will be critical to biotechnology's success. The problems in biotech are too large for any one individual, laboratory, or even discipline to tackle. What's more, they believe the future will bring an even tighter connection between industry and academia, in large part because industry has the resources to make ideas reality. The increasingly intimate contact between industry and academia opens opportunities for researchers.

The Fort Wayne, Indiana, *News Sentinel,* in an article titled "Cloned Cows Show No Signs of Premature Aging," wrote:

They look like regular cows, but they harbor a secret: put their cells under a microscope and they look astounding young. Massachusetts scientists have cloned six cows that are causing a stir because their cells show none of the worrisome premature aging that researchers previously found in Dolly the cloned sheep. The finding could ease fears that cloned cells age too fast to be useful against diseases (p. 10).

In fact, the cloned cows have cells that appear as young as those of newborn calves. Unlike Dolly, the cows were cloned from cells nearing the end of their life span. If even old cells can have their aging clock rewound, then scientists might be able one day to clone customized replacement tissues for patients suffering from diabetes, Parkinson's, or other diseases. In an article titled "Economy," the author writes, "Get ready for the bioeconomy which will supplant our infoeconomy. Bioeconomy will give new meaning to the smell of money" (*Time*, 2000, p. 21).

Best known are the dozens of bioengineered drugs already on the market. Most of these save lives by treating existing problems. One of the biggest shifts in biotech in the decades to come will be the way it transforms the health care paradigm from treatment to prediction and prevention. Health care today is really sick care. The sick-care business model made money by filling hospital beds. Currently, we're in the managed care model. It is transitional, lasting one or two decades. Here, you make money by emptying beds. In the bioeconomy, health care will work on a preventive model, making money by helping people to avoid having to enter a hospital in the first place.

Problems will spread as much as benefits do. Each era produces its own dark side. The industrial era was accompanied by pollution and environmental deregulation. The major problem of the information age is privacy. In the bioeconomy, the issues will be ethical ones. Cloning, bioengineered foods, eugenics, genetic patenting, and certainly inherited diseases are just a few of the many developments already creating a storm.

All of this will make Baby Boomers a unique generation. They will be the first to span three unique economies. Born at the end of the industrial period, they will spend their entire careers in the information age and will end their days watching their grandchildren negotiate the bioeconomy.

Generation Xers will be different. During their working years, they will experience two major economic shifts: first, from the crunching to the connecting halves of this information economy, and second, from a microwave-based connected universe to a cell-based world of biologic and bionomics. Those in Generation Y (Nexters) may have to go through three.

In a *Popular Mechanics* article by Jim Wilson from October 2000, titled "Science's Greatest Unsolved Mysteries," the author writes:

Cancer cells share a similar characteristic. They are immortal. As long as they are fed, they will continue to divide. Not so for healthy cells, where a kind of timer built into the end of chromosomes limits the number of times a cell can replicate itself. These timers are called telomeres. Think of them as the plastic caps on each end of your shoelaces that prevent the cord from unraveling. Each time a cell reproduces, a tiny bit of the telomere is knocked off. When it is gone, the cell stops dividing. With 46 chromosomes, humans have 92 of these life-span clocks. (p. 55)

An article by Rick Weiss, titled "Science Nears Revival of Dead Species" from the *Washington Post*, in October 2000, reads:

Bessie, an ordinary cow on an Iowa farm, is pregnant. But she's not having a cow. Developing inside her uterus is an endangered species called an Asian gaur, a heavily muscled, hump-backed, ox-like animal native to the bamboo jungles of India and Burma.

Bessie's gaur, named Noah and due to be born next month, was cloned from a single skin cell taken from a dead gaur. It is the first endangered species ever to be cloned, and the first cloned animal to gestate in the womb of another species (p. 10).

Already the Massachusetts scientists who created Noah are laying plans to clone endangered giant pandas, including perhaps the National Zoo's Ling-Ling and Hsing-Hsing, who died in 1992 and 1999, and whose cells sit frozen in liquid nitrogen in Frederick, Maryland.

The more radical prospect of bringing back extinct animals raises even more profound environmental and ethical questions. Would it be right, for instance, to bring back a species whose native habitat is gone or so fractured that the creature could survive only in the zoo?

"Cash Cow," an October 7, 2000 article by Emma Young in *NewScientist*, reads:

A clone of Mandy, a prize dairy cow, raised $82,000 at an auction on Friday at the World Dairy Expo in Madison, Wisconsin. It was the first time a clone had been offered for commercial sale, says biotechnology company Infigen.

Infigen is so confident in its techniques that the clone has not yet been created. But the promised exact genetic copy fetched nearly seven times the price of Mandy's normal calves. . . .

"At this state in development of the technology, this is probably a publicity issue rather than the start of a genuine commercial service," says Harry Griffin of the Roslin Institute near Edinburgh, where the Dolly the sheep was cloned. . . .

Mandy will be cloned in December. . . . The heifer will be due nine months later.

The term *biotechnology* is generally used to describe a wide range of technologies and businesses whose aim it is to understand, alter, or direct the function of a wide set of organic cells, including plant, animal, and human.

Biomaterials is in wide use in the health care field to describe those technologies related primarily to human tissues.

Bioterials is used to describe the combination of two fields, biology and new materials (Oliver, 2000, p. 14).

Whether it be *Time Magazine, BusinessWeek, New Scientist,* the *Washington Post, Popular Mechanics,* or even your hometown newspaper, it is becoming increasingly obvious that we are moving into a new and very different era, an era we have yet to even begin to scratch the surface, one that brings, based on previous periods of economic adjustment, significant opportunity and potential.

Management Philosophies and Organizational Designs

Following from the previous period in time, the contingency and systems managerial approach continue to prevail. As well, the contingency organizational design model and the matrix and matrix permutations described earlier continue to date through this period.

Chapter 21

Career Development—Models

I cannot recall how many times in my life I felt as though I was sitting somewhat stagnant, wasting my time, not knowing what was next or which way to go. I knew I had talent, credentials, and many ideas, but I just wasn't sure which direction was right for me at that time in my life. I just couldn't decide. To add to the confusion is the instance that you have no idea even what is available, or in other words, the thought that there has to be more, but you're not sure what it is, let alone how to get there.

Sometimes if a job we want doesn't materialize, and we continue meandering to no avail, we might begin to feel a sense of insecurity. We start to question our own self-worth, wondering if we really have what is required to find that next higher position or ideal job. Feelings of low self-worth, even in the most optimistic among us, can lead to depression, being tired, not caring much about anything, and the spiral continues downward. It's a scenario down an emotional rat hole that nobody wants to chase.

I've spent many of my nearly thirty years in industry counseling others, in one capacity or another, on how to move to that higher-level job or how to position themselves for that next, more exciting assignment. The conversations have always been centered around the idea of moving from where they know they are now (point "A") to some other assignment or position (point "B"). In fact, I've led or participated in the design and implementation of at least seven institutionalized career development processes. And, in all cases, the processes were essentially the same. The only significant difference was whether the career development process originated with the employee or the company. In today's social contract, career development almost always originates with the employee, as organizations have steered away from the older materialistic and paternalistic models and the career development models that came with them.

On occasion, the conversations would step back from the gap analysis of determining how to move from point "A" to point "B," and center around the predecessor question of, "What's available for me (the employee) to do." This is a slightly more interesting question and one that requires an understanding of what parallel or peer opportunities might exist within the same discipline or within another discipline. For example, if I'm performing a task in software engineering, what parallel tasks are there in systems engineering or even program management? These types of questions are interesting in that our knowledge of a discipline is very specific and to move to another discipline means we can readily cross over and have sufficient knowledge to be immediately productive in the destination discipline. Now, here's the rub. Let's say I am sufficiently knowledgeable in software engineering and have gained some level of success such that my salary and my grade are reasonably high. Then, I want to transfer to another discipline where I do not have sufficient senior-level knowledge and can therefore only function at a lesser level. The problem is the destination function can hire someone of possibly considerably lesser salary and grade to perform, perhaps even better than I can. In fact, the destination discipline may even be able to hire someone right out of college to perform that destination function for a fraction of my current compensation. This therefore, is the problem with cross-discipline movement.

Continuing our climb up the cognitive scale resides an even more fascinating question, "What am I (the employee) really best suited to do?" To answer this, as professionals, we usually begin the process by looking at the employee's knowledge, skills, and abilities. But this approach is somewhat superficial. It proceeds on the premise the employee's knowledge, skills, and abilities are aligned with the employee's true fundamental personality preferences. For example, I might be in a profession that requires me to communicate in front of large groups, when, in fact, I may not like that type of activity and really do exhibit a rather introverted or reserved type of personality. Or, another example, I might be in finance doing detailed number crunching when in fact I may be a bigger picture type of individual and find working with details boring, and perhaps even worse, I may exhibit a short attention span when involved in detailed-oriented tasks, therefore, forgetting or appearing to be somewhat sloppy and lacking precision. Thus, it is not safe to assume that since I've been working in a discipline performing a set of tasks that this is a natural derivation of my personality. I may simply be in the wrong discipline, or in the least, performing the wrong tasks.

The problem we perpetuate when counseling someone on career choices is that we frequently begin our process with a gap analysis of how to get from point "A" to point "B." And, if we do look at the problem from a bigger perspective, maybe we look at other roles or responsibilities in the same or a different discipline and make an assessment on which role the individual could move into. Seldom, however, do we actually try to assess the true personality preferences of the individual, to determine which type of function or task the individual might best be able to contribute.

The actual counseling process, then, is inverted. Instead of first asking what type of personality preferences an individual possesses, then mapping those preferences to some form of task or responsibility within a function, we, in fact, frequently begin at the other end by trying to suggest how the employee should move from point "A" to point "B," without knowing if he or she should be in the job at point "A" to begin with, let alone in the job at point "B." Figure 21.1 depicts this inverted relationship.

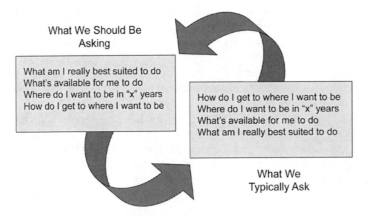

What We Should Be
Asking

What am I really best suited to do
What's available for me to do
Where do I want to be in "x" years
How do I get to where I want to be

How do I get to where I want to be
Where do I want to be in "x" years
What's available for me to do
What am I really best suited to do

What We
Typically Ask

Figure 21.1. The Four Levels of Decision

I happen to be a prolific reader. In my earlier years I enjoyed reading technical books, which seemed to coincide with my professional interests. As I chronologically aged, I began to show an interest in psychology, an understanding of motivation and why we do what we do. Always having been a planner, I wanted to know what was going to happen to me as time passed. By that, what changes would I experience from a cognitive, psychological, and biological perspective? I wanted to be ready for what was to come. I've never really liked surprises, and in fact, I've preached for years to my sons to plan for the worst and hope for the best and you will never be too disappointed. The direction of my interest, coupled with my insatiable need to be prepared, led me to the study of gerontology and ultimately to the concept of cohort groups. Gerontology (the study of the aging process) seemed to go hand in hand with the four basic groups discussed in nearly all recent literature: Veterans, Boomers, Generation Xers, and Generation Y/Nexters. It is most interesting when you overlap the cohort groups onto the phases of human life. There is a very natural mapping that seems to complement each concept.

It has been the study of the four basic cohort groups, coupled with the case for action, that really helped me to recognize the need for this topic. Recent literature discusses what has been termed an expectancy-reality gap. This gap is probably best described by Charlotte Shelton and Laura Shelton in *The NeXt Revolution*. The authors write that there is a reason why Generation Xers are feeling unhappy and dissatisfied about work. They continue, "Due to the success of Boomer women, Xers grew up with a very different set of expectations. We set our career goals high, based on achievements of our mothers, Oprah, Diane Sawyer and others . . . our parents', teachers', and career counselors' great expectations for my generation have, unfortunately, created a sense of entitlement" (2005, p. 25).

The basic logic behind Shelton and Shelton's statement is that Boomer mothers were the first generation of mothers to be primarily in the workforce. When they entered the workforce, they really didn't necessarily have any preconceived notions of what to expect in terms of advancement. What they found was a labor force that behaved like a sponge, soaking up however many of these individuals our society could provide. And the rewards came quickly. There were promotions and salary increases at an unequivocal pace. As these Boomer mothers gained in education and knowledge, they continued to receive promotions seemingly without end. The Boomer mothers, then, told their daughters and sons that they could have it all. All their children had to do was get a college education, and like themselves, they would receive these many riches associated with promotions and salary. The Boomer mothers weren't the only ones saying this; high school and college counselors were also saying it. This generation, Generation X, therefore, grew up thinking all this was theirs on graduation. What they found, however, was something quite different. They found the hours required to get ahead to be hard and long. They found jobs they really didn't like doing. They found promotions and salary increases frequently came with paying their dues in tenure. On the whole, they became somewhat disenchanted with the promised working life. Couple this, then, with their being told they would have thirteen to fifteen careers in their lifetime, versus two to three when I graduated from college, and it's easy to see how this generational cohort believed the next great job was just around the corner. The obtain-job quit-job cycle just continued.

In fact, although this chapter is not about the numerous dimensions of generational similarities and differences, there are many authors who describe our newest generation, Generation Y/Nexters, as being somewhat different minded than previous generations. Huntley (2006) describes Generation Y:

in the face of all this; an insecure job market, the diminished value of a university degree, [college] debt and ridiculous housing prices—how have Yers reacted? They have realistic adjustments to the world's instability by taking unstable employment as a given and adopting a self-reliant, survival-of-the-fittest attitude to career success. Most are repelled by the idea of a "job for life", the kind of employment stability understood by their parents and grandparents . . . so Yers have reworked employment insecurity into vocational freedom and the opportunity to travel, experience new workplaces, expand skills and stave off boredom. Above all else, they value flexibility and diversity in their working lives . . . The bulk of Gen Y will constitute a volatile sector of the workforce, switching career paths, companies, taking off traveling, downshifting and moving home to take on further study. A job for life isn't an option. And even if it was, they aren't investing enough in work to want that. . . . They want an interesting job that can fund a balanced life, one that involves a harmony of work, relationships, friends, fun travel and life experience. (pp. 96–102)

Huntley goes on to talk more specifically about Generation Y's lack of direction by saying,

talking about the future is a challenging task for people of any age. But, when it comes to Generation Y, and the question of where its members are going, what they plan to do with their lives, is about as palatable as a week-old pizza. And, I'm talking about ten or twenty years hence. For most of them "the future" is five years. They are highly educated with big dreams and huge expectations. But in making important choices about their careers and their lives, they are more often than not rudderless. Generation Y has always lived with pressure and high expectations. While their optimism and energy is hard to curtail, they are still susceptible to the kinds of problems Xers faced as young adults—despair, lack of direction, depression and suicidal thoughts. (p. 175)

Jean Twenge, in her 2006 book *Generation Me,* makes comparable arguments. Twenge says, "this generation enters a world where college admissions are increasingly competitive, good jobs are hard to find and harder to keep, and basic necessities like housing and health care have skyrocketed in price" (p. 2).

Anya Kamenetz says in *Generation Debt,* "researchers use five milestones of maturity: leaving home, finishing school, becoming financially independent, getting married and having a child. By this definition, only 46 percent of women and 31 percent of men were grown up by age 30 in 2000, compared with 77 percent of women and 65 percent of men of the same age in 1960" (2006, p. 4).

Whether it's disenchantment or disengagement, dealing with uncertainty and shattered expectations is where this chapter comes in. It's an opportunity to help others to recognize what they really want in terms of employment, and then pursue it. Whether it's Shelton and Shelton, Huntley, Twenge, Kamenetz, or Tamara Draut in her 2005 book *Strapped*, there is the realization that there is no perfect job, but, in the pages to follow, we will show that there is a job that complements our personality preferences, and helping to find that job is the process proposed in this book.

Fortunately, for me, the times in my life where I wasn't sure which direction to go were few, far between, and generally short lived. I began my professional career in software engineering. From there I transitioned very naturally into systems engineering, program management, and human resources. The path seems somewhat disjointed, but actually, it is very much aligned once it is understood how it overlaps with my roles and responsibilities at the time. What I've discovered as I've moved from one discipline to the next is that each discipline offers something from which others could benefit. It's amazing how much overlap there is when we're talking about the management of people and the creation of processes. It could be argued it is exactly the experience of working in these many disciplines and the decisions associated with each that has provided me the insight to write this book.

This section on career development is about identifying which direction to go and taking the required steps to get you there. It's about reflection, life direction, understanding one's skills, knowledge, preferences, pragmatism, and persistence. Career development is about gaining control over your life. It's about taking action and achieving your potential. I've been very fortunate in my life. I have been provided opportunities to learn more than I could ever have imagined. As an admitted lifelong learner, I feel very blessed to have been afforded such rich and rewarding opportunities, both personally and professionally. In learning, I've discovered the more you learn and know, the more you recognize how very much there is yet to learn. The more we learn, the more we recognize the gray areas in discussions and that not everything is as it seems. Learning helps to eliminate unfounded biases and prejudices. Learning exposes us to yet more opportunities grow as human beings.

This chapter evolved in concept over many years of recognizing that the same principles I have been associated with in my professional life are exactly those principles used in making key life direction decisions. The thought process, activities, and manner in which we document how we move forward are the same as those very processes, activities, and attendant products used in designing some of the most sophisticated hardware and software systems in the world. In essence, career development in this chapter is based on the principles of rocket science! Gaining control of our lives is no different than the very rational, methodical, logical, and pragmatic manner in which we make decisions in designing the most complex software and hardware technological systems that protect our very lives on a daily basis.

Interestingly, as I peruse the many books on my shelves on this topic and the hundreds more in bookstores, the prescribed approaches to gaining control and moving forward are very similar. The process employed seems to be fundamentally based on understanding what you want in life and then, in some seamless manner, pursuing it. Most of us recognize it's really not quite that simple. If it were, then we wouldn't need so many books on the topic. I'm not sure I've ever seen a book with a sufficiently detailed plan for moving forward. This chapter will build on this basic body of knowledge, by providing a plan and much more. We will detail a process so unmistaken that it will do what is being suggested; it will help to move you forward.

Moving forward, based on the processes and methodologies used to build the greatest software and hardware technology in the world and the very principles used to defend our nation, will help each of us attain that future frontier that we so much desire but aren't sure how to obtain.

Moving Forward—The Four Questions

When you think about it, returning to our previous discussion, there really are four very different questions associated with getting to where we want to be. The first question is, "What am I really best suited to do?" With that, then, "What's available for me to do?" Then the longer-term perspective, "Where do I want to be 'x' years from now?" and finally, having already made that decision, "How do I get there from here?" These four questions, answered in this order, form the underlying premise of what this book is all about.

When this chapter was originally conceived, the focus was on how to help others get to where they want to be, without having given any real thought to the fact that many, including myself on numerous occasions, weren't really sure where that was, let alone how to get there. Figuring out where we want to be "x" years from now, as it turns out, is the harder of the two latter questions. In looking at the literature, there are numerous books on "how to get there" once you know where "there" is. There are considerably fewer books, however, on how to determine where "there" is.

So I decided to focus on helping others by examining a series of questions. Four different questions, four different activities, all required in the order given, to end up where you intended to end up.

- What am I really best suited to do?
- What's available for me to do?
- Where do I want to be in "x" years?
- How do I get to where I want to be?

The sections that follow are sequenced in accordance with the above four questions and preceded by a call to action. The call to action is intended to provide a sense of urgency and an open discussion that helps us to realize we must move forward in our career decision process. In other words, we must minimize our uncertainty in purpose, goals, or direction—the premise, in fact, of this entire chapter. Indirection, uncertainty, and/or a lack of goals all contribute to false starts and wasted time and energy. Their very nature is counterproductive and emotionally draining as we struggle to get where we believe we fit the best. The call to action is simply intended to provide an awareness heightening.

In looking at "What am I really best suited to do?" we'll examine a model that can be used to help us better understand ourselves in terms of strengths and weaknesses. The purpose of this, again, is to help us in determining which type of job might best fit our preferred way of collecting, assimilating, and applying information.

The section on "What's available for me to do?" will take our newfound knowledge of our preferences and help to match those preferences to types of occupations. In doing so, we begin to gain an understanding of where our true contentment might lie. There is nothing worse than being in a job that every Sunday we dread the thought of going back to work to on Monday. Like most other professionals who have been the workforce for any period of time, I have experienced these problem jobs many times. Fortunately, they were relatively short-lived.

The section on "Where do I want to be in 'x' years?" can be applied to the previous sections or simply stand alone. I say this because our preferences for the type of work we would like to do may not be the type of work we need to do at this time. There are many reasons—some may be financial, others may be organizational or even geographical. So when answering "Where do I want to be in 'x' years?" that objective assignment may not be where I could excel the most at, but instead, where I have the opportunity to be at this time in my life. To this end, we should not look at our careers through rose-colored glasses. There are going to be many times when we don't like what we are doing, whether it be the job, people, location, or any number of other reasons. It is true, however, that we all have had substandard jobs that we experienced at one point or another in our lives. The objective of this book is to help us recognize why some jobs might not be as good as others, especially as they relate to our preferences for collecting, assimilating, and applying accumulated knowledge.

The last section of this chapter deals with "How do I get to where I want to be?" This question, which is really at the bottom of the cognitive scale, is perhaps the most methodological. Here we will examine a process that identifies activities and attendant products that we can use to help us figure out the path from point "A" to point "B." The process, as discussed above, truly is premised on the basic principles of rocket science in the sense that it is the underlying practice associated with basic program and project management. Getting things done, then, whether it be moving our career forward or managing a highly sophisticated real-time military systems, follows the same process.

What Am I Really Best Suited to Do?

As I moved from managing engineering resources to human resources and back to managing engineering resources once again, I have had the fortunate opportunity to be involved in literally hundreds of conversations with employees who are trying to figure out where they want to be, or, once they believe they know, how can they get there from where they are. The conversations are nearly routine. I ask almost the same questions every time: "What do you like to do?" "Where is your passion?" I follow these basic questions up with a battery of second-tier questions like, "What are you doing when you feel at your peak, that you are really excelling, being the most you can be?" "Do you like to work as part of a team, or would you prefer to work alone?" "Do you like to work with facts, or do you prefer to develop bigger picture ideas?" "Do you prefer logical and objective analysis, or are you people-centered and prefer more of a participatory orientation?" "Do you prefer organization and structure, or do you prefer spontaneity and adaptability?"

What I'm really trying to get to is what natural characteristics or preferences, this individual possesses. This section is about better understanding ourselves. It's about understanding our strengths and weaknesses, our preferences for how we collect information, assimilate, and ultimately reapply that information to new situations. It's about understanding how we make informed decisions and at what point in our data-gathering process we feel comfortable enough to make those decisions. This section will examine basic characteristics that can lead to a natural selection of careers that might work best for each of us.

There are many models for delving into our psychological selves. Human resource management texts are loaded with them. In fact, nearly every human resource management text has a chapter or two on the topic of managing careers. They typically begin by addressing the roles and responsibilities of the individual, manager, and organization. Some even address the slightly more interesting concept of a person's career stage, which takes us through a form of career evolution as we chronologically age.

In this section, we want to focus on better understanding ourselves through our preferred way of doing things, such as how we gather, store, retrieve, reflect on, and apply information. The underlying premise is the more we understand about ourselves, the better our decisions will be and the more effectively we will be able to implement those decisions. Our personality preferences can help us decide what we want to do and how to improve our chances of getting what we want. Of course, our Myers-Briggs Type Indicator (MBTI) results are not the only source of information useful in career development; our skills, abilities, interests, and values, as well as information about jobs themselves—their availability, entrance requirements, and growth potential—must also be considered (Hammer, 1993, p. 2). In other words, in this chapter, we should gain a better understanding of our preferences, which then leads us to the next section on which occupations are most applicable. The material presented below evolved from numerous sources dealing with the topic of the MBTI personality inventory. Reference material for the MBTI can be found from the Center for Applications of Psychological Type (CAPT).

What's Available for Me to Do?

When asking the question "How can I increase my job satisfaction?" Allen Hammer (1993) discusses the following.

Because every individual is unique, and even jobs with the same title can be very different from one another, an exact fit or match between a person's preferences and the characteristics required by the job is rare (when this does happen, you may hear the person say, "I can't believe I'm getting paid to do this!"). More often, there are degrees of fit. Some of the things about the job will provide opportunities for you to use your preferences, while other tasks will require you to "work against the grain" of your preferences. Even if a good match does exist, you may not have the opportunity (some would call it a luxury) to take advantage of it. Or, you may have the opportunity, but decide that other factors are more important. For example, some people choose jobs because of geographical location, salary, or proximity to family or friends, rather than for reasons directly related to their personality preferences. Those familiar with type theory will recognize that many of these reasons are probably also related to personality preferences.

If you do choose to enter, or are already working in, an occupation that does not tend to attract individuals of your type, type theory would predict that you:

- May experience difficulty communicating or agreeing with your coworkers.
- May see problems differently. You may even speak a "different" language.
- May see the use of your preferences not rewarded with promotion, salary increase, or increased responsibility with the same frequency of your coworkers.
- May eventually experience stress or dissatisfaction if you are required to work "against the grain" of your preferences for too long, and this may even lead to burnout or lack of productivity.

It is also possible, of course, that you possess particular knowledge, skills, or abilities that are valued in the occupation. However, if you are experiencing any of the stresses associated with being in an occupation that is not a good fit for your preferences, and if you cannot, or choose not, to change jobs, then you have two other choices to increase your job satisfaction. You can try altering the job to better fit your personality, or adapting yourself to better fit the job. Obviously, these alternatives are not mutually exclusive. You could try both at once, or first one and then the other. There are other options as well, such as not working at all or going back to school.

Matching Preferences to Occupations

Over the years, millions of people in hundreds of different occupations have taken the MBTI. Data from many of these people has been collected at CAPT (Hammer, 1993, p. 14). The CAPT Atlas of Type Tables provides a useful introduction to exploring the relationship between career choice and MBTI type. The Atlas of Type Tables is a compilation of more than 300 occupations reported by more than 250,000 people who have taken the MBTI. For each of the sixteen types, these occupations have been ranked for how "attractive" or "popular" the occupation is for that type. An occupation is considered "attractive" to that type if the number of people found in that occupation is significantly greater than would be expected based on the representation of that type in the base population (the entire database). For example, if 10 percent of the 250,000+ people in the entire database were ISTJs, and if everyone entered careers randomly, or for reasons that had nothing to do with their type preferences, then we would expect that all occupations would also have about 10 percent ISTJs. However, when we look at the actual proportions of types in many occupations, we see far more, or far fewer, based on the frequencies of the type in the entire population. For example, we see far more ISTJs choosing careers as managers of small businesses than we would expect based on chance.

Findings such as these suggest that there is something about this career that ISTJs find attractive. This "something" probably is related to a good match between a person's preferences and tasks that are used in that job. Type theory suggests that people choose occupations, in part, because they believe the occupation will provide opportunities to express their type preferences, greater job satisfaction, rewards for using their strengths, and tasks and problems that they find interesting (Hammer 1993, p. 14).

Better Understanding Available Occupations

Ideally, at this point we have a better understanding of our preferences for how we attract, retain, assimilate, and apply information. We should also have an understanding of how our type preferences map to most and least attractive occupations. This section, then, focuses on how to learn more about the many occupations available.

Probably the best original source for learning about occupations comes from the U.S. Department of Labor Bureau of Labor Statistics, which has information on hundreds of different types of jobs documented in the *Occupational Outlook Handbook*. According to their website, the "*Occupational Outlook Handbook* is a nationally recognized source of career information, designed to provide valuable assistance to individuals making decisions about their future work lives."

The *Occupational Outlook Handbook* is revised every two years. Generally, it categorizes jobs into broad-band collections based on type of work, not necessarily content. For example, occupational categories include management, professional, service, sales, administrative, farming, construction, installation, production, transportation, and armed forces.

The handbook provides information for each job on:

- The training and education needed
- Earnings
- Expected job prospects
- What workers do on the job
- Working conditions

To continue our example, if you select management as an occupational category, you will get the following two job subcategories to select from:

Management and business and financial operations occupations

I. Management occupations
- Administrative services managers
- Advertising, marketing, promotions, public relations, and sales managers
- Computer and information systems managers
- Construction managers
- Education administrators
- Engineering and natural sciences managers
- Farmers, ranchers, and agricultural managers
- Financial managers
- Food service managers
- Funeral directors
- Human resources, training, and labor relations managers and specialists
- Industrial production managers
- Lodging managers
- Medical and health services managers
- Property, real estate, and community association managers
- Purchasing managers, buyers, and purchasing agents
- Top executives

II. Business and financial operations occupations
- Accountants and auditors
- Appraisers and assessors of real estate
- Budget analysts
- Claims adjusters, appraisers, examiners, and investigators
- Cost estimators
- Financial analysts and personal financial advisors
- Insurance underwriters
- Loan officers
- Management analysts
- Meeting and convention planners
- Tax examiners, collectors, and revenue agents

If, from the above two subcategories, you select financial managers out of the management occupations subcategory, you will get the following pages of descriptive information:

Significant Points

- About 3 out of 10 work in finance and insurance industries.
- A bachelor's degree in finance, accounting, or a related field is the minimum academic preparation, but many employers increasingly seek graduates with a master's degree in business administration, economics, finance, or risk management.
- Experience may be more important than formal education for some financial manager positions—most notably, branch managers in banks.
- Jobseekers are likely to face competition.

Nature of the Work

Almost every firm, government agency, and other type of organization has one or more financial managers who oversee the preparation of financial reports, direct investment activities, and implement cash management strategies. Because computers are increasingly used to record and organize data, many financial managers are spending more time developing strategies and implementing the long-term goals of their organization.

The duties of financial managers vary with their specific titles, which include controller, treasurer or finance officer, credit manager, cash manager, and risk and insurance manager. *Controllers* direct the preparation of financial reports that summarize and forecast the organization's financial position, such as income statements, balance sheets, and analyses of future earnings or expenses. Controllers also are in charge of preparing special reports required by regulatory authorities. Often, controllers oversee the accounting, audit, and budget departments. *Treasurers* and *finance officers* direct the organization's financial goals, objectives, and budgets. They oversee the investment of funds, manage associated risks, supervise cash management activities, execute capital-raising strategies to support a firm's expansion, and deal with mergers and acquisitions. *Credit managers* oversee the firm's issuance of credit, establishing credit-rating criteria, determining credit ceilings, and monitoring the collections of past-due accounts. Managers specializing in international finance develop financial and accounting systems for the banking transactions of multinational organizations.

Cash managers monitor and control the flow of cash receipts and disbursements to meet the business and investment needs of the firm. For example, cash flow projections are needed to determine whether loans must be obtained to meet cash requirements or whether surplus cash should be invested in interest-bearing instruments. *Risk* and *insurance managers* oversee programs to minimize risks and losses that might arise from financial transactions and business operations undertaken by the institution. They also manage the organization's insurance budget.

Financial institutions, such as commercial banks, savings and loan associations, credit unions, and mortgage and finance companies, employ additional financial managers who oversee various functions, such as lending, trusts, mortgages, and investments, or programs, including sales, operations, or electronic financial services. These managers may be required to solicit business, authorize loans, and direct the investment of funds, always adhering to federal and state laws and regulations. (Chief financial officers and other executives are included with top executives elsewhere in the *Occupational Outlook Handbook*.)

Branch managers of financial institutions administer and manage all of the functions of a branch office, which may include hiring personnel, approving loans and lines of credit, establishing a rapport with the community to attract business, and assisting customers with account problems. The trend is for branch managers to become more oriented toward sales and marketing. It is important that they have substantial knowledge about all types of products that the bank sells. Financial managers who work for financial institutions must keep abreast of the rapidly growing array of financial services and products.

In addition to carrying out the preceding general duties, all financial managers perform tasks unique to their organization or industry. For example, government financial managers must be experts on the government appropriations and budgeting processes, whereas health care financial managers must be knowledgeable about issues surrounding health care financing. Moreover, financial managers must be aware of special tax laws and regulations that affect their industry.

Financial managers play an increasingly important role in mergers and consolidations and in global expansion and related financing. These areas require extensive, specialized knowledge on the part of the financial manager to reduce risks and maximize profit. Financial managers increasingly are hired on a temporary basis to advise senior managers on these and other matters. In fact, some small firms contract out all their accounting and financial functions to companies that provide such services.

The role of the financial manager, particularly in business, is changing in response to technological advances that have significantly reduced the amount of time it takes to produce financial reports. Financial managers now perform more data analysis and use it to offer senior managers ideas on how to maximize profits. They often work on teams, acting as business advisors to top management. Financial managers need to keep abreast of the latest computer technology in order to increase the efficiency of their firm's financial operations.

From the above, the U.S. Department of Labor offers an enormous amount of very good data on each job within the *Occupational Outlook Handbook*, including information on employment, job outlook, earnings, and related occupations. They also provide a wealth of sources for additional information. So, knowing the type of occupation you might be interested in, you should be able to gain considerable additional information even further helping to make an informed decision.

Where Do I Want to Be in "X" Years?

This is where most career development models begin. On entering the discussion, you'll be asked, "Where do you want to be in 'x' years"? Ideally, you have an advantage. Having read through the previous material, you should know a little more about the predecessor questions of, "What am I really best suited to do?" and "What's available for me to do?" If you recall the lead-in discussion, how can you really know where you want to be in "x" years, without first knowing what it is you like doing and how that maps to what's available?

As discussed in the introduction to this material, I cannot tell you how many times in my life I didn't know where I wanted to be in two, five, or ten years from now. I didn't even know what was available for me, let alone how to get there. Sometimes in life we have what are called "unknown unknowns" (Springer, 2005, p. 45). These are the many things that we don't even know about. Their very existence is something that we would not even have ever thought to exist. Good examples of these are diseases. AIDS, for example, was a disease that we didn't even have any idea existed or ever would exist. It was totally an unknown entity and never conceived as something that might have existed. AIDS, therefore, is what we would call an "unknown unknown." Once we recognize that something does exist that we had never previously suspected, then it becomes known to us, although we don't know much, if anything, about it. We call this a "known unknown." In other words, we know that it exists, but that's the extent of what we know. After some period of time, once we begin to research the phenomenon, we eventually learn something more about it, making it a "known known." In this case, we know that it exists and we know what it is, how it comes to exists, and how to control it.

So at some points in our lives, we are in the "unknown unknown" phase, where we have no idea what is even available to us as a future opportunity. Sure, we can all imagine careers as teachers, bus drivers, restaurant workers, and the like, since we have had exposure to these occupations in our lives. But, what else exists? I routinely talk with young people on college campuses and it is not uncommon that they ask questions along the lines of, "What do you do?" or "What types of work are there for me to do when I graduate?" Even these bright young future professionals, who recognized the field they had an interest in and then pursued education in that field, are still not sure what's available for them to do once they achieve their great success.

I guess, then, we shouldn't feel bad that we may not know "where" we want to be in life. Although, it doesn't stop the unsettling feeling of wandering aimlessly from day to day, truly believing there is something greater out there, something better that we would each enjoy more or feel a greater contentment over. That feeling of meandering aimlessly is perhaps one of the worse feelings in the world. During my times dealing with this emotion, I felt as though I was wasting my time and the many precious years of my life.

There is one thing, however, that happens when you truly believe there is more—that very thought of knowing something greater exists—which tends to guide us like a compass to make good decisions over bad ones. Wanting to be something greater and knowing it will someday materialize tends to help us stay the course. It acts as a greater conscience. For example, I grew up extremely poor. I didn't know what was available to me when I was nearing the completion of high school, but I knew I didn't want to be poor anymore. I knew I had to go to college to be something, but what, I had no idea. I remember in the beginning of my senior year in high school there were representatives from the many college campuses around my home state of Indiana visiting our high school. I knew my strengths were in math and science, and I really enjoyed a couple of computer courses I had taken, so I walked up to a guy from Indiana University and asked one question, "What can I go into for the fewest number of years and make the most amount of money?" He asked me a few basic questions on what I liked, and then replied, "See that man over there from Purdue University? He has a program called computer science that I think might satisfy what you're looking for." The rest, as they say, was history. I signed up for computer science at Purdue, never looked back, never questioned my decision, and only focused on achieving my goal, although I had no idea what it would bring in the end.

I remember so many times not knowing what good would come from my obtaining a bachelor's degree in computer science from Purdue, but knowing that something good would, indeed, happen. It wasn't until I began my interviewing process as I neared graduation that I really started to get an idea of what was available to do.

So, as you can see, sometimes we don't know where we will end up, but we do believe that we are doing the right things to get us somewhere else. And to this end, we use our belief in something else, a longer-term greater good, to guide our short-term decisions we make in life. I tell my sons this routinely. I constantly remind them to "remember the bigger picture and let that guide your short-term decisions." My older son in particular, who tremendously enjoys being a free spirit and traveling, I have reminded him so many times of this that he now interrupts me in mid-conversation and says, "Yes, Dad, I know, see the bigger picture and make smart choices." I don't care if I'm repetitive with my children, if it helps them to make smart choices.

One of things I've learned as I've gained more experience (I like to say "gained more experience" versus "gotten older," since it sounds better), is the more I do, the more I recognize what else there is to do. In other words, the more we experience, the more we begin to see the many possibilities where we might fit in, and, to this end, the more we recognize what it takes to pursue one of these possibilities, whether it be more education or specialized training.

Now we have to focus on the topic question of "Where do we want to be in 'x' years?" The answer to this question stems from the quantitative discussion on the many activities of the program/project management process. It begins with the chapter on defining the requirements.

How Do I Get to Where I Want to Be?

A this point, we sort of have a feeling for what our personality preferences are, we might even have a feel for the type of work that lends itself to those preferences, and perhaps, we might even have a longer-term perspective on what we would like to do some years out. Now, then, given we have some feel for where we are and where we want to be, our next task is to determine how best to get from point "A" to point "B," and that's where basic career development models come in.

Career Models

There are many forms of career development models. Some models, as we stated earlier, are employee-driven, while others are organizationally driven. Those organizationally driven models, however, are becoming fewer and fewer, heading the way of the dinosaurs.

Now, with that said, it's important to differentiate between career development and training for a given task or job. Training is very much in the interest of a company or organization. It enhances the skills of its workforce, therefore increasing the likelihood of growing the business. Career development, however, is something much different. Career development prepares one for a career. It may include training along the way, but it is greater than simply preparing someone for the next short-term assignment. Now, one could argue that a sufficiently large number of training opportunities over a prolonged period of time might actually, by default, lead to a career development model, although it was never intended to be one. In this section, when we talk about career development models, we are talking about planned, bigger picture coordinated and orchestrated cohesive set of initiatives, assignments, education, and training.

Understanding the Basic Model

At the basic level, a career development model might look like figure 21.2.

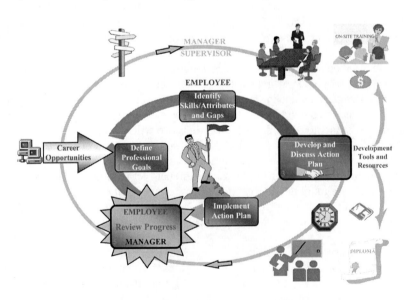

Figure 21.2. Basic Career Development Model

The model has five basic steps or phases:

- Employee defines his or her professional goals,
- Employee identifies skills, attributes, and gaps,
- Employee develops an action plan and then proceeds to discuss the plan with his/her supervisor,
- Employee implements the action plan with the manager's approval, and
- Employee and manager monitor the action plan for applicability as time goes on and adequacy.

Now, in most models, how one accomplishes these five steps can be somewhat cryptic. In some cases, templates are provided, in others, words describing what could happen. In our model, we are actually going to focus on using the same process as that used in designing real-time embedded hardware and software-integrated computer systems—in other words, that used in rocket science.

Succession Planning as a Career Development Model

We would be remiss if we didn't address career development from a succession planning perspective. Within my current industry and business, the number one reason cited by people leaving the organization, today and in the past two years, has been a lack of career opportunity, or, more appropriately stated, a lack of known career opportunities.

Current career development takes place through one of three sources: (1) the function/discipline manager, (2) the program or work organization manager, and/or (3) the corporate-provided career development model.

In each of these three cases, the perspective of career development is focused on those aspects most applicable to the career coach, as detailed below. In common, however, is the underlying premise that each coaching opportunity is bounded by a short-term and narrowly focused perspective, therefore lacking in the breadth of the solution.

Functional managers, or discipline-specific managers, are responsible for making sure resources are available to work the many current and upcoming programs. To this end, they work to identify what programs, by type, size, and complexity, are forthcoming, and what skills will be required. Then, the functional managers determine which individuals with which skills will become available in time to work on the target programs. The final step of the career matching process is to match the available supply with the future demand. From a career development perspective, then, the functional manager works diligently to determine where a given individual will be placed on a continuous basis, from program to program. By virtue of the functional manager's perspective being a six- to twelve-month horizon, the career development advice is quite naturally going to be limited to this same relative short time period. The responsibilities of the functional managers themselves are bound by perspective and time, and are generally limited in scope to program opportunities.

The program or work organization performs career development from the same short-term perspective. The program manager's perspective of work to be performed is nearly always limited to the length of his or her program, and, quite naturally, is bound by this fixed time period. Individual employee career development, therefore, is equally bound to this time period. And, in fact, the program manager relies on the functional/discipline manager to make career development choices outside the time bounds of the given program's duration, a hand in glove approach to a perceived holistic career development model.

The program manager, therefore, worries about the individual during the length of the program, while the functional manager worries about development across programs within the six- to twelve-month program planning window.

The company provides a third opportunity for career development, namely, self-identification of where an individual would like to be in some forward-thinking period of time. The company-sponsored website for career development basically relinquishes the maternal/paternal responsibilities for career development by placing the burden for future desired position in the hands of the individual. The corporate model begins by asking the employee to visualize where she or he wants to be, following up with a gap analysis between where the employee is now and that desired end state. The problem with this approach is the inevitable question from the individual requesting career development guidance, "What's available for me to do?"

It is this question that goes only partially answered in any of the above three provided opportunities for career development. To fully answer the question means to have a plan for succession for each and every individual in the target employee population pool. In other words, we can tell employees what they will be doing within the context of a given program (program manager), across multiple programs (functional manager), or assist them if they know where they want to end up over time, but there exists another perspective, that being peer-level tasks or responsibilities within or across disciplines.

Succession planning is performed for some minimal immediate leadership positions within the organization, but the bulk of the organization lies well below these few higher-level positions. In fact, more than 90 percent of the target exempt population falls outside of the current succession planning model.

Succession planning, if done properly, is a full-time, fully supported effort to determine successors in time-phase with required attendant training. At the highest level, the process is composed of identifying positions, successors who are ready now, in one to three years, three to five years, and so on, and the required next assignments and training and education to prepare these future successors for their target positions. And although simple in theory, it clearly is exhaustively rigorous in practice. Constant updates coupled with advancing and statusing of development plans require dedicated attention, but, in the end, solves the number one reason nearly 50 percent of the population leaves current industry and business, namely, lack of career opportunity or knowledge of one.

Utilizing an effective succession development model provides a clear and known career path for each individual employee and the required development to advance to those many next positions. Additionally, utilization of a succession development model removes the number one reason for attrition, namely, a lack of known career opportunities.

Understanding Our Career Development Model
In this section, our career development model consists of the following activities:

- Identify the requirements (completed in the previous section)
- Group the requirements into categories of things, such as activities or events
- Determine who has responsibility for each activity or event
- Create a schedule for completing the activities and events

On the surface, our model somewhat resembles most other career development models. We'll see, however, that our model brings consistency to the process, ultimately forming a coherent set of activities and attendant products along the way.

Let's assume our requirements were identified as in figure 21.3.

Notice, on the surface, it appears we have identified requirements whose highest importance have to do with ENTJ MBTI preferences and support internal satisfiers of motivation. Note also that one or more items can have the same relative importance.

From our requirements, then, and after reviewing the Department of Labor occupations from their *Occupational Outlook Handbook*, we've decided the right long-term job is to be the chief learning officer at a major firm. This job satisfies all the highest-priority requirements and is something our company has, so it is reasonably possible to aspire to the position. Note also, if this position were obtained, it would satisfy our requirement to grow our salary and be a part of an executive profit sharing (hygiene factors).

Now, we have to ask ourselves what are we missing in terms of education, experience, and training to get to where we want to be. Based on our previous efforts in preceding chapters, we have a pretty good idea of what type of job would make a good match. Figure 21.4 reflects this gap analysis between where we are at this point in time and where we want to be.

Importance	Requirement
1	Job should be at a relatively high level in organization
2	Job should support systems-level problem solving
3	Job should have career growth potential
3	Job should utilize organizational skills
3	Job should require vision
4	Select a geographical region which has pronounced seasons (Spring, Summer, Fall, Winter); but not too cold or too hot
5	Job should have management responsibility
6	Job should support development of others
7	Grow current salary
8	Be a part of an executive profit sharing plan

Figure 21.3. Initial Job Requirements

Category	Gap
Education	Need education in international affairs
Education	Need understanding of andragogy
Education	Need understanding of curriculum design
Location	Wrong geographical location. Position isn't where I am.
Responsibility	Not in the career path for position
Responsibility	Need more similar experiences
Training	Need training in Organizational Effectiveness
Training	Need Organizational Development training

Figure 21.4. Requirements Gap Analysis

If we were to create an organizational depiction of these gaps, it may look like figure 21.5.

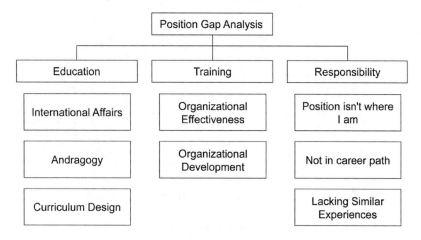

Figure 21.5. Gap Analysis—Chart Depiction

Once we have our requirements organized, it's time to determine who has primary and perhaps even secondary responsibility for each. To depict this, it's best to use a spreadsheet type of table as in figure 21.6.

Category	Gap	Responsibility	
		Employee	Manager/Department/ Organization
Education	Need education in international affairs	P	S
Education	Need understanding of andragogy	P	S
Education	Need understanding of curriculum design	P	S
Responsibility	Wrong geographical location. Position isn't where I am.	P	S
Responsibility	Not in the career path for position	S	P
Responsibility	Need more similar experiences	S	P
Training	Need training in Organizational Effectiveness	P	S
Training	Need Organizational Development training	P	S

Figure 21.6. Career Development Responsibility Assignment Matrix

Notice when it comes to responsibility, our manager/department/organization has the primary role and we have a secondary one. One could argue this either way, the supposition is that the organization has to make the opportunity available to us once we have identified our intentions to pursue it. The other way to view this is that we have primary responsibility, in that we could leave our current company and pursue work in another. In the instances where we are talking about education and training, the assumption is that we're willing to pursue it with or without the company's financial support. What's important with a responsibility assignment matrix is that we determine to the best our situation will allow, who has which responsibility for our meeting our objectives. This becomes especially important when we sit with our current manager and go over our plan.

Now, to summarize our efforts, we have a pretty good idea of our preferences from MBTI; we have had a good opportunity to match those preferences to any number of job types; we followed our process to define our requirements, organize those requirements, and identify who has primary and/or secondary responsibility for accomplishing those requirements. And now, it's time to create some form of schedule that reflects the anticipated completion of our many activities (figure 21.7).

Activity/Event	20xx												20xy		
	J	F	M	A	M	J	J	A	S	O	N	D	J	F	M
Need education in international affairs	■	■													
Need understanding of andragogy				■	■										
Need understanding of curriculum design							■	■							
Wrong geographical location. Position isn't where I am.										■	■	■			
Not in the career path for position										■	■	■			
Need more similar experiences										■	■	■	■	■	
Need training in Organizational Effectiveness									■	■					
Need Organizational Development training											■	■			

Figure 21.7. Career Development Schedule of Activities

There we have it. Following the same process, essentially, as that used to design, develop, and implement our most sophisticated electronic systems, we have successfully created a plan made of activities and attendant products to move our career in the direction most suited for us based on our psychological preferences.

Are we done? Is this it? Basically, yes.

For nearly twenty-five years I've been following the research and speaking on generational similarities and differences. Only now are we beginning to better understand the attitudes and energies in job and career pursuits from our two most recent entries into the job market, Generation X and Generation Y/Nexters. The literature has proliferated on what motivates these two generational cohorts in their work life and pursuits. Generation X, it is said, suffers from what has been termed an "expectancy-reality gap," while Generation Y suffers from this same "expectancy-reality gap," until such time when they do find that ideal job, are content to settle for a series of lesser jobs that fund a life of fun, travel, and time with friends. Both generations are looking to find that ideal job, the one that provides financial security and personal fulfillment.

Moving forward is about identifying which direction to go and taking the required steps to get there. It's about reflection, life direction, understanding one's skills, knowledge, preferences, pragmatism, and persistence. Moving forward is about gaining control over your life. It's about taking action and achieving your potential.

Moving forward, based on the processes and methodologies used to build the greatest software and hardware technology in the world and the very principles used to defend our nation, will help each of us attain that future frontier that we so much desire but aren't sure how to obtain.

Chapter 22

Succession Planning—
Providing Opportunities for Growth

Effective succession planning provides for individual personal and professional growth and career opportunities. Succession planning creates a highly integrated and synchronized effort to recruit, develop, and retain an organization's personnel. Figure 22.1 depicts the interrelatedness of these three key elements to organizational continuation.

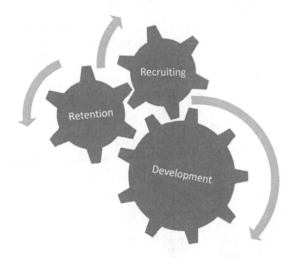

Figure 22.1. Highly Integrated, Fully Synchronized Effort

Simply stated, *succession planning* is a *process* of *developing* talent to meet the needs of the organization *now* and in the *future*. Every time a manager makes a work assignment, he or she is preparing someone for the future by building that worker's ability. Work experience builds competence, and different kinds of work experience build different kinds of competence (Rothwell, 2010).

Why is Succession Planning Important?

Succession planning is a tool to protect against any number of anticipated or unanticipated events within an organizational setting. There is no shortfall of literature discussing the worldwide aging of the world's population. This aging, coupled with a perceived shortfall of skilled labor, directly necessitates an organization's ability to develop and promote talent from within. The added benefit of developing and promoting from within is an organizational benefit through the retention of company knowledge. New hires involve relocation, training, and indoctrination, which have been documented to carry costs averaging $10,000 to $50,000 per hire. These costs do not include the time required to understand an organization's policies, practices, procedures, and culture. If a new hire does not feel a sense of belonging to the new organization, then the cost has little to no return on new hire investment.

Effective succession planning provides for a ready-made workforce. Literature reveals a happy workforce is a more productive workforce. Succession planning also provides an organization's workforce with a purpose aligned to career advancement. This concept of personalizing the greater vision converts external energy into internal energy; which creates the required thrust for sustaining organizational goals and vision.

Who is Succession Planning For?

Succession planning can be used at any level in the organization. Positions more commonly discussed in the literature are executive, senior managers, and leadership teams. Succession planning, however, can be used at any level or for any position in an organization. Succession planning can be especially useful in sustaining hard to fill positions.

Activities of Effective Succession Planning

The first step in implementing a succession plan is to perform a job analysis on each position within the position tree. This provides an understanding of the required knowledge, skills, and abilities to perform in the target position(s). With this knowledge, each individual in the succession planning hierarchy can be analyzed relative to the below:

- What are their knowledge, skills, and abilities
- What training would they need to move up
- What education would they need to move up
- What assignments would be most beneficial to prepare for next move
- How long in current position and how long before ready for next position

Below is a depiction of a format used for the planning of a succession plan (Norman, 1986). Figure 22.2 depicts the identification of potential successors by position within the position tree hierarchy, while figure 22.3 depicts each current incumbent's personal characteristics.

Each individual, then, must have an individual development plan (IDP). The IDP is the mapping medium between where an employee is at the current time and what is required to progress to the next level. The IDP takes into account the following:

- Identify next position in succession tree
- Determine time required for preparation
- Determine what training or education is required in preparation for next move
- Determine what resources will be required to gain the necessary training and/or education
- Determine what interim assignments, tasks, or responsibilities the employee should assume or be part of

What Do We Do When a Position Vacates?

When someone vacates a position there is a series of steps that are immediately enacted based on the above planning effort.

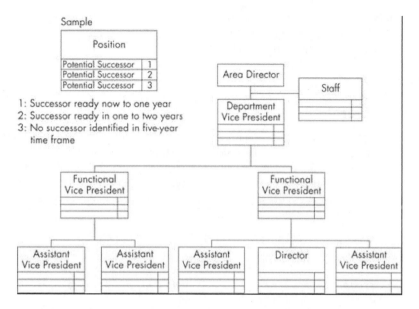

Source: Norman H. Carter, "Guaranteeing Management's Future through Succession Planning,"
Journal of Information Systems Management (Summer 1986), 19.

Figure 22.2. Potential Successors by Position

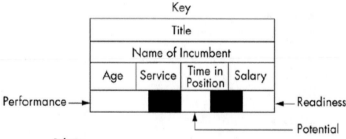

Performance Rating   Definition
X   New—in position less than three months. Not evaluated.
1   Unsatisfactory results and performance.
2   Marginal—does not meet requirements of position (with learning
     discounted). Attitude and/or initiative not acceptable.
     Remedial action indicated.
3   Satisfactory—generally meets job requirements but room for improvement.
     If in a major learning phase, considerable room for improvement.
4   Above average—surpasses overall job requirements but lacks strength in
     some areas.
5   Superior—some elements of performance may rate as exceptional, but
     overall performance falls below an exceptional rating.
6   Exceptional—general all-around excellence in quality/quantity of work,
     initiative, self-development, new ideas, and attitude. Rapid learner.

Potential
A   Outstanding—can advance two levels above present position.
B   Considerable—can advance at least one level above present position
     and/or assume substantial added responsibility at present level.
C   Some—can assume added responsibilities at present level.
D   Limited—at or near capacity in present position.
E   Key capacity in current position—vital technical knowledge precludes
     movement.
X   New—in position less than three months. Not evaluated.

Readiness
R/O   Qualified to move now.
R1   Within one to two years.
R2   Within two to four years.
N/A   Current level appropriate.

Source: Norman H. Carter, "Guaranteeing Management's
Future through Succession Planning,"
Journal of Information Systems Management (Summer 1986), 20.

Figure 22.3. Position Incumbent Characteristics

- Present the list of available candidates to the hiring manager
- Select the best fit for the vacant position
- Backfill the selected candidates newly emptied position through the iteratively defined process
- Backfill the lowest position vacated, if necessary, with others internally or an outside fresh hire

Things to Remember

It is important to heighten awareness that there can only be one person in each named position. Even though an individual may have sufficient knowledge, skills, and abilities, there may not be an opening for that individual to promote into (i.e., there must be an available opportunity for promotion). It is equally important that others who may be qualified are considered even if they are from another "outside" function. In other words, someone from the business office may be qualified to fill a position in the administrative professional discipline, and vice versa. Generally, then:

- There can only be 1 president, provost, dean, etc.
- Even though an employee is ready for the next position, there must be an opportunity (see above)
- Look at everyone for peer/parallel level rotations and fills, versus vertical moves; across disciplines (e.g., program management to marketing)
- Assess each individual still in the pipeline to determine their potential/applicability for advancing

Final thoughts on effective succession planning:

- Creates a process that is *fair*
- Provides *equitable* opportunity
- Promotes personal and professional *growth*
- Creates a *career progression*
- *Reduces turnover*—we know we have opportunities we can be prepared for
- Maintains and retains *corporate knowledge*
- Common business sense—*$$*

Who is Responsible?

Succession planning should be assigned to a single individual. This approach creates accountability for ongoing focused effort and helps to ensure effective implementation. To help guide and provide insight into shareholder interests, there should be an advisory board composed of representatives from the stakeholder groups. Term of membership can be determined by the implementing organization, typically no more than two years.

Chapter 23

The Business Case for Diversity and Inclusivity

Decision making, or making decisions, can be discussed in terms of both a quantitative process and a qualitative process. The literature on both is nearly insurmountable. When I search Amazon for books with the titles or keywords *decision making,* it returns nearly one quarter of a billion hits—that's a lot of literature on any subject!

My intent in this section is not necessarily to discuss tools and techniques for making good decisions, but instead, to lay a foundation for better understanding the approaches to making better, more informed decisions.

The quantitative discipline for making better decisions is referred to as management science. According to authors David R. Anderson, Dennis J. Sweeney, Thomas A. Williams, Jeffrey D. Camm, and R. Kipp Martin, in their book entitled *An Introduction to Management Science: Quantitative Approaches to Decision Making* (2011), management science is an approach to decision making that makes extensive use of quantitative analysis. In addition to *management science,* another widely known and accepted name is *operations research.* Many use the terms management science and operations research interchangeably. The scientific management revolution of the early 1900s, initiated by Frederick W. Taylor, provided the foundation for MS/OR. But modern management science/operations research is generally considered to have originated during the World War II period, when teams were formed to deal with strategic and tactical problems faced by the military. These teams, which often consisted of people with diverse specialties (e.g., mathematicians, engineers, and behavioral scientists), were grouped together to solve a common problem through the utilization of the scientific method. After the war, many of these team members continued their research on quantitative approaches to decision making.

Two developments that occurred during the post-World War II period led to the growth and use of management science in nonmilitary applications. First, continued research on quantitative approaches to decision making resulted in numerous methodological developments. Probably the most significant development was the discovery by George Dantzig, in 1947, of the simplex method for solving linear programming problems. Many more methodological developments followed, and in 1957, the first book on operations research was published by C. W. Churchman, R. L. Ackoff, and L. E. Amoff.

Concurrently with these methodological developments, there was a virtual explosion in computing power made available through digital computers. Computers enabled practitioners to use the methodological advances to successfully solve a large variety of problems. The computer technology explosion continues; personal computers are now more powerful than the mainframe computers of the 1970s. Today, variants of the post-World War II methodological developments are being used on personal computers to solve problems larger than those solved on mainframe computers in the 1980s.

Problem solving can be defined as the process of identifying a difference between the actual and the desired state of affairs and then taking action to resolve the difference. For problems important enough to justify the time and effort of careful analysis, the problem-solving process involves the following seven steps:

- Identify and define the problem.
- Define the set of alternative solutions.
- Define the criterion or criteria that will be used to evaluate the alternatives.
- Evaluate the alternatives.
- Choose an alternative.
- Implement the selected alternative.
- Evaluate the results, and determine if a satisfactory solution has been obtained.

Decision making is the term generally associated with the first five steps of the problem-solving process. Thus, the first step of decision making is to identify and define the problem. Decision making ends with the choosing of an alternative, which is the act of making the decision.

Quantitative analysis truly provides a framework to evaluate selected alternatives based on sound rational and methodical thought processes. The management science approach is taught in colleges and universities around the world and usually involves one or more semesters of study.

On the qualitative side of the decision-making discussion, there is probably nothing more read in recent times than the work by Daniel Goleman entitled *Emotional Intelligence*. Emotional intelligence (EI) has been researched and reported on as the foundation on which solid, thoughtful decisions are made. In Goleman, Boyatzis, and McKee's book *Primal Leadership*, the authors discuss the four dimensions of emotional intelligence and the six styles of leadership (2002, p. 3). Within the four dimensions of emotional intelligence (self-awareness, self-management, social awareness, and relationships management), there are eighteen competencies. These competencies are the vehicles of primal leadership. Even the most outstanding leader will not have all competencies. Effective leaders, though, exhibit at least one competency from each of the domains.

The four domains and their competencies, from Goleman's *Emotional Intelligence* (1995, pp. 3–10), are listed below:

Self-Awareness

- Emotional self-awareness: Reading one's own emotions and recognizing their impact and using "gut sense" to guide decisions.
- Accurate self-assessment: Knowing one's strengths and limits.
- Self-confidence: A sound sense of one's self-worth and capabilities.

Self-Management

- Emotional self-control: Keeping disruptive emotions and impulses under control.
- Transparency: Displaying honesty, integrity, and trustworthiness.
- Adaptability: Flexibility in adapting to changing situations or overcoming obstacles.
- Achievement: The drive to improve performance to meet inner standards of excellence.
- Initiative: Readiness to act and seize opportunities.
- Optimism: Seeing the upside in events.

Social Awareness

- Empathy: Sensing others' emotions, understanding their perspective, and taking active interest in their concerns.
- Organizational awareness: Reading the currents, decision networks, and politics at the organizational level.
- Service: Recognizing and meeting follower, client, or customer needs.

Relationship Management

- Inspirational leadership: Guiding and motivating with a compelling vision.
- Influence: Wielding a range of tactics for persuasion.

- Developing others: Bolstering others' abilities through feedback and guidance.
- Change catalyst: Initiating, managing, and leading in new directions.
- Building bonds: Cultivating and maintaining relationship webs.
- Teamwork and collaboration: Cooperation and team building.

The best, most effective leaders act according to one or more of six distinct approaches to leadership. Four of the styles—visionary, coaching, affiliative, and democratic—create the kind of resonance that boosts performance. The other two—pacesetting and commanding—should be applied with caution.

The Six Styles of Leadership

- *Visionary.* The visionary leader articulates where a group is going, but not how it gets there, setting people free to innovate, experiment, and take calculated risks. Inspirational leadership is the EI competence that most strongly undergirds the visionary style. Transparency, another EI competency, is also crucial. If a leader's vision is disingenuous, people sense it. The EI competency that matters most to visionary leadership, however, is empathy. The ability to sense what others feel and understand their perspectives helps a leader articulate a truly inspirational vision.
- *Coaching.* The coaching style is really the art of the one-on-one. Coaches help people identify their unique strengths and weaknesses, tying those to their personal and career aspirations. Effective coaching exemplifies the EI competency of developing others, which lets a leader act as a counselor. It works hand in hand with two other competencies: emotional awareness and empathy.
- *Affiliative.* The affiliative style of leadership represents the collaborative competency in action. An affiliative leader is most concerned with promoting harmony and fostering friendly interactions. When leaders are being affiliative, they focus on the emotional needs of workers, using empathy. Many leaders who use the affiliative approach combine it with the visionary approach. Visionary leaders state a mission, set standards, and let people know whether their work is furthering group goals. Ally that with the caring approach of the affiliative leader and you have a potent combination.
- *Democratic.* A democratic leader builds on a triad of EI abilities: teamwork and collaboration, conflict management, and influence. Democratic leaders are great listeners and true collaborators. They know how to quell conflict and create harmony. Empathy also plays a role. A democratic approach works best when as a leader, you are unsure what direction to take and need ideas from able employees. For example, IBM's Louis Gerstner, an outsider to the computer industry when he became CEO of the ailing giant, relied on seasoned colleagues for advice.
- *Pacesetting.* Pacesetting as a leadership style must be applied sparingly, restricted to settings where it truly works. Common wisdom holds that pacesetting is admirable. The leader holds and exemplifies high standards for performance. He or she is obsessive about doing things better and faster, quickly pinpointing poor performers. Unfortunately, applied excessively, pacesetting can backfire and lead to low morale as workers think they are being pushed too hard or that the leader doesn't trust them to get their job done. The EI foundation of a pacesetter is the drive to achieve through improved performance and the initiative to seize opportunities. But a pacesetter who lacks empathy can easily be blinded to the pain of those who achieve what the leader demands. Pacesetting works best when combined with the passion of the visionary style and the team building of the affiliate style.
- *Commanding.* The command leader demands immediate compliance with orders, but doesn't bother to explain the reasons. If subordinates fail to follow orders, these leaders resort to threats. They also seek tight control and monitoring. Of all the leadership styles, the commanding approach is the least effective. Consider what the style does to an organi-

zation's climate. Given that emotional contagion spreads most readily from the top down, an intimidating, cold leader contaminates everyone's mood. Such a leader erodes people's spirits and the pride and satisfaction they take in their work. The commanding style works in limited circumstances, and only when used judiciously. For example, in a genuine emergency, such as an approaching hurricane or a hostile take-over attempt, a take-control style can help everyone through the crisis. An effective execution of the commanding style draws on three EI competencies: influence, achievement, and initiative. In addition, self-awareness, emotional self-control, and empathy are crucial to keep the commanding style from going off track.

The literature, then, on decision making is significant. The number of books on quantitative to qualitative foundational skills is proliferate. The discussion on decision making very naturally progresses into a discussion on leadership traits and/or characteristics themselves. It's hard to not make mention of leadership when talking about decision making. The very essence of leadership, and management for that matter, is premised on characteristics of qualitative descent.

As stated in the beginning of this section, it isn't my intent to go any further with this discussion than to heighten awareness to the basic elements of effective decision making. Understanding the tools, techniques, and methodologies in practice can be further understood once the reader better acquaints himself or herself with the above. I believe, however, it should be somewhat apparent that numerous sections of this book further compare and contrast management and leadership in terms of traits and characteristics. There is also a major discussion on generational personalities.

Business Case for Diversity and Inclusivity: It's All about Growth

A number of years back we used to be required to attend what was then referred to as diversity training. Diversity training, in almost every case, was one of the most boring discussions we could have. It centered on the legal aspects of being sued for discrimination in the workplace. The topic was frequently presented by human resources or the legal department. Nobody wanted to go; there was absolutely nothing positive about the training, and from year to year it never really ever changed.

The problem with that previous training was that it never answered the fundamental question of what benefits accrue the organization from thinking from a diverse perspective or even valuing inclusivity (a term not then known or used). Company performance and profitability was tied to legal implications from lawsuits. Most of us at the time knew there had to be a better way to express the value of diversity in the workforce other than to avoid litigation. We desperately wanted a concept or model we could sell that resonated with each employee.

Then, around the late 1990s, the concept of diversity in the workforce took a decidedly different turn. We began talking about diversity as more than simply a race or gender issue and started looking at it as an array of diverse characteristics representative of the general employee population. The familiar things associated with age, race, gender, religion, physical ability/disability, and national ethnicity were still identified, as they should be, but additional characteristics such as family situation, sexual orientation, veteran status, language spoken, work experience, education, thought, geographical location, functional discipline, and international experience all came into the fold, contributing toward a more complete perspective of diversity in the workplace. The identification of these additional characteristics also ushered in new presentation material with a different slant. Now we talked about:

- diversity being an imperative for business survival
- diverse teams making better decisions and better decisions making us more competitive
- creating an atmosphere that helped great ideas to thrive
- celebrating our uniqueness

During this time we also began talking about creating an inclusive culture and creating metrics for measuring such. Strategic objectives were being created in most every organization that talked about hiring and promoting at all levels; recognizing, developing, and using diverse employee talent; increasing the use of mentoring; building relationships and alliances with local communities and highly diverse colleges and universities; and building a bidirectional line of open and honest communication. All of this was backed by numerous programs and initiatives intended to support the stated strategic objectives. Things were starting to solidify in terms of actions and commitments. The entirety of all of these things was years beyond our previous training. We had moved away from compliance-related training into logical reasoning attendant to increasing growth in our organizations.

During this same time, I watched a video by Joel Barker entitled *Wealth, Innovation and Diversity*, which in my opinion was the best, most explicit depiction of why we should value diversity in our organizations. Barker presented something comparable to figure 23.1.

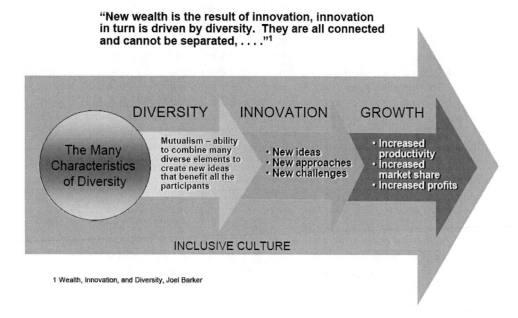

Figure 23.1. Growth, Innovation, Ideas, and Inclusion

In this video, Barker says the following:

Now it is time to begin to connect wealth, innovation, and diversity more clearly. We've seen how diversity sets the stage for new ideas and how mutualism manifests those ideas into new combinations. Another way to describe these new ideas is as innovations. And successful innovations add new value to the world. New value creates new wealth. And, according to the Economist magazine, as much as 40 percent of all the increased wealth in the world each year comes from innovation. So ongoing innovation enlarges the economic pie from which the whole world can dine. While there are several kinds of innovations, I have found that one kind, in particular, adds the most new value and the most new wealth. I have labeled these "paradigm-shifting" innovations.

What Barker refers to as "paradigm-shifting" innovations, we previously discussed as "disruptive technologies." Disruptive technologies are those technologies that exist in the gaps of pure disciplines, at the intersection of the brilliance of pure disciplines. In this scenario, disruptive technologies require the recognition of the value of other disciplines—one of our diversity characteristics, as you may recall.

Around 1999, I remember attending an NAACP luncheon in downtown Fort Wayne, Indiana. It was intended to provide yet additional insight into the value of diversity. While the session itself wasn't as detailed as that presented above, it did stir my emotions. I remember halfway through the session getting up and making a phone call to my boss, saying that I wanted to start a diversity council in our company. His comment, being always open to new initiatives, was, "Go ahead and do it. Sounds great to me." After returning to the office, I did just that. I pulled the demographics from our facility and selected quantities of individuals to be representatives for our diversity council. In staying with our philosophy that diversity was more than compliance characteristics, I selected representation from as many of the multitude of diverse characteristics as I could find. I really wasn't sure what to expect. I remember pulling together our first collection of individuals called the diversity council. One of the first questions I was asked in that opening session was, "Isn't diversity supposed to be gender and race predominantly?" I knew right then and there if our own group possessed a lack of understanding, and couldn't differentiate between diversity as we defined it and compliance characteristics, the general population was certainly going to be confused.

To help the general employee population better understand what we meant by diversity, we would take each diversity-related characteristic and do an entire sixteen-foot-wide by nine-foot-tall display every other month. The displays received a lot of attention. In fact, the displays received so much attention that other businesses within our overall company began borrowing our displays for their facilities. Over the years our diversity council changed personnel, as most time spent was voluntary, but the passion was always there. I really believe we got it, and it was our purpose in life to help others better understand it. We never meant to change people's minds on a given diverse characteristic, only to heighten their awareness to all aspects of that characteristic in hopes they would develop a more open mind to differences. Having grown up in a very diverse neighborhood as a child, I never really felt animosity against an entire diverse characteristic, but that wasn't to say I didn't like certain people, whether they be mean, rude, or obnoxious.

Interestingly enough, the generations of people we call "Generation X" and "Generation Y/Nexters" really do get it. They are the most accepting of differences in people. In fact, most in these two cohort groups don't see any value in even discussing varying diversity characteristics. They simply already accept these many differences. In fact, as I go around the country doing generational awareness presentations, I routinely hear stories that are indicative of how open these cohorts are to diversity of every kind. At no time has anyone in either of these two groups led me to believe they would even waste one minute on gender, race, or ethnicity discussions. They take it for granted that people from all diverse groups are their friends, colleagues, parents, or grandparents. Inclusivity and acceptance of diversity is their norm, as I hope someday will be the case for all human beings.

Chapter 24

Effective Communication Skills

In its broadest sense, communication may be considered a chain of events in which the message serves as the basic link. The chain connects the transmitter to the receiver. Feedback provides some assurance of consistency in the encoding and decoding process.

Looking back through the window of time provides some fascinating communication milestones:

- 20000 BC—Approximate date of earliest prehistoric cave drawings
- 3500 BC—Egyptians developed hieroglyphics
- 2500 BC—Egyptians invented papyrus
- 1800 BC—First true alphabet developed in Middle East
- 540 BC—First public library in Athens
- 300 BC—Hindus invented numerals
- 63 BC—Shorthand system invented
- AD 105—Chinese developed paper
- AD 1477—First printing press
- AD 1591—First post office in England
- AD 1822—First phonograph
- AD 1837—Telegraph invented
- AD 1876—Telephone invented
- AD 1877—Phonograph invented
- AD 1923—Television invented
- AD 1965—First telecommunications satellite system launched
- AD 1975—Sony introduced Betamax
- AD 1978—Magnavox introduced the first laser video disc player

A few observations related to our advances in communications technology:

- Communication is a basic human activity.
- The world has become smaller because of advances in communications technology.
- Communication is not always accomplished successfully.
- To communicate effectively requires clarity of mind and singleness of purpose.
- Conviction produces authoritative statements that can be carried into the hearts of receivers.
- Effective communication between two or more people requires a meeting of the minds.

Figure 24.1 reflects the basic communications model.

The model depicted in this figure illustrates how a message is sent through some form of communication medium to the receiver. Notice that the message is encoded by the sender and decoded by the receiver. The process of encoding and decoding is very specific to the individuals involved.

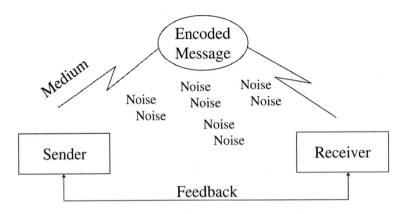

Figure 24.1. Basic Communications Model

Numerous aspects of an individual's life impact the ability to encode and decode a given message. For example, during a negotiation, we may be on edge, looking for some form of hidden meaning in what was being said. This obviously taints our perspective of the incoming message. And further, anything that gets said might be interpreted in a manner inconsistent with the intent of the sender. It is easy to see, therefore, how anger, fear, uneasiness, and even joy, happiness, or any other emotion can cause disruption in the manner in which the message is encoded or decoded. How often have we heard another party say, "That's not quite what I meant." This type of statement is clearly a miscommunication, in that the intended message was either encoded incorrectly or simply decoded differently than that intended.

Encoding and Decoding Skills

Encoding skills include writing and speaking. Decoding skills include listening and reading.

Written Communication

When involved in written communication:

- Determine the purpose of the message.
- Collect and evaluate the facts needed.
- Organize the material into principal topics.
- Prepare first draft using conversational style of writing (i.e., write like you speak).
- Consider the intended receiver (who is the audience?).
- Review the text.

Major advantages of written communication include:

- Displays authority
- Usually more accurate than verbal communication
- Verifiable
- There exists a degree of permanence
- High retention rate by receiver
- Makes for accurate and speedy reproduction

Major disadvantages of written communication include:

- If the situation is changing, the written text may be outdated soon
- It may not take into account the reading ability of the recipient
- Slower feedback than oral communication

Speaking Skills

When making a presentation or simply speaking with another individual, the following should be considered.

What are you selling?—This asks why you are making the presentation.

To whom are you selling it?—Know your audience!

Against what are you competing?—Consider the emotional needs of your audience. For example:

- If there exist fear on the part of the listener, the message might curtail his or her prestige, authority, or advancement opportunities.
- The listener might be unwilling to take on something new.
- The listener might be unwilling to leave the beaten path.
- In what environment is the message to be received? Is it friendly, supportive, hostile, or, is there organized hostility? Organized hostility is the worst kind of environment to speak in. If the organization has properly done its homework, the message is already anticipated and appropriate or inappropriate responses are most likely waiting.

Basic Rules for Addressing an Audience

Talking in front of people can very intimidating, to say the least. Even the most experienced speaker has about two to five minutes of initial adjustment. During this time, frequently, the speaker is looking for a friendly member of the audience to look to for reassurance that things are progressing well. When I speak in front of people, I routinely look for those individuals who smile or nod in a positive manner. Seeking out these people and further looking to them during the speech help to make me feel more comfortable with the presentation. Body language on the part of the audience, the speaker's self-confidence, the speaker's knowledge of the subject matter, time of day/night, physical aspects of the speaker (is he or she hungry, etc.) all go a long way to the overall quality of the speech by the presenter.

Basic rules when addressing an audience that will help to make the presentation a more meaningful experience for the receivers include:

- Keep the presentation simple and brief.
- Rehearse the presentation.
- Speak clearly.
- Keep your back to the wall.
- Speak at an even rate of speed.
- Maintain eye contact.
- Stand erect and control nervous habits. I forever had a bad habit of playing with the change in my pocket. Once this was brought to my attention, I immediately ceased this annoyance.
- Use pause for effect.
- Relax and smile. Chances are that you know as much and most generally more than most everyone in the room. There will always be someone with comparable knowledge to yours, but that's generally the exception, not the rule.
- Avoid excessive statistics.
- Avoid jargon.
- Reaffirm your points in closing.

- Allow time for questions.
- Remember:
  - Visual contact, facial expression, body language, and clothing account for 55 percent of the entire presentation.
  - Tone of your voice accounts for 38 percent of the presentation.
  - The content of the presentation, that is, the words themselves, accounts for only 7 percent of the presentation.

Questions After the Presentation

After any presentation there will generally be two categories of questions asked:

- Probing: "What are your thoughts about . . ." "I'm wondering what your reaction might be to . . ." These types of questions cause the speaker to think more deeply about the subject matter.
- Confrontational: These types of questions are a deliberate attempt to focus the speaker on an area she or he might be avoiding. Confrontation can be positive, if handled openly and honestly without it becoming personal.

Probing questions, which require something other than a "yes" or "no" response, fall into three basic groupings:

- Open-ended: "What is the most effective way to read, write, speak, listen, observe, and visualize?"
- Means-ends: "How do I get the time, energy, and budget to do what is important?" This type of question is looking for how to do something, while conveying the ultimate end objective.
- Means-only: "What do I look for . . ." "Where would I find . . ." This type of question is similar to the above, only it does not provide insight into the final outcome.

Nonverbal Communication Skills

Nonverbal communication skills, as the words imply, are those skills that are basically seen as opposed to heard. They generally fall into four broad categories.

- Physical—includes facial expressions, sense of touch and smell, and body motions
- Aesthetic—creative expression, such as playing instrumental music, dancing, painting, and sculpturing
- Signs—mechanical in nature, such as signal flags, twenty-one-gun salute, horns, and sirens
- Symbolic—makes use of religious entities or other status

Listening Skills

Effective listening is very difficult. It takes a special form of patience. Most of us tend to be thinking about what we are going to say when the speaker is done, and therefore miss some of what is being said. This is complicated by the fact that we can generally think faster than an individual can speak. This "downtime" allows our mind to wander in a different direction rather than to be focused on the speaker. Our ability to context-switch between what we are thinking about and the speaker is directly related to our being able to participate in an effective communication exchange.

A good listener:

- Usually make more informed decisions, because inputs received are more thorough
- Learns more in a given period of time, therefore saving time
- Encourages others to listen to what he or she says because the listener appears more attentive and better mannered

Listening is hard work. It is characterized by:

- A faster heart rate
- Quicker blood circulation
- A small rise in body temperature

A set of guidelines to follow when listening are:

- Prepare to listen—you can't listen if you are talking.
- Recognize your own biases—understand your personal frame of reference. This also implies that you not only understand your frame of reference, but that of the speaker as well.
- Resists distractions—good listeners look and act interested.
- Keep an open mind—don't feel threatened or insulted.
- Find an area of interest—find ways to make the message relevant to yourself.
- Acknowledge the speaker—let the speaker know that he or she has your attention.
- Show some empathy—this creates a climate that encourages others to communicate openly and honestly.
- Hold your fire—be patient, don't interrupt. Let the speaker finish her or his thoughts completely.
- Listen critically and delay judgment—thorough listening produces enlightened judgment.
- Judge the content not the delivery—ask for clarity when you don't understand. (although recall, when we discussed basic rules for addressing an audience, that only 7 percent of the presentation is content-related).
- Capitalize on thought speed—we think four times faster than the communicator speaks; what, therefore, do we do with the extra time?

Reading Skills

Effective reading skills are essential to our very existence and provide a depth of understanding. Efficient reading skills, the speed at which we read, are taught in numerous speed reading seminars around the globe. Key factors to consider when reading are:

- Comprehension is our ability to understand what is read.
- Determine the writer's point of view.
- Determine whether you accept or reject the thesis of the argument.
- Be discriminating in what you read—effective managers read only the most applicable material. It is not uncommon that I will receive as many as forty e-mail messages and twenty phone calls in a day. To be honest, I do not have time to read every e-mail. Therefore, it is only natural that I might spend more or less time on a given e-mail depending on its perceived applicability at the time.

Skipping Judiciously

When confronted with having to read large amounts of information, it is important to be able to read enough information to become knowledgeable on the subject, but not have to read every word. To this end, skimming or skipping through the material becomes necessary. The process described below may of value for this purpose:

- Scan the table of contents for a rough idea of what the book or material is all about.
- Read the first couple of sentences of paragraphs of those sections with greatest applicability.
- Read thoroughly those sections that require greater understanding.

Communication Barriers

In the communications model presented earlier, the message that was sent from the sender and encoded was passed through some form of communication medium. As the message passes through this medium, there is noise and the like that permutes the message into something potentially different than that which was sent. This noise may be identified as barriers to effective communication. Below are listed other barriers to effective communication:

- Noise—noise can be actual static or anything that distracts from the intended message.
- Lack of feedback—one of the most detrimental effects on a speaker can be a lack of feedback. Even as employees, we want to know what others think of our performance, whether it is good or bad, at least we know. With knowledge about how we are performing, we can make informed decisions on how to enhance our performance or simply take other action.
- Incorrect medium of communication—all too often we want to send a message and choose a medium that may be inappropriate. For example, if we were to ask our boss for a raise, we probably would choose a personal medium where we set up a meeting time and sit down to discuss our concern. It would be less effective if we were to ask for our increase through an e-mail or the like.
- Mental barriers—
  - arrogance of the sender
  - assumption about the sender's logic or rationality
  - sender assumes that he or she is logical or rational
  - sender's misconceptions, self-interest, or strong emotions
  - receiver not ready to receive
  - problems with word selections
  - use of abstract words; the more specific one can be, the more doubt that gets removed during the decoding process
  - time and space barriers—finding out the ship is sinking after we are vertical is of lesser value than knowing earlier
  - empathy and other relationships—seeing ourselves through the eyes of others

Organizational Communication

When we talk about communication channels within an organization, we are usually referring to one of three basic categories:

- Formal—formal channels are those channels established by virtue of the organization's design hierarchy. They are usually clearly identifiable and have a strong relationship to the reporting relationships of the managers and supervisors in the organization.
- Informal—informal communication channels are those typically between peers or others in the horizontal portion of the organization. In this category are work groups.
- Unofficial—these are typically socially oriented groups, that is, friendships, cliques, and the like.

Overloading is a concept used to describe too much information being passed through a given channel. Going back to an earlier example, it's easy for our e-mail basket to overflow. When I receive forty e-mails in a given day, it's not possible to effectively manage that quantity of input and tend to other daily matters. Therefore, one might suggest that my e-mail medium is overloaded.

It's also important to recognize the audience's needs and the benefits to them of receiving the message. The more relevant a message to the receiver, the more likely the message will be focused on and subsequently understood as intended.

Conducting an Effective Meeting

In a nutshell, conducting an effective meeting can be simply stated in a few quick steps:

- Establish meeting objectives
- Prepare meeting agenda
- Determine timing and physical arrangements
- Identify and invite people who can make a contribution
- Brief participants in advance
- Consider matters of protocol

Chapter 25

Change Management—People, the Hardest Part

When we discuss change management in the context of program/project management, we typically think of contract or program changes. While this is true, that type of change management is covered elsewhere in this text. This chapter's discussion of change management is premised on the idea change happens all the time and is no more prevalent than when bringing together a new program, in possibly a new business, and generally more often than not with a new team of colleagues. To this end, it is imperative we discuss change management as it impacts individuals involved in a new endeavor. The impact of this type of change is relatively the same as in any other change involving emotional reactions—and all change involves emotional reaction. While it is critical to understand the vision, goals, and objectives of the change, and the processes, methodologies, practices, and technologies employed to help ensure the change, there is probably nothing more important than managing the emotional impact of the change. Doing a Google search on the phrase "culture trumps strategy" reflects numerous organizations, company presidents, and book authors using it. To a large extent, I agree. Maintaining a healthy perspective while initiating and managing the currents of change is critical.

This chapter will examine change management from four perspectives:

- Within the context of organizational development
- Models of change management
- Change management as a process
- Activities or phases of the change management process
- Why change fails

Organizational Development—The Context of Change

In looking at change, it is important to understand the larger organizational development (OD) umbrella process. This section will review organizational change definitions and types, the definition of OD, and the historical development of OD.

Organizational change can be either remedial or developmental. Remedial change is designed to change or modify an existing situation, essentially to remedy the situation. For example, remedial change might be designed to improve poor performance of a product or service, reduce burnout in the workplace, or perhaps address large budget deficits.

Developmental change is designed to make a successful situation even more successful. Examples of this type of change include expanding the number of customers served or increasing the already good sales of a product or service.

Change can also be unplanned or planned. Unplanned change occurs because of a major, sudden surprise to the organization or business. Examples of this might include the loss of a senior- or executive-level manager, a public relations issue (think Tylenol), or a product performance issue (again, Tylenol).

Planned change, on the other hand, occurs when leaders recognize the need for a situational change and therefore organize, plan, and execute in accordance with a predefined set of activities on a specified timeline.

OD provides an overarching framework for better understanding organizational change. OD is an adaptive process for planning and implementing change. It is intended to create an environment where the organization can, in time and with training, lead its own change.

OD has many different yet similar definitions. Cummings and Worley (2009) define OD as "a systemwide application and transfer of behavioral science knowledge to the planned development, improvement, and reinforcement of the strategies, structures, and processes that lead to organization effectiveness" (pp. 1–2).

The key elements of most all definitions of OD include:

- Applies to changes in the strategy, structure, and/or processes of an *entire system*
- Is based on the application of leadership, group dynamics, strategy, and other related behavior science interventions
- Oriented to improving organizational effectiveness

Cummings and Worley suggest there are five predecessor stems of organizational development: laboratory training, action research, normative, quality of work life, and strategic change.

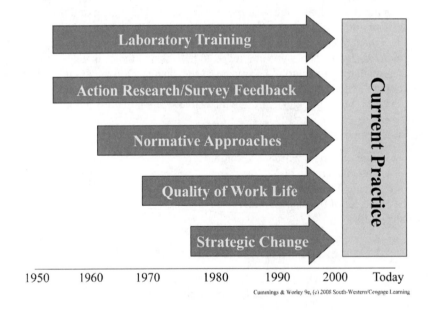

Cummings & Worley 9e, (c) 2008 South-Western/Cengage Learning

Figure 25.1. Five Stems of Organizational Development

Laboratory Training

This original type of training was referred to as sensitivity training. The intent was for groups to be taped as they operated in a given situation. They would subsequently review the taped sessions, observe their own and others' behavior, and ideally learn how to move forward in a more congenial and effective manner. This form of team building is one of the most common forms of OD today that stems from this early historical behavioral approach. This type of training provided awareness that feedback was critical to human improvement, and the lessons learned from this experience were transferrable to other related situations.

Action Research

Action research is designed to be closely aligned to organizational members with an intent to be iteratively incorporated into a solution space. In action research, data is collected, action planning is jointly designed with the leadership team, the identified actions are implemented, and subsequent data is collected, thereby creating yet another iteration.

Normative Approaches

Normative approaches believe a human relations approach represents the "one best way" to manage organizations. They tend to center around leadership historical pursuits, namely, trait leadership theories and behavioral leadership theories. These two approaches have predominately given way to a contingency view that acknowledges the influence of the external environment, technology, and other forces.

Quality of Work Life

Quality of work life focuses on how employees can contribute more to running the organization so it can be more flexible, productive, and competitive. Employee involvement, total quality management, six sigma, lean, department quality teams (DQT), and similar initiatives fall under this type of movement.

Strategic Change

Strategic change involves improving the alignment among an organization's environment, strategy, and organizational design. It includes efforts to improve both the organization's relationship to its environment and the fit between its technical, political, and cultural systems.

There are three major trends shaping change in organizations:

- *Globalization* envelops the global economy with emerging new markets, changing the markets and environments in which organizations operate, as well as how they function.
- *Information technology* (IT) includes the equipment or interconnected system that is used in the automatic acquisition, storage, management, movement, control, display, switching, interchange, transmission, or reception of data or information. IT has redefined the traditional business model by changing how work is performed, how knowledge is used, where work is performed, and how the cost of doing business is calculated.
- *Managerial innovation* involves new organizational forms, such as networks, strategic alliances, multinational corporations, and virtual corporations. It provides organizations with new ways to think about how to manufacture goods and deliver services.

Models of Change Management

There are numerous models of change management. Four of these models are:

- Lewin's Model
- Action Research
- Appreciative Inquiry (Positive Model)
- General Model

Lewin's model, named after Kurt Lewin, is concerned with unfreezing, moving, and refreezing. During unfreezing, there is an effort to reduce the many forces that are in favor of maintaining the current state. Lewin suggests (Cummings and Worley, 2009) "decreasing those forces maintaining the status quo produces less tension and resistance than increasing forces for change and consequently is a more effective change strategy" (p. 24). Lewin's model is depicted in figure 25.2.

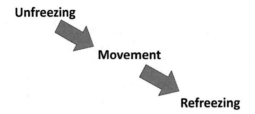

Figure 25.2. Lewin's Model of Planned Change

Action research is a planned change model in which the organization-provided information is used to develop and guide subsequent change action. The basic phases of this model include identifying the problem, gathering data, working with leadership to develop a joint action plan, performing the action, and then continuing to gather additional information in preparation for a subsequent cyclical event. Figure 25.3 depicts this model.

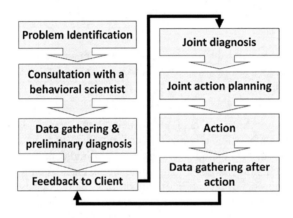

Figure 25.3. Action Research Model

The positive model, or what is commonly called appreciative inquiry, is another planned change model where the effort is focused on what the organization is doing well. This, then, forms subsequent action with a new envisioned future state. This model is depicted in figure 25.4.

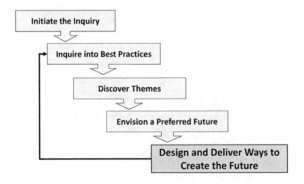

Figure 25.4. Appreciative Inquiry Model (Positive Model)

Cummings and Worley provide what they term a general model of planned change (figure 25.5). In this model, they suggest four basic phases of planned change. Phase one is the act of entering into the contract for planned change. This phase is designed to get everybody on board with the concept. It recognizes resources and cultural implications will be required and exist. Phase two is diagnosing the problem. This is very similar to other planned change models in that it involves gathering information and data, analyzing the situation based on the gathered information, and then preparing a planning and implementation (phase three) approach. Institutionalizing the change and evaluating the effectiveness and efficiency of the change is phase four.

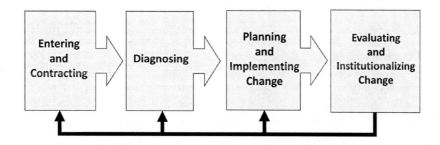

Figure 25.5. General Model of Planned Change

Activities or Phases of the Change Management Process

Change is not the same thing as transitioning. Change and transitions are different in that change is an event, it's situational. Examples include such things as receiving a new boss, new office, and even new processes. Transition, on the other hand, is a process with activities and attendant products. Transitions can be extremely emotional. They have the potential for tremendous upheaval. Individuals in the transitional phase of change are likely to experience emotions similar to those experienced during a grieving process.

The basic process for change includes three concepts:

- Letting go of the current and previous state
- Moving through the transitional aspects of the change
- Forging a new beginning

The starting point of letting go of the current and previous state is dealing with the many challenges of leaving the old behind. This includes such things as emotional ties, new infrastructure changes, and the inevitable organizational changes attendant to people, processes, practices, and methodologies. Things as simple as how an employee might fill out a travel expense report become highly emotionally charged process changes.

During this initial phase, we should recognize the potentially crippling personal effect of the process (likened to Kübler-Ross model of grieving):

- Denial—this can't be happening
- Anger—why do we have to be going through this?
- Bargaining—what if we simply did . . .
- Depression—loss of things past and loss of future differences to current people, practices . . .
- Acceptance—I understand and recognize my limited ability to change it, so let's make do

It is important during this phase that we recognize who is losing what. Leaders must:

- Understand exactly what is changing
- Understand the potential for secondary changes and what they may be
- Understand who is going to be losing something—department heads, line workers
- Recognize the "way things are" is what helps individuals feel comfortable and at home
- Understand that if everyone is going to feel a loss of something big in the "organization's history," for example, mergers, then a major effort to celebrate the past is important
- Understand the loss is extremely personal to each individual—it probably doesn't work to suggest, "I know how you feel."

During this time, exaggerations may become commonplace. In fact, "overreacting" is relative, not the same for everyone. Generally, it is the losses, not the changes, to which people are reacting. It is a piece of each individual's world being lost, not necessarily our piece. Additionally, overreaction is actually quite "normal" and not "overreaction" at all. This is no different than any one of us when dealt a stressful situation, especially one that might impact our ability to provide for ourselves or our family.

According to Bridges (2009), it is important that we make known what is over and what isn't. There are three potential side effects of not being clear on this:

- People will not stop doing anything; they will try to do it all
- People make their own decisions about what to keep doing and what to stop, causing inconsistency and chaos
- People toss out all of the past stuff; loss of good things, information, processes, practices, and so forth may occur

Bridges says we should celebrate the endings of the past. Treat the past with respect; do not denigrate the past. Let people keep a piece of the past; create a banner of historical accomplishments and provide a vision of continuity from the past to the future. During the many mergers of the defense industry, we used to create a multi-panel wall display from beginning to current of products produced by the organization being merged. In doing this, everyone involved could see the many great things that had been created, and perhaps most importantly, feel a sense of pride and completeness of this previous time.

Why Change Fails

Change fails for numerous reasons. Perhaps no one has thought about endings or planned to manage their impact on individuals as described above. Perhaps the end result was not clearly communicated. It may very well be a compelling logic wasn't conveyed to justify the change being proposed. Niccolò Machiavelli basically felt unplanned incremental change is worse than planned intentional action. He said, "in taking possession of a state, the conqueror should well reflect as to the harsh measures that may be necessary, and then execute them at a single blow. . . . Cruelties should be committed all at once." Dragging out a change with changing end results is detrimental to a successful change.

During the change process:

- People's anxiety rises and their motivation falls
- People miss more work than any other time
- Things not done well in the past will get worse and done "less" well
- People will be overloaded; priorities will get confused; information will be miscommunicated; important tasks will go undone
- People will become polarized:
  - Some move forward
  - Others want to go back

- • Discord rises
- • Teamwork is undermined
- • Loyalty is variable
- • The organization becomes vulnerable to outside attacks
  - • Disorganized and tired, people respond slowly
  - • People may look for ways to "pay back" the organization
  - • People may even sabotage the organization

Change can be a tremendous rush for some. There is not necessarily "that's the way we've always done it" mentality. In many instances, it is a chance to seek disruptive technologies, policies, and practices; those not found in the pureness of the past, but instead at the intersection of the past and the future. In William Bridges' *Managing Transitions*, he writes:

the outlook, attitudes, values, self-images, and ways of thinking that were functional in the past have to "die" before people can be ready for life in the present. Moses took care of transition's ending phase when he led his people out of Egypt, but it was the 40 years in the neutral zone wilderness that got Egypt out of his people. It won't take you 40 years, but you aren't going to be able to do it in a few weeks either. (2009, p. 43)

Transition is a tremendous opportunity for innovation. During this time:

- • Provide training on "thinking out of the box"
- • Help employees to "see" what innovation looks like
- • Form groups to look for innovation between the "purity" of the existing products/services (i.e., in the gaps)
- • Emphasize diversity of thought—growth comes from innovation; innovations comes from ideas; ideas come from people—all people (inclusivity)

In discussing the new world being created, define the purpose behind and outcome being sought by the proposed changes. Paint a portrait of how the end will look; explicitly create a visualization of the good stuff. Be sure to identify a step-by-step plan for phasing in the end result (plan), and provide as many as possible with roles to play in the plan and the eventual outcome. In doing this last step, the individuals undergoing the change, the ones most likely impacted, become part of the solution and are not left to sit at the sidelines waiting for a communication of how the change is progressing.

It is most important to avoid problems with defining the purpose for the change. In some instances, there may not be a purpose; none that stands up to scrutiny anyway. There may be an idea, but it is not communicated effectively; in this instance, management will lose their followers. Or perhaps the proposed purpose isn't the real purpose; it is a smoke screen to hide the real purpose. For example: we're simply looking to restructure a bit; real reason: we're looking to reduce our workforce.

To quote Heraclitus, a Greek philosopher known for his doctrine of change being central to the universe (535 BC–475 BC), "the only constant is change."

Appendix A

Evaluating the Program Plan

Once the program management planning phase for the program has been completed, the program team is ready to begin execution. The newly created plan will form the basis for all immediately identifiable activity. We say all immediately identifiable activities, because, as most program managers recognize, a plan will inevitably change. But, from the beginning one might ask, "How good is the plan that the program team is preparing to execute?"

To answer this question, we need to perform some form of evaluation of the plan. As one might guess, even performing an evaluation has a process. What follows is a complete program management plan evaluation. For this evaluation, a program was selected to use in implementing the program management planning process. The program was an awarded cost-plus contract consisting of engineering development with production options. The contract value was approximately $40,000,000 at sell price, and extended over a five-year period. Of the $40,000,000 selling price, $20,000,000 was for engineering development, leaving $20,000,000 for production options. Two of the five years were dedicated to the development of the product, with the remaining three years dedicated to the product's production. What follows in the remaining paragraphs is an overview of a process for performing an evaluation.

Committee of Stakeholders

The process for performing an evaluation begins with the creation of a committee of stakeholders. A committee of stakeholders should be formed that represents organizational interests and the program under study. The committee plays an integral role by assisting in the following:

- Generating the program's goals and objectives
- Generating evaluation instruments
- Validating data-gathering items and instruments

Primary Activities

The primary activities associated with performing an evaluation include:

- Identify and organize the stakeholder group
- Develop goals and objectives
- Develop data collection instruments
- Identify the target program
- Collect data
- Perform analysis of data
- Report findings to the stakeholders

Figure A.1 depicts these activities and their proposed duration.

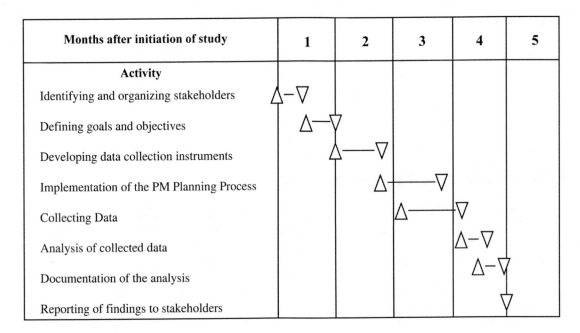

Figure A.1. Evaluation Process Activities

Note, of course, that the duration of each activity varies based on the complexity of the program being evaluated. Figure A.1 is for illustrative purposes only.

Interviewing Program Participants

Part of the process of collecting data is interviewing program participants who participated in the development of the program management cost, schedule, and technical performance measurement baseline. When selecting program participants to be interviewed for the evaluation, is it important that they represent numerous applicable disciplines. In building a home, the disciplines might include:

- Plumbers
- Electricians
- Masonry
- Framers
- Finishers

When working with an organization that develops hardware and/or software systems, the disciplines would most likely be:

- Hardware engineering
- Software engineering

- System engineering
- Accounting
- Quality assurance

Outcome-Based Evaluation Methodology

There are many types of evaluation methodologies that could be used. This discussion assumes the use of an outcome-based evaluation methodology. Outcome-based evaluation utilizes the following steps:

- Identify the desired outcomes of the program to be studied
- Identify behaviors acceptable as evidence that the outcomes have been realized
- Create data collection instruments and procedures to collect data to determine whether the acceptable behaviors have been demonstrated
- Execute the data collection procedures to collect the data
- Transcribe the data, which provides individuals other than the researcher of the particular study with the opportunity to make their own interpretations of the results
- Interpret the data and make judgments as to whether the behaviors acceptable as evidence were demonstrated, the outcomes were satisfied, and the questions can be addressed from the findings

The data collected helps to determine whether the behaviors acceptable as evidence were demonstrated and the outcomes subsequently satisfied.

For example, given the outcome, "create a cost, schedule, and technical performance measurement baseline," behaviors acceptable as evidence that this baseline was not only created, but created with adequacy, might include:

- Was the work adequately defined?
- Are tasks depicted as time-phased interdependent activities?
- Have resources been assigned to activities?
- Has a time-phased resource budget been generated?

Our objective, then, is to collect evidence that these activities were properly performed, supporting our making judgments about the adequacy of the objective being satisfied, that is, that a cost, schedule, and technical performance measurement baseline was created.

A sample interview item that might be asked of our program participants could be: "Which documents did your functional organization use to extract its stated and derived requirements?"

This question serves two purposes:

- It establishes whether requirements were identified at all.
- It establishes whether requirements were identified from the right contract documents.

Another sample interview item might be: "Please describe the organization and sequencing of the work to be performed." This second question allows judgments to be made as to the quality of the baseline, with implications to the three formal contract documents:

- Statement of work
- Specification
Contract provisions

An example of a sample Likert Scale item might look like figure A.2.

	SA	A	U	D	SD	Statement
1.	1	2	3	4	5	The contract statement of work provided a vital source for program requirements
2.	1	2	3	4	5	The contract specification provided a vital source for program requirements
3.	1	2	3	4	5	Other functional organizations provided a source for program requirements

Figure A.2. Sample Likert Scale Question

Following are samples of multiple-choice questions that might be used as a data collection instrument.

- Relative to identifying the requirements for purposes of organizing the work, I believe that:
  - all contract documents were thoroughly scanned
  - all contract documents were minimally scanned
  - some contract documents were scanned more thoroughly than others
  - not all contract documents were scanned
- Relative to the assignment of costs to the work breakdown structure elements, I am convinced:
  - all costs were allocated appropriately based on sound evidence
  - costs are allocated appropriately in most cases
  - costs allocated do not appear to consider the actual effort of the work to be performed
  - when implemented, most cost estimates will require major revisions

Figure A.3 depicts a sample observation form as a data collection instrument for evaluation.

1. **Used contract statement of work, specification and/or contract provisions for extracting program stated or derived requirements**

   No utililzation   ( )   ( )   ( )   ( )   Continuous utilization of
   of documents   documents

2. **Used higher-level schedules for purposes of generating lower-level schedules.**

   No utilization of   ( )   ( )   ( )   ( )   Continuous use of
   higher-level   higher-level schedules
   schedules

Figure A.3. Example of an Observation Form

Summary of Outcome-Based Evaluation Data Analysis Method

The list below, then, summarizes the data analysis method for outcome-based evaluations.

- Identify outcomes that represent the desired outcomes for the program to be studied
- Identify behaviors/activities acceptable as evidence that outcomes have been satisfied
- Create data collection instruments and procedures to collect data that subsequently aid in the determination of whether the behaviors acceptable as evidence have been demonstrated
- Execute the data collection procedures to collect the data as defined by the data collection instrument methodology
- Transcribe the resultant data collected. This provides individuals, other than the researcher, with the opportunity to read the results of data collection instruments and make their own interpretation of those results
- Interpret the transcribed data and make judgments as to whether:
    - the behaviors acceptable as evidence were demonstrated
    - the outcomes were satisfied
    - the research questions can be addressed from the findings

Appendix B

Executing the Program Plan

A great deal of the thought in this chapter comes from the work of Quentin Fleming (1992).

Once the performance measurement baseline has been established, the next step is to monitor and report progress against the plan. While it might seem fitting to do a comprehensive review of all cost and schedule budgets, a more efficient way is to monitor performance on an exception basis, commonly referred to as management by exception.

In a management cost/schedule control system, performance variances cause particular attention to be focused only on those areas that have exceeded reasonable, previously set limitations. These reasonable limits are called "variance thresholds" and are nothing more than outer limit cost and schedule parameters. Any time such parameters or thresholds are exceeded, the management cost/schedule control system procedures call for special type of analysis to take place and for formal reporting of the results of the analysis to the customer. These special analyses are documented in what's called "variance analysis reports" (VARs) or, sometimes, "performance analysis reports" (PARs). Therefore, in a management cost/schedule control system, when a performance threshold has been penetrated beyond a previously agreed to limit, a flag is waved, indicating some form of action is required.

The customer, behaving in much the same manner as the program manager, sees only a small portion of these VARs. The customer, therefore, is also managing by exception, only at a higher level. Internal to the company, however, program management may go through all variances to assess their full impact on the program, and take corrective action before the problem becomes sufficient enough to be raised to the customer.

Variance thresholds may be expressed in either absolute terms (e.g., $10,000 over or under a budget value; or ten days ahead or behind schedule) or as a percentage of some particular base (e.g., 10 percent ahead or behind a cost value or schedule date). Positive variances, an under-budget or ahead of schedule condition, are sometimes allowed to exist at twice the value of a negative condition. This is true because typically positive variances are more likely related to a poor plan than to poor performance. However, there is no universal agreement on this issue, and many organizations set the same threshold values for both positive and negative variances. A chronic positive performance condition could, however, be reflecting a more fundamental problem, for example, the basic method for planning the work in the first place, that is, the distribution of effort in the budgeted cost of work scheduled (BCWS).

During the contract's performance period, management cost/schedule control system variance thresholds may be tracked at three distinct points of reference:

- Cumulative to Date—reflecting performance on a cumulative, or total basis, through the current reporting period.
- Current Month—focusing only on the last month of performance.
- Estimate At Complete—which incorporates all actions to date and makes a projection to the end of the program.

It is not uncommon for the buying customer to impose thresholds at the cumulative to date point, and if it's a government customer, for all three points to be imposed. There is a group of management cost/schedule control system followers that believe reporting at all three points is excessive. This group takes the position that cumulative to date thresholds are all that should be required for good performance monitoring. They claim that the current month threshold is too prone to accounting fluctuations to measure progress, and results only in excessive paperwork (VARs).

As well, there is a mixed opinion on the value of setting estimate at complete (EAC) thresholds. Some claim that the EAC is too subjective. However, since one of the primary purposes of imposing a management cost/schedule control system is to obtain a reliable EAC, it seems a weak argument to suggest that EAC isn't worth monitoring.

We need to also remember that a management cost/schedule control system is simply a quantitative tool to assist the program manager in managing his or her program. It, by itself, is not the entirety of the skills or tools required to manage a program effectively.

A variance analysis report will vary significantly in format as the tool and the organization change. Figure B.1 depicts an example of a company and tool-specific variance analysis report.

A few things to take note of in figure B.1:

- All of the formulas are properly displayed, so that anybody reading the VAR can tell how the figures were calculated.
- Monthly and cumulative (cum) numbers are provided for each primary activity. In this case, the PES project level and the software development effort.
- Notice also the thresholds on the right side of the form. There are no standard thresholds for the industry; each customer, or minimally the contractor, imposes these prior to contract award. It is, as stated above, the manner in which management by exception takes place, and therefore, is really very subjective and up to the program manager and/or the customer. The program manager might, in some cases, set tighter thresholds than the customer so that the program manager will see a problem before it hits the customer's higher-level thresholds.

All variance analysis reports should meet four basic requirements:

- They should be prepared by the responsible cost account manager, the one closest to the variant condition, and not by an outside planner, scheduler, or budgeter.
- They must explain separately each cost and schedule variance and its present and potential impact to the program.
- They should state the actions taken, or to be taken, to solve the problem.
- The variance analysis report should be reviewed with, and approved by, the next higher level of management.

What the formalization of the variance analysis process does in effect is to require that a contractor go through a series of defined steps any time its performance is outside of the plan by a previously tolerance. It also requires such analysis be documented, so that a contractor's program manager and, if required, the customer may trace through each problem area at a subsequent date.

In summary, then:

Variance thresholds:

- Are pre-established at the beginning of the program
- Identify areas requiring management attention
- Need not match the contract thresholds set by the customer
- Can be changed over time

PES02
PAGE 1

7/16/20xx
11:22:07

Purdue Electronic Systems
Detail Variance Analysis
DATA AS OF: JUN-20xx
Selection Criteria: ALL DATA INCLUDED

LEGEND: Latest Revised Estimate (LRE) = Actuals thru JUN-20xx + ETC thru end of project
Out of Tolerance (OT) -- Elements with "*" are out of tolerance

$$\text{Cost Variance (CV)} = \text{BCWP} - \text{ACWP} \qquad \text{Cost Variance in \% (CV\%)} = \frac{CV}{BCWP} \qquad \frac{\text{CUM BCWP}}{\text{CUM ACWP}}$$

$$\text{Schedule Variance (SV)} = \text{BCWP} - \text{BCWS} \qquad \text{Schedule Variance in \% (SV\%)} = \frac{SV}{BCWS} \qquad \frac{\text{CUM BCWP}}{\text{CUM BCWS}}$$

$$\text{Independent Estimate At Complete (IEAC)} = \frac{BAC}{CPI} \qquad \text{To Complete Performance Index (TCPI)} = \frac{\text{BAC-CUM BCWP}}{\text{LRE-CUM ACWP}}$$

$$\text{\% Spent1} = \frac{\text{CUM ACWP}}{BAC} \qquad \text{\% Spent 2} = \frac{\text{CUM ACWP}}{LRE} \qquad \text{\% Complete} = \frac{\text{CUM BCWP}}{BAC}$$

$$\text{Cost Performance Index (CPI)} = \frac{\text{CUM BCWP}}{\text{CUM ACWP}}$$

$$\text{Schedule Performance Index (SPI)} = \frac{\text{CUM BCWP}}{\text{CUM BCWS}}$$

Thresholds:
Mon SV (+/-) = $5,000	and 10.00% of	BCWS
Cum SV (+/-) = $10,000	and 7.00% of	BCWS
Mon CV (+/-) = $5,000	and 10.00% of	BCWP
Cum CV (+/-) = $10,000	and 7.00% of	BCWS
LRE (+/-) = $25,000	and 5.00% of	BCWS

WBS ID / DESCRIPTION (* = cost account)	Hours	Tot Burd $	Max Allowed Var (+/-)	OT	Schedule Variance	Schedule Variance %	Cost Variance	Cost Variance %	Other Analysis
PES PROJECT									
Mon BCWS	23,703	1,886,424							
Mon BCWP	28,184	1,521,797	2,370	*	4,481	18.90%			
Mon ACWP	25,090	1,404,303					3,094	10.98%	
Cum BCWS	160,986	9,526,819	11,269	*					
Cum BCWP	144,671	8,564,396			-16,315	-10.13%			
Cum ACWP	147,804	8,666,205					-3,133	-2.17%	
BAC	734,583	41,390,975							CPI: 0.988
LRE	734,822	41,135,102							SPI: 0.899
IEAC	734,822	41,883,009							TCPI: 1.011
									%SPNT1: 20.94%
									%SPNT2: 21.07%
									%COMPL: 20.69%
SOFTWARE DEVELOPMENT									
Mon BCWS	23,518	1,283,304	2,352	*	-4,260	-18.11%			
Mon BCWP	19,258	987,560							
Mon ACWP	13,564	686,775					5,694	29.57%	
Cum BCWS	66,747	3,701,520	4,672	*	-9,459	-14.17%			
Cum BCWP	57,288	3,156,370							
Cum ACWP	53,814	2,957,139					3,474	6.06%	
BAC	434,132	22,990,528							CPI: 1.067
LRE	434,760	23,017,730							SPI: 0.853
IEAC	434,760	21,539,360							TCPI: 0.989
									%SPNT1: 12.86%
									%SPNT2: 12.85%
									%COMPL: 13.73%

Figure B.1. Example Variance Analysis Report

Variance analysis report:

- Is required when variances exceed the thresholds
- Analysis is at the cost account level
- Is a memo for the record

As part of the variance analysis report, causes of the problem must be reported. When discussing the cause of the problem:

- Discuss cost variance and schedule variance separately
- Clearly identify the reason for the variance
- Isolate significant labor rate variances
- Place emphasis on the qualitative, not quantitative, aspects of the problem
- Place emphasis on the specific, not the general
- Place emphasis on only the significant problems, not all problems

When discussing the impact on the program:

- Describe the specific cost, schedule, and technical impact to the program
- Address the intermediate schedules
- Describe the impact to other cost accounts
- Assess the need to revise the estimate to complete the job

Under the corrective action planning portion of the variances analysis report:

- Describe specific actions to be taken to alleviate or minimize the impact of the problem. Examples of poor corrective action plans:
  - None required
  - I plan to work harder
  - I should be able to make up the overrun downstream
- Include the individual or organization responsible for the required action
- Include schedules for the actions and get well dates
- If no corrective action is possible, explain why
- Include results of corrective action plans from previous variance analysis reports
- Examples of poor causes cited for variances include:
  - This cost account is overrun because I spent more than I planned
  - I am overrun because engineering charged more hours than we had agreed
  - I am overrun because I worked more hours than I planned to
  - I used more computer time than I planned to
  - It took longer than I thought

In government contracting, there are three primary management cost/schedule control system report types:

- Contract funds status report (CFSR)—prepared by accounting and the program manager to advise the customer of the funds spent and funds remaining to complete.
- Cost performance report (CPR)—prepared by the program manager to explain the status of the program, reasons for variances from plan, and corrective action undertaken. Requires written analysis of current and cumulative to date variances.
- Cost/schedule status report (C/SSR)—prepared by the program manager to explain the status of the program, reasons for variances from plan, and corrective action undertaken. Requires written analysis of cumulative to date variances only.

Figure B.2 depicts an example of a cost performance report specific to a tool and organization.

Item	Current Period Budgeted Cost Work Sched	Current Period Budgeted Cost Work Pref	Current Period Actual Cost Work Perf	Current Period Variance Sched	Current Period Variance Cost	Budgeted Cost Work Sched	Budgeted Cost Work Pref	Actual Cost Work Perf	Variance Sched	Variance Cost	At Completion Budget	At Completion Latest Revised Est	At Completion Var
AB													
SYSTEM ENGINEERING													
& DESIGN	200.9	173.7	211.2	-27.2	-37.5	2434.4	2273.1	2523	-161.3	-249.9	3606.2	3817.5	-211.3
LABOR	80.4	69.5	85.1	-10.9	-15.6	963.1	898.5	1014.9	-64.5	-116.4	1429	1535.8	-106.8
MATERIAL	0	0	0.1	0	-0.1	0	0	0.3	0	-0.3	0	0.3	-0.3
OTHER DIRECT COSTS	0	0	0.1	0	-0.1	0	0	0.8	0	-0.8	0	0.8	-0.8
TRAVEL	0	0	0	0	0	0	0	0	0	0	0	0	0
OVERHEAD	120.6	104.2	125.9	-16.3	-21.6	1471.3	1374.5	1506.9	-96.8	-132.4	2177.2	2280.5	-103.3
ABAA													
SYSTEM ENGINEERING													
& DESIGN	171.8	117.7	171.8	-54.1	-58.5	2164.6	2060.2	2404.7	-104.4	-344.5	2984.2	3304.1	-319.9
LABOR	68.7	47.1	71.7	-21.7	-24.6	855.6	813.8	969.1	-41.8	-155.3	1181.6	1331.3	-149.7
MATERIAL	0	0	0.1	0	-0.1	0	0	0.3	0	-0.3	0	0.8	-0.3
OTHER DIRECT COSTS	0	0	0.1	0	-0.1	0	0	0.8	0	-0.8	0	0.8	-0.8
TRAVEL	0	0	0	0	0	0	0	0	0	0	0	0	0
OVERHEAD	103.1	70.6	104.2	-32.5	-33.6	1309	1246.4	1434.4	-62.7	-188.1	1802.7	1971.7	-169
12345													
SYSTEM ENGINEERING	96.1	69.9	151.1	-26.1	-81.2	1862.9	1824	2202.2	-38.9	-378.2	1862.9	2210.1	-347.2
LABOR	38.4	28	61.6	-10.5	-33.6	735.1	719.5	887.4	-15.6	-167.9	735.1	890.7	-155.6
MATERIAL	0	0	0.1	0	-0.1	0	0	0.3	0	-0.3	0	0.3	-0.3
OTHER DIRECT COSTS	0	0	0	0	-0.1	0	0	0.8	0	-0.8	0	0.8	-0.8
TRAVEL	0	0	0	0	0	0	0	0	0	0	0	0	0
OVERHEAD	57.7	42	89.3	-15.7	-47.3	1127.8	1104.5	1313.7	-23.3	-209.3	1127.8	1318.4	-190.6
98765													
DOC SUPPORT (SYSTEM)	75.7	47.7	25	-28	22.7	301.7	236.2	202.4	-65.6	33.7	327.8	228.2	99.6
LABOR	30.3	19.1	10.1	-11.2	9	120.5	94.3	81.7	-26.2	12.6	130.9	92.1	38.8
MATERIAL	0	0	0	0	0	0	0	0	0	0	0	0	0
OTHER DIRECT COSTS	0	0	0	0	0	0	0	0	0	0	0	0	0
TRAVEL	0	0	0	0	0	0	0	0	0	0	0	0	0
OVERHEAD	45.4	28.6	14.9	-16.8	13.7	181.2	141.9	120.7	-39.3	21.1	196.9	136.2	60.7
45678													
SYSTEM ENGR. MGT.	0	0	0	0	0	0	0	0	0	0	672.6	746.5	-73.9
LABOR	0	0	0	0	0	0	0	0	0	0	267.4	300.4	-33
MATERIAL	0	0	0	0	0	0	0	0	0	0	0	0	0
OTHER DIRECT COSTS	0	0	0	0	0	0	0	0	0	0	0	0	0
TRAVEL	0	0	0	0	0	0	0	0	0	0	0	0	0
OVERHEAD	0	0	0	0	0	0	0	0	0	0	405.2	446.1	-40.9

Dollars In Thousands

Figure B.2. Example Cost Performance Report

There are numerous detailed activities to be performed by either the program manager, administrator/planner, cost account managers, or functional managers. Figure B.3 depicts these activities in the form of an execution phase responsibility assignment matrix.

EVM Implementation Task	Functional Responsibility			
	Program Office		Functional Organization	
	Program Manager	Administrator/ Planner	Cost Account Managers	Functional Managers
1. Determine Performance Monthly			P	
2. Coordinate Budgeted Cost For Work Performed (BCWP) Input With Cost Account And Functional Managers		P	S	S
3. Calculate Budgeted Cost For Work Performed And Input To Cost System		P		
4. Analysis Of Status Reports		P		
5. Update Schedules And Evaluate		P	S	
6. Review Cost/Schedule Data	S	P		S
7. Prepare Variance Analysis And Estimate At Completion As Required		S	P	S
8. Request And Review Variance Analysis	P			
9. Initiate Cost Account Changes As Required	S	P	P	
10. Approve Changes to Cost Account Budgets	P	S	P	S
11. Maintain Baseline Control	S	P		
12. Update And Review Cost System Plan As Required		P		

P - Primary Responsibility
S - Secondary Responsibility

Figure B.3. Execution Phase Responsibility Assignment Matrix (RAM)

Appendix C

Changes to the Program Plan

The program management change management process defines the process by which program management identifies and manages the changes that impact the program during planning and execution. This process defines the management and control of the changes to the program baseline, which is established during program planning. Change management provides the planning organization and the program organization (PO) with a methodology to identify external and internal sources of change, to determine a change's impact on the program, and to communicate this impact to the customer and upper management in order to begin the process of implementation or elimination of the change.

The change management process is highly dependent upon effective documentation and communication. If the documentation and communication process is not completely implemented, the change management process will not be completely effective. Change identification and communication of change impact are totally dependent upon effective program organization communication and thorough documentation of the change and the events causing the change. All channels of the program organization communication network must be open and functioning properly for a change to be detected in time to control its impact.

Another process on which change management is totally dependent is defining the requirements—in particular, the generation of the requirements database. Generation of the requirements database requires the identification of all program requirements (technical, supportability, cost, schedule, and programmatic) and the mapping of each identified requirement to an element of work in the extended contract work breakdown structure (CWBS). It is this process that provides the basis for determining if, later in the program, a new requirement has been added or an existing requirement has been deleted or modified.

The change management process is highly dependent upon effective documentation and communication and requirements management.

There are three basic strategies for dealing with change:

- Proactive—based on change control through early identification and resolution before the change can have an impact on the program. The change is controlled by planning the change into the program before the change is executed.
- Reactive—a reactive strategy relies on detection of the change, through variance analysis, after the change has impacted the program. Reactive strategy employs corrective action.
- Inactive—-an inactive change allows the change to impact the program with no corrective action

It is the responsibility of each member of the planning organization and the program organization to adopt a proactive strategy toward change, by being aware of the requirements identified in the requirements database that drive his or her functional assignment, and by immediately communicating and documenting any suspected change, whether caused internally or externally, to the program manager.

General requirements for dealing with change in the change management process include:

- A change will be incorporated into the program baseline only after the contract modification has been negotiated, unless otherwise directed by the commercial customer or government contracting officer in writing.
- Incorporate the change only after it has been planned in and approved by the program manager.
- Conversion of an informal change to a formal change should occur as soon as it is detected. Informal changes will be defined as changes identified via an informal documentation and communication path, from either an external or an internal source. The detrimental aspect of informal changes is that they may be incorporated without change to the program baseline and remain undetected until a cost account variance has been exceeded.

Figure C.1 depicts the change management process.

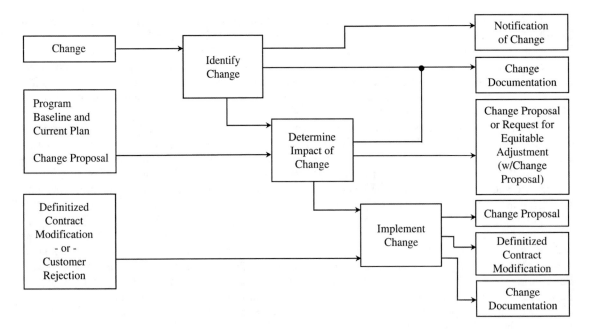

Figure C.1. Change Management Process

Identifying the change is the responsibility of each member of the PO. Any informal changes should be documented in writing. If the change is a contract change, the requirement is either:

- New
- A deletion of a requirement
- Modification of an existing change

If the program's cost, schedule, or performance measurement baseline has been impacted, then sometimes an organization will require a special form be filled out called a baseline change request (BCR). It is good practice to use a form of this nature for purposes of fully documenting the requested action. Before any action is executed to incorporate the change, a separate charge number is usually established simply to capture the accumulated costs associated with determining the impact of the potential change. In all cases, the customer should be notified if the change has an external impact.

Figure C.2 depicts the identify change aspect of the change management process.

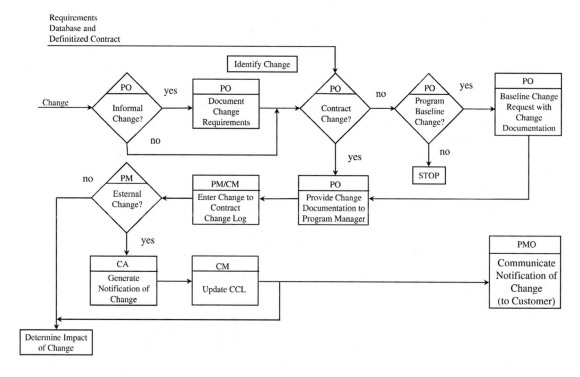

Figure C.2. Identify the Change Process

The process for identifying the change will be executed when a suspected change has occurred to the contract baseline or program baseline. Except as indicated, this activity will be the responsibility of the cognizant program organization member, utilizing the requirements identified in the requirements database and in the definitized contract, and should consist of the following:

- Informal Change?—the change requirement(s) will be documented in writing when the change is informal.
- Contract Change?—compare the suspected change with the requirements in the requirements database and the definitized contract. If the suspected change is a new requirement, a deleted requirement, or a modified existing requirement, then a change to the definitized contract has occurred. (Be aware of so-called derived requirements. Each derived requirement should be considered a new requirement, a change to the definitized contract, unless system engineering can demonstrate that the derived requirement is totally in support of an existing requirement.) If the program performance baseline has been affected by the change, in either budget or schedule, then a baseline change request is required.
- Program Baseline Change?—a baseline change request (BCR) is required when the suspected change alters the program baseline plan identified in the program management planning phase. Otherwise, the change management process is stopped.
- When a definitized contract change has occurred, the change document will be provided to the program manager.
- A separate charge number(s) should be established by the cost manager (CM) to accumulate costs for determining the impact of potential changes. The change will be entered into a contract change log (CCL) by the program administrator.

- External Change?—a formal notification of change should be prepared by the contract admin-istrator (CA) and submitted to the customer when the change is customer induced. The CCL will be updated to indicate submittal of the notification of change.

When determining the impact of the change, it is the responsibility of the program manager and the program organization member to:

- Convene a meeting to discuss the significance of the impact within a reasonable period of time of the change identification. The meeting should include, as a minimum, the impacted program organization members.
- Estimate a rough order of magnitude impact to cost, schedule, and technical performance baseline.
- Determine if impact is negligible; if so, then the change might be submitted to the customer as good will. In this case, the organization would submit a no-cost change proposal to the customer.
- Submit a change proposal to the customer for any external change requested, and make sure the change proposal is accompanied by a request for equitable adjustment (REA)

Figure C.3 depicts the process flow for determining the impact of the change as part of the change management process.

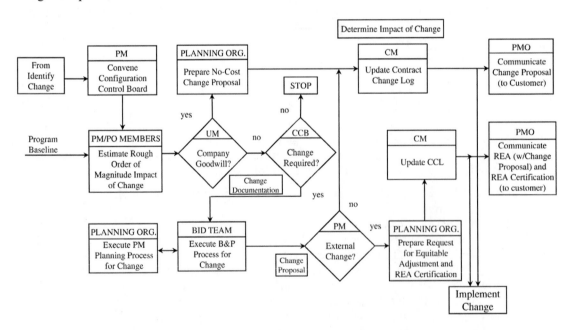

Figure C.3. Determine Impact of the Change Process

Implementing the change is the primary responsibility of the program manager. The customer, in gov-ernment contracts, may direct a change be implemented prior to negotiation under terms of the definitized contract.

If the customer rejects the change proposal, then in government contracts, a request for equitable ad-justment may be filed through the claims process as defined by the contract. If, in this case, no request for equitable adjustment was filed, then the work was performed without monetary compensation.

Implementing the change consists of the following:

- Customer-Directed Change?—when a customer directs that a change be implemented before the change has been negotiated and this direction is allowed under the definitized contract, the following should occur:
  - The PM and CM establish special charge number(s) to segregate the cost of execution of the implemented change.
  - A BCR should be executed using the change proposal's updated plan to modify the program baseline.
  - The updated program plan should be executed in accordance with the program management process after the baseline change request has been incorporated.
  - The impact (cost, schedule, etc.) of planning the change before and after negotiation of the change should be included in the change proposal.
- The REA and/or change proposal should be negotiated in accordance with the bidding process.
- Definitized Contract Modification?—when the contract modification is received, a baseline change request should be executed to incorporate the change or, in the case of a directed change (government work only), any modifications to the change proposal as a result of negotiations. The updated program plan should be executed in accordance with the program management process after the baseline change request has been approved.
- REA?—when a customer rejection is received and the change is external, the claims process is executed. The claims process receives as input all formal and informal change documentation produced during the change management process. Otherwise, for internal changes a customer rejection terminates the change management process.
- Update the CCL to indicate receipt of the customer input.

Figure C.4 depicts the process flow for implementing the change as part of the change management process.

Recognizing Changes

Effective management of contract changes requires recognition of changes before they occur, or as soon thereafter as possible. To recognize changes, program management (program manager, contract administrator, program office personnel, and cost account managers) must be familiar with: (a) what is required by the contract; (b) the change provisions in their contract; and (c) the law (Federal Acquisition Regulations [FAR], Uniform Commercial Code [UCC], etc.) governing their contract.

When referring to the following text it is imperative that program management recognize that the company can be either a buyer or a seller, who is either the prime contractor, subcontractor, or lower-tier subcontractor.

To enhance change recognition and processing, answers to these questions are provided in the text that follows:

- What is a change?
- What determines how a contract is changed?
- How do contractual relationships affect changes?
- Why are government contract changes unique?
- Why do changes occur?
- When are changes likely to occur?
- What are the elements of a change?
- Common name given to changes.
- What types of change orders can occur?
- Who has authority to order changes?

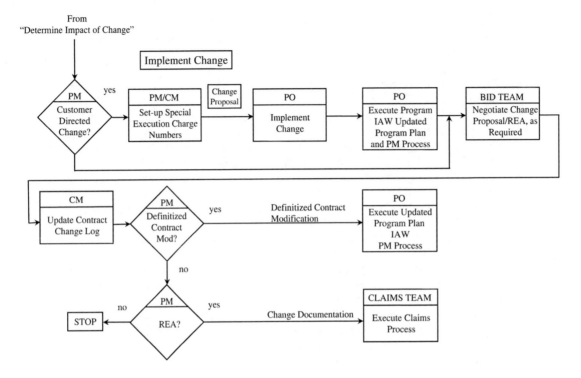

Figure C.4. Implementing the Change Process

- When can changes be ordered?
- What changes can be ordered?
- What response does a change order require?
- When is changed work performed?
- How does compensation for changes occur?

What Is a Change?

Simply stated, a contract change has the effect of making the work different than: (a) required by the contract and (b) planned and baselined in the performance measurement baseline (PMB).

A change does not necessarily imply a requirement for more work; it may require less work, or merely different work. If it affects the PMB (e.g., cost, schedule, technical performance, work breakdown structure, or other aspect of performance), it is a change.

These two contexts, the contract and the PMB, are both relevant to the change management process. Since the objective of the program management process is to plan, organize, and implement work in conformance with contract requirements, these two contexts, although not identical, are very closely related. Both are equally the concern of the program manager, program office personnel, and cost account managers, for the following reasons.

- Senior management has asserted that programs will be managed to the contract requirements.

- PMB variances will frequently provide the first indication that an informal or constructive change has occurred (refer to the sections on informal changes or constructive changes below).
- The PMB provides a barrier to performing work that is not required by the contract.

Performance Measurement Baseline

In the PMB context, changes or revisions have the effect of making the cost, schedule, or technical performance *different* from the *planned* budget, *planned* schedule, and/or *planned* technical performance as defined by cost accounts. *Different than planned* is the operative term.

The PMB forms the baseline for all work authorized by the contract and includes: (a) the CWBS and its attendant dictionary; (b) the responsibility assignment matrix (RAM); and (c) all approved cost account plans. Cost account plans and their associated work/planning packages define, in terms of planned: budget, schedule, and technical performance requirements, the work to be performed. The PMB is established at or very near the time of contract award. Once established, all changes to the PMB must be preceded by a baseline change request approved by the program manager.

Changes to the PMB may be necessitated by contract changes or by internal conditions that require re-planning within the scope of the contract. Scope, as it applies to the PMB, is bounded by three parameters: the contract budget base, the contract schedule, and the contract performance requirements.

Internal conditions causing the work to be different than planned and requiring changes to the PMB are cost, schedule, or technical problems that have caused the original plan to become unrealistic, therefore, requiring (a) reorganization of the work or people to increase efficiency of operations; or (b) different engineering or manufacturing approaches than originally contemplated.

Whenever a significant variance occurs or re-planning becomes necessary, the cost account manager should perform an in-depth review of cost, schedule, or technical problems to determine if any informal changes have occurred.

Contract

From a contract perspective, the change management process is concerned with any change that has the effect of making the work different than required by the contract. The operative words are *required* and *by the contract.*

Contract changes fall into two broad categories: formal and informal. For more detail, refer to the sections on formal changes, formal change orders, informal changes, and informal change orders.

The contract is the paper or papers that collectively contain the parties' agreements concerning the work that is to be performed; it includes the following:

- A specification and/or statement of work
- Deliverable, contract line items (CLINs) and a contract data requirements list (CDRLs)
- Delivery schedule
- Price (ceiling, target, or both) for fixed-price contracts or cost (target, ceiling, or both) for cost-reimbursement contracts
- All specifications and standards incorporated by reference
- When so stipulated by the contract, the contractor's proposal
- Any other documents that form the bases for the agreement
- An order of precedence for contract documents.

Government Contracts

Many government contracts are completely formed (definitized) at the time of award, when the contract is signed by both parties. Anything prepared or referenced at a date later than contract award, or any subsequent desire, suggestion, or direction expressed by a customer representative is not generally part of the contract.

Government contracts *not* completely formed (definitized) at the time of contract award include indefinite-delivery, time and materials, labor-hour, letter contracts, and agreements (basic ordering agreement [BOA]). These contract types are definitized subsequent to contract award via a bilateral (negotiated) contract modification, at a time determined by the contracting officer. Between contract award and contract definitization, desires, suggestions, or directions expressed by a government representative may be part of the contract. Prior to incorporating any new work or changed work into the PMB, the contract administrator will obtain written confirmation from the contracting officer.

Commercial Contracts

In commercial contracting it is much easier to enter into or change a contract. Absent specific contract language to the contrary, any change, whether written or verbal, that is offered and accepted in good faith by parties having either actual or apparent authority, constitutes a contract (new or revised). It is literally possible to fall into a contract. Therefore, in commercial contracting it is imperative that the program manager, program office personnel, and cost account managers understand and adhere to their contract change provisions, especially when discussing planned or actual changes.

What Determines How a Contract Is Changed?

A contract's change clause or provisions determine how contract changes will be accomplished. Contracts involving the government are significantly different from most commercial contracts.

How Do Contractual Relationships Affect Changes?

Prime contracts with the government are governed by the FAR and some variant of the FAR. The FAR includes several types of change clauses, which may be used, with one or more contract types.

Subcontracts with government prime contractors, or one of the prime's subcontractors, are unique forms of commercial contract in that FAR clauses may be flowed down from the prime's contract. Alternatively, the subcontract may include change provisions or clauses very similar to the government's clauses.

Contracts with other governments are treated as government contracts, if they are foreign military sales (FMS) or U.S. government financed. Otherwise, they are commercial contracts and the change provisions are whatever the parties agree to in the contract.

Commercial contracts include any change clauses or provisions agreed to by the parties. Typically, changes will be agreed to by the parties prior to performing the change, and neither party will have the right to unilaterally direct or make a change. Any change implemented or demanded without mutual agreement will constitute a breach of the contract.

Why Are Government Contract Changes Unique?

Government contract changes are substantially different from most commercial contracts in the following regards:

- The government can unilaterally issue a change order for in-scope changes without prior contractor approval.
- The contractor has a duty (legal obligation) to perform in accordance with the change order.
- The contractor is obligated to provide the government a written notification of change for any change.

Why Do Changes Occur?

From program management and change management perspectives, it is very important to know whether a change is internally (the company) or externally (buyer or seller) driven.

Changes are frequently initiated by both the buyer and seller because of:

- Information unknown at the time of contract award that later becomes available (e.g., defective specifications, impossible requirements, superior knowledge, etc.)
- Differing interpretations of a requirement
- Bid or solicitation mistakes
- Overly optimistic estimates
- Unanticipated limitations on funding
- The urgency of the requirement (e.g., acceleration of performance)
- Advances in technology
- Requirements that are either ambiguous, inconsistent, or inaccurate

An ambiguity is more than a mere disagreement; it is an uncertainty of meaning (e.g., a requirement is either vague or easily interpreted in multiple ways). An inaccuracy is an error (e.g., 10 seconds versus 1.0 second). An inconsistency exists when a requirement has been defined more than once, the definitions differ, and the difference cannot be resolved by application of document precedence (e.g., the system spec states: [a] The radio will weigh ten pounds maximum; and [b] The radio will weigh five pounds maximum).

Internally Driven Changes

Internally driven (ordered) changes are caused by acts or omissions of the party to the contract (i.e., the company) and do not occur at the behest of the customer, a subcontractor, or some other outside force.

Internally driven changes can affect the company's contract with the buyer (government or prime), or seller (subcontractor), or both.

Certain changes of this type may occur as the result of manufacturing problems, supply problems, labor inefficiencies, or other factors causing negative variances from plan. Others may stem from the discovery or application of an improved or different process or product component, resulting in positive variances from plan, or in superior performance at no change in cost or schedule. In either case, a corresponding change to the performance measurement baseline (program plan) is implied.

Internally driven changes fall into two broad groups: formal and voluntary. Refer to the sections on formal changes and voluntary changes.

Externally Driven Changes

Externally driven changes are caused by acts or omissions of the other party to the contract (i.e., the customer or subcontractor). These are the more commonly occurring of all changes and require the most attention by program management.

Externally driven changes can affect the company's contract with the buyer (government or prime), or seller (subcontractor), or both.

Externally driven changes may also occur as a consequence of circumstances, which are *not* the responsibility of the company. Indeed, certain external changes may occur that are neither the responsibility of the company nor its customer nor its subcontractor. Included in this type are acts of God or of the public enemy, fires, floods, epidemics, and strikes, to the extent that such causes are unforeseeable and beyond the control, fault, or negligence of the parties.

Externally driven changes fall into two broad groups: formal and informal. Refer to the sections on formal changes and informal changes.

When Are Changes Likely to Occur?

Changes can occur at any time during the life of a contract. Changes are more likely to occur: (a) at or immediately following contract award, (b) during reviews or meetings, (c) when the buyer/government furnishes property, (d) whenever there is a failure to cooperate, or (e) during the process of inspecting/testing contract/subcontract deliverables.

At or Immediately Following Contract Award

When a contract is awarded on a competitive basis, the requirements of the contract awarded may differ from the solicitation requirements that were bid and negotiated by the competing parties. Differences usually reflect the customer's desire to improve the contract based on information gained during the competition phase.

During Reviews or Meetings

Reviews (program, design, test readiness, CDRL, etc.) or meetings (technical interchange, working groups, etc.) frequently provide a forum for discussing requirements ambiguities, inaccuracies, and/or inconsistencies, as well as differences in the parties' interpretations of requirements.

System requirements reviews (SRR), system design review (SDR), preliminary design review (PDR), and critical design review (CDR) are almost certain to expose requirements ambiguities, inaccuracies, inconsistencies, and/or differing interpretations that are properly resolved via formal contract modifications, executed as soon after each review as possible. It is *always* in the best interest of the parties to formally resolve issues relating to contractual requirements when they arise. It is imperative that program management (either buyer's, seller's, or both) incorporate changes into their program's performance measurement baseline as soon as, but not before, changes are confirmed by the other party (i.e., buyer or seller) to the contract.

Common attempts at resolving differing requirements interpretations are:

- The buyer (e.g., government) insists the seller (e.g., the company) embrace the buyer's clarifications and perform accordingly.
- To assign one of the parties an action item(s) to analyze the requirement(s) and to either recommend solutions for, or to resolve, specification inconsistencies and inaccuracies.

When the Buyer/Government Furnishes Property

Delivery of buyer/government-furnished property: (a) later than the date specified by the contract; (b) other than specified by the contract (substitution); (c) not suitable for the intended use; or (d) that is defective are likely to be compensable contract changes.

Impact to contract performance due to operational failures or latent defects incurred during the intended use of the subject property also constitute constructive/compensable changes.

Whenever There Is a Failure to Cooperate

The buyer may be said to fail to cooperate when its representatives:

Fail to take an affirmative act that is needed for the seller to perform the contract successfully
- Interfere with the seller's performance
- Are tardy in acting upon virtually any kind of submittal that is required before seller's performance can go forward
- Are negligent in coordinating the work of several sellers who are working simultaneously on the same product

One area where a failure to cooperate may occur more frequently than others involves contractor/subcontractor data requirements lists (CDRLs/SDRLs). A failure to: (a) submit draft CDRLs/SDRLs to the buyer as scheduled, (b) submit draft CDRLs/SDRLs that are complete and accurate, (c) review draft CDRLs/SDRLs and deliver comments to the seller in a timely fashion, (d) approve final CDRLs/SDRLs in accordance with contract terms, (e) perform inspections or witness tests in accordance with approved test plans/procedures, (f) perform inspections or witness tests in a timely fashion, and (g) accept deliveries in accordance with contract requirements are all likely to constitute constructive/compensable changes.

Program management, especially cost account managers, should be alert to the potential for changes due to their involvement as either a buyer representative receiving and using data from subcontractor(s) (SDRLs) or as a seller representative submitting data (CDRLs or SDRLs) to the customer, or both. Involvement will include (a) either generating or reviewing documents or both; or (b) generating comments, or incorporating comments, or both.

During the Process of Inspecting/Testing Contract Deliverables

In the process of inspecting or witnessing testing of contract deliverables, the government sometimes imposes requirements that go beyond contract terms. Government inspectors or witnesses may impose a higher standard of performance, improperly reject work, interfere with performance, or enforce (mandate) excessive test requirements. Any of these actions are likely to constitute constructive/compensable changes.

What Are the Elements of a Change?

Changes are made up of two elements: the change element and the order element.

Change Element

The change element may describe the change requirements in terms of why, what, when, how, and/or available fund or agreed to price.

In general, the change element relates to the difference between (1) the work as the parties bargained for when the contract was awarded or when the contract was last modified, and (2) the work to be performed, or the work being performed, or both.

Changes have been given a variety of common names, which relate to the change element, for example, cardinal change that implies the change in an out-of-scope change. (For more detail, refer below to sections on cardinal changes or out-of-scope change.)

As it relates to constructive change doctrine, the change element is:

- That part of the actual performance that went beyond the minimum standards, demanded by the terms of the contract, that was ordered by the government
- Any interpretation of the contract that is either incorrect or unreasonable, which makes the contractor's work more costly.

Order Element

The order element identifies whose acts or omissions caused the change. There are several types of changes orders. Refer to the section on what types of orders can occur.

Common Names Given to Changes

Changes are frequently referred to as cardinal, compensable, constructive, or formal. Each name generally reflects a single aspect of a change. Therefore, it is likely that several names will apply to a single change, for example, an informal change may also be called a compensable change, a constructive change, or an in-scope change. Some common names given to changes, with their meanings, are as follows.

Administrative Changes

Administrative changes are not changes that affect either the change management process or the PMB, as they do not affect the work performed or the substantive rights of the parties. Examples include changing the mailing address or the paying office.

Cardinal Changes

Cardinal changes are out-of-scope changes that constitute a breach of government or commercial contracts. Refer to the section below on out-of-scope changes.

Compensable Changes

Compensable changes are changes meriting an adjustment to the contract price, or schedule, or both, to provide damaged party's consideration for changed performance. Note: both parties may be entitled to consideration.

Constructive Changes

Constructive changes are a special category of informal changes existing only within government contracting. Constructive changes are never formal; they are seldom readily identifiable as a change; and they do not originate from procedures designed to contain their effects. Constructive changes may not be identifiable until their cost and schedule impacts are noticed and attributed to an act or omission of the government.

The constructive change is a legal artifice of government contacting that the courts have used to maintain certain of the parties' rights and obligations under a contract in spite of government conduct that would, in a commercial contract, be construed as a breach of contract. See also the sections on constructive change orders, constructive notice, and recognizing constructive changes.

Engineering Changes

An engineering change proposal (ECP) will be prepared for any change in the program technical baseline that affects the contract. This applies equally to unsolicited and solicited (or directed) ECPs. The format of an ECP will be in accordance with the contract, customary practices of the cognizant general or business area manager, or as specified by the customer, as applicable.

Formal Changes

Formal changes include documentation that, as a minimum, specifies what is to be changed. Formal changes may also include when and/or how the change is to be implemented, a negotiated price, and delivery schedule. Refer to the section below on formal change orders.

For government contracts, formal changes are documented using a Standard Form 30, Amendment of Solicitation/Modification of Contract, or telegraphically under unusual or urgent circumstances (FAR 43.201 (c)). Formal changes may be referred to as bilateral or unilateral contract modifications. Refer to the section below on bilateral changes or unilateral changes.

For commercial contracts, methods for implementing contract changes are prescribed by and specific to each contract. Formal changes are executed in writing and signed by authorized persons representing the parties prior to performing the changed work. The change document typically includes the negotiated change, price, and delivery schedule.

Forward Priced Changes

Forward priced changes are formal changes, which are bid, negotiated, and priced prior to the start of work. Priced options are a category of forward priced changes.

Informal Changes

Informal changes are (a) often effected by means other than writing, (b) ordered by someone other than the contracting officer, (c) the most likely to threaten a program's success, and (d) frequently the cause of contract disputes (claims, in government contracting; breach, in commercial contracting.).

Informal changes have the practical effect of formal changes in that they (1) reflect the same customer intent to influence performance as would a formal change, and (2) they require adjustment to, or result in a variance relative to, the current performance measurement baseline. Informal changes, by their very nature, often do not clearly reflect a corresponding intent to adjust the contract price or schedule to accommodate the changed performance.

In government contracting, informal changes includes a special category, constructive changes. Refer to the section on constructive changes.

In commercial contracting, informal changes are synonymous with voluntary changes (refer to the section on voluntary changes). Such changes frequently occur as a result of conversations between engineers representing the parties, or as a result of a business decision involving customer relations.

In-Scope Changes

In-scope changes apply to government contracts only.

In-scope changes are considered to be within the general scope of the contract so long as the modified job is essentially the same work as the parties bargained for when the contract was awarded. As an example, five hundred radios versus fifty radios are essentially the same work.

Negotiated Changes

The preferred way of amending a contract is through a negotiated change. Such changes meet the same tests of validity as does the underlying contract; for example, some aspect of (changed) performance is promised or allowed in exchange for some valuable consideration, and the agreement is freely entered into by both parties without coercion on either side (i.e., the change is not directed).

In government contracting, negotiated changes are bilateral changes.

For commercial changes, negotiated changes may be either formal (written) or informal (oral). However, formal changes are preferred as a matter of policy, for obvious reasons.

Out-of-Scope Changes

Out-of-scope changes constitute breach of contract for both government and commercial contracting. The legal department should be consulted prior to notifying the customer that a change is out-of-scope.

In government contracting, out-of-scope changes are considered outside the general scope of the contract, as they have the effect of making the work as performed essentially *not* the same work as the parties bargained for when the contract was awarded—as an example, developing a general purpose computer versus developing a radio. Changes of this type are frequently confused with in-scope changes or informal changes.

In commercial contracting, out-of scope changes are any changes not agreed to by the parties prior to their implementation (price of the change need not be discussed).

Unilateral Changes

Unilateral changes include (a) administrative changes, (b) change orders in accordance with the contract change clause, (c) changes authorized by clauses other than change clauses (e.g., property clause, options clause, suspension of work clause, etc.), and (d) termination notices.

Voluntary Changes

Voluntary or volunteered changes occur when one party provides, and the other accepts, a different (usually higher) level of performance than required by the contract without consideration and without actually changing the contract.

Performing work pursuant to a change order issued by someone who is *not* the contracting officer may be interpreted as performing volunteered work.

Voluntary changes are the opposite of compensable changes and are often confused with informal changes.

What Types of Change Orders Can Occur?

Changes to contracts may be ordered in substantially different ways depending on whether the contract is government, commercial, or a mix of government and commercial. Each type supports different conventions with respect to unilateral (directed) changes, duties of the parties, scope of the contract, and the like.

Government contracts with prime contractors and prime contractor contracts with subcontractors generally include a change clause that permits the government to unilaterally order in-scope-changes to the contract.

Constructive Change Orders

Constructive change orders can occur (a) as the result of contacts between government and the company employees, (b) when the government requires the company to perform to defective government-furnished specifications, or (c) when government-furnished property is furnished late or in a condition that is unsuitable for its intended use.

During the performance of a government contract, there are frequent contacts between employees of the government and the company on many facets of the contract work. Any one of these contacts can give rise to: (a) a constructive order, written or oral, to perform work that does not specifically identify the work as a change to the contract; and (b) liability for a constructive change.

The most common variety of constructive change order occurs when the government insists that the company follow an interpretation of the contract (frequently referred to as a "clarification") that calls for a more expensive level of performance. It is an axiom of government contract law that a contractor is entitled to follow the least expensive means to achieve the specified performance of the contract.

As a general rule, clarifications are compensable changes whenever something more is required of the contractor than the least expensive, reasonable, and logical interpretation of the contract terms permit. Two possible exceptions are: (a) when the contractor fails to seek clarification of a known patent or obvious ambiguities prior to contract award; and (b) the contractor's current interpretation is not consistent with interpretations stated or implied in the contractor's proposal or during negotiations.

Action item resolution frequently calls for a more expensive level of performance. Accordingly, action item resolution is likely to be a compensable change. Compensable efforts include (a) efforts to arrive at a mutually acceptable resolution and (b) efforts to incorporate the acceptable resolution into the performance measurement baseline (changed performance).

Government Directives

Government directives may be formal change orders or constructive change orders; the difference being determined by the authority of the person ordering the change. Refer to sections in this chapter on formal change orders, informal change orders, and who has authority to order/make changes.

Formal Change Orders

Formal change orders are those executed in writing by someone specifically authorized to modify the contract. Distinctions between formal and informal changes differ significantly between government and commercial contracting.

In the case of government contracting, formal change orders may only be issued by the principal contracting officer (PCO) or by the administrative contracting officer (ACO) when authority has been delegated to the ACO in writing. Formal government change orders are accomplished by use of the Standard Form 30 (SF 30), Amendment of Solicitation/Modification of Contract, or telegraphic message under unusual or urgent circumstances, provided that certain criteria are met. Change orders may be effected by bilateral or unilateral contract modifications. Because the government's right to make changes is provided in the contract change clause, neither consent of the contractor nor new consideration is necessary for a change order to be issued. Similarly, disagreement on an equitable adjustment does not render the change ineffective. Refer to the section in this chapter on bilateral contract modifications or unilateral contract modifications.

In the case of commercial contracting, it is much easier to change the contract. Absent specific contract language to the contrary, any change, whether written or verbal, that is offered and accepted in good faith by parties having either actual or apparent authority constitutes a new contract. It is literally possible to fall into a contract. Therefore, in commercial contracting a formal change order is a change order enacted within the provisions of the contract. Informal change orders are treated as either a contract breach or a voluntary change. Refer to the section in this chapter on who has authority to order changes.

Unilateral Contract Modifications

Unilateral changes (or unilateral modifications) are unique to government contracts and afford the government the ability to order in-scope changes to the contract without the contractor's consent. Further, the contractor has a duty to proceed, that is, he or she must execute the change order or be held in breach of the contract.

Informal Change Orders

For government contracts, refer to sections in this chapter on constructive change orders and government directives.

For commercial contracts, the company should respond in the same manner as prescribed for formal change orders.

Who Has the Authority to Order Changes?

Authority to order contract changes varies significantly between government and commercial contracts. Laws recognize several doctrines relating to authority: actual, implied, and apparent (or ostensible).

Government Contracts

The company's program managers, contract administrators, and cost account managers must be aware of (a) the authority of the various government personnel with whom they deal, such as contracting officer (CO), administrative contracting officer (ACO), contracting officer's technical representative (COTR), program manager, project engineers, inspectors, and the like, as each person has specific limitations (i.e., actual authority) regarding what they can and cannot do; and (b) each company representatives' signature authority, as well as the authority they and other program personnel exercise or induce the government or subcontractors to reasonably believe exists.

Government Team

It is the company's responsibility to accurately ascertain that person who purports to act for the government stays within the bounds of her or his authority.

The CO, and when she or he has delegated authority in writing to an ACO, are the only two government agents having requisite actual authority to issue a change order or to modify a contract.

Prior to responding to a contract modification or change order issued by the ACO, written delegation of authority will be obtained from the CO.

Neither the program manager, COTR, nor other agents of the government have the requisite actual authority to issue change orders or direct changes. However, acquiescence, implied authority, and ratification have been found by the courts to be exceptions to the lack of actual authority.

Acquiescence

If an authorized official (CO or ACO) does not expressly ratify the unauthorized act of an agent, but knows of and does not challenge or impeach the act, it may be concluded that the CO/ACO has authorized the act through acquiescence (e.g., the government PM, COTR, or agent directs a change in the presence of the CO/ACO and his or her direction is not challenged, it may be concluded that the CO/ACO has authorized the act through acquiescence).

Constructive Notice/Knowledge

The CO/ACO may be deemed to have constructive notice or knowledge of a fact if: (a) she or he would have discovered the fact through the exercise of reasonable care; or (b) the person committing unauthorized acts prepared extensive daily written reports, even though the reports did not indicate to whom they were distributed.

Implied Authority

Implied authority is usually found when the authority appears to be an integral part of the duties that have been assigned to the particular person who required the change. Most government employees found to have implied authority have involved delegations of authority by contracting officers to persons like project managers, engineers, inspectors, and other persons who are directly involved in contract administration.

Ratification

Ratification is the adoption of an unauthorized act, which results in the act being given effect as if it were authorized originally. Ratification may sometimes be found by the court when the contracting officer normally relies on an inspector and is in constant communication with him or her; then knowledge of any change orders issued by him or her is imputed to the contracting officer.

Contractor Team

The law as it relates to the authority of the contractor team involved in the performance and administration of the contract differs significantly from that of the government team. Two doctrines dealing with contractor team authority are actual authority and apparent (or ostensible) authority.

Actual Authority

Within the company, signature authority for contracts and bids or amendments or modifications thereto for materials to be furnished or services to be rendered to the U.S. government, to any department, agency, or division thereof, or to other purchasers of the corporation or its subsidiaries' products or services is delegated in writing to various individuals, at varying dollar levels, by the company president. Signature authority for memorandums of understanding (MOUs), memorandums of agreement (MOAs), teaming agreements, license agreements, license and technical assistance agreements, and joint venture agreements is delegated in writing to various officers of the corporation, by the board of directors. Joint venture agreements must also receive approval of the board of directors.

Information relating to specific individuals and their dollar levels can be obtained from the division contract directorate of the legal department.

Apparent Authority

Apparent (or ostensible) authority is that authority that, though not actually granted, a contractor knowingly permits its agent to exercise, or which he or she holds the agent out as possessing.

The company may place an agent of the corporation in a position giving rise to liability under the doctrine of apparent authority in the following ways: (a) by appointing the agent to a managing position (i.e., contracts manager, project director, etc.) or (b) whenever another party (i.e., the government, a subcontractor, a vendor, etc.) is induced by the company to reasonably believe that such an agency exists, even though no actual authority was, in fact, conferred on anyone. If the company fails to correct the erroneous impression of an apparent authority relationship, the company will continue to be liable to third parties who act thereunder in good faith.

When Can Changes Be Ordered?

Contracts usually include language (change clauses) that affords both buyer and seller the flexibility to initiate in-scope changes or changes within the general scope of the contract.

Government contract change clauses provide contracting officers the right to issue written change orders directing the contractor to make changes without the contractor's consent. A government change clause or similar provision will be included in nearly all contracts involving the government (prime contractor or subcontractor).

For commercial contracts without change provisions, any change to the work that the parties bargained for when the contract was awarded constitutes a breach of contract.

What Changes Can Be Ordered?

Contract change clauses are frequently specific as to what kind of changes can be ordered.

In government contracting, changes that the contracting officer can unilaterally order are specifically delineated in the contract change clause. Change clauses vary as a function of contract type. Program management office personnel and cost account managers should ask their contract administrator to identify which of the following changes are permissible on the contract they are performing:

- Specifications (including drawings and designs)
- Drawings, designs, or specifications when the supplies to be furnished are to be specifically manufactured for the government in accordance with the drawings, designs, or specifications
- Statement of work or description of services to be performed
- Time or place of services to be performed
- Manner or method of performance or work
- Place of inspection, delivery, or acceptance
- Method of shipment or packing of supplies
- Place of delivery
- Amount/type of buyer/government-furnished facilities, equipment, materials, services, or site

For commercial contracts, what, when, and to what extent changes will be permitted are as negotiated by the parties to the contract.

What Response Does a Change Order Require?

Notification of all company-initiated changes, formal change orders, or informal change orders (including constructive change orders or government directives) should be given the customer in writing by the contract administrator within time limitations established by the contract, or as soon after receipt or detection of the order as practical.

To ensure timely customer notification, notices can be transmitted in two parts: (a) brief description of the change and identification of the party issuing the order; and (b) detailed description(s) of the change(s), its/their impact to work bargained for when the contract was awarded or last modified, and the added cost (dollars and schedule) to perform work in accordance with the change order.

Accordingly, program management office personnel and cost account managers will notify the contract administrator, in writing, whenever they believe they are in receipt of a change order (formal, constructive, or directive).

Responses to Formal Change Orders

As a minimum, all formal change orders must be acknowledged, in writing, by the contract administrator within the time limits specified by the contract. Other actions taken by the company will be as specified in the change order or as directed by the business area manager or program management, or both.

For government contracts, the company is required by law to provide the contracting officer with specific information prescribed by the notification of change clause (Federal Acquisition Regulation (FAR) 52.234-7).

For commercial contracts, company change notifications will provide all information required by the contract's change provisions. In the absence of specific change notification requirements, the contract administrator should provide essentially the same information as required for government contracts.

Responses to Informal Change Orders

When the company considers that the government has effected or may effect a change in the contract that has not been identified in writing and signed by an authorized agent, it is necessary that the company notify the government in writing as soon after receipt or detection of the order as practical, but definitely prior to receipt of final payment.

Constructive Notice/Knowledge

The CO/ACO may be deemed to have constructive notice or knowledge of a fact if:

- He or she could have discovered the fact through the exercise of reasonable care.
- The government has actual knowledge of the facts, which constitute the constructive change.
- The person committing unauthorized acts prepared extensive daily written reports, even though the reports did not indicate to whom they were distributed.

To minimize the company's reliance on constructive notice/knowledge, program management personnel (program manager, program management office personnel, and cost account managers) will provide the contract administrator with the information required to submit a formal notice to the government.

When Is Changed Work Performed?

Prior to starting any work that is either different than defined or not defined (changed work) in the PMB, the PMB should be revised in accordance with an approved BCR. Further, the contract administrator will obtain written authorization, from the buyer's contracting officer, prior to the program manager giving approval to any BCR involving changed work initiated at the behest of any buyer representative.

Government Contracts

When changes are implemented or when changed work is performed is determined in part by the type of change order.

Commercial Contracts

Prior to their execution, formal changes will be agreed to by the parties to the contract in writing. As a minimum, change agreements will include the negotiated description for each change and either the separate or aggregate delivery schedule(s) or price(s).

Appendix D

Program Planning Master Process Flow

This appendix is a deeper dive on pre-contract award program planning.

Prior to contract award, there are a number of activities that a program should perform to create an integrated cost, schedule, and technical performance measurement plan. After contract award, these activities will form a performance measurement baseline that accurately reflects the program's definitized awarded contract. This pre-award program planning provides the program with a solid foundation from which execution of the program may commence with minimal post-contract award baseline updating effort. Program planning, therefore, is composed of activities that, when implemented both prior to and after contract award, provide the program and its management team with an efficient mechanism for effectively executing and managing the program with minimal post-contract award delay.

All activities discussed below, as part of pre-contract award, are depicted in an overall program management planning process flow in figure D.1. Viewing this overall process flow prior to reading the following paragraphs will provide a more complete and comprehensive perspective.

The program planning master process flow diagram depicts the basic activities of the planning process prior to contract award. After contract award these same process activities are revisited to update and make correct previous planning thoughts and product outputs from the activities of the program/ project management process. Notice in the process flow the twenty identified entities strategically placed between the activities of the overall process. The first of these is titled "definitions," followed by "contract types." These twenty entities are essential elements, to be read as "chapters" or parts of chapters, presented in this text to heighten awareness to what the subsequent process activities are. In a few instances, information is presented in this section that is not previously discussed elsewhere, namely "establish the program management library." In this scenario, process flows and templates are presented to further enhance understanding. In other areas discussed relative to this process flow, no charts or process flows are presented, as these areas are discussed in great length in their corresponding chapters.

Establish Planning Organization

Establishing the planning organization is an activity that identifies and organizes the required planning resources for the program. The program's planning personnel are the individuals responsible for establishing the program's integrated cost, schedule, and technical performance measurement plan. These personnel may (and should) be responsible for the subsequent execution of the program in accordance with the program's baseline plan.

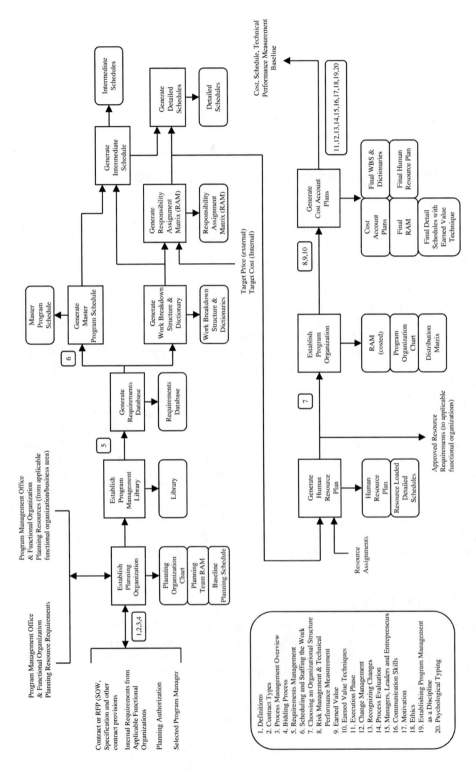

Figure D.1. Program Planning Master Process Flow

Products

Establishing a planning organization requires the generation of three products:

- Planning organization chart—a hierarchical, graphical depiction of the program planning team's personnel and management structure.
- Planning team responsibility assignment matrix—a matrix depiction of the activities required to establish the performance measurement baseline and the specific program planning resource assigned to those activities.
- Baseline planning schedule—a time-phased integrated networked schedule depicting the activities required to establish the program's performance measurement baseline.

Inputs

Inputs to this activity are:

- Program manager selected by business area director (BAD)
- Contract or request for proposal (RFP) (SOW, specification, and other contract provisions) from external customer or BAD
- Internal requirements from functional organizations
- Equipment/facility and material resources
- Planning authorization document

Processing

The program manager of the program is initially responsible for defining the program's planning organization resource requirements. Once defined, the program manager conveys these identified needs to the functional managers and business area directors. The functional managers and business area directors make tentative personnel assignments to the program manager for purposes of planning the program. These resource assignments should be made with the intent of making these individuals a part of the long-term program team (i.e., beyond the initial planning).

After acceptance, or negotiation of alternative personnel, the program manager will initiate two activities: (a) the generation of the planning organization chart and the planning team responsibility assignment matrix (with the program's management office), and (b) the generation of the baseline planning schedule (with the program's planner).

These products, once generated, will be approved by the program manager and subsequently distributed by the program management office in accordance with a predefined program distribution list. Figure D.2 depicts the process flow for this activity.

Outputs

Outputs from this activity, then, are the three products: (a) planning organization chart, (b) planning team responsibility assignment matrix, and (c) baseline planning schedule.

Establish Program Management Library

Establishing the program management library is an activity that is intended to: (1) increase communication between program personnel, (2) enhance communication between the program's management team and their customer, and (3) centralize documentation that supports program decisions, progress, and program change. The program management library is a vehicle for effective communications management. The program management library supports a uniform and orderly categorization of program documentation that subsequently provides for more effective communications within the program and with external sources.

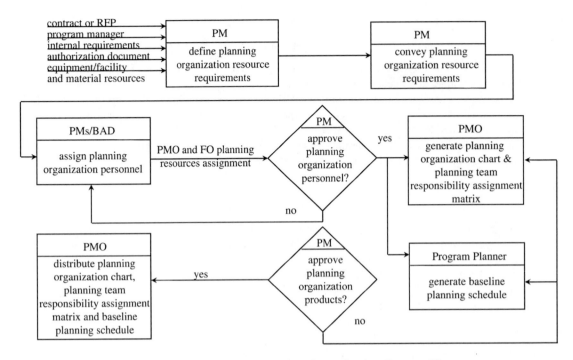

Figure D.2. Establishing Planning Organization Process Flow

The program management library is generally maintained in a centrally located file cabinet. The information maintained within may be physical master documents or pointers to electronic versions. The program management library, to be effective, must be maintained through processes similar to those described in standard configuration management literature. That is, fundamentally, all data to be placed in the library should be organized chronologically by subject, dated, approved (if required), and a sign-out sheet provided for those program individuals wishing to temporarily remove placed documents.

Products

The product of establishing the program management library is the program management library itself. More importantly, however, is the type of program information to be placed in the library and its handling. There are a number of products that should be generated as a result of good program management practices. These products, persons responsible for assuring library retention, originators, and persons responsible for approval (if required) are depicted in figure D.3.

Inputs

Inputs to this activity are all correspondence and specifically those items listed in figure D.3.

Processing

There are two fundamental issues to be dealt with prior to placing an item into the program management library: (1) does the item being placed in the program management library require approval, and (2) if the item is to be distributed, as well as placed in the program management library, to whom should it go, and who on the program should be involved in distributing it.

	Responsible for Retention	Originator	If Approval is Required
Contract	CA	Customer	PM/CA
Contract Mods	CA	Customer	PM/CA
Contract Data	DM	Various	
Contract Correspondence			
Incoming	CA	Customer	
Outgoing	CA	Various	PM
Meeting Minutes			
Internal	PM	Various	PM
External	PM/CA	Various	PM
Action Item List	PM	PM	PM
Program Events Calander	PM	PM	PM
Significant Events	PM	Various	PM
Program Directives	PM	PM	PM
Telecons	Various	Various	PM
Earned Value Management Files			
Dictionaries	Administrator	Various	PM
Schedules	Administrator	Planner	PM
C/SSR & CPR's	Administrator	Proj. Accountant	PM
Variance Analysis	Administrator	CAMs	PM
Corrective Action	Administrator	CAMs	PM
Baseline Change Requests	Administrator	CAMs	PM

Figure D.3. Example Data to be Placed in Program Management Library

This activity, then, is more involved than simply to create a program management library. It also includes those facets associated with the handling, distribution, and placement of program data/information. If a piece of program information is considered to be formal, then the contract administrator needs to be involved in its distribution and filing. If the item is a contract data item to be distributed to the customer, then both contract administration and data management are involved. Preparing a document for delivery to the customer involves the proper reproducing, marking, and pricing, and this should be performed in accordance with the requirements specified by data management and configuration management practices.

Establishing the program management library, therefore, is a prerequisite to the handling, distribution, and placement of program data. The establishment of the program management library follows the process flow depicted in figure D.4.

Outputs

Output from this activity is the creation of a program management library, properly distributed program data (in accordance with the program's distribution list), and properly placed/filed program data/information.

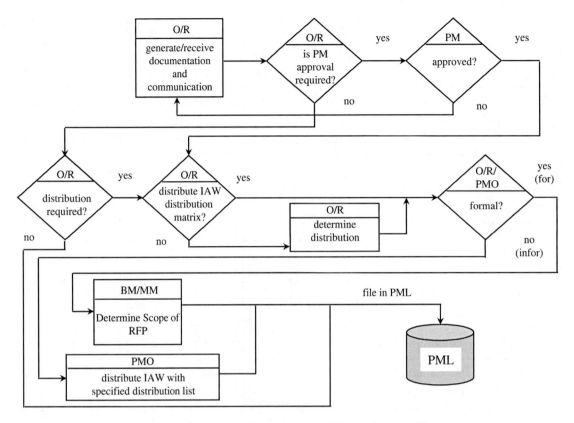

Figure D.4. Program Management Library Process Flow

Generate Requirements Database

Requirements management involves five steps: (1) requirements identification, (2) requirements analysis, (3) requirements allocation, (4) a means for requirements verification, and (5) requirements traceability. Generating a requirements database necessitates that stated and derived requirements be identified and categorized on placement into the requirements database, and that some basic information be associated with each requirement, providing subsequent traceability to lower-level design activities. One measure of effective program planning and successful execution is the thoroughness of the steps involved in identifying, categorizing, and allocating contractually stated and derived requirements.

Requirements identification is the process of collecting both stated and derived requirements from both internal and external sources. External documentation, which provides a source for program stated and derived requirements, includes the contract statement of work, contract specification and contract provisions. Internal documentation, which provides a source for program derived requirements, includes specific functional organization processes.

An explicitly stated requirement is one that announces, for example, "The programming language used in this program shall be the Ada programming language." A derived requirement is one that the contractor has placed upon itself as a result of direction given by the stated requirement. An example of this type of requirement is when the contractor decides to use Company A's Ada programming language compiler instead of a Company B's Ada programming language compiler. The intention to use the Company A's Ada programming language compiler is self-imposed, but nevertheless a requirement. The customer only stated that the programming language had to be Ada, not that the Ada programming language compiler had to be Company A's.

Requirements analysis is an activity that separates like requirements into groups under umbrella higher-level requirements. This activity creates a hierarchical depiction of related requirements.

Requirements allocation is the assignment of a given requirement or family of requirements to a piece of the system for implementation and subsequent satisfaction. For example, the requirement to program the software in the Ada programming language might be given to the software group working on the program. The understanding is that the software group will be responsible for insuring this requirement is satisfied. Within the software group, the requirement may be further allocated to a specific subset of individuals, such as the software support group.

Staying with our current example, the software support group will also identify the type of testing required to demonstrate that the requirement has been satisfied. This verification method may fall into one of four categories: (a) analysis, (b) demonstration, (c) inspection, or (d) test.

The last item dealing with requirements management is requirement traceability. Requirement traceability is the process by which a requirement is traced from its original statement in a contract, or related document, to the actual piece of the total system, which is responsible for implementing a means to satisfy the requirement.

The requirements database provides the program with a means of tracking all program requirements through each phase of the program's life cycle. A preliminary requirements database is established during the bid and proposal phase.

Generate Master Program Schedule

Schedules provide the time frame for resource allocation, establish a baseline for current status, and forecast completion dates of scheduled work. A program contains a hierarchy of related levels of schedules, beginning with the master program schedule, with each succeeding lower level more fully identifying and expanding the activities necessary to meet the program requirements. Management of these activities begins with the master program schedule, incorporates the intermediate schedule, and culminates in the detailed schedules. As a management tool, the intermediate schedule and detailed schedules are typically depicted as an interdependency network. The interdependency network depicts the interrelationships between the numerous program activities.

A program's master schedule is incrementally created beginning with the identified activities and milestones provided in the contract.

Products

A master program schedule is the sole product of the generating a master program schedule activity.

Inputs

Input to this activity is the requirements database. The requirements database contains stated and derived schedule requirements. Stated requirements are derived from the contract or request for proposal. Internally derived requirements are defined from within the processes of the functional organizations that are performing work within the program. For example, the design engineering functional organization process specifies that a review is required (such as a preliminary design review). Even if there is no stated external customer requirement for such a review, the preliminary design review should be depicted on the appropriate schedules as an event, and should occur unless the program manager and functional manager agree to delete the requirement.

Processing

Figure D.5 depicts the process flow for generating the master program schedule. Processing for this activity is the responsibility of the program planner, utilizing the requirements database and consists of the following:

- Depicting:
  - Contract deliveries
  - Major customer review/decision points and major contractual schedule events
  - Buyer furnished equipment/material and delivery dates
  - Buyer review/approval dates
  - Summaries of all program activities and key schedule events
  - Schedule reserve
- The program manager reviews the master program schedule. If the master program schedule requires changes, it will be returned to the program planner; otherwise, the program manager will demonstrate approval by signing the master program schedule. The master program schedule should be generated in accordance with in accordance with the following requirements:
  - Depict the master program schedule as an interdependency network or Gantt chart
  - Identify early, late, and baseline dates for each summary and event
  - The scheduling process should be performed with approved tools. Approved tools will ensure the use of a consistent format throughout the company.
  - The schedules should be generated utilizing top-down development. The master program schedule should be generated and approved before generating the intermediate schedules. The intermediate schedules should be generated and approved before generating detailed schedules.
  - Traceability exists from each lower-level schedule element to a uniquely identifiable upper-level schedule element; that is, a lower-level schedule element completely supports the next higher schedule element.
  - Since the master program schedule functions as a reporting tool to company management and to the customer, it should reside on only one page. When adequate visibility for contract data requirements lists and contract line item numbers is precluded in the one page format, then the master program schedule may be augmented by supplemental schedules for contract data requirements lists and contract line item numbers.
  - The master program schedule should be released with schedule reserve depicted (if applicable). Schedule reserve may be depicted and taken at any point in the master program schedule. Schedule reserve consists of time retained for later use. This schedule reserve could then be used later, when unplanned activity occurs. These unplanned activities would otherwise have negatively affected the schedule of in-scope work, had not schedule reserve been planned at the start of the program. The inclusion of a schedule reserve is at the discretion of the program manager and will be used later as required. The inclusion of a schedule reserve potentially eliminates the later need to submit a change request to the external customer or business area director. Lower-level schedules should be generated to show completion of the activities no later than the dates of the accelerated schedule activities created when schedule reserve was taken.

Outputs

Output from this activity is the master program schedule.

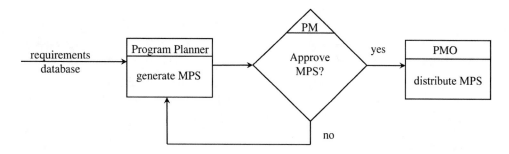

Figure D.5. Master Program Schedule Process Flow

Generate Preliminary Extended CWBS and Dictionary

In parallel with generating the master program schedule, the work breakdown structure provided by the customer may be extended to reflect the program's current understanding of the work and its organization. attendant to the work breakdown structure are dictionaries that describe what the work is to be performed, as depicted in the currently extended work breakdown structure.

Extending the work breakdown structure and creating attendant dictionaries is the first step in planning the costs of the program. Cost planning is concerned with defining the relationship between the elements of work to be performed under the contract, allocating budget to the elements of work, defining who is responsible for performing the work, and selecting preliminary cost accounts (CAs).

The CA is the management control point at which actual costs can be accumulated and compared to budgeted costs for work performed. A CA is a control point for cost, schedule, and technical performance planning, work execution, and performance measurement. Cost account responsibility is assigned to a cost account manager (CAM).

The historical MIL-STD-881, military standard for work breakdown structures for defense material items, provides an overview of the various types of work breakdown structures encountered in a typical U.S. Department of Defense contract.

Products

Generating a preliminary extended contract work breakdown structure (CWBS) and dictionary requires the generation of two products:

- Extended contract work breakdown structure—a hierarchically oriented depiction of the work to be performed and its organization.
- Extended contract work breakdown structure dictionary—a detailed textual description of the work depicted in the extended contract work breakdown structure.

Inputs

Inputs to this activity are:

- Specification, statement of work (SOW), and other contract provisions.
- Requirements database
- Product family tree

Processing

Figure D.6 depicts the process flow for generating the extended CWBS and dictionaries. The program management office (PMO) has primary responsibility for processing of this activity. The processing of this activity is a combined effort of the PMO and functional organizations (FOs) and consists of the following:

- Expand (augment) the contract provided CWBS to form the extended CWBS. The initial expansion should be to one level below the reporting level. This expansion is generated by incorporating the individual functional organization's work breakdown structure into the program's extended CWBS template. Individual elements of the CWBS do not need to be expanded equally.
- Developing the dictionary, which unambiguously describes the work to be accomplished under each element of the extended CWBS.
- The program manager (PM) reviews the extended CWBS and dictionary. If the extended CWBS and dictionary requires changes, it is returned to the PMO, otherwise the PM demonstrates approval by signing the extended CWBS and dictionary.

Detailed requirements for generating the extended CWBS and dictionaries are as follows:

- For each contract there should be a single CWBS generated that defines all authorized work.
- Since the CWBS forms part of the contract, it should be defined before the contract is signed. This definition will generally be accomplished during the proposal and/or negotiation phase of the procurement, since it requires concurrence between the customer and the contractor.
- The program management office representatives on the proposal team are responsible for coordinating the CWBS with the customer. Normally, our government customers are restricted by regulation to providing a contract work breakdown structure no lower than level three. The program management office representatives should make every effort to avoid letting the CWBS partition the work into unnatural or unmanageable packages. Unless otherwise required by the customer, the CWBS should be in accordance with the requirements and should be organized consistently with the product family tree.
- The extended CWBS dictionary correlates with the basis of the work depicted in the intermediate schedules and detailed schedules.
- The program management office, with support from the functional organizations (FOs), is responsible for determining the initial top-down costs of the work identified.
- Each extended CWBS element summarizes into only one higher-level element.
- The degree to which CWBS elements are extended is governed by the following:
  - Contract reporting level.
  - The complexity and criticality of elements of work to meet contract requirements.
  - The cost of elements of work.
  - The visibility needed by management for control of the element of work.
- The extended CWBS dictionary identifies quantities of all deliverables, relevant CLINs, and data items.
- All work for each subcontractor should be separately identified within the CWBS, using one or more extended CWBS elements according to the nature of the work. Each subcontract should be represented as a CA. A subcontract should consist of a purchase order (PO) that contains a statement of work. A subcontract is required if the supplied item or service is unique, and a PO is insufficient to define requirements.
- The following requirements apply to subcontract CAs:
  - The subcontractor's statement of work (SOW) should include the work described in the extended CWBS dictionary for the subcontract CA work packages (WP).

- The subcontractor's cost reporting structure (level) should be the WPs identified within the subcontract CA.
- The subcontractor work breakdown structure (SWBS) should be generated for the subcontract CA and extend to at least the CA WP level.
- Effort to monitor the subcontract should be in one or more WPs in the subcontract CA.
- CAMs that use a subcontractor's product in their CA are responsible for monitoring the technical aspects of that product.
- The subcontract CA should have the following minimum set of items:
- Cost account "material" is any hardware, software, or service that is planned and controlled by an identifying part number, model number, or detailed description. Cost accounts for material should include:
  - Material used for destructive tests or internal setup for pilot runs (overbuy)
  - Shrink (anticipated loss, damage, etc., based on historical rates)
  - Vendor setup charges
  - Vendor burn-in tests
  - Minimum buy costs
  - Procurement and transportation (material burden)
  - Licenses and maintenance fees
  - Purchased material inspection (PMI), if applicable (based on historical rates)
  - Be a direct charge resource that includes: all assets purchased for a program from sources outside of the company, inter-divisional purchases, and internal transfers
- Requirements in the requirements database at the CWBS level should be mapped to the extended CWBS level in accordance with any existing functional organization extended CWBS templates. The extended CWBS elements that do not map to a requirement should be deleted from the extended CWBS.
- Recurring and nonrecurring effort should be divided into separate elements. Generally, recurring and nonrecurring should become subsidiary elements under each element to which the distinction applies.
- No work should be associated with summary level elements.
- If the element identifiers in the extended CWBS are incompatible with the type(s) of identifiers the company cost accounting system requires, the extended CWBS should provide a cross-reference between the extended CWBS element identifiers and the company cost accounting system identifiers.
- Extended CWBS should be updated as required. After cost accounts have firmed, the extended CWBS should be extended to the work package level.
- The dictionary should define the scope of work of each extended CWBS element.
- A description of the technical content, associated risks, and cost category (direct, recurring, nonrecurring, material, etc.) should be provided for each element of the extended CWBS.

Outputs

The output from this activity is the extended contract work breakdown structure and its supporting dictionary.

Generate Preliminary Responsibility Assignment Matrix

The intent of the preliminary responsibility assignment matrix (RAM) is to initially assign target costs to groupings of work identified as cost accounts. Generating the preliminary responsibility assignment matrix is performed subsequent to the generation of the extended CWBS and dictionaries.

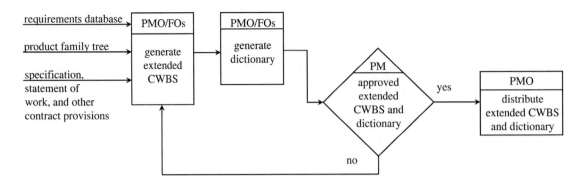

Figure D.6. Extended CWBS and Dictionary Process Flow

Inputs

Inputs to this activity are the following:

- Contract target price (external/internal)
- Cost proposal or cost estimate
- Extended CWBS and dictionary

The external contract target price is provided by a marketing process for the proposal phase and by the contract administrator for an external contract. The internal contract target price is provided by the business area director. The internal contract target price is internal research and development (IR&D), bid and proposal (B&P), internally funded effort in direct support of an external contract, or other internally funded effort. The cost proposal or cost estimate is provided by accounting to the program management office. The cost estimate is an initial top-down estimate generated to allocate budget to CWBS elements prior to any bottom-up estimating.

The difference between the preliminary RAM and the final baseline RAM are those changes resulting from continuation of the planning process.

Processing

Figure D.7 depicts the process flow for generating the preliminary RAM. The processing of this activity is the responsibility of the program management office (PMO) and functional organization (FO) managers, with support of accounting and consists of the following:

- Development of the budget consists of the following:
  - Subtract target profit or fee from contract target price, yielding contract target cost.
  - Add budget of any internally contracted work and authorized unpriced work (AUW), yielding contract budget base (CBB) (as applicable).
  - Subtract any management reserve from the difference of the CBB and the AUW, yielding the budget for performance measurement baseline (PMB).
  - Subtract any undistributed budget.
  - Subtract general and administrative (includes G&A, IR&D, B&P, tax, interest, and cost of money) costs yielding a distributed budget.
  - Allocate the distributed budget to each extended CWBS element.
- Considering the type, magnitude, duration, management visibility/control, and risk of the work and functional organization involved, initially define cost accounts (CAs) to one level

below reporting level or the level required to satisfy requirements for a CA. Costing updates should be reflected in the final baseline RAM.
- Has extended CWBS changed? The extended CWBS will be changed if elements are (re)allocated to satisfy requirements for establishing CAs.
- The program manager (PM) should review the preliminary RAM. If the RAM requires changes, it needs to be returned to the program management office (PMO); otherwise, the PM demonstrates approval by signing the preliminary RAM.

Detailed requirements for generating the preliminary RAM are as follows.

- Assign CAs—initially CAs are defined in the extended CWBS at one level below the reporting level (normally at level four).
- Allocate the distributed target budget to each CA to match the work identified in the extended CWBS dictionary using similar-to analysis from historical data.
- Establish charge number structure based on CAs. No charge number should be used for charges into more than one CA. Prior to contract award, the charge number structure should be constructed using pseudo CA charge numbers.

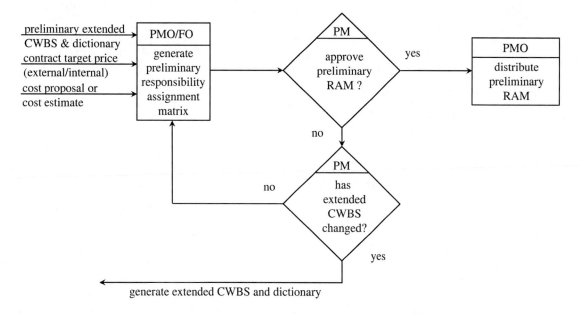

Figure D.7. Generating the RAM Process Flow

Outputs

Output for this activity is the preliminary RAM.

Generate Intermediate Schedules

The intermediate schedules are a hierarchically lower decomposition of the work to be performed, as initially depicted in the master program schedule. The intermediate schedules simply continue to decompose the activities depicted in the master program schedule into lower-level subactivities. This further evolution of identified work culminates in the lowest level of schedules produced, detailed schedules.

Inputs

Inputs to this activity are:

- Master program schedule
- Requirements database
- Extended CWBS and dictionary

Processing

Figure D.8 depicts the process flow for generating the intermediate schedules. Processing for this activity is the responsibility of the program planner, utilizing the master program schedule (MPS), requirements database, and extended CWBS and dictionary, and it consists of the following:

- Developing the summary level activities identified on the MPS into greater detail.
- Identifying the following associated with the further developed summaries/subprojects:
  - Key events
  - Duration of summaries/subprojects
  - Fixed start/completion dates
- MPS affected? The MPS is affected when any MPS date is changed as a result of intermediate schedule development
- The program manager (PM) reviews the intermediate schedule. If the intermediate schedule requires changes, it is returned to the program planner; otherwise, the PM demonstrates approval by signing the intermediate schedule.

The intermediate schedule should be generated in accordance with the following requirements:

- Depict the intermediate schedule as an interdependency network

- Identify early, late, and baseline dates for each summary, subproject, and event

- Identify relationships (dependencies—successor/predecessor) between key events

- Identify the float (slack time) of each summary and event

- Identify the critical path(s)

Outputs

The output for this activity is the intermediate schedule.

Generate Preliminary Detailed Schedules

Detailed schedules depict the lowest level of visibility into the activities on the program. They are the bottommost schedules in the schedule hierarchy, preceded by intermediate and master-level schedules. The intent of developing lower-level schedules is to identify discrete elements of work that can be managed.

The detailed schedules expand each intermediate schedule summary/subproject into multiple activities to the extent necessary or desired and adds schedule events that satisfy the requirements of the intermediate schedule. The detailed schedules are working schedules that depict horizontal dependencies and are, therefore, used on a daily basis by the cost account managers (CAMs) to manage their work.

Products

The products of generate preliminary detailed schedules are the many lower-level detailed schedules.

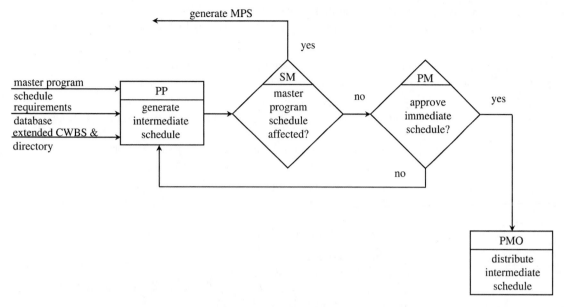

Figure D.8. Generate Intermediate Schedule Process Flow

Inputs

Inputs to this activity are:

- Intermediate Schedule
- Other functional organization (FO) documents (trade studies, system engineering management plan, manufacturing plan, integrated logistics support plan, software development plan, hardware development plan, etc.)

Processing

Figure D.9 depicts the process flow for generating the detailed schedules. There are a couple of things that could happen as a result of creating the detailed schedules: (1) the end dates in the interdependency network may no longer be acceptable, and (2) the intermediate schedule may have been affected. All processing activities below are associated with these two potential problems.

Processing for this activity is the responsibility of the CAMs. Processing consists of the following:

- Develop the summaries/subprojects identified on the intermediate schedule (IMS) into greater detail (activities). It is imperative that contractual requirements not be modified during this process.
- Answer the following when generating activities:
  - Is work missing or not required?
  - Does the work definition need modification to satisfy the requirements of the CA?
  - Should the work be broken down further?
  - Should the requirements be broken down further (generate sub-requirements)?
- IMS affected? The IMS is affected when any IMS date is changed as a result of detailed schedule development

- The program manager (PM) reviews the detailed schedules. If the detailed schedules require changes, they are returned to the program planner; otherwise, the PM demonstrates approval by signing the detailed schedules.

If detailed schedules do not map into the dates established by their parent intermediate schedules, then the following options are available for reconciling differences:

- Identification of alternate plans for accomplishing the work
- Reevaluating interpretations of the requirements to ensure the requirements are satisfied but not exceeded
- Evaluated use of additional or higher skilled resources to accomplish the work
- Reevaluated schedule/risk tradeoffs

Part of generating the preliminary detailed schedules may involve negotiating the detailed schedules. This activity is performed when the interdependency network (IDN) is unacceptable and the cost account managers (CAMs) have attempted to reconcile the differences. This activity is the responsibility of the program planner and CAMs. Processing consists of the following:

- Negotiate for the adjustment of IMS date(s)
- Negotiate for an adjustment of detailed schedule date(s)
- Detailed schedules affected? The detailed schedules are affected when any detailed schedule date is changed as a result of negotiating detailed schedules
- Requirements changed? The requirements have been changed as a result of this activity when:
  - Requirements have been reallocated
  - Requirements have changed (reinterpreted)

Once the detailed schedules have been deemed acceptable and no impacts to either the intermediate or master schedules have been realized, then from the detailed schedules work packages and planning packages should be identified. Processing for this activity is the responsibility of the CAMs.

Once the detailed schedules have been approved and it has been verified that the intermediate and master schedules are consistent, then the schedule baseline is established and is ready for the program manager to sign off. The program planner is responsible for establishing the schedule baseline by recording all early dates as baseline dates.

Outputs

Output from this activity are the detailed schedules.

Generate Human Resource Plan

The objective of this activity is to formulate a concise, meaningful, and practical program-level strategy for managing human resources in the manner most favorable to fulfill the program goals.

Resource planning as a philosophy requires that resources be identified for each detailed schedule activity and be loaded against that activity in the program's scheduling tool. The human resource plan (HRP), then, is an automated, time-phased report, by activity, CWBS element, or program, generated by the program planner utilizing the program's scheduling tool.

Development of the HRP is an iterative process. A "first look," high-level initial plan is done early in the program planning stage. After completion of generate cost account plans, an updated plan is developed using the cost accounts as a basis.

Products

The end product of generate human resource plan is a time-phased human resource plan.

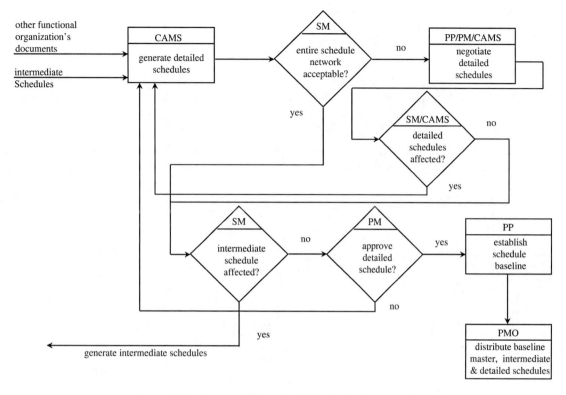

Figure D.9. Generate Detailed Schedules Process Flow

Inputs

Inputs to this activity are:

- Extended contract work breakdown structure (CWBS) and dictionary
- Preliminary responsibility assignment matrix (RAM)
- Resource assignments (not an initial input; done three months prior to the scheduled start date of a work package)
- Requirements database

Processing

Figure D.10 depicts the process flow for generating the human resource plan. Processing for this activity consists of the following:

- Identify human resources—this activity is the responsibility of the functional organization (FO) planning resources, with program management office (PMO) assistance, utilizing the extended CWBS and dictionary, and preliminary RAM. Processing consists of determining respective FO personnel requirements and preparing an individual FO input, in accordance with the resource loading procedures for the program's scheduling tool.
- Integrate FO inputs into the resource plan—this activity is the responsibility of the program planner, utilizing the individual FO inputs and intermediate schedule.

- Assign resources by name—this activity is the responsibility of the functional managers (FMs)/business area directors (BADs), cost account manager (CAM), and program planner
- HRP meet program requirements? The PM determines if the HRP meets program requirements

Two additional details for consideration after resources have been loaded are: (a) has the intermediate schedule been affected, and (b) has the preliminary RAM been impacted? If either the intermediate schedule or preliminary RAM has been impacted, then modifications are required and need to be made in accordance with their respective paragraphs of this section.

- The PM reviews the human resource plan. If the human resource plan requires changes, it is updated; otherwise, the PM demonstrates approval by signing the human resource plan.

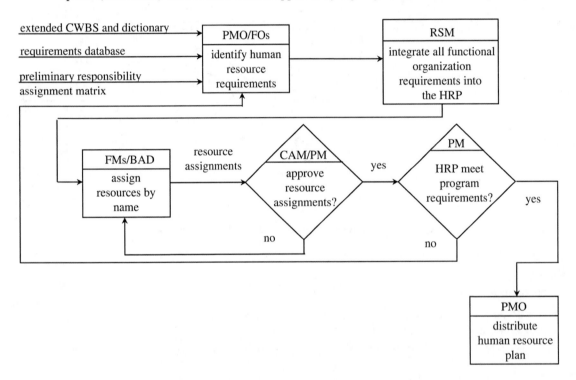

Figure D.10. Human Resource Plan Process Flow

Outputs

Output from this activity is the human resource plan.

Establish Program Organization

The program personnel, while they may be the same personnel involved in the creation of the program's baseline, are those individuals responsible for execution of the program in accordance with the program's created and approved performance measurement baseline.

The program organization consists of personnel whose function it is to execute the program in accordance with the program's created and approved performance measurement baseline. The program organization consists of all personnel assigned to the program depicted in an organization chart. The program responsibility assignment matrix is the intersection of the program organization personnel (to the cost account level) with those extended contract work breakdown structure (CWBS) elements identified as cost accounts (CAs).

Products

Establish program organization has two products: (1) program organization responsibility assignment matrix and (2) program organization chart.

The program organization preliminary responsibility assignment matrix has exactly the same format and intent as the preliminary RAM generated as part of the "generate preliminary RAM" activity. The intent of the program organization responsibility assignment matrix is twofold: (1) associate program individuals with the identified work to be performed and (2) assign budgets to cost accounts.

Inputs

Inputs to this activity are:

- The company organization
- Extended CWBS

Processing

Figure D.11 depicts the process flow for generating the program organization. Identifying the program organization is required prior to the generation of the preliminary RAM. The program organization is based on a more refined understanding of the way in which work is to be organized for execution on the program. The extended CWBS provides the initial perspective of how the program's work is organized. The program management office, with assistance from the functional organizations, will allocate key program personnel as responsible persons for the successful execution of the identified work elements. These key personnel will then form the program's management structure and be depicted on the program organization chart.

Once the program's organization has been identified and approved, the next activity is the assignment of identified work elements from the extended CWBS to responsible individuals. This assignment of work elements is physically depicted in the preliminary responsibility assignment matrix. The CWBS elements on the vertical axis of the preliminary RAM are only those representative of major elements of work, known as cost accounts. The individuals shown on the preliminary RAM as being responsible for the work elements are known as cost account managers (CAMs).

Outputs

Output from "establish program organization" is the program organization responsibility assignment matrix (RAM) and program organization (PO) chart.

Post-Contract Award

The last activity in the program management planning process is the generation of cost account plans. This activity is represented here as a post-contract award activity because final contract information related to requirements, schedules, and costs will not be known until after the contract has been awarded and definitized; however, it is possible to create cost accounts prior to contract award. These pre-contract awarded cost accounts will simply have to be revisited after contract award, and creating cost accounts prior to contract award provides little benefit.

The cost, schedule, and technical performance measurement baseline, however, is not complete until the cost accounts have been generated.

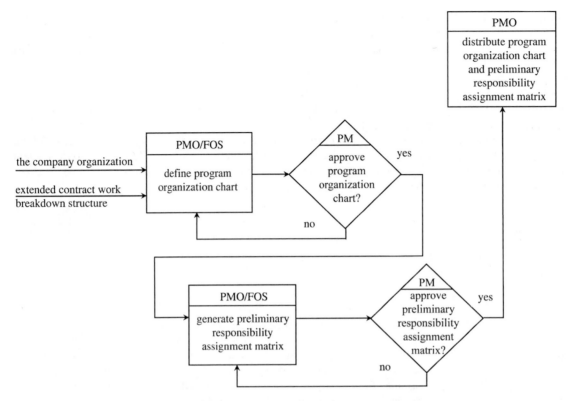

Figure D.11. Program Organization Process Flow

Generate Cost Account Plans

Generate cost account plans involves the detailed planning of the contract SOW, budget, and schedule, via work packages (WPs) and planning packages (PPs). A CA is a control point for cost, schedule, and performance planning, work execution, and performance measurement. CA responsibility is assigned to a cost account manager (CAM).

Successful completion of "generate cost account plans" concludes the planning phase of the program management (PM) planning process and therefore establishes the program's performance measurement baseline.

Products

The product of "generate cost account plans" are the program's cost account plans.

Inputs

Inputs to this activity are:

- Detailed schedules
- Requirements database
- Extended contract work breakdown structure (CWBS) and dictionary
- Human resource plan (HRP)
- Program organization responsibility assignment matrix (RAM)

- Other functional organization (FO) documents (trade studies, system engineering management plan, manufacturing plan, ILS plan, software development plan, hardware development plan, etc.)

Processing

Figure D.12 depicts the process flow for generating the cost account plans. Processing of this activity consists of the following subprocesses.

Schedule/Cost All Resources

This activity is the responsibility of the CAM, utilizing the WP descriptions from the extended CWBS dictionary and HRP.

Resolve Cost Account Scope

This activity occurs when the CA target cost is exceeded and cost reduction has been attempted by the CAM. This activity is the joint responsibility of the CAM(s), PM, and functional organizations (FOs). If requirements changed, then requirements in the requirements database need to be reallocated/changed as a result of this activity. As well, if CA target costs changed, then CA target cost in the RAM may need to be reallocated/changed as a result of this activity. Otherwise, work definition changes.

Assign Earned Value (EV) Technique/Define EV Milestones

This activity is the joint responsibility of the CAM and project accountant and consists of the following:

- Planning package? Earned-value techniques/milestones are not required for PPs until they become work packages. This is because performance is not measured against PPs.
- Begin this activity after the PM approves the following:
  - The human resource plan (HRP) for the CA
  - Intermediate schedule
  - The CA budget
- Specify a single earned-value technique for each WP.
- Provide an attendant description for each earned value milestone.
- Schedule earned-value milestones associated with travel in relation to the technical work that they are supporting.
- Earned-value techniques/earned-value milestones/CAP OK? Earned-value techniques are correct when they meet the requirements stated in company-specific guidelines. Earned-value milestones and attendant descriptions are correct when they are defined in accordance with the requirements stated in this activity. The CAP is correct when the CAM has confirmed its completeness and accuracy in accordance with this process.
- Extended CWBS dictionary affected? The extended CWBS dictionary should be updated whenever a WP description is modified.

The last item performed by the program manager and the project accountant are the establishment of cost and schedule variance thresholds. Cost and schedule variance thresholds should satisfy the following requirements:

- Variance thresholds should be imposed by contract and/or self-imposed by the PM.
- Self-imposed variance thresholds should be communicated via a program directive.
- Thresholds are determined by establishing plus and minus percentage and dollar amounts.

Approve Cost Account Plans (CAPs)

This activity is the responsibility of the CAMs, FM(s), and the PM, and it consists of demonstrating approval by signing all CAPs. Signature of the CAPs indicates approval and becomes a contract between the cost account manager and program manager and authorizes the work.

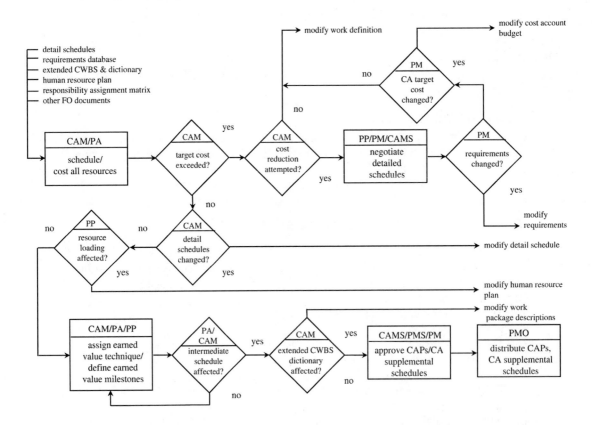

Figure D.12. Cost Account Plans Process Flow

Outputs

Outputs from this activity are the approved cost account plans.

Glossary

0/100 (EV Technique)
The earned-value technique for work packages having a planned duration of *one* accounting period where the BCWP earned for starting work is 0 percent of BAC and the BCWP earned for completing the planned work is 100 percent of BAC.

25/75 (EV Technique)
The earned-value technique for work packages having a planned duration of *two* accounting periods where the BCWP earned for starting work is 25 percent of BAC and the BCWP earned for completing the planned work is 75 percent of BAC.

40/60 (EV Technique)
The earned-value technique for work packages having a planned duration of *two* accounting periods where the BCWP earned for starting work is 40 percent of BAC and the BCWP earned for completing the planned work is 60 percent of BAC.

50/50 (EV Technique)
The earned-value technique for work packages having a planned duration of *two* accounting periods where the BCWP earned for starting work is 50 percent of BAC and the BCWP earned for completing the planned work is 50 percent of BAC.

Accounting Calendar
A calendar, unique to each year, that is established and used by the accounting FO to identify accounting periods (weeks and months).

Accounting Calendar Month (ACM)
An accounting month (three to five weeks in duration), as defined by the accounting calendar.

Accounting Period
See accounting calendar month.

Action Item List (AIL)
A product of the documentation and communication process that documents all action items generated in a specific program area, including action item identification, progress, closure (solution), and archiving. The AIL is an attachment to the appropriate meeting minutes.

Activity

- A discrete element of work or task in a project that occurs over time and consumes resources.
- A work package, planning package, or task.
- A class of scheduling objects that includes activities, summaries, hammocks, and subprojects.

Activity-on-Node

An activity-oriented scheduling method that demonstrates the critical path; also called the precedence diagram method (PDM) for scheduling.

Actual Cost of Work Performed (ACWP)

The costs actually incurred and recorded in accomplishing the work performed within a given time period.

Actual Direct Cost

Those costs identified specifically with a contract, based upon the contractor's cost identification and accumulation system as accepted by the cognizant defense contract audit agency (DCAA) representatives. (See direct costs.)

Adjustment

See program adjustment.

Aliasing

A technique used to relate functional CWBS elements to product CWBS elements for the purpose of collecting costs on a product basis.

Analysis

See program analysis.

Applied Direct Costs

The amounts recognized in the time period associated with the consumption of labor, material, and other direct resources, without regard to the date of commitment or the date of payment.

Apportioned Effort (EV Technique)

The earned-value technique for work packages (WPs) measuring work "related in direct proportion to work measured by one or more other WPs," where the apportioned value of BCWP earned is based on the BCWP earned by the other applicable WPs. As an example, WP#1's BCWS for the first period is $1,000. WP#2's BCWS is $100, as it is budgeted to cost 10 percent of WP#1's effort planned for the first period (i.e., 10 percent $BCWS_{WP\#1} = BCWS_{WP\#2}$). Assume only 50 percent of WP#1's planned work ($1,000 x 50 percent = $500) is completed during the first period; then BCWP earned by WP#2 would be 10 percent of 500, or $50.

Asset Number

The company-assigned identification number assigned to equipment for inventory and tracking purposes.

Authorized Unpriced Work (AUW)

Work authorized *in writing* by the buyer's contracting officer that has not been negotiated.

Authorized Work

Effort that is required in the performance of a definitized contract, or effort authorized in writing, by the buyer's contracting officer, prior to having a definitized contract.

At-Completion Variance (ACV)

See variance at completion.

Balanced Set

Typically refers to the complete set of parts and/or subassemblies required by the bill of material to manufacture a single end item. However, a balanced set may also be used when referring to a subassembly, as opposed to an end item.

Baseline

See program baseline, performance measurement baseline, or contract baseline.

Base Material Cost (BMC)

Prior to contract negotiations, it is the anticipated vendor's price for material, usually based on a quote obtained by purchasing from the vendor, or an advertised price (e.g., catalog price). Following contract negotiations, it is the negotiated material cost minus management reserve (i.e., BMC = BCWS $_{Material}$ = BMC$_{Negotiated}$ - MR).

Bid Manager

The person responsible for managing proposal preparation, delivery, and post submission activities.

Budget at Completion (BAC)

The total budgeted cost for work scheduled (BCWS).

Budgeted Cost for Work Performed (BCWP)

Credit earned for work completed at the program or work package level.

- For a program BCWP is the sum of the budgets for completed work packages and completed portions of open work packages, plus the appropriate portion of the budgets for level of effort and apportioned effort.
- For a work package, BCWP is a value (dollars or person-hours) earned during each accounting period by accomplishing scheduled work and is all or part of the budget at completion for the work scheduled, as determined by the WP's earned-value technique established prior to the start of work.

Budgeted Cost for Work Scheduled (BCWS)

Budget for planned work at the program or work package level.

- For a program BCWS is the sum, by accounting period, of the budgets for all work packages and planning packages.
- For a work package or planning package, BCWS is the budgeted cost of the work planned for completion during each accounting period.

Build/Version

An event that depicts a predetermined state of development for a hardware configuration item (HWCI) and/or computer software configuration item (CSCI).

Build/Version Schedule
An intermediate-level supplemental schedule depicting only those activities required to complete a build or a new version, of a configuration item.

Burden (Labor)
The sum of all indirect cost incurred within a specific labor pool (e.g., design engineering, assembly shop, etc.).

Burden Rate
A standard percentage of total direct cost incurred within a specific labor pool, periodically determined by the accounting FO, which is used when bidding/estimating contracts, to compensate for all indirect expense incurred by the labor pool.

Business Area Director (BAD)
The person responsible for managing a business area.

Buyer-Furnished Equipment (BFE)
Equipment furnished by the customer, which is used during contract execution.

Buyer-Furnished Information (BFI)
Software and/or documentation furnished by the customer, which is used during contract execution.

Buyer-Furnished Material (BFM)
Material furnished by the customer, which is consumed during contract execution.

CAP Worksheet (CAPW)
A form, prescribed by PACE II, which is used during cost account planning to transmit detailed work package/planning package data between the planner (CAM or FO planning resource) and the cost manager.

Charge Number
A job order number assigned, by the accounting FO, to a cost account to collect and report actual costs.

Child

- Any scheduling object (e.g., node, milestone, activity, subproject, etc.) whose start or finish is controlled by virtue of its connection to other objects.
- An element of the requirements breakdown structure, work breakdown structure (contract or extended), or cost breakdown structure residing one level lower in the breakdown structure.

Change Order
See contract change order.

Communications Management
The program management function responsible for managing a program's internal and external formal documentation and communication.

Company Investment

- Internally contracted work completed with company funds.
- Any "contractual effort" funded from company profit in accordance with a contract's cost sharing provisions. Investment is normally funded via an approved internal request for expenditure (RFE).

Company Organization
The organization that illustrates the arrangement of jobs and positions from the president to each employee.

Configuration Item

- An aggregation of hardware and/or computer software or any of its discrete portions, which satisfies an end-use and is designated by the customer or the company for configuration management.
- Any item required for logistic support designated for separate procurement.

Configuration Item Schedule
An intermediate-level supplemental schedule depicting only those activities required to complete a build or a new version of a configuration item.

Connection (Schedule)
A sequential workflow link (dependency) between activities that is used to calculate the activity's early and late schedule.

Constraint (Schedule)
A date limitation imposed on the start and/or finish of an activity or event. Events having constraints are frequently called "targeted" or "fixed" events.

Contract Administrator (CA)
See contract manager.

Contract Baseline
A baseline formed by the paper or papers that collectively contain the parties' agreements concerning the work that is to be performed, including: (a) a specification and/or statement of work; (b) contract deliverables, line items (CLINs), and data (CDRLs); (c) delivery schedules; (d) price (ceiling, target, or both) for fixed-price contracts or cost (target, ceiling, or both) for cost-reimbursement contracts; (e) all specifications and standards incorporated by reference; (f) when so stipulated by the contract, the contractor's proposal; (g) any other documents that form the bases for the agreement: and (h) an "order of precedence" for contract documents. The contract baseline is established by the definitized contract.

Contract Budget Base (CBB)
The value of all negotiated contract costs, plus the estimated cost of authorized unpriced work (AUW).

Contract Change Order
A written order, signed by the buyer's contracting officer, directing the contractor to make a change that the contract "changes" clause authorizes the contracting officer to order without the contractor's consent.

Contract Data Requirements List (CDRL)
A list of various types of data to be prepared by the contractor in accordance with contract requirements and delivered to the buyer.

Contract Line Item Number (CLIN)
A unique number defined by the contract and assigned to each contract deliverable.

Contract Manager
The contract management FO person assigned to the communications management function, responsible for managing *external formal* documentation and communication, except CDRL data item management and delivery.

Contract Reporting Level
The CWBS level, agreed to by the customer and contractor, at which formal cost performance reporting to the customer is required. The contract reporting level is normally level three (i.e., CWBS element AAA, AAB, etc.).

Contract Target Cost (CTC)

- The negotiated cost for the original definitized contract and all contractual changes that have been definitized, but excluding the estimated cost of any authorized, unpriced changes. The CTC equals the value of the budget at completion plus management reserve, when there is no authorized unpriced work.
- The cost specified in incentive contracts that is compared to total allowable contract cost to arrive at a difference that is used to adjust negotiated profit or fee, based on the contract's incentive formula.

Contract Target Price
The negotiated price of the contract (CTC plus profit or fee).

Contract Work Breakdown Structure (CWBS)
The complete work breakdown structure (WBS), for a contract, provided by the customer in the contract or developed by the contractor in accordance with the historical MIL-STD-881A (or latest revision/document) and the contract statement of work. This document must be accompanied by the CWBS dictionary.

Control Identification (CID) Number
See job order number.

Cost Account (CA)

- An intersection of the extended contract work breakdown structure (CWBS) and organizational structure (OS) at which budget, statement of work (technical performance), schedule, and functional responsibility for work is assigned by the program manager to a cost account manager.
- The management control point at which (a) actual costs of work performed (ACWP) can be accumulated and compared to budgeted costs for work scheduled (BCWS) and work performed (BCWP); and (b) cost, schedule, and technical performance variances are monitored and reported.

Cost Account Authorization Document (CAAD)
A form used by the program management office to formally authorize work. The CAAD must include, as a minimum, the cost account job order number, statement of work, scheduled start and completion dates, budget, and manager's name. The CAAD must be approved by the program manager and functional manager, and be agreed to by the cost account manager.

Cost Account Identifier
Typically the same identifier as the extended CWBS element, normally at the fourth level (e.g., AABA, AABC, etc.), which intersects with a program organization to form the basis for the cost account.

Cost Account (CA) Supplemental Schedule
A product of the schedule planning process (but approved in the cost account planning process), which is below the intermediate schedule and depicts a cost account's summary schedule, work package schedules, planning package schedules, interface events, and other applicable milestones. CA supplemental schedules are program baseline documents.

Cost Account Manager (CAM)
The person responsible for managing a cost account.

Cost Account Plan (CAP)
A product of the cost account planning process that provides a summary of the time-phased work allocated to a cost account in terms of budget and schedule. The CAP includes summary information, work/planning packages, EV milestones description list, and MAS for material CAs. The CAPs are program baseline documents.

Cost Account Planning (CAP)
The program management planning process used for developing the cost account plans and the spend plan. Cost account supplemental schedules are approved in this process.

Cost Breakdown Structure (CBS)
A product of the cost planning process that (a) assigns budget (initially target budget) to each extended CWBS element, (b) provides identification of cost accounts, (c) identifies where charge numbers for direct charges will be required, and (d) budget (initially target budget) allocated to G&A, cost of money, undistributed budget, performance measurement baseline, management reserve, contract budget base, current target cost, and authorized unpriced work. The CBS is a program baseline document.

Cost Management
The program management office function responsible for managing and maintaining program-level work definition and program cost data using an approved software tool (e.g., MPM®), and the cost requirements performance management function.

Cost Objective
A contract, organizational division, function, or other work unit for which cost data are desired and for which provision is made to accumulate and measure the cost of processes, products, jobs, and so forth.

Cost of Capital Assets under Construction
An imputed cost determined by applying a cost-of-money rate to the investment in tangible and intangible capital assets while they are being constructed, fabricated, or developed for the contractor's own use.

Cost of Money (COM)
Facilities capital cost of money and cost of money as an element of the cost of capital assets under construction.

Cost of Money Rate

- The cost of money rate for any accounting period is the arithmetic mean of the interest rates specified by the Secretary of the Treasury pursuant to Public Law 92-41.
- Where the cost of money must be determined on a prospective basis the cost of money rate shall be based on the most recent available rate published by the Secretary of the Treasury.

Cost Performance Report (CPR)
A standard Department of Defense (DoD) form, submitted monthly to the customer, having five reporting formats: (1) WBS, (2) functional categories, (3) baseline, (4) manpower loading, and (5) problem analysis. Formats 1 (WBS) and 2 (functional categories) show current period, cumulative-to-date, and at-completion status.

Cost Planning (CP)
The program management planning process used for developing the extended CWBS and dictionary, the extended CWBS/CLIN matrix, and the cost breakdown structure.

Cost/Schedule Control System Criteria (C/SCSC)
A methodology described in DoD Instructions 5000.1 and 5000.2 and the C/SCSC "Joint Implementation Guide," which is imposed as a requirement for government contracts above specified dollar-values, and is composed of EVM, on-site implementation review, and extensive progress reporting.

Cost Variance (CV)
The difference between BCWP and ACWP (i.e., CV = BCWP - ACWP).

Critical Path
Any path through a schedule having a float equal to or less than zero.

Current Target Cost
See contract target cost.

CWBS Cost Reporting Level Schedule
An intermediate-level supplemental schedule that depicts the program level at which costs are being reported to the customer.

CWBS Dictionary
A document that includes, for each CWBS element, a name and definition of the product(s)/service(s) being developed/manufactured/provided. This document must identify the elements used for cost reporting to the customer and must accompany the CWBS.

CWBS Template
Generic CWBS structures, developed by functional organizations, that are used as a basis to develop a program specific CWBS, when a CWBS is not specified in the contract.

Data Item (Contract Data Requirements List)
An individual document identified as a deliverable item in the contract data requirements list.

Data Item (Database)
The smallest unit of data stored in a database. Data items are defined within process product standards.

Database

A collection of interrelated data items stored together with controlled redundancy to serve one or more applications; the data are stored so that they are independent of programs (or people) that use the data; a common and controlled approach is used in adding new data and in modifying and retrieving existing data within a database. A system is said to contain a collection of databases if they are entirely separate in structure.

Data Manager (DM)

The data management FO person assigned to the communications management function, responsible for management and delivery of the data items specified in the CDRL, which is part of *external formal* documentation and communication.

Definitized Contract

A negotiated and signed agreement that completely defines in writing the funding, delivery schedule, and technical performance requirements for all research and development, supplies, and/or services to be furnished by the contractor. The definitized contract establishes the contract baseline.

Dependency (Schedule)

See connection.

Design Engineering

Functional organizations existing within company divisions consisting of hardware engineering, software engineering, and drafting.

Detailed Schedules

A product of the schedule planning process that is the lowest level of the schedule hierarchy, which depicts activities and events and their interdependency. The detailed schedule may be presented as a Gantt chart or an interdependency network. Resources are applied to and status is entered into these schedules. Detailed schedules are program baseline documents.

Direct Cost

Any costs that can be identified specifically with a particular final cost objective. (See actual direct costs.)

Discrete Effort

Tasks that have a specific end product or end result.

Discrete Milestone

A milestone that has a definite scheduled occurrence in time, signaling the finish of an activity, such as "release drawings," "submit CDRL Data Item," and/or signaling the start of a new activity. Synonymous with the term objective indicator.

Documentation and Communication

The program management process used for (a) managing and maintaining all written program documentation and communications and (b) generating the program management library and various products including program directives, meeting minutes, program events calendar, action item lists, management presentations, telecons, and trip reports.

Earned-Value Management (EVM)
A methodology for program management that is composed of tracking cost and dollarized schedule at specific management points called cost accounts. Tracking requires establishing and maintaining a performance measurement baseline (PMB), comparing performance to the PMB, and implementing corrective action with formal reporting for deviation from the PMB, which exceed specified thresholds.

Earned-Value (EV) Milestone
A discrete milestone used to earn credit for work performed (BCWP). The value of BCWP allocated to an EV milestone (milestone weight) reflects both the amount of work that must be performed to achieve the milestone and the value of BCWP, expressed as a percentage of BAC and earned as a result of achieving the milestone.

Earned-Value (EV) Milestone Description Worksheet
A form, prescribed by an organization, which is used during cost account planning to transmit EV milestone information for each work package between the planner (cost account manager (CAM) or functional organization (FO) planning resource) and the cost manager.

Earned-Value (EV) Milestones Description List (EVMDL)
Part of the cost account plan that provides the list of EV milestones and their descriptions for every WP in a CA.

Earned-Value (EV) Technique
One of ten methods of establishing BCWP, during each accounting period, based on BAC and the amount of scheduled work completed for a work package.

Element (CWBS, Extended CWBS)
A work unit identified by a unique designator. Each element has an associated dictionary and all contract/internal work requirements identified in the RBS. Elements may be summary-level, cost accounts or work/planning packages.

Element of Cost (EOC)
Direct cost for labor, material, other direct costs (ODC), and travel.

Estimate at Completion (EAC)
Actual direct cost (ACWP) to date plus the estimate of costs for authorized work remaining (ETC) (i.e., $EAC = ACWP_{Cum} + ETC$).

Estimate-to-Complete (ETC)
An estimate of actual direct cost to complete the remaining authorized work.

Event (Schedule)
- A objective or milestone, often associated with the start or finish of a project or phase of work, or an important hand-off point between tasks.
- An occurrence or milestone represented, for example, by a triangle or diamond.
- An occurrence at a point in time, often associated with the start or completion of a key activity. Events do not consume time or resources.

Event Description List (EDL)
A product of the schedule planning process that identifies each MPS and IMS schedule event (milestone) by name and provides a description of how the event is accomplished. The event description list is a program baseline document.

Execution
See program execution.

Extended Cost

- The material cost determined by the monthly quantity multiplied by the unit price.
- The total cost for a particular item of material (i.e., unit cost x total number of units).

Extended CWBS (ECWBS)
A product of the cost planning process that is the contractor's extension of the CWBS to the lowest level required for management control. The contractor will generally expand the CWBS by partitioning CWBS elements into smaller and more specific units of work, such as units separated by functional area or by time. In conjunction with the extended CWBS dictionary, the extended CWBS is a program baseline document.

Extended CWBS/CLIN Matrix
A product of the cost planning process that provides a detailed cross-reference between each extended CWBS element and the contract line item number (CLIN) that funds the work described in the extended CWBS element. The extended CWBS/CLIN matrix is a program baseline document.

Extended CWBS Dictionary
A product of the cost planning process that is coupled with the extended CWBS and that includes, for each extended CWBS element, (a) a name, definition, and completion criteria of the product(s)/service(s) being developed/manufactured/provided; (b) risk (cost/schedule/performance); (c) applicable elements of cost (e.g., labor, material, subcontractor, other direct costs); and for applicable elements, (d) work/planning package descriptions, in *product/service-oriented* terms (lowest elements only). In conjunction with the extended CWBS, the extended CWBS dictionary is a program baseline document.

External Formal Documentation and Communication
Any documentation or communication, transmitted by buyer's or seller's contracting officer, that results in complying with contract requirements or changes to the contract baseline.

External Informal Documentation and Communication
Any documentation or communication *not* requiring compliance with or a change to the contract.

Facilities Capital Cost of Money
An imputed cost determined by applying a cost-of-money rate to facilities capital employed in contract performance.

Final Cost Objective
A cost objective that has allocated to it both direct and indirect costs and, in contractor's accumulation system, is one of the final accumulation points.

Finish-to-Finish Connection
A workflow dependency that states that the successor activity (child) cannot finish until its predecessor activity (parent) has finished.

Finish-to-Start Connection
A workflow dependency that states that the successor activity (child) cannot start until its predecessor activity (parent) has finished.

Finish Float
The number of workdays the finish of an activity can slip before it causes another activity to slip.

Fixed Event
An event with an imposed date limitation.

Float (Schedule)

- "Free" float is the number of workdays an activity can slip before it causes another activity to slip.
- The difference between an activity's earliest finish date and latest finish date (i.e., spare time). Float is also referred to as slack time. See also finish float and start float.

Formal Documentation and Communication
Any documentation or communication resulting in compliance with or a change to the contract baseline and/or program baseline (including the performance measurement baseline).

Formal Reprogramming
A re-planning of the effort remaining on the contract that requires prior written customer approval and is based on a new budget allocation, which exceeds the contract budget base. The excess budget is referred to as the operating budget.

Freeze Period
A period, typically the current and subsequent reporting periods, during which customer approval is required prior to changing the BCWS for any work that is part of the performance measurement baseline.

Functional Discipline Work Breakdown Structure
A WBS template that has been developed by each functional discipline describing the way that the functional discipline performs its work.

Functional Manager (FM)
The person responsible for managing a functional organization.

Functional Organization (FO)
An organization associated with a specific functional discipline including contract management (administration), quality assurance, subcontract management (administration), system engineering, design engineering, operations, purchasing, configuration management, data management, specialty engineering, and so forth.

Functional Organization by Process (Schedule Perspective)
An intermediate-level supplemental schedule that depicts the intermediate schedule specific to one functional organization.

Functional Organization (FO) Planning Resources
Resources from functional organizations, assigned to planning organization functions other than the program management office, that execute the PM planning process.

Gantt Chart
A timescaled chart that represents activities as bars and depicts relative durations of activities without depicting workflow dependencies.

Gantt/Milestone Chart
A Gantt chart that also depicts program milestones.

General and Administration (G&A) Expense

- As defined in the PM cost management tool, an aggregate of indirect expenses that include: corporate general and administrative (G&A), division G&A, bid and proposal (B&P), and independent research and development (IR&D) allocated only to final cost objectives.
- Expenses, representing the cost of management and administration of a business area, which are grouped into a separate indirect cost pool and allocated only to final cost objectives.

General and Administration (G&A) Rate

- As defined in the PM cost management tool, a standard percentage of total burdened direct cost, periodically determined by the corporate accounting FO, that is used when bidding/estimating contracts, to compensate for: corporate G&A, division G&A, B&P, and IR&D expenses.
- A standard percentage of total burdened direct cost, periodically determined by the corporate accounting FO, that is used when bidding/estimating contracts, to compensate for general and administration expense.

Government-Furnished Equipment (GFE)
Equipment furnished by the government, which is used during contract execution.

Government-Furnished Information (GFI)
Software and/or documentation furnished by the government, which is used during contract execution.

Government-Furnished Material (GFM)
Material furnished by the government, which is consumed during contract execution.

High Risk
See significant risk.

High-Value Material
Those material items that constitute 80 percent of the program's material cost, but only represent about 20 percent of the total quantity of material items.

Holding Account
An inventory account outside the performance measurement system where actual material costs are accrued until material is released to build, at which time, the actual cost of released material is transferred to the proper cost account.

Horizontal Integration
The development of work flow dependencies among all schedule elements so that the impact of the expansion, compression, delay, or acceleration of one schedule element is reflected in all affected elements.

Horizontal Traceability
The ability to trace work flow dependencies among all schedule elements so that any impact due to expansion, compression, delay, or acceleration of one element can be identified and located.

Human Resource Plan (HRP)
A product of the resource planning process that (a) details a program's human resource requirements, and (b) provides a program-level summary for schedule and cost of human resources. The HRP is a program baseline document.

Incremental Cost
Cost depicted over time or at specified times.

Incremental Funding Period
That portion of a program performance period funded by the contract, when total contract funding is not authorized at the time of contract award.

Incremental Funding Requirement (IFR) (Incremental Contract Funding)
The provision (or recording) of budgetary resources for a program or project based on obligations estimated to be incurred within a fiscal year when such budgetary resources will cover only a portion of the obligations to be incurred in completing the program or project as programmed. This situation differs from full funding, where budgetary resources are provided or recorded for the total estimated obligations for a program or project in the initial year of funding.

Indirect Costs
Costs, which because of their incurrence for common or joint cost objectives, are not readily subject to treatment as direct costs. (See overhead.)

Internal Replanning
Replanning actions required to incorporate *change in scope* that are performed, by cost account managers at the direction of the program manager, for remaining effort *within* the contract budget base.

Informal Documentation and Communication
Any documentation or communication *not* resulting in compliance with or a change to the contract baseline and/or program baseline (including performance measurement baseline).

Instant Contract
The negotiated contract including all change orders or supplemental agreements existing at any particular instant during the life of the contract.

Interdependency Network (IDN)
See network diagram/chart.

Interface Event
- A schedule activity that provides a link between two levels of schedule hierarchy.

- An event that demonstrates interaction between levels of schedule hierarchy. An interface event is a single entity that resides in two different places (the subproject in which it was created and the subproject's parent node). Interface events are used to identify hand-off points between subprojects as well as the start and finish of a subproject. Interface events remember their schedule when project files are separated, and automatically link together again when united in the same project file.

Intermediate Schedule (IMS)
A product of the schedules planning process existing one level below the master program schedule (MPS) that (a) depicts significant events and activities required to meet MPS milestones; (b) depicts key internal milestones including receipt of critical material and long lead items; (c) depicts transmittal of buyer-furnished equipment, information, or material to subcontractors and/or receipt of subcontractor deliverables; (d) contains interrelated activities or summarization's of lower-level schedules (e.g., cost account supplemental schedules); (e) provides horizontal integration for lower-level schedules; and (f) is vertically integrated with the MPS and all lower-level schedules. For small programs the MPS and IMS can be the same schedule. Large programs may have more than one IMS. The IMS is a program baseline document.

Internal Formal Documentation and Communication
Any documentation or communication resulting in compliance with or a change to the program baseline.

Internal Informal Documentation and Communication
Any documentation or communication *not* requiring compliance with or a change to the program baseline.

Internal Milestones
Any milestone not contractually stated or derived that is required to give management visibility to critical or significant events.

Internal Requirement
Includes, but is not limited to, requirements stated in (a) BAD directives, (b) program management process standards, (c) company standard practice instructions (SPIs), (d) company engineering standards, or (e) other departmental procedures or processes.

Internal Requirements from Functional Organizations (FOs)
Any requirements stated or derived, as a result of performing functional organization processes and procedures.

Inventory Control Plan
A part of the procurement plan in the material management plan (MMP), which includes inventory (a) handling details, (b) location information, (c) quantities, (d) tracking and rotation data, and (e) costs.

Job Order (JO) Number
A number, assigned by the accounting FO, to collect and report actual costs. (See also charge number.)

Job Title
Classification of a given job (e.g., senior engineer).

Latest Revised Estimate (LRE)
See estimate at completion.

Ledger Variance (Material)
A conversion factor, unique to each material item, used to convert standard cost to actual cost, when material is transferred from a holding account to a cost account. Ledger variance is computed by dividing "the actual cost of the item based on the most recent buy" by "the item's standard cost."

Level of Effort (LOE)
Effort of a general nature (e.g., liaison, coordination, follow-up, etc.), which does not produce definite end products or results (e.g., CDRL, hardware assembly, software module, test results, etc.).

Low Risk
See negligible risk.

Low Run-Rate Material (LRRM)
Engineering materials for systems or modules that exceed a quantity build of six or more. The determining factor is that it will *not* be built in a production environment (i.e., with flow charts, paced lines, etc.). $BCWS_{LRRM}$ is time-phased based on the point of issue, in balanced sets, using cost from the negotiated cost proposal minus any management reserve. $BCWP_{LRRM}$ is earned when material is issued from the holding account to the assembly activity. $ACWP_{LRRM}$ is based on "standard cost" plus "ledger variance."

Make/Buy Analysis Plan
A part of the material management plan that details what parts and assemblies will be manufactured by the company or purchased from a vendor or subcontractor.

Management Presentations
A product of the documentation and communication process that documents a presentation, related to the program, given to internal management.

Management Reserve (MR)
An amount of the total allocated budget withheld by the program manager for management control purposes, rather than being designated for the accomplishment of a specific task or set of tasks. MR is within the scope of the contract, but it is not part of the performance measurement baseline (i.e., not within the scope of any cost account). MR is synonymous with management reserve budget. (See also cost reserve.)

Manufacturing Cost
Direct cost plus applicable burden (e.g., labor burden, P&T, etc.). Manufacturing cost does not include general and administrative (G&A), cost of money (COM), or profit/fee.

Master Program Schedule (MPS)
A product of the schedule planning process that provides the top-level summary of all program contractual effort, significant events, and/or milestones including (a) hardware/software deliveries; (b) major customer reviews/decision points; and (c) buyer-furnished equipment, information, and material delivery dates. The MPS shall dictate the time frames for the development of all lower-level schedules (e.g., IMS and detailed schedules). The MPS is a program baseline document.

Material
- A direct charge resource that includes all assets purchased for a program from (a) sources outside of the company, (b) inter-divisional purchases, and (c) internal transfers.
- Buyer- or government-furnished material used in the fabrication of a contract end item.

Material Acceptance Plan

A part of the material management plan that details how material will be accepted by the company prior to being sent to stock.

Material Analysis Sheet (MAS)

Part of the cost account plan used by the CAM (a) during planning to establish BCWS; and (b) during execution to (1) alert the CAM of potential schedule variance; and to (2) record the data required to calculate and monitor material Usage variance, price variance, and cost variance, at both item and cost account levels. For nonrecurring material *only*, the MAS is also used to establish the value of BCWP earned when material is received.

Material Attrition

See material shrink.

Material Cost Variance

The sum of material usage variance and material price variance (i.e., $CV_{Material} = UV_{Material} + PV_{Material}$).

Material Disposition Plan

A part of the material management plan that details how material that is no longer required will be disposed.

Material Price Variance

The difference for a material item between the committed or actual unit price and the budgeted unit price. Material price variance is synonymous with price variance.

Material Shrink

Production or development material that ends up as material scrap. Production material is scrapped for various reasons (e.g., defective vendor material, obsolete material due to engineering change notice (ECN) activity, excess material, manufacturing scrap, floor loss, etc.). Development material may be scrapped as a result of obsolescence, screening, burn-in, destructive testing, stress testing, and so forth.

Material Shrink Rate

- Production—a standard percentage of purchased material costs, periodically determined by the accounting FO for each business area, which is applied to production material bids to cover the required material overbuy necessary to account for material that ends up as material scrap.
- Development—an engineering estimate of additional material items that are added to development material bids to account for anticipated losses due to obsolete material, screening, burn-in, destructive testing, stress testing, and so forth.

Material Usage Variance

The difference, for a material item, between the actual quantity used and the quantity budgeted. Usage variance in terms of actual consumption is derived from an item-by-item comparison of the company's purchase order written report with the cost account material analysis sheet. Material usage variance is synonymous with usage variance.

Meeting Minutes
A product of the documentation and communication process that documents the significant decisions and status reported during internal and external (customer, subcontractor, etc.) program meetings.

Milestone
See event.

Milestone Weights (EV Technique)

- The earned-value technique for long-term effort (more than two months) where earned-value (BCWP) is reported based on accomplishment of milestones, which have each been assigned a predetermined value of BCWP (milestone weight).
- The values assigned to EV milestones, which reflect both a predetermined amount of work that must be completed to achieve the milestone (BCWS) and the value of BCWP earned, as a result of achieving the milestone.
- The percentages of work package/planning package BAC assigned to the EV milestones (e.g., Milestone Weights are MS#1 = 20%, MS#2 = 30%, and MS#4 = 50% of the BAC).

Milestone Weights with Percent Complete (EV Technique)
An earned-value technique that can be used when a series of measurable units of work are *essentially equal* in value. Milestones must be scheduled in each month within which measurable units are performed. BCWS for each milestone shall be equal to the percentage of the total units planned for completion at each milestone occurrence multiplied by BAC (e.g., Milestone #1 = 10 of 100 units or 10% are planned for completion; BAC = $1,000; therefore, BCWS = 10 % of $1,000 = $100). BCWP for each milestone is earned based on "the percentage of total units actually completed by the milestone date" multiplied by BAC (e.g., Milestone #1 = 9 of 100 units or 9% actually completed; BAC = $1,000; therefore, BCWP = $90).

Moderate Risk
A risk that can potentially cause some disruption of schedule, increase in cost, degradation of performance, or some combination thereof, which special management emphasis and close monitoring will probably be able to overcome. Moderate risks have low/high, medium/medium, low/medium, or high/high probability of occurrence/seriousness of impact.

Multi-Functional Organizational Effort
Effort within a cost account that is to be completed by more than one functional organization.

Negligible Risk
Risk that has little potential to cause disruption of schedule, increase in cost, or degradation of performance. Normal effort and normal monitoring will probably be able to overcome difficulties. Negligible risks have a low or medium probability of occurrence and a low seriousness of impact.

Negotiated Contract Cost
The cost negotiated by the parties for the following types of contracts: cost plus fixed fee (CPFF), cost plus incentive fee (CPIF) or fixed price incentive fee (FPIF).

Network Diagram/Chart
A schedule that shows a grouping of discrete elements of work or tasks, as bars in a time-scaled format, with workflow connections.

Nonrecurring Material (NRM)
Material used by engineering to develop an end item and its associated tools and test equipment, and to build five or less end items (e.g., prototype systems or modules). $BCWS_{NRM}$ is planned using the material analysis sheet and is time-phased based on anticipated receipt dates. $BCWP_{NRM}$ is earned in the reporting period that the material is physically received. $ACWP_{NRM}$ is actual cost accrued during the reporting period that the material is physically received.

Operating Budget
The total budget in excess of the contract budget base (applicable only to reprogramming).

Operations
A functional organization consisting of material logistics, manufacturing, manufacturing engineering, tooling, test equipment, hybrid microelectronics, and facilities maintenance.

Organization
A social entity, which is goal-directed, has a deliberately structured activity system, and an identifiable boundary.

Original Budget
The budget established at, or near, the time the contract was signed, based on the negotiated contract cost.

Organizational Breakdown Structure (OBS)
A redundant term for organizational structure.

Organizational Structure (OS)
The formal pattern, illustrated in chart form, of how people and jobs are grouped (arranged) in an organization.

Other Direct Cost (ODC)
Include direct costs for travel, outside engineering, equipment rental/lease and maintenance, facilities rental/lease, CADAM, and so forth. Rented/leased equipment/facilities must be used in support of only *one* contract.

Overhead
Indirect labor and material, supplies and services costs, and other charges, which cannot be consistently identified with individual projects.

Parent

- Any scheduling object (e.g., node, milestone, activity, subproject, etc.) having successor objects (children). Parent is another term for predecessor.
- An element of the requirements breakdown structure, work breakdown structure (contract or extended), or cost breakdown structure residing one level higher in the breakdown structure.

Parent-Child Relationship
An association existing between (a) a predecessor (parent) scheduling object (e.g., node, milestone, activity, subproject, etc.) and any other successor scheduling object (child); or (b) elements in adjacent levels (e.g., level 2 and 3) of the requirements breakdown structure, work breakdown structure (contract or extended), or cost breakdown structure.

Parts Control Plan
A part of the material management plan that details all aspects of component selection.

Percent Complete (EV Technique)
The earned-value technique were BCWP is earned monthly based on a formula, established prior to work authorization, which incorporates objective factors for determining the percentage of the total effort completed (e.g., BCWP = number of drawing completed divided by the number of drawing budgeted multiplied by BAC). Monthly BCWS is calculated using the same formula as BCWP, with the exception that "number of drawings completed" is replaced by "number of drawings *planned* to be completed."

Performance Management
The program management function responsible for requirements identification, requirements mapping to the CWBS and extended CWBS, and performance measurement planning and execution. Requirements are separated into five perspectives (categories): (1) technical, (2) supportability, (3) programmatic, (4) cost, and (5) schedule.

Performance Measurement Baseline (PMB)

- The baseline for all work authorized by the contract that includes (a) the contract work breakdown structure (CWBS) and its attendant dictionary; (b) the responsibility assignment matrix (RAM); (c) the budget baseline log; and (d) all approved cost account plans. Cost account plans and their associated work/planning packages define the work to be performed, in terms of planned budget, schedule, and technical performance requirements.
- The time-phased budget plan against which contract performance is measured. The PMB is formed by the budgets assigned to scheduled cost accounts and the applicable indirect budgets. The PMB equals the total allocated budget less management reserve.

Performance Planning (PP)
The program management planning process used for developing the requirements breakdown structure and the technical, programmatic, and supportability performance measurement plan.

Performing Organization
A defined unit within the company's organizational structure, which applies the resources to perform the work.

Planned-Value Profile (PVP)
A value profile, spanning an objective's performance period, which defines projected, time-phased, demonstrable values for the performance objective, that are attainable with planned resources. A PVP is used for performance management (technical, supportability, and programmatic).

Planning
See program planning.

Planning Authorization Document
A document approved by the business area manager that defines the program planning scope and authorizes the program manager to expend funds to perform the pm planning process. During the bid phase this document is the bid request (BR) document.

Planning Distribution Matrix
A product of the program organization planning process consisting of a cross reference of the planning organization functions and the planning documents available/produced. The planning distribution matrix forms a distribution list for all documents required/used during a program's planning phase.

Planning Organization

- A product of the program organization planning process that consists of an organization comprised of program management office resources and all functional organization (FO) planning resources assigned to plan a program, or portion thereof, in accordance with the PM planning process.
- The organization that executes the PM planning process.

Planning Organization Resource Requirements
A product of the program organization planning process that consists of human resources required for the planning process. The document includes both functional organization planning resources and program management office resources.

Planning Package (PP)
Part of the cost account plan that provides a logical aggregation of work within a cost account, normally the far term effort, that can be identified and budgeted in early baseline planning, but is not yet defined into one or more work package(s).

Planning Package Descriptions
Planning package descriptions are part of the extended CWBS dictionary. Descriptions state engineering or manufacturing approaches contemplated to accomplish tasks, produce products, services provided, or purchase materials in accordance with all RBS requirements assigned to the planning package.

Precedence Diagram Method (PDM)
A network scheduling technique that depicts activities (or tasks) on nodes.

Predecessor
Any scheduling object (e.g., node, milestone, activity, subproject, etc.) controlling the start or finish of another scheduling object, by virtue of the connection between the objects.

Price Variance
See material price variance.

Prime Costs
Any costs that can be identified specifically with a particular final cost objective. (See direct cost.)

Process Control Data (PCD)
Data collected at process control points and used to measure the effectiveness of the process and the resultant products.

Process Control Point (PCP)
Strategic points within a process where process control data are collected.

Process Product Standard ("Product Standard")

Process product standards are documents created, derived, manipulated, or modified as a result of performing the specified process. Product standards include detailed content and format requirements.

Procurement and Transportation (P&T) Expense

Expenses, representing a business area's cost of procuring (a) material and/or (b) subcontractor services or products, which are grouped into a separate indirect cost pool and allocated only to final cost objectives.

Procurement and Transportation (P&T) Rate

A standard percentage of total direct cost for material or a subcontract, periodically determined by the accounting FO for each business area, that is used when bidding/estimating contracts, to compensate for procurement and transportation expense.

Procurement Plan

A part of the material management plan that (a) details how material will be procured, (b) provides schedule and cost information, and (c) includes an inventory control plan.

Procuring Activity/Agency

The command in which the procuring contracting office (PCO) is located. It may include the program office, related functional support offices, and procurement offices. Examples of procuring activities are AFSC/ESD, AFLC/OC-ALC, DARCOM/MIRADCOM, CECOM, and NAVAIRSYSCOM.

Program

- An activity that has the attributes of a definite starting point, clearly defined objectives, a definite ending point, and requiring resources to execute.
- A specific activity or phase for a product that is clearly delineated by the type of funding applied: independent research and development (IR&D), bid and proposal (B&P), contract, or company investment.
- A set of activities in the life of a specific product's development and deployment. (This definition is broader than the scope of the program management planning process.)

Program Adjustment

One of four major activities in the program management process during which corrective actions alternatives for over-threshold conditions identified during program analysis are examined and decisions are made to select corrective action plan(s).

Program Administration Management

The program management function responsible for all program-level administration, process metrics data collection, the programmatic requirements performance management function, and cost account management of the program management office.

Program Analysis

One of four major activities in the program management process during which cost, schedule, and performance data collected during program execution are compared to the program baseline and over-threshold conditions are identified.

Program Baseline

- The complete planning baseline derived from the internal requirements and the contract baseline.
- The baseline that includes all planning product standards (RBS, MPS, IMS, event description list, detailed schedules, extended CWBS and dictionary, extended CWBS/CLIN matrix, CBS, HRP, EFP, MMP, spend plan, PO, PO distribution matrix, RAM, RT, RAPs, TPSPMP, CAPs, CA supplemental schedules, and program directives).
- The program baseline includes the performance measurement baseline.

Program Directive

A product of the documentation and communication process, issued by the program manager, that provides special program instructions and/or procedures that are not specified in the contract or the program management process standards and guides. Program directives are program baseline documents.

Program Events Calendar

A product of the documentation and communication process that provides a variable-day horizon calendar of upcoming program and non-program significant events.

Program Execution

One of four major activities in the program management process during which deliverables are produced and cost, schedule, and performance data are collected.

Program Management (PM)

- The program function responsible for (a) managing all program facets (i.e., technical, programmatic, supportability, cost, schedule) and their attendant risks during all program phases (planning, execution, analysis, and adjustment) in accordance with the (i) BAD's direction, (ii) contract, (iii) company program management processes, (iv) company engineering standards and guides, and (v) company standard practice instructions; (b) approving all external and internal formal documentation and communication.
- A professional discipline concerned with the function of program management.

Program Management Library (PML)

A repository for all program external and internal formal documentation and communication. The PML is generated in the documentation and communication process.

Program Management Office (PMO)

The group of functions and corresponding personnel that are responsible for program-level planning, execution, analysis, adjustment, administration, and so forth. The PMO includes the following functions: program management, cost management, schedule management, secretarial, program administration management, risk management, resource management, and communications management.

Program Management Organization

See program organization (PO).

Program Management Process Flowchart
The top-level flow diagram depicting the (a) four phases of program management (planning, execution, analysis and adjustment), (b) processes performed during each phase, (c) inter-process relationships, and (d) significant inputs/outputs.

Program Manager (PM)
The person responsible for performing the program management function.

Program Office
See program management office (PMO).

Program Organization (PO)

- A product of the program organization planning process, depicted in an organizational chart format, which consists of all functions and associated personnel responsible for executing the program. The PO is a program baseline document.
- All personnel assigned, directly or indirectly, to a program, up to an including the program manager.

Program Organization (PO) Distribution Matrix
A product of the program organization planning process that is a cross reference of program organization functions and program documents that forms a distribution list for those documents during the execution phase of a program.

Program Organization Planning
The program management planning process used for developing the planning organization resource requirements, planning organization, planning distribution matrix, program organization, program organization distribution matrix, and responsibility assignment matrix.

Program Planning

- One of the four program management requirements.
- A major activity in the program management process. Program planning is composed of program organization planning, performance planning, cost planning, schedule planning, resource planning and cost account planning. Completion of the program planning activity produces the program baseline.

Program Risk
The probability of not achieving a program's cost, schedule, technical performance, supportability, and/or programmatic requirements.

Programmatic Risk
Risks associated with obtaining and using applicable resources that are outside of the program's direct control, but can affect the program's direction (e.g., manufacturing, environmental facilities, government test facilities, etc.).

Project
See program.

Project Accountant (PA)

The person assigned to the cost management function, responsible for managing and maintaining program-level work definition and program cost data, and cost requirements performance management.

Project Tree (Schedule)

The graphic representation of the project structure, which shows how subproject networks relate to one another hierarchically and is used to change network views.

Project Tree Chart

The schedule breakdown structure (schedule hierarchy).

Pseudo-Asset Number

Artificial asset numbers, assigned to work/planning package assets during planning prior to asset assignment, which are used to identify where each asset is used, when more than one of an asset type is involved. A pseudo-asset number is replaced by the actual asset number when the assignment is made.

Pseudo-Name

Artificial names assigned to work/planning package human resources, during planning prior to assignment, which are used to identify where each resource is used, when more than one resource of a specific type is involved. A pseudo-name is replaced by the actual name when the assignment is made.

Release Order Notification (RON)

The primary work authorization document used within the company to authorize a program manager to expend company resources to perform contract or company-funded activities.

Reporting Periods

Periods that normally run concurrent with accounting periods, except where specified differently by the contract. Cost performance report (CPR) and cost/schedule status report (C/SSR) are normally due to the customer in a predefined number of days after the end of each accounting period.

Reprogramming

See formal reprogramming.

Resource Code

A two-character code defined by the company standard resource code (resource deck) used, in the human resource plan, to represent (a) resource description, (b) labor grade (range of salary costs), and (c) element of cost (labor, material, other direct costs (ODC), and travel).

Resource Deck

A cost tool database, created from accounting data by the program management office, comprised of rate tables, burden template, and element of cost (EOC) table.

Resource Management

A program management office function responsible for management of program-level human, material, equipment, and facility resources.

Resource Manager (RSM)
The person assigned to the resource management function who is responsible for management of program-level human, material, equipment, and facility resources.

Resource Planning (RSP)
The program management planning process used for developing the human resource plan, equipment/facility plan, and material management plan.

Responsibility Assignment Matrix (RAM)
A product of the program organization planning process, depicted in a matrix format, which consists of (a) intersections of the Program organization structure with cost breakdown structure elements (extended CWBS depicting CA budgets) at the cost account level. The intersection identifies the CAM responsible for the management of the CA. When budget information on the CBS appears on the RAM, it is called a costed RAM. The RAM is a program baseline document.

Risk

- The combination of the probability of an event occurring and the seriousness of the impact (consequence) of the event.
- The condition of having outcomes with known probabilities of occurrence, not certainty of occurrence.
- A measurable probability of consequence associated with a set of conditions or actions. Generally, in the Department of Defense (DoD) risk has a negative connotation—that action must be taken to avoid failure.

Risk Abatement
Mitigation of risk through timely implementation of management actions consistent with the chosen risk handling method.

Risk Analysis

- Involves an examination of the change in consequences caused by changes in the risk-input variables.
- An examination of risk areas or events to determine options and the probable consequences for each event in the analysis.

Risk Assessment

- The process of examining all aspects of a program with the goal of identifying areas of risk and their corresponding potential impact.
- The process of subjectively determining the probability that a specific interplay of performance, schedule, and cost, as an objective, will or will not be attained along the planned course of action.

Risk Assumption
A conscious decision to accept the consequences of the risk occurring.

Risk Avoidance
The non-selection an option because of potentially unfavorable results. Selection of an option because of its lower risk is also risk avoidance.

Risk Control
The process of continually monitoring and correcting the condition of the program.

Risk Drivers
The technical, programmatic, and supportability risk facets.

Risk Handling
Any action or in-action taken to address risk issues identified and evaluated during the risk assessment and risk analysis efforts.

Risk Handling Methods
One of four risk handling methods: avoidance, assumption, control, and transfer.

Risk Identification
An organized thorough approach to seek out the real risks associated with the program and document them in straight forward English language narrative statements. The basic risk identification question is, "What are the events or facts that may reasonably occur that will prevent the achievement of program goals?"

Risk Management

- Relates to the various process used to manage risk.
- All actions taken to identify, assess, and eliminate or reduce risk to an acceptable level in selected areas (e.g., cost, schedule, technical, producibility, etc.) and the total program.

Risk Prioritization
The process of organizing and stratifying risks based on a risk rating scheme and risk quantification data.

Risk Quantification
The process of taking quantitative risk information and transforming it into quantitative risk estimates in terms of probability of occurrence and potential impact to cost, schedule or performance (technical, supportability, or programmatic), based on the advice of experts.

Risk Transfer
The sharing of risk through joint ventures, make-versus-buy decisions, or contractual agreements (prime or subcontract) such as performance incentives, cost sharing, warranties, and so forth.

Rolling Wave Planning
A planning technique using a combination of work packages and planning packages where all near-term (normally the next 120 days) work is defined in detail, by work packages, with the remaining far-term work is defined by planning packages. As time progresses, planning packages are progressively converted to and superseded by work packages (the rolling wave).

Schedule Acceleration
See schedule reserve.

Schedule Element
Another term for the activity class of scheduling objects (e.g., activities, milestones, subprojects, etc.).

Schedule Management
The program management office function responsible for constructing, maintaining, and statusing program-level schedules (MPS, IMS, and detailed schedules with CAM assistance) and the schedule requirements performance management function.

Schedule Manager (SM)
The person assigned to the schedule management function, responsible for constructing, maintaining, and statusing program-level schedules and schedule requirements performance management. Typically referred to as the program planner.

Schedule Perspectives
Intermediate-level supplemental schedules created to view schedule data from various perspectives such as build/version, functional organization by process, configuration item, CWBS cost reporting level, or cost account.

Schedule Planning (SP)
The program management planning process used for developing the master program schedule, intermediate schedule, detailed schedules, and CA supplemental schedules.

Schedule Risk
The risk to a program in not meeting a milestones (e.g., schedule growth).

Schedule Reserve
Time retained for later use, by the program manager, obtained by accelerating contractual dates in the MPS.

Schedule Variance (SV)
The difference between BCWP and BCWS (i.e., SV = BCWP - BCWS).

Shrink Rate
See material shrink rate.

Significant Risk
Risk that is likely to cause significant disruption of schedule, increase in cost, or degradation of performance, or any combination thereof, although special management emphasis and close monitoring occur. Significant risks have high/high, high/medium, or medium/high probability of occurrence/seriousness of impact.

Significant Variances
Those differences between planned and actual performance that require further review, analysis, or action. Appropriate thresholds are established as to the magnitude of variances that, when exceeded, require variance analysis reports (VARs).

Skill Code
A code used by various functional organizations that provides information on an individual's experience, field of expertise, and education.

Spend Plan
A product of the cost account planning process that is a periodically revised document and provides the time-phased expenditure estimate ($ACWP_{Cum\text{-}to\text{-}date} + ETC$), fees, and price at the program level.

Specialty Engineering
The functional organization consisting of reliability engineering, maintainability engineering, testability engineering, environmental engineering, component engineering, integrated logistics support, electromagnetic engineering, human factors engineering, and system safety engineering.

Standard Cost (Material)
The weighted value, at the piece part level as determined by purchasing. For example, in some instances based on a maximum of the five most recent buys during the previous twenty-four months.

Start Float
The number of workdays the start of an activity can slip before it causes another activity to slip, assuming the activity's duration is held constant.

Start-to-Start Connection
A workflow dependency that states that the successor activity (child) cannot start until its predecessor activity (parent) has started.

Subcontract Management Plan
A part of the material management plan that details how subcontractors will be selected and managed.

Subcontract Work Breakdown Structure (SWBS)
The subcontractor's SWBS is relatable to the prime contractor's extended CWBS and defines all of the subcontractors contractual effort and cost reporting requirements.

Substantial Risk
See significant risk

Summary-Level Extended CWBS Element
An extended CWBS element, above the cost account level, that identifies sub-elements where work is defined, rather than detailing work to be performed. Detailed work definitions should only appear in the lowest level extended CWBS elements.

Summary Planning Budget
Budget that cannot be immediately identified with a cost account, but may be identified with a summary-level extended CWBS element.

Subproject
An activity-type scheduling object used to summarize a group of activities performed (a) by one functional group (e.g., software engineering) or (b) within a cost account. Subprojects are schedule-driven by interface events, which are used to integrate detailed work and other subprojects.

Successor
Any scheduling object (e.g., node, milestone, activity, subproject, etc.) whose start or finish is controlled by virtue of its connection to other objects.

Supplemental Schedule
A summary view of schedules that accurately reflects schedule detail contained in more than one node of the project tree. Supplemental schedules are frequently used to depict CDRL delivery schedules, functional organization schedules, extended CWBS-oriented schedules, and cost account schedules. Supplemental schedules cannot be statused.

Supportability Risk
Risks associated with fielding and maintaining systems or products, which are currently being developed or have been developed and are being deployed.

System Engineering (SE)
The functional organization responsible for (a) system requirements analysis, requirements allocation, and system design, and (b) for the technical and supportability requirements performance management function.

System Engineering Manager (SEM)
The system engineering FO person assigned to the performance management function, responsible for the technical and supportability requirements.

Target Budget
A budget for a CA established by the program manager, during cost planning, which the cost account manager is expected to meet, or better, during cost account planning.

Targeted Event
An event with an imposed date limitation.

Target Profit/Fee
The excess of the amount realized from sales of goods over the cost thereof in a given transaction or over a given period. Profit is the term used with fixed-price contracts. Fee is used with cost-reimbursement contracts

Technical Risk
The risk associated with evolving a new design to provide (a) a greater level of performance than previously demonstrated, or (b) the same or a lesser level of performance subject to one or more new constraints.

Telecon
A product of the documentation and communication process that documents, using the standard company form, external telephone conversation affecting the program. Telecons are external informal documentation and communication.

Top-Down Planning
A method of planning schedule, cost, and performance that begins with the top level and systematically decomposes or subdivides requirements, products, and/or work into increasing levels of detail.

Total Allocated Budget
The sum of all budgets allocated to the contract. Total allocated budget consists of the performance measurement baseline (all direct costs plus burden, cost of money, general and administrative expense, undistributed budget) and all management reserve. The total allocated budget will reconcile directly to the

contract budget base. Any differences will be documented as to amount and cause. In the case of reprogramming, the total allocated budget is the sum of the contract budget base and the operating budget.

Total Cost
Total cost is the sum of manufacturing cost (i.e., direct costs plus burden), cost of money, general and administrative expense, undistributed budget, and management reserve.

TPS Milestone
A milestone identified by the parameter's planned-value profile, at which time the value of the parameter is measured and/or analyzed. Where a TPS milestone exists within a CA, the EV milestone for that event shall be identical to the TPS milestone (i.e., the EV milestone description shall be identical to the TPS milestone description).

TPS Variance
The difference between the measured and/or analyzed parameter value and the parameter's planned-value profile value at the TPS milestone, the time at which the parameter is being measured/analyzed.

Trip Report
A product of the documentation and communication process that documents, using the standard company form, all trips made to support the program. Trip reports are external informal documentation and communication.

Undistributed Budget
Authorized budget applicable to contract effort that has not been distributed to cost accounts.

Usage Variance
See material usage variance.

Variance
See cost variance, material (cost, price, and usage) variances, schedule variance, significant variance, TPS variance, variance at completion.

Variance Analysis Report (VAR)
A report prepared by the cost account manager and submitted to the program manager whenever a cost, schedule, or performance (technical, supportability, or programmatic) variance occurs. The report states the cause of the variance, impact to the cost account, and provides a corrective action plan that includes expected recovery dates.

Variance at Completion (VAC)
The difference between budget at completion (BAC) and estimate at completion (EAC) (i.e., VAC = BAC - EAC).

Variance Threshold

- Thresholds for cost or schedule variances are expressed two ways: (a) plus or minus a percent, and (b) plus or minus a dollar amount (e.g., +/- 10% and +/- $5,000).
- Thresholds for TPS variances are expressed as "maximum" and/or "minimum" parameter values.

- More than one threshold for an item may be established by the program manager or CAM. A lower threshold can be an informal indicator that a problem may be developing. When the highest threshold is exceeded, a variance analysis must be performed and a formal variance analysis report must be submitted to the program manager.

Vertical Integration

The development of relationships between all levels of schedule information to ensure that each level of the schedule supports the program objectives of the top-level schedule and correctly reflects the status of the detail in the lowest level(s) of the schedule.

Vertical Traceability

The ability to trace the relationships between all levels of schedule information to ensure that each level of the schedule supports the program objectives of the top level and correctly reflects the status of the detail in the lowest level(s) of the schedule.

Work Breakdown Structure (WBS)

A product-oriented family tree composed of hardware, software, services, and data that completely defines the project/program. A WBS (a) displays and defines the product(s) to be developed or produced, or services to be provided, and (b) relates the elements of work to be accomplished to each other and to the end item. (See contract work breakdown structure, extended contract work breakdown structure, and subcontract work breakdown structure.)

Work Package (WP)

Part of the cost account plan that is a detailed short-span job, or material items, identified by the contractor for accomplishing work required to complete the contract. A work package has an assigned EV technique.

Work Package Descriptions

Work package descriptions are part of the extended CWBS dictionary. Descriptions state engineering or manufacturing approaches contemplated to accomplish tasks, produce products, provide services, or purchase materials in accordance with all RBS requirements assigned to the work package.

Bibliography

Abrams, D. (2011). *Man down: Proof beyond a reasonable doubt that women are better cops, drivers, gamblers, spies, world leaders, beer tasters, hedge fund managers, and just about everything else.* New York: Abrams.

Ackerman, S. (2011, July 26). Navy's next laser mashes up machine guns and death rays. Wired On-Line. http://www.wired.com/dangerroom/2011/07/navys-next-laser-mashes-up-machine-guns-and-death-rays.

Alsop, R. (2008). *The trophy kids grow up: How the Millennial Generation is shaking up the workplace.* San Francisco: Jossey-Bass.

Anderson, D. R., Sweeney, D. J., Williams, T. A., Camm, J. D., and Martin, R. K. (2011). *An introduction to management science: Quantitative approaches to decision making* (13th ed.). Mason, OH: South-Western Cengage Learning.

Arias, E. (2006). United States life tables, 2003. *National Vital Statistics Reports* (Center for Disease Control and Prevention), *54*(14).

Barker, J. (2006, October 10). Wealth, innovation and diversity video. Retrieved from http://www.media-partners.com/leadership/wealth_innovation_and_diversity.htm

Begley, S. (2007, July 2). When Does Your Brain Stop Making New Neurons? *Newsweek*, 62–64.

Berger, K. S., and Thompson, R. A. (1998). *The developing person through the life span* (4th ed.). New York: Worth.

Berk, L. E. (2009). *Development through the lifespan* (5th ed.). Boston: Pearson Education.

Bertoline, G. (2011, March 23). *Future college of technology: A vision-based detailed analysis and implementation plan.* Presented at the Purdue University College of Technology Dean Search Seminar. http://www.tech.purdue.edu/About_Us/Office-of-the-Dean/documents/Bertoline-presentation.pdf.

Bodnar, A. G., Ouellette, M., Frolkis, M., Holt, S. E., Chiu, C.-P., Morin, G. B., Harley, C. B., Shay, J. W., Lichsteiner, S., and Wright, W. E. (1998, January 16). Extension of life-span by introduction of telomerase into normal human cells. *Science, 279*, 349–352.

Boone, E. J., Safrit, R. D., and Jones, J. (2002). *Developing programs in adult education: A conceptual programming model* (2nd ed.). Long Grove, IL: Waveland.

Boroush, M. (2010). *NSF releases new statistics on business innovation* (NSF 11-300). Washington, D.C.: National Science Foundation.

Boyd, D., and Bee, H. L. (2011). *Lifespan development* (6th ed.). New York: Pearson Education.

Bridges, W. (2009). *Managing transitions: Making the most of change.* Philadelphia, PA: Perseus Books Group.

Brown, E. (2007, August 13). A Path out of the forest. *Forbes*, 92–94.

Business-Higher Education Forum (BHEF). (2005). *A commitment to America's future: Responding to the crisis in mathematics and science education.* Washington, D.C.: Business-Higher Education Forum.

Cateora, P. R. 1990. *International marketing* (7th ed.). Homewood, IL: Irwin.

Centro Nacional de Investigaciones Oncologicas (CNIO). (2012, May 14). First gene therapy successful against aging associated decline: Mouse lifespan extended up to 24% with a single treatment. *Science Daily*. http://www.sciencedaily.com/releases/2012/05/120514204050.htm

Cherniss, C., and Adler, M. (2000). *Promoting emotional intelligence in organizations*. Alexandria, VA.: American Society for Training and Development.

Chomik, R., and Whitehouse, E. R. (2010). *Trends in pension eligibility ages and life expectancy, 1950-2050*. OECD Social, Employment and Migration Working Papers No. 105. http://dx.doi.org/10.1787/5km68fzhs2q4-en

Choyce, R. (1992, January). Why become a project management professional? *PM Network*, 32–33.

Cibinic, J., and Nash, R. (1998). *Formation of government contracts* (3rd ed.). Washington, D.C.: CCH, Inc.

Cloned cows show no signs of premature aging. (2000, April 27). *News Sentinel*, p. 10.

Collins, M. (2011, March 15). Worker confidence on having enough money for retirement hits 20-year low. *Bloomberg.com*. http://www.bloomberg.com/news/2011-03-15/worker-confidence-on-retirement-money-at-20-year-low-ebri-says.html

Cummings, T. G., and Worley, C. G. (2009). *Organizational development and change* (9th ed.). Mason, OH: South-Western Cengage Learning.

Dessler, G. (2000). *Management: Leading people and organizations in the 21st century* (2nd ed.). Upper Saddle River, NJ: Prentice Hall.

Dillow, C. (2011, July). How to make a giant chain gun even deadlier: Give it a laser cannon. *Popular Science On-Line*. http://www.popsci.com/technology/article/2011-07/how-make-deadly-chain-gun-even-deadlier-add-laser-cannon

Dolan, K. A. (2006, April 17). Offshoring the offshorers. *Forbes*, 75–76.

Draut, T. (2005). *Strapped: Why America's 20- and 30-somethings can't get ahead*. New York: Doubleday.

Dugas, C. (2011, March 15). More workers have a gloomy retirement outlook. *USA Today*, p. A1.

Dychtwald, K. (1999). *Age power: How the 21st century will be ruled by the new old*. New York: Tarcher Putnam.

Dychtwald, K., Erickson, T. J., and Morison, R. (2006). *Workforce crisis: How to beat the coming shortage of skills and talent*. Boston, MA: Harvard Business School Press.

Dychtwald, M. (2003). *Cycles: How we will live, work and buy*. New York: Free Press.

Ellis, B. (2011, March 15). Most workers have saved just $25,000 for retirement. *CNNMoney.com*. http://money.cnn.com/2011/03/15/retirement/retirement_confidence/index.htm

Encyclopedia Americana. (1996). Danbury, CT: Grolier Incorporated.

Erickson, T. (2008). *Retire Retirement: Career Strategies for the Boomer Generation*. Boston, MA: Harvard Business Press.

Federal Acquisition Regulations System, 48 C.F.R. (2011).

Finn, J. (2008, August 20). The power of older workers. *Inc. 5000*. http://www.inc.com/inc5000/2008/articles/retirees.html

Fishman, T. C. (2005, March 1). How China will change your businesses. *Inc. Magazine*. http://www.inc.com/magazine/20050301/china.html

Fitzgerald, C., and Kirby, L. (Eds.). (1997). *Developing leaders: Research and applications in psychological type and leadership development*. Palo Alto, Calif.: Davies Black.

Fleming, Q. W. (1992). *Cost/schedule control systems criteria: A management guide to C/SCSC* (2nd ed.). Chicago: Probus Publishing Company.

Fossel, M., Blackburn, G. and Woynarowski, D. (2011). *The immortality edge: Realizing the secrets of your telomeres for a longer, healthier life*. Hoboken, NJ: John Wiley & Sons, Inc.

Frame, J. D. (1999). *Project management competence: Building key skills for individuals, teams, and organizations*. San Francisco: Jossey-Bass.

Frey, R. (1999). *Successful proposal strategies for small businesses: Using knowledge management to win government, private-sector, and international contracts.* Boston: Artech House.

Gibbons, M. T. (2004). The year in numbers. Washington, D.C.: American Society of Engineering Education (ASEE).

Gibson, J. L., Ivancevich, J. M., Donnelly, J. H., and Konopaske, R. (2011). *Organizations: Behavior, structure, processes* (14th ed.). New York: McGraw-Hill/Irwin.

Gioia, J. (1992, November). Comprehensive program management. *PM Network*, 5–7.

Goldberg, B. (2000). *Age works: What corporate America must do to survive the graying of the workforce.* New York: Free Press.

Goldstein, L. S. B., and Schneider, M. (2010). *Stem cells for dummies.* Indianapolis, IN: Wiley Publishing Company.

Goleman, D. (1995). *Emotional intelligence.* New York: Bantam Books.

Goleman, D., Boyatzis, R., and McKee, A. (2002). *Primal leadership: Learning to lead with emotional intelligence.* Boston: Harvard Business Review Press.

Grady, J. O. (2010). *Systems management: Planning, enterprise identity, and deployment* (2nd ed.). Boca Raton, FL: CRC Press.

Graff, H. F., and Krout, J. A. (1971). *The adventure of the American people* (3rd ed.). New York: Rand McNally.

Grayson, Jr., C. J., and O'Dell, C. (1988). *American business: A two-minute warning.* New York: Free Press.

Gurian, M. and Annis, B. (2008). *Leadership and the sexes: Using gender science to create success in business.* San Francisco: Jossey-Bass.

Hammer, A. (1993). *Introduction to type and careers.* Washington, D.C.: Consulting Psychologists Press.

Hankin, H. (2005). *The new workforce: Five sweeping trends that will shape your company's future.* New York: AMACOM.

Helman, R., Copeland C., and VanDerhei, J. (2011). *The 2011 Retirement Confidence Survey: Confidence drops to record lows, reflecting the "new normal"* (Issue Brief No. 355). Washington, D.C.: Employee Benefit Research Institute. http://www.ebri.org/pdf/surveys/rcs/2011/EBRI_03-2011_No355_RCS-11.pdf

Hennigan, W. J. (2011, July 26). Flying robotic seagull attracts flock of birds. *Los Angeles Times*, Business. http://latimesblogs.latimes.com/technology/2011/07/robot-bird-drone-festo-ted.html.

Herman, R., Olivo, T., and Gioia, J. (2003). *Impending crisis: Too many jobs, too few people.* Winchester, VA: Oakhill Press.

Higgins, J. M. (1994). *The management challenge: An introduction to management.* New York: Prentice Hall.

Hoban, F. T. (1992, August). An overview of training and development strategies for NASA project management. *PM Network*, 44–49.

Howard, P. J. (2006). *Owner's manual for the brain: Everyday applications from mind-brain research* (3rd ed.). Austin, TX: Bard Press.

Huntley, R. (2006). *The world according to Y: Inside the new adult generation.* Sydney, Australia: Allen & Unwin.

Johansson, F. (2004). *The Medici effect: What elephants and epidemics can teach us about innovation.* Boston, MA: Harvard Business School Press.

Johnson, L. and Learned, A. (2004). *Don't think pink: What really makes women buy—and how to increase your share of this crucial market.* New York: AMACOM.

Johnson, M., and Johnson, L., (2010). *Generations, Inc.: From Boomers to Linksters—managing the friction between generations at work.* New York: AMACOM.

Jonas, N. (1986, March 3). The hollow corporation. *BusinessWeek*, 57.

Kamenetz, A. (2006). *Generation debt: Why now is a terrible time to be young*. New York: Riverhead Books.

Kerzner, H. (2009). *Project management: A systems approach to planning, scheduling and controlling* (10th ed.). Hoboken, NJ: Wiley.

King, C. G. (1992, August). Multi-discipline teams: A fundamental element of the program management process. PM Network, 13–22.

Kinsella, K., and Velkoff, V. (2001). *An aging world: 2001* (International Population Reports, Series P95/01-1). Washington, D.C.: U.S. Government Printing Office.

Kirsch, I., Braun, H., Yamamoto, K., and Sum, A. (2007). *America's perfect storm: Three forces changing our nation's future.* Princeton, NJ: Educational Testing Service.

Kotlikoff, L. J. 2004. *The Coming Generational Storm: What you need to know about America's economic future.* Cambridge, MA: MIT Press

Kowalski, T. J. (1988). *The organization and planning of adult education.* Albany, NY: SUNY Press.

Krell, E. (2011, June). The global talent mismatch. *HR Magazine*, 68–72.

Ladika, S. (2006, April). The brain race. *HR Magazine*, 69.

Land, R. E. (2012, Spring). Engineering technologists are engineers. *Journal of Engineering Technology.* 32–39.

Lang, R., Alfonso, M., and Dawkins, C. (2009, May). American Demographics—Circa 2109. Planning, 10–15.

Levinson, D. J. (1978). *The seasons of a man's life.* New York: Ballantine.

Likert, R. (1967). *The human organization: Its management and value.* New York: McGraw-Hill.

Lohr, S. (2011, January 1). When innovation, too, is made in China. *New York Times, Business Day*. http://www.nytimes.com/2011/01/02/business/02unboxed.html.

Loo, D. (2011a, July 18). Big pharma launches a talent raid in China. *Bloomberg Businessweek*, 21–22.

Loo, D. (2011b, July 11). Move over Boston, China eyes biotech too. *Bloomberg Businessweek*, 20–21.

Marcel, J. (2000, September 29). A white rabbit that glows in the dark. *The American Reporter*, 6(1430). http://www.ekac.org/amrep.html.

Marrewa, A. (1998). *The feminine warrior: A woman's guide to verbal, psychological, and physical empowerment.* New York: Kensington.

Marston, C. (2007). *Motivating the "What's in it for me?" workforce: Manage across the generational divide and increase profits.* Hoboken, NJ: Wiley.

Memmott, M. (2011, June 15). 2 million 'open jobs'? Yes, but U.S. has a skills mismatch. *The Two-Way: Breaking News from NPR*. http://www.npr.org/blogs/thetwo-way/2011/06/15/137203549/two-million-open-jobs-yes-but-u-s-has-a-skills-mismatch.

Montfort, N. (1999, November 1). BioTech (Innovators in the biotechnology industry). *Technology Review*, 92.

Murk, P. J., and Wells, J. H. (1988, October). A Practical Guide to Program Planning. *Training & Development Journal*, 45–47.

Muschany v. United States. (1994). Retrieved from http://supreme.justia.com/cases/federal/us/324/49/

Naisbitt, J., and Aburdene, P. (1990). *Megatrends 2000: Ten new directions for the 1990's.* New York: Avon Books.

National Academy of Sciences. (2010). *Rising above the gathering storm, revisited: Rapidly approaching Category 5.* Washington, D.C.: National Academies Press

National Federation of Independent Business (NFIB). (2011). The benefits of hiring semi-retired workers. *NFIB.com*. http://www.nfib.com/business-resources/business-resources-item?cmsid=50011

National Human Genome Research Institute (NHGRI). (2007). *A guide to your genome.* National Human Genome Research Institute. http://www.genome.gov/Pages/Education/AllAbouttheHumanGenomeProject/GuidetoYourGenome07.pdf

National Institutes of Health (NIH). (n.d.). Human genome project fact sheet. National Institutes of Health Website. http://report.nih.gov/nihfactsheets/ViewFactSheet.aspx?csid=45&key=H.

National Science Foundation (NSF). (2006). Science and engineering indicators 2006. Arlington, VA: National Science Foundation.

National Science Foundation (NSF). (2010). Science and engineering indicators 2010. Arlington, VA: National Science Foundation.

Norman, Carter, H. (1986, Summer). Guaranteeing management's future through succession planning. *Journal of Information Systems Management*, 19.

Oliver, R. W. (2000). *The coming biotech age: The business of bio-materials*. New York: McGraw Hill.

Organisation for Economic Co-operation and Development (OECD). (2011). *Pensions at a glance 2011: Retirement income systems in OECD and G20 countries*. OECD Publishing. http://dx.doi.org/10.1787/pension_glance-2011-en

Overly, S. (2011, June 19). For science and tech companies, immigration debate strikes a different tone. *The Washington Post, Capital Business*. http://www.washingtonpost.com/...ness/capitalbusiness/for-science-and-tech-companies-immigration-debate-strikes-a-different-tone/2011/06/16/AGmWoxbH_story.html

Park, A. (2011, June 13). Cracking cancer's code: Tumor DNA holds the key to beating the disease. *Time*, 69–71.

PEW Research Center. (2008). Men or women: Who's the better leader? Retrieved from http://www.pew-socialtrends.org/2008/08/25/men-or-women-whos-the-better-leader/

Plunkett, J. (2010). *The next boom: What you absolutely, positively have to know about the world between now and 2025*. Houston, TX: BizExecs Press.

PMI (2013). Project Management Institute Jordan Chapter. Retrieved from http://www.pmi-jo.org/public/English.aspx?Lang=3&Page_Id=211

Pollack, A. (2011, May 18). *A blood test offers clues to longevity*. New York Times, Business Day. http://www.nytimes.com/2011/05/19/business/19life.html?pagewanted=all

Powell, B. (2011, June 27). The end of cheap labor in China. *Time*, 1–4.

Price, M. T. (1992, October). A process approach to project manager training. *PM Network*, 17–26.

Puliyenthuruthel, J., and Kripalani, M. (2005, February 14). India: Good help is hard to find. *Business-Week*, 52.

Rathe, J. (2010, January 9). The perception that older workers are less productive than younger ones is false. *RetiredBrains.com*. http://retiredbrains.blogspot.com/2010/01/perception-that-older-workers-are-less.html

Rawe, J. (2000, May 22). Economy. *Time Magazine, 155*(21), 21–22.

Reinhardt, A. (2006, January 30). Angling to be the next Bangalore. *BusinessWeek*, 62.

Robbins, S. (1998). *Organizational behavior: concepts, controversies, applications* (8th ed.). Upper Saddle River, NJ: Prentice Hall.

Robbins, S. (1999). *Management* (5th ed.). Upper Saddle River, NJ: Prentice Hall.

Rosenburg, N., and Birdzell, L. E. (1986). *How the West grew rich: The economic transformation of the industrial world*. New York: Basic.

Rothwell, W. J. (2010). *Effective Succession Planning: Ensuring leadership continuity and building talent from within*. New York: AMACOM.

Rue, L. W., and Byars, L. L. (1989). *Management: Theory and Application* (5th ed.). Homewood, IL: Irwin.

Ruskin, A. M. (1992, April). Concerns of project managers: Project risk management. *PM Network*, 30–37.

Sacks, D. (2006, January/February). Scenes from the culture clash. *Fast Company*, 73–75.

Santrock, J. W. (1999). *Life-Span Development* (7th ed.). New York: McGraw Hill.

Saunders, N. (2005, November 5). A summary of BLS projections to 2014. *Monthly Labor Review*. http://www.bls.gov/opub/mlr/2005/11/art1full.pdf

Scarborough, N. M. (1992). *Business: Gaining the competitive edge*. Needham Heights, MA: Allyn & Bacon.

Schuster, S. (2011, June 28). Genetic sequencing may aid survival of Tasmanian devil. *USA Today*, 9A.

Serruya, M. D., Hatsopoulos, N. G., Paninski, L., Fellows, M. R., and Donoghue, J. P. (2002). Instant neural control of a movement signal. *Nature, 416*(6877), 141–142.

Sheehy, G. (1998). *Understanding men's passages: Discovering the new map of men's lives*. New York: Random House.

Shelton, C., and Shelton, L. (2005). *The neXt revolution: What gen X women want at work and how their Boomer bosses can help them get it*. Mountain View, CA: Davies-Black.

Shenkar, O. (2005). *The Chinese century: The rising Chinese economy and its impact on the global economy, the balance of power, and your job*. Upper Saddle River, NJ: Wharton.

Smith, G. (2008 May 21). Mexico: Pumping out engineers. *BusinessWeek*. http://www.businessweek.com/stories/2006-05-21/mexico-pumping-out-engineers

Smith, P. (1986). *Taking charge: A practical guide for leaders*. Washington, D.C.: National Defense University Press.

Smith, J. W., and Clurman, A. (1997). *Rocking the ages: The Yankelovich report on generational marketing*. New York: Harper Business.

Social Security Administration (SSA). (2005). Social Security: A Brief History. Washington, D.C.: Social Security Administration. http://www.ssa.gov/history/pdf/2005pamphlet.pdf

Sorrel, C. (2011, July 26). IBM's mighty morphin' touchscreen keyboard tailors itself to your hands. *Wired On-Line*. http://www.wired.com/gadgetlab/2011/07/ibms-mighty-morphin-touchscreen-keyboard-tailors-itself-to-your-hands

Springer, M. L. (2005). *A concise guide to program management: Fundamental concepts and issues*. West Lafayette, IN: Purdue University Press.

Sternberg, S. (2011, June 28). The Pitch for Stem Cells. *USA Today*, 1A.

Stinnett, W. D. (1992, May). Lone wolf teams: Reconciling the need for collaboration with the need for individual accomplishment. *PM Network*, 21–25.

Strauss, W., and Howe, N. (1991). *Generations: The history of America's future, 1584 to 2069*. New York: William Morrow and Co.

Taylor, P., Kochhar, R., Morin, R., Wang, W., Dockterman, D., and Medina, J. (2009). America's changing workforce: Recession turns a graying office grayer. Washington, D.C.: Pew Research Center. http://pewsocialtrends.org/files/2010/10/americas-changing-workforce.pdf

Tulgan, B. (2009). *Not everyone gets a trophy: How to manage Generation Y*. San Francisco: Jossey-Bass.

Twenge, J. M. (2006). *Generation me: Why today's young American's are more confident, assertive, entitled—and more miserable than ever before*. New York: Free Press

United Nations (2011, May 3). World population to reach 10 billion by 2100 if fertility in all countries converges to replacement level. *United Nations Press Release*. http://esa.un.org/unpd/wpp/other-information/Press_Release_WPP2010.pdf

U.S. Bureau of Labor Statistics. (2013). Current population survey employment projections. Retrieved from http://www.bls.gov/emp/ep_chart_001.htm

Van Fleet, D. D., and Peterson, T. O. (1994). *Contemporary Management* (3rd ed.). Boston: Houghton Mifflin.

Vance, A. (2011, May 2). Pacific Biosciences' $600 million decoder ring. *Businessweek*, 57–59.

Vandeveer, R. (2011, April). *Alternative model proposed during a brainstorming session*. Technology Leadership and Innovation (TLI) Combined Advisory Board Meeting. West Lafayette, Indiana.

Veale, J. (2009, February 10). South Korea's pet clone wars. *Time World.* http://www.time.com/time/world/article/0,8599,1878398,00.html

Vergano, D. (1999, May 25). Of transgenic mice and men. *USA Today,* 11D.

Vergano, D. (2012, May 16). Paralysis victims use brain signals to control robotic arm. *USA Today.* http://www.usatoday.com/news/health/story/2012-05-15/robotic-arm/55004238/1?csp=34news.

Wallace, P. (1999). *Agequake: Riding the demographic rollercoaster shaking business, finance, and our world.* London: Nicholas Brealey Publishing.

Waters, R. (2011, March 21). A sales surge for gene sequencing machines. *Businessweek,* 58–60.

Weiss, R. (2000, October 14). Science nears revival of dead species. *Washington Post,* p. 10.

Welsh, A. (1992, May). The future of project management. *PM Network,* 5–6.

Wilson, J. (2000, October). Science's greatest unsolved mysteries. *Popular Mechanics, 177*(10), 52–57.

Woolhouse, M. (2011, January 23). Underemployed and overeducated—and maybe the nation's best hope. *Boston Globe.* http://www.boston.com/business/articles/2011/01/23/study_tempers_pessimism_over_worker_shortage/

World Economic Forum (WEF). (2011). Global talent risk—Seven responses. Geneva, Switzerland: World Economic Forum. http://www3.weforum.org/docs/PS_WEF_GlobalTalentRisk_Report_2011.pdf

Young, E. (2000, October 7). Cash cow. *NewScientist.* Retrieved from http://www.newscientist.com/article/dn50-cash-cow.html

Yukl, G. (2002). *Leadership in Organizations* (5th ed.). Upper Saddle River, NJ: Prentice Hall.

Zakaria, F. (2011, June). Innovate better: Everyone agrees it's key to America's future. But where do we focus innovation, and how do we fund it?. *Time Magazine,* 30–32.

Zakaria, F. (2012). *The post-American world: Release 2.0.* New York: W. W. Norton.

Zells, L. (1992, May). Applying Japanese total quality management to software project management. *PM Network,* 32–35.

Zemke, R., Raines, C., and Filipczak, B. (2000). *Generations at work: Managing the clash of Veterans, Boomers, Xers, and Nexters in your workplace.* New York: AMACOM.

Index

Note: Page numbers in italics refer to illustrations.